MODERN SCOTTISH HISTORY
1707 TO THE PRESENT

D0931608

MODERN SCOTTISH HISTORY
1707 *to the* PRESENT

VOLUME 2 : THE MODERNISATION OF SCOTLAND, 1850 TO THE PRESENT

Edited by
Anthony Cooke, Ian Donnachie,
Ann MacSween and Christopher A Whatley

TUCKWELL PRESS

In association with
THE OPEN UNIVERSITY IN SCOTLAND

and
THE UNIVERSITY OF DUNDEE

First published in 1998 by
Tuckwell Press Ltd
The Mill House
Phantassie
East Linton
East Lothian EH40 3DG
Scotland

Original texts copyright ©
the editors and contributors severally 1998

All rights reserved
ISBN 1 86232 073 X

British Library Cataloguing-in-Publication Data
A catalogue record for this book is available on request
from the British Library

Designed by James Hutcheson

Typeset by Hewer Text Ltd, Edinburgh

Printed and bound by
Cromwell Press, Trowbridge, Wiltshire

Preface

This volume and the series of which it is part have as their central purpose the study of the history of Scotland from 1707 until the present. The series seeks to combine the products of more recent research and general findings by some of the most prominent scholars working in the subject with the enthusiasm of those who wish to study it either in a systematic way or simply by reading one or more of these volumes at leisure.

Now is a particularly appropriate moment to bring this scholarship and the wider audience together. There is enormous latent enthusiasm for Scottish history, particularly, but not exclusively, of the modern period. This springs from a variety of sources: the new political agenda in Scotland following the 1997 Referendum; the higher profile of Scottish history in school, college and university curricula; the enhanced interest in local and family history; the success of museums and heritage ventures devoted to the more recent past; and the continuous flow of books on so many aspects of Scottish history. However, explicitly academic publications, with a few honourable exceptions, have been little read by any but specialists, so new findings have frequently had little impact on general perceptions of Scotland's more recent past.

There are two main aims encapsulated in these volumes, which are overlapping and complementary. The first is to present an overview of recent scholarly work, drawing on the approaches and findings of political, economic, social, environmental and cultural historians. This should be illuminating not only for those seeking an up-to-date review of such work, but also for anyone interested in the functioning of Scotland today - the essential historical background of present-day issues and concerns. The second, equally important, aim is to help readers develop their own historical skills, using the volumes as a tool-kit containing a wide range of primary sources and more detailed readings on specific topics. This and the other volumes in the series differ from most conventional academic publications, in that the focus is on **doing** history, rather than just absorbing the facts. The volumes are full of ideas on sources and methods that can be followed up by the interested reader.

Given the vast scope of the subject, we have had to put some limits on the coverage. The timescale is the early eighteenth century to the late twentieth century, a period for which sources not only abound but can also be readily understood and critically assessed. There is no attempt to give a detailed historical narrative of the period from the Union of 1707, which can readily be found elsewhere. Rather we present a blend of topics and themes, selected with a view to providing readers with a reasonably comprehensive introduction to recent work and a context and stimulus for further reading or investigation. Although there is an organisational divide at 1850, many of the themes are explored continuously over the whole period. Hence the first volume begins with the Union of 1707 and Jacobitism, and covers topics including industrialisation, demography, politics, religion, education, class, the environment, and culture, as well as looking at the differences between Highland and Lowland society and economy. The second volume from 1850 to the present also covers a wide range of topics. Some of these, such as industrialisation, demography, urbanisation, religion, class, education, culture and Highland and Lowland society are continued while new topics include the state, Scottish identity, leisure and recreation. The third and fourth volumes contain carefully selected readings to accompany the topic-theme volumes and are likely to prove an invaluable resource for any reader wishing to pursue a particular subject in greater depth or perhaps investigate it in a local or regional project. The fifth volume in the series is a collection of primary sources for the history of modern Scotland designed to accompany the other volumes. It makes accessible between the covers of one book many of the documents of national and local importance from the eighteenth century and beyond and provides a unique and detailed insight into the period.

This book forms one part of the University of Dundee/Open University collaborative course, Modern Scottish History: 1707 to Present. This is an honours level undergraduate course for part-time adult learners studying at a distance, and it is designed to develop the skills, methods and understanding of history and historical analysis with modern Scotland as its focus. However, these volumes are designed to be used, either singly or as a series, by anyone interested in Scottish history. The introduction to recent research findings, together with practical exercises, advice on the critical exploitation of primary sources, and suggestions for further reading, should be of wide interest and application. We hope it will encourage users to carry their enthusiasm further by investigating, for example, some aspect of their own community history based on one or more themes covered in the series.

A series of this kind depends on the efforts of many people, and accordingly there are many debts to record. Our enthusiasm was shared by the Scottish Higher Education Funding Council which provided a generous grant to fund the development of the course. Within the University of Dundee, Professor David Swinfen, Vice Principal, has played a valuable supporting role. The authors produced their contributions to agreed formats and deadlines. While they are responsible for what they have written, they have also been supported by other members of the writing team and our editorial and production specialists. The material was developed collaboratively, reflected too in the cooperation and support we have had from our publisher, Tuckwell Press. Particular thanks to Tracey Walker and Johanne Phillips, the Project Secretaries, for their administrative support. Thanks also to Karen Brough and Jen Petrie who transcribed some of the texts for the articles and documents volumes.

USING THIS BOOK

Activities

Volumes 1 and 2 are designed not just as a text to be read through but also as active workbooks. They are therefore punctuated by a series of activities, signalled by a different format. These include short questions, exercises, and prompts for the reading articles in Volumes 3 and 4 or documents in Volume 5. Conversely the readings and documents refer back to topics/themes discussed in detail in Volumes 1 and 2.

References

While this book is free-standing, there are cross-references to other volumes in the series. This is to aid readers using all the books. The list of books and articles that follows each chapter generally follows the scholarly convention of giving details of all works cited. They are not intended as obligatory further reading.

Series Editors

Contents

PREFACE v
ILLUSTRATIONS x
PICTURE ACKNOWLEDGEMENTS xi
CONTRIBUTORS xiii

14   The State   1
      Ian Levitt
15   National Identity: From British Empire to European Union   25
      Richard J Finlay
16   The Highlands since 1850   47
      Ewen A Cameron
17   Industrialisation and Industrial Decline   73
      Peter L Payne
18   Demography   95
      Bill Kenefick
19   Urbanisation   119
      R J Morris
20   Religion   142
      Callum G Brown
21   Women and Gender Relations   161
      Arthur McIvor
22   Lowland Agriculture and Society   188
      Gavin Sprott
23   Class   210
      J Foster
24   Education   235
      Robert Anderson
25   Leisure and Recreation   257
      Robert A Lambert
26   Culture and Identity   277
      Christopher Harvie

INDEX   299

Illustrations

Sir John McNeill	4
Robert Munro	13
St Andrew's House, Edinburgh	19
Excerpt from *The Diary of John Sturrock*	27
Hugh McDiarmid	41
John Murdoch	53
The Napier Commission	55
Camperdown Works, Dundee	78
Welder – John Brown Shipyard, Clydebank, 1965	85
Scotland: civil counties and regions	97
District and regional administrative areas, 1991	102
Population density, 1991	103
The Murraygate, Dundee, 1875	128
Stewart's Court, Dundee, 1876	129
Princes Street, Edinburgh, bypass scheme, 1949	137
Bishop Forbes of Brechin	144
Free Church General Assembly, 1888	145
Trade union committee, Stanley Mills, Perthshire, 1915	174
Glasgow clippies, *c.* 1915	175
Farmworkers at Morphie, St Cyrus, Montrose, 1903	190
Advertisement, *c.* 1937, for the Ferguson-Brown tractor and system	200
Claas Super combining barley, 1954	204
Bleachers' strike, Almondbank, Perthshire, 1920	224
To the Workers - Call to Arms!	228
Sir Henry Craik	244
Scotland Street School, Glasgow	246
'Baxter's old half-time school', Dundee	247
Young stag, Invernate Forest, 1934	267
Botanists on Ben Lawers, 1932	270
The snow fields of Cairngorm	273
Alasdair Gray, *Lanark*	296

Picture Acknowledgements

The following are thanked for permission to reproduce illustrations in their collections:

Cambridge University Press: *illus 42*; Dundee University Archives: *illus 36, 37, 40, 41, 45, 46, 48, 49, 55, 59*; HMSO: *illus 43, 44*; National Library of Scotland/ Alasdair Gray: *illus 63*; National Museums of Scotland, Scottish Life Archive: *illus 52, 53, 54*; Royal Commission on the Ancient and Historical Monuments of Scotland: *illus 35, 58*; Scottish National Portrait Gallery: *illus 33, 38, 57*; Springburn Museum Trust: *illus 51*; The Trustees of the National Library of Scotland: *illus 56*; University of St Andrews Photographic Collection: *illus 60, 61*.

Dundee University Archives

The illustrations from Dundee University Archives, 36, 37, 40, 41, 45, 46, 48, 49, 55, 59, are a small selection from the extensive photographic collections held by the University. The collections include photographs of the jute and other related industries, the University and its predecessor institutions and the Scottish landscape. The Michael Peto Collection contains *c*. 200,000 photo-journalistic prints and negatives mainly featuring people and work in Britain, Europe and Asia. They include many personalities of politics and the arts during the 50s and 60s and many backstage scenes of the London Ballet featuring Nureyev and Fontaine.

The Archives are situated in the Tower Building basement of the University. For further information contact: The University Archivist, Tower Building, The University, Dundee DD1 4HN, Tel: 01382 344095, Fax: 01382 345523 or see the Archives' world wide web site at : http://www.dundee.ac.uk/Archives/

List of Contributors

Robert Anderson, Professor of Modern History, Department of History, University of Edinburgh. Has published *Education and Opportunity in Victorian Scotland* (1983), *Education and the Scottish People, 1750–1918* (1995), and other works on Scottish educational history and modern French history.

Callum G Brown, Senior Lecturer, Department of History, University of Strathclyde. Has published extensively on religious, social and cultural history, including *Religion and Society in Scotland since 1707* (1997).

Ewen A Cameron, Lecturer in Scottish History, University of Edinburgh. Interests are Scottish and Irish rural history. Author of *Land for the People? The British Government and the Scottish Highlands, c. 1880–1925* (1996).

Anthony Cooke, Senior Lecturer, Institute for Education and Lifelong Learning, University of Dundee. Has published widely on the history of adult education and on textile history including recent publications on the cotton mills at Spinningdale, Sutherland and on Stanley Mills, Perthshire for Historic Scotland.

Ian Donnachie, Senior Lecturer in History and Director of the Centre for Scottish Studies, The Open University in Scotland. Among his publications are *Historic New Lanark* (1993) and *The Companion to Scottish History* on CDRom (1996), both jointly with George Hewitt.

Richard J Finlay, Senior Lecturer in History, University of Strathclyde. Has published widely on Scottish identity and Scottish politics since 1700, including *A Partnership for Good?* (1997).

John Foster, Professor of Applied Social Studies, University of Paisley. Has published widely on working-class and labour history in the nineteenth and twentieth centuries, including *A Class Struggle and the Industrial Revolution* (1974) and *Paying for the Piper: Capital and Labour in the offshore Oil Industry* (1996), jointly with C Woolfson and M Beck.

Christopher Harvie, Professor of British and Irish Studies at the University of Tüebingen, Germany. Author among other works of *No Gods and Precious Few Heroes: Scotland since 1914,* which he is updating for its fourth edition.

William Kenefick, Lecturer in Scottish History, Department of Modern History, University of Dundee. Interests include labour history, particularly waterside labour and the role of the Irish; is currently preparing *Rebellious and Contrary: Glasgow Dockers, 1853–1932*.

Robert A Lambert, Institute for Environmental History, University of St Andrews. Writes on the environmental history of Britain, nature conservation, leisure, countryside recreation and tourism. Editor of *Species History in Scotland* (1998).

Ian Levitt, Professor of History, Department of Historical and Critical Studies, University of Central Lancashire. Has published widely on government administration and the development of social provision, including *The Scottish Office, 1919–59* (1995).

Arthur McIvor, Senior Lecturer in History, University of Strathclyde. Research interests are labour and industrial relations history, women's history and the history of occupational health. Recently published *Organised Capital* (1996), and co-edited *Roots of Red Clydeside, 1910–1914* (1996) with W Kenefick.

Ann MacSween, Project Manager, Distance Learning: Modern Scottish History Project, University of Dundee. Author of a number of books and articles on the archaeology of Scotland, including *Prehistoric Scotland* (1990).

R J Morris, Professor of Economic and Social History, Department of Economic and Social History, University of Edinburgh. Author of several publications on urban history and the British middle classes including *Class, Sect and Party, 1800–1850* (1990). Founding editor of *History and Computing*.

Peter L Payne, Professor Emeritus of Economic History, University of Aberdeen and sometime Colquhoun Lecturer in Business History at the University of Glasgow. Has written widely on many aspects of the modern Scottish economy, including *Growth and Contraction: Scottish Industry, c. 1860–1990* (1992).

Gavin Sprott, Keeper of the Department of Social and Technological History in the National Museums of Scotland. Has published a range of papers on his two main areas of interest, farming history from the eighteenth century to the present, and the farming background of Robert Burns.

Christopher A Whatley, Professor of Scottish History, Department of Modern History, University of Dundee. Author of numerous publications on eighteenth-century Scottish economic and social history including *The Industrial Revolution in Scotland* (1997).

The State

Ian Levitt

INTRODUCTION

As Scottish economic and social life became more complex, governments, often against their better judgement, were forced to become increasingly interventionist. This chapter explains how the state tackled the numerous problems of administration which arose after 1850. We will be examining this topic under the following sub-headings:

- The Scottish Board and representative opinion 1850–1880
- The Scottish Secretary, franchise reform and Liberal Unionism, 1880–1914
- The Scottish Secretary of State and collective provision, 1914–31
- St Andrews House and Labour Unionism, 1931–50

When you have completed work on this chapter, you should have a good understanding of how different governments perceived the role of the state and how the decisions they took affected Scotland during the second half of the nineteenth and the twentieth centuries.

In 1850 the number of civil servants employed by the Government on Scottish Administration totalled less than 50. The annual cost of the administration, which included the Lord Advocate's department and a number of Boards and other offices was £32,000, a total somewhat less than the £35,000 spent on the British Secret Service. Nominally the Home Secretary was responsible for Scottish Administration, but in practice much of this was delegated to the Lord Advocate, a member of the Government, but not in the Cabinet. By 1950 the number of civil servants employed totalled more than 6,000 at a cost of £100,000,000 per annum and Scottish Administration was the responsibility of the Secretary of State for Scotland, who did sit in the Cabinet. His principal office was the newly built St Andrew's House in Edinburgh, some 400 miles from Westminster. The Scottish Office which administered the Scottish Secretary's services was based on four departments, the Scottish Home Department (with responsibility for law and order, the prisons, the fire services and the fishing industry), the Department of Health (with responsibility for the National Health Service, housing and town and country planning), the Department of Agriculture and the Scottish Education Department (Milne 1958; Gibson 1985; Kellas 1989).

Much of the growth in Scottish Administration can be attributed to similar issues affecting other Western industrial societies. On the one hand there was a general reaction against the philosophy of laissez-faire and the 'night-watchman' State. New

forms of statutory provision emerged that stressed collectivism and the redistribution of economic rewards, seen most succinctly in State-subsidised housing, National
Insurance and the promotion of health care. On the other hand, there was a
widespread view that private enterprise, by itself, did not necessarily generate
general economic well-being and without Government measures to stimulate
investment and support education, the productivity of labour – and hence employment – would decline. However, to regard the development of Scottish Administration as part of the 'natural' growth of Government can be misleading, for as a
Scottish Office review in 1948 pointed out, much of the growth appeared haphazard
and not necessarily in accordance with Scottish 'sentiment' (Scottish Office 1948).
For instance, the review noted that during the Second World War the Scottish
Secretary had been given responsibility for town and country planning and for the
North of Scotland Hydro-electricity Board, but responsibility for the development of
industry was given to the Board of Trade. Similarly, despite the opposition of local
authorities and the indigenous air industry the Ministry of Civil Aviation assumed
responsibility for Scottish Air Services. Moreover, after 350 years of a separate Poor
Law, social security provision was removed from Scottish control and given to the
National Assistance Board, a British ministry. In essence to appreciate the growth of
the British State in Scotland and the relative balance of responsibility, it is necessary
to take into account three issues, first, the nature of domestic administration at a
time of laissez-faire economic policy, second, the nature of Scottish 'sentiment' in a
more democratic age and third, the rising demand for collective provision and a
higher level of welfare (Fry 1987; McCrone 1992; Levitt 1992; Lynch 1993; Finlay
1994).

1. THE SCOTTISH BOARD AND REPRESENTATIVE OPINION, 1850–1880

In the period after the 1832 Reform Act, which extended the franchise to the
wealthier middle class, a succession of Whig Governments began to reorganise
public services according to the principle of utilitarianism. By the early 1850s a
central Government Board in England held responsibility for managing the Poor
Law and the nascent health services. Similar boards existed for the management of
asylums and prisons, and a department of the Home Office monitored the provisions
of the Factory Acts. Utilitarian government implied that provision was broadly
uniform throughout the country and much of this was achieved through the power
of the Government to issue Orders and regulations governing local services. The
central boards were invariably assisted by regionally-based civil servants to insist
that the regulations were applied, irrespective of past customs and the opinion of the
local electorate. The period had witnessed a succession of protests, most notably
those organised by the chartists against the workhouse provisions of the New Poor
Law, but, in general, the intellectual force and logic of utilitarianism gradually
established a centripetal form of government administration. Boards of Guardians
and local authorities settled down to a period when there was an expectation that a

central view of provision would emerge, but that negotiation with district inspectors would ensure some degree of autonomy over its implementation and its impact on the rates.

Scotland was not immune from the influence of utilitarianism and by the mid-1850s there were central boards for the administration of the Poor Law, mental welfare and prisons. There was also a Fisheries Board, whose work lay primarily with the Scottish herring industry, but also had some responsibility for the industry in England. However, important differences emerged in the evolution of Scottish public administration. The desire to influence and control forms of social development and mitigate chartist dissent certainly existed, but neither the local landowner nor the professional urban classes were prepared to accept London control over Scottish provision. The Act of Union had left domestic management largely in local hands and in areas of social and education provision, like the Poor Law, a distinct and separate style of administration emerged (Paterson 1994). The professional classes, particularly lawyers used to a separate legal code, were unwilling to accept the primacy of a Lord Chancellor whose background was the English Bar. The medical schools were similarly opposed to a British administration which might favour the clinical view of the London medical schools and diminish their ability to attract students.

In 1845 the Scottish Poor Law was reformed and placed under the supervision of an Edinburgh-based board, headed by a full-time chairman and assisted by three sheriffs (representing the counties), the Lord Provosts of Edinburgh and Glasgow (representing the urban burgh), the Solicitor-General and two Crown appointees (Levitt 1988). Technically a sub-department of the Home Office, the Board held no power to issue Orders. Instead it acted in a semi-judicial capacity, issuing regulations for the building of poorhouses and for the distribution of medical relief and heard appeals by paupers against inadequate relief. Nevertheless the Board's preferred mode of operation was through the publication of circulars issuing guidance to parishes and its district inspectors, first appointed in 1852, were specifically instructed that they should avoid 'the appearance of superceding' the local authority.

The Board, which became the model of subsequent boards, was based on the principle of patronage. Its first chairman, appointed during a Conservative Government, was Sir John McNeill, a Tory, who had been a diplomat and was a confident of Queen Victoria. His secretary, a wealthy Perthshire landowner, was also a Tory, as were subsequent chairmen and secretaries. Occasionally the Board consulted the Lord Advocate on matters of legal principle, but there is little evidence that the Home Secretary took much interest in its deliberations. In fact, the Board, like the Prison Board and the Board of Lunacy (established after the 1856 Lunacy Act), conducted its business with a deliberate view of incorporating 'representative' opinion into its administration and unlike the English Poor Law Board attracted little Parliamentary comment or inquiry. McNeill sought to ensure that one of the Crown nominees was a Whig (**Document 85**) and that the sheriffs and Lord Provosts would not raise objection to the gradual implementation of a uniform Scottish

33 Sir John McNeill, first Chairman of the Board of Supervision for the Relief of the Poor (1845-68). *Scottish National Portrait Gallery: Hill & Adamson Collection.*

policy. By the 1870s although there were technical differences between Scottish and English law, in practice, much the same kind of person received Poor Relief or was committed to an asylum, or sent to prison. The Fisheries Board managed the Scottish and English industries alike. The same applied to public health which was added to the Board of Supervision's responsibilities in 1867. Despite numerous attacks by Liberal MPs alleging that the Scottish Boards lacked political control and were too independent of Parliament, both the 1869 Scottish Poor Law Committee and the 1870 Scotch Offices Commission confirmed that no alternative scheme was likely to reduce the cost of central administration without an increase in staff or greater London control. The Boards' representative element, their availability in Edinburgh and their refusal to cajole local authorities into accepting Government 'orders' had ensured considerable institutional support. A belief in *laissez-faire* economics meant few preferred increased Government, if the Scottish boards appeared to work.

EXERCISE I

In the mid-nineteenth century, why do you think the Scots seemed keen on representative boards? What administrative advantages do you think they contained? Do you perceive any problems they might have had?

Briefly, your responses should include the following points; the retention of political control over Scottish affairs in Edinburgh, ease of communication with Scottish institutions and the extent of enfranchisement. You might also mention how far the mid-Victorian Scot accepted the principles of *laissez-faire*.

2. THE SCOTTISH SECRETARY, FRANCHISE REFORM AND LIBERAL UNIONISM, 1880-1914

One reason for the failure to reform the Scottish Board and place them under a Scottish minister had been the desire of Liberal MPs to combine greater political control with enhanced local democracy (Morton 1996). The principal difficulty they faced was that outside the burgh, the franchise was severely restricted and, in practice, the landward areas of Scotland were heavily controlled by the landowner and other large property owners. In addition, the thrust of public policy, headed by those in education and public health was to increase the rates; piped water, systems of sewerage and new schools did not come cheap. 'Intelligent' opinion wanted further provision, but the disenfranchised working class, as George Trevelyan, a Liberal MP pointed out, would not pay unless directly represented (Hansard 1876). An 'epistolary' style of central administration might satisfy the Edinburgh lawyer or landowner, but seemed too distant from the working class's view of Scottish democracy.

Disraeli's Conservative administration, 1874–80, had considered appointing a Parliamentary Under Secretary at the Home Office to deal with Scottish business, but recognised that the appointment would challenge the authority of Lord Advocate, without a commensurate increase in Scotland's political status. Gladstone's electoral triumph in 1880, based on the populist Midlothian campaign, brought the issue of Scotland's political control back into focus. Soon after the election a group of Liberal MPs petitioned the Government for the creation of a Scottish Secretary to represent the Scottish interest more directly in Parliament. The Lord Advocate, they said, had too many legal duties to focus on political matters and lacked sufficient ministerial status to influence the Government. A number of Lords Advocate had not been MPs, which had further disenfranchised Scotland. Many local authorities, they argued, complained that the Home Office was dominated by English concerns and often relegated Scottish Bills to occasional late night sittings, usually with less than a half hour for debate.

Gladstone's Government, nominally Liberal but dominated by the Whigs, rejected the petition. It believed that introducing a 'national' or territorial element into British administration would cut across utilitarian thought and the earlier reform of public administration. It was his Government in 1870 that decided against creating a separate Scottish Board of Education. Provision in Britain was managed by a Committee of the Privy Council, whose principal aim was the creation of a system of uniform schooling for the working class. The Conservative Opposition held similar objections and feared that a Scottish administration would be dominated by the domestic concerns of Highland land reform, temperance and church disestablishment. They also feared that the prospective extension of the franchise to the working class would democratise the local authority and sweep away the influence of the Tory landowner. (The Liberals intended to extend the vote to all male householders at the next General Election.) However, in March 1883 Lord Rosebery, the Parliamentary Under Secretary at the Home Office with special responsibility for Scottish affairs, similarly petitioned the Government and repeated the comments he had made earlier in the Lords (Hanham 1965). He told the Lords:

> No Lord Advocate has ever been in the Cabinet. It really is a considerable disadvantage for the country to have its Chief Officer permanently excluded from the Cabinet. There is another disadvantage. For every other part of the country and every other Department of the Government there is a permanent staff, and when a new Minister comes into one of these Departments he finds the traditions and arrangements of their Office working on, whatever political changes occur. But there is no such tradition for Scotland. Everything has to be begun again *de novo* on the accession of a Lord Advocate . . . But there is another side, which I think still more serious and important. The words 'Home Rule' have begun to be distinctly and loudly mentioned in Scotland. At the Convention of Royal Burghs this year there was a Motion brought forward urging that a separate and subordinate legislature should be set on foot to consider Scotch questions. That Motion was not largely entertained; but it is a significant sign of the times that . . . under present circumstances it should be heard.
>
> (House of Lords Debates, 1881)

Sir William Harcourt, the Home Secretary, accepted much of what Rosebery said, but refuted the view that the Home Office had neglected to support 'first rank' Scottish Bills, or failed to appreciate Scottish 'conditions' (Rosebery 1883; Harcourt 1883). However, he did concede that expectations had been raised – 'which had to be satisfied' – and proposed the establishment of a Scottish Local Government Board, headed by a 'President'. The minister, who would sit in Parliament, would have 'oversight' of the other Boards and be based in London. The President would have the rank of Lord Privy Seal, a position somewhat between a parliamentary under secretary and a Cabinet minister, like the Home Secretary or the Lord Chancellor. Nevertheless Harcourt's Bill attracted severe criticism from backbench MPs and the Bill was withdrawn. As the press pointed out Scottish opinion wanted more than a London-based minister for sewerage, lunatic asylums and fisheries (*Glasgow Herald* 1883; *Times* 1883). Edinburgh was the natural centre of Scottish administration.

The Conservatives sensed the Government's discomfort and in a complete *volte face* joined a campaign established by the Convention of Royal Burghs for a Scottish Secretary (Mitchell 1990). At an open meeting in Edinburgh in January 1884, organised by the Convention, Lord Lothian spoke vigorously in favour of establishing a Scottish Secretaryship (*Scotsman* 1884). Lothian told the meeting that the Treaty of Union had guaranteed that certain areas of Scottish administration would be 'managed independently' from England and although his Party favoured the Union, it was not in favour of 'absorption'. Scottish 'manners', 'customs', laws and administrative practices had their own distinct heritage. The appointment, he added, would raise Scottish politics above class interests and provide a focus to unite the electorate behind a common cause – maintaining Scotland's interest in the Union and 'remove other temptations to tamper with the integrity of the Empire'. The view of the Conservatives was quite simple. If the Act of Union was to survive working class enfranchisement it meant a different kind of Scottish administration, capable firstly of ensuring that British ministers took account of Scottish interests in the formulation of policy, secondly of ensuring that Parliament allocated more time for Scottish business and thirdly of 're-invigorating' Scottish consciousness with a new sense of national 'solidarity'.

With some reluctance Gladstone agreed to a wider measure, though it fell to Lord Salisbury's minority administration in 1885 to pilot the Bill through Parliament. (Salisbury accepted that the Bill had become 'non-political', though the utilitarian Whigs tried unsuccessfully to prevent the Scottish Secretary assuming control of education.) The first Scottish Secretary, the Duke of Richmond and Gordon, took office in August that year, with his administrative 'headquarters' established symbolically, not in Edinburgh, but at Dover House (an ex-Admiralty building) in Whitehall. The Scottish Office, as it became known, was staffed by a permanent under secretary and a half-dozen clerks, all drawn from existing Whitehall departments. The Scottish Secretary's powers included the promotion of Scottish Bills, the control of the Scottish Boards, law and order (the functions previously exercised by the Home Office) and Crown patronage. He also assumed the vice-presidency of a newly created Scotch Education Department, an arrangement designed to pacify Whig opinion. The SED, whose office was established in London, remained a sub-department of the Privy Council and technically the Scottish Secretary's actions were subject to review by the Lord President. Its Departmental secretary reported directly to the Scottish Secretary and not through the Scottish Office. However, the Scottish Secretary with the ministerial rank of a Lord Privy Seal, was not a Secretary of State with an automatic right to a seat in the Cabinet. His seat in the Cabinet depended on the personal inclination of the Prime Minister. A further Act in 1887 clarified the Scottish Secretary's powers and confirmed he was the Government's principal minister for Scottish affairs.

The new Scottish Secretary faced three particular issues affecting the duties of his office. First, the office implied that there was a definite Scottish administration with a distinctive Scottish policy which other ministries would have to accept. The Scottish electorate would hardly believe the reform unless the Scottish Secretary was seen to exercise power. Second, the Act did nothing to alter the nature or the constitution of the Boards, except that they now reported to him, rather than the Home Secretary – and they had not been used to political interference. Third, the Treasury brief to his officials had been clear, the Scottish Secretary was to avoid action which might promote further political devolution. The Scottish Secretary's primary task was to ensure that the Liberal voter, the majority opinion in Scotland, remained satisfied with the Union and Westminster control.

The immediate issue facing the Scottish Secretary was an outbreak of unrest in the Western Highlands, where the crofting community faced higher rents and the threat of eviction (Hunter 1976). A bill was quickly produced to give the crofter a measure of protection over tenure and at the same time introduce schemes of emigration. However, the Scottish Office also continued with the Home Office's policy of rigorously policing the area, using, at times, a number of secret agents to assess the likelihood of further disturbances. By 1887 the emergency was over, but it left the legacy of an administration dedicated to maintaining law and order and the break-up of traditional patterns of Highland living. The early Scottish Secretaries, particularly Arthur Balfour, Lord Salisbury's minister, 1886–7, judged that what-ever the crofters' apparent popular support, the new urban classes had no wish to subsidise a redundant community from increased taxation. The Scottish Secretary's position was further enhanced when Salisbury's Chancellor of the Exchequer, George Goschen, agreed that the level of Treasury support for public education in Scotland should not be less than its share of UK wealth, which according to probate and excise duty was assumed to be eleven-eightieths (Anderson 1995). Although the announcement was meant to quell public unease over Scotland's entitlement to the various grants then available, the 'Goschen formula', as it became known, soon became the yardstick with which to measure other allocations between England and Scotland. As the Treasury commented, the Scottish Secretary assumed that future Scottish grants would be increased in proportion to any increase in England, irrespective of purpose or the relative state of wealth between the two countries (Treasury 1896).

The Boards presented the Scottish Secretary with a different problem. Their membership had been decided by Act of Parliament and, in the case of the Board of Supervision, although the Scottish Secretary could sack the chairman if he did not agree with his policy, he could not do the same with the sheriffs or the Lords Provost of Edinburgh and Glasgow. As George Trevelyan, Gladstone's Scottish Secretary, 1892–95, discovered, when they did object, there was little he could do. (He had wanted to extend Poor Relief to the unemployed, then illegal in Scotland and abolish the property qualification for parochial board electors.) In 1894 Trevelyan persuaded the Cabinet to support the Board's replacement with a Local Government Board, composed of the Scottish Secretary (as president), the solicitor-general, the permanent under-secretary and three appointed members, drawn from those in local government and the legal and medical professions. In Parliament he commented:

> These three officers, with a salaried secretary, will constitute what I may call the inner circle of the Local Government Board in Scotland. That is a much larger Board in England, which in truth consists of no one but the President; but the circumstances of Scotland differ very much from those of England. The work has to be done on the spot in Edinburgh, and only a general control can be exercised in London . . . You will then have in Edinburgh a small, compact, and, I think, well-established group of administrators who will be entirely confined to the work of their Department, and in London during the Session you will have a Parliamentary Minister who is really and truly responsible to Parliament for the information he gives it, and for the policy of the Board.
>
> (*Hansard* 1894a)

The 1894 Local Government Act placed the Scottish Secretary as the effective head of domestic administration, though Scottish opinion believed that he should consult with 'representative' opinion before taking action, or agreeing British policy with the Cabinet. (Trevelyan also extended the franchise in parochial board elections to adult householders, broadly identical to the Parliamentary franchise). The Local Government Board model was used as the basis for the constitution of the Congested Districts Board (established in 1897 to deal with land reform and emigration in the crofting community), the Board of Agriculture (established in 1912 to introduce schemes of agricultural improvement and land settlement) and the Highlands and Islands Medical Board (established in 1913 to improve medical services) (Day 1918; Mackay 1996).

The third issue, political devolution, posed the Scottish Office with a special difficulty. Its officials knew that the Conservatives were opposed to further devolution. However, after 1886 the Liberals were pledged to supporting Irish Home Rule and a number of backbench MPs pressed for a similar measure for Scotland. This was intensified in 1889 when the numerically greater number of Scottish Liberals successfully amended the Local Government Bill during the Committee stage of the Bill (a group of English MPs had failed to attend), only to find the Conservatives reversing the amendments at the Third Reading. The amendments, affecting the power of the County Councils to purchase property and decide the regulations affecting public health, were designed to increase Scottish autonomy from Westminster. Motions supporting Home Rule were introduced in 1889, 1892 and 1893 and although defeated the Liberal Government accepted that a Scottish Select (or Grand) Committee should be established. It would consider the Committee stage of Scottish Bills and be composed of the 70 Scottish MPs with the addition of 15 other members. In the House of Commons Trevelyan argued that this would ensure Scottish Bills could be passed more quickly and with greater consideration given to the views of Scottish MPs. He commented;

> We offer the Scottish members a proposal for enabling them, at one of the most important periods of process in the manufacture of their Bills, to have those Bills moulded in accordance with Scottish opinion. This year the Scottish members have not been very fortunate in the Ballot; and yet I already see on the Table of the House at least eight very important Scottish Bills, and I know that a good many more are in preparation. It requires almost endless patience and perseverance, and it requires almost humiliating appeals to the indulgence of English members to get one of these Bills occasionally passed between 12 and 1 o'clock in the morning . . . What is the House in Committee on Scottish business? Before that Committee has gone 10 minutes all the Members except the Scottish Members have left the House. No one but a Scottish Member speaks; but I am sorry to say that the Members who are in the precincts of the House come in to vote.
>
> (*Hansard* 1894b)

Trevelyan made it clear that the Committee would not discuss Bills dealing with foreign policy, trade and industry, the armed forces or Government finance. Nevertheless the proposal caused alarm amongst Conservative MPs. In the Commons Arthur Balfour argued that it would be difficult for a Government to reverse amendments to a Bill approved by a predominately Scots Committee, if it reflected the majority opinion of Scottish MPs. He sensed it represented the first stage towards Home Rule and commented:

> The idea that we can legislate either for Ireland, or Scotland, or Wales, or England, and that that legislation passed for these countries does not react upon the other countries, is a fantastic absurdity. It must be followed in the long run by a similar proposal for England; and if Scotland is to be excluded from her share of legislating for England, the result will be that Scotland will not have a greater but a lesser power over the legislation not merely of the United Kingdom, but of Scotland itself, than she possesses at the present moment. I say that no greater danger menaces the political interests of Scotland than the danger that by our insane action we may arouse England to a sense that she is an oppressed nationality, and compel her to use the power which she undoubtedly possesses to

exclude from all share in her affairs those who do not happen to live within her borders.

(*Hansard* 1894c)

The *Scotsman* declared that a Grand Committee, dominated by the interests of the Highland crofter and Lowland temperance campaigner, would 'provincialise' Scotland (1894). The *Glasgow Herald* took a similar position and accused Trevelyan of 'vestry patriotism' (1894). It added that Scotland, with its much smaller population and industry, was heavily dependent on 'free trade' with England. The Government reluctantly accepted a Conservative amendment that the committee should be increased by a further 15 non-Scottish MPs to equal the Party balance in the House of Commons. The Bills remitted were to be restricted to non-controversial measures and to English measures which had been examined by the full House. Salisbury's third administration, 1895–1900, abandoned the committee (the Conservatives remained a minority party in Scotland), but the Liberals re-established it in 1907 with a similar membership and restriction on what Bills could be discussed.

By the 1900s the Scottish State had evolved a distinctive form. In Parliament Scottish Bills received much greater attention and few local authorities complained that it was impossible to secure the passage of purely local measures. In Edinburgh the Boards continued to administer Scottish services much as in the past with little complaint as to their administrative competence. MPs, local councils and the public identified with the Boards and recognised their authority to speak on Scottish issues. However, the Boards now contained a visible and identifiably political element – the Scottish Secretary – who since 1892 had been a member of the Cabinet. The Scottish Secretary's role was to ensure that on the one hand the Scottish interest was represented in Whitehall, and on the other that domestic opinion understood the benefits of maintaining the Union (Jalland 1979). His dual role, embodying the 'national spirit' in London and maintaining political control over Scottish 'extremism' differed radically from the functions of other ministers, but the failure of successive Home Rule Bills to excite Scottish interest and the relative ease at which new Boards were accepted indicated how far the 1885 Act had incorporated the enfranchised worker.

EXERCISE 2

Why did Scottish opinion object to the absorption of Scottish administration into a British framework of ministerial control? Why did the Conservatives so fear a Scottish Parliament? What do you think is meant by the term 'Liberal Unionism'?

Your response here should refer to the widening of the franchise and a concern to counter class divisions with an appeal to the uniqueness of Scottish historical tradition. Some thought should also be given to the fear of Scottish radicalism developing its own agenda for the Highlands, public expenditure and the urban society. A reference to the interests of the Scottish business community might also be considered.

3. THE SCOTTISH SECRETARY OF STATE AND COLLECTIVE PROVISION, 1914–31

The Liberal Government, 1906–10, had pledged itself to the principle of 'free trade' and cheap food, largely to retain the support of the working class (Dyer 1996). However, under pressure from the newly formed Labour Party and the trade unions, it began to restructure the provision of welfare. By 1914, the majority of British workers benefited from a national scheme of Health Insurance and a growing number were also covered for unemployment. Necessitous schoolchildren received free school meals and a local authority infant and maternity service had been established. A reform of the Poor Law was also pledged. Nevertheless, in Scotland these measures were not seen as sufficient to mitigate the growing level of poverty and satisfy the electorate's demand for additional welfare (Harvie 1993). Scottish housing conditions, with over 40% of the population living in one or two rooms (over four times the proportion in England), became notorious as a breeding ground for TB and the principal cause of the much higher level of infant mortality. Outside the principal cities hospital provision remained negligible and the lower rateable capacity of Scottish local authorities meant much greater resistance to extending statutory services. A Government inquiry on the British mining industry in 1908 reported on the comparatively poor state of housing for the Scottish miner and its likely effect on worker productivity and trade union militancy. As a result the Scottish Secretary ordered the Local Government Board to conduct its own inquiry which confirmed much of what the report had said. Another Board report was authorised on the measures that Glasgow had taken to control the spread of TB. It indicated that local authority measures to provide hospital care were practically useless unless patients could be found new housing. In 1913, after further pressure from the trade unions, the Government agreed to appoint a Royal Commission on the state of Scottish housing. The First World War interrupted the Commission's work and before it could report the Government had introduced the Rent Restriction Act (after a 'strike' of tenants in Glasgow), an extension of unemployment benefit to most workers and the break-up of the Poor Law. Following the report of the Royal Commission (in 1917), the Government announced a crash post-war programme of 'reconstruction', in which the State would subsidise the provision of local authority housing. In Scotland over 200,000 new houses were thought necessary to replace the slums and meet 'general' needs. Other schemes of health and welfare were also announced.

Lloyd George's 'khaki' election in December 1918 returned the war-time coalition Government with a substantial majority, pledged to continue the programme of 'reconstruction'. However, in Scotland, despite the poor showing of the Labour Party, many MPs and the press had sensed a shift in attitude of the working class towards the State and established political values. The Scottish Secretary, Robert Munro, had been an erstwhile campaigner for Home Rule, but saw that the Liberal Party's commitment to political reform did not necessarily coalesce with Labour's demands for the nationalisation of industry and the radical restructuring of economic rewards. The outbreak of industrial militancy during the War continued and on Clydeside the Government feared the prospect of a general strike, fuelled by unemployed demobilised soldiers. Munro tried unsuccessfully to persuade Lloyd George to raise the status of the Scottish Secretary to a Secretary of State – to symbolise Scotland's contribution to the war and its importance to the Union – but was persuaded to accept a restructuring of the Scottish Office. A division was established especially to look after law and order; as one Scottish civil servant pointed out, the future looked dominated by the problems of industrial unrest, unemployment and crofter disturbances (Scottish Office 1921). The Cabinet also retreated from establishing a separate Scottish Ministry of Health to correspond with the English Ministry of Health. Instead a Board of Health was established under the 'Presidency' of the Scottish Secretary, with the additional appointment of a Parliamentary Under-Secretary. The Board, based in Edinburgh, took over the functions of the Local Government Board, the Highlands and Islands Medical Board and the Scottish National Health Insurance Commission. (The latter had been established in 1911). Munro told the Commons that a separate ministry, with a brief that looked too close to Labour's interests, was felt bound to diminish the Scottish Secretary's status in Cabinet and his authority as Scotland's principal representative in London (Scotsman 1919).

34 Robert Munro, Secretary of State for Scotland and first President of the Scottish Board of Health (1919-22). From WT Pike (ed) 1904 Contemporary Biographies, No 12, (WT Pike & Co), Edinburgh.

The election of a Conservative Government in 1922, at the same time as Labour's broad sweep of seats in Central Scotland, heightened Scottish political tension (Donnachie 1989). Ten of Glasgow's seats were captured by members of the Independent Labour Party and wiped out the last vestige of city support for the Liberals. The new MPs, many of them with a background in the war-time pacifist movement and in organising the 1919 Glasgow general strike, immediately pressed the Government to reverse the policy of economic retrenchment introduced to counter inflation. The housing programme had been one of the most severely affected, with only 25,000 out of an estimated need of 200,000 being built. In 1921 unemployment in Scotland reached 22% of the workforce and riots over cuts in benefit occurred in Dundee, Glasgow, Aberdeen and a number of other industrial centres.

Lord Novar, the Scottish Secretary, initially supported retrenchment, but in March 1923 accepted that, without a higher level of housing grant, few local authorities would continue with the subsidised programme. He also accepted that the private house-building market could not meet more than a quarter of the estimated need, unlike England where two thirds of the new housing was expected to be for owner-occupation. However, the Cabinet rejected Novar's claim and told him that Government could not provide an additional subsidy without doing the same in England. It was impossible, the MPs were told, to ask the English worker to agree additional taxation to finance a higher level of need in Scotland (Hansard 1923).

The 1924 minority Labour Government restored some of the benefits that had been cut in 1921 and agreed a new housing subsidy under the Minister of Health, John Wheatley, the Clydeside MP. Nevertheless, Scottish Labour MPs felt dissatisfied with Westminster and its failure to address specifically Scottish problems and in May introduced a Home Rule Bill to establish a Parliament in Edinburgh (see **Document 86**). The Parliament would have control of the Scottish Secretary's work and a number of other services, but not including defence, foreign policy, international trade and the currency. In principle, the Government supported the measure, but refused to consider its re-introduction when Conservative MPs 'talked out' the Bill during the Second Reading. The Government felt that Scottish support for the measure was not as great as the MPs believed (see **Document 87**). Some of the opposition was due to a fear that a Scottish Parliament would be dominated by a particular brand of the militant socialist – trade unionists, ex-Irish nationalists and Highland radicals. But equally many businessmen felt that it would not be able to increase the level of collective provision without additional taxation. Opposition of local authorities had forced the Government to abandon a rate-supported scheme of public hospitals. For similar reasons of Scotland's low rateable capacity a significant number had failed to consider the Wheatley Act, despite the prospect of an increased grant. The attitude of the trade union movement was also equivocal. In 1920 the railwaymen's union successfully opposed a Government proposal to establish a Scottish regional railway, largely on the grounds that it would be less profitable than the continuation of the existing companies, with their links to the English midlands and the south. Other trade unions, particularly the skilled, remained concerned that a Scottish Parliament might lead to employers abandoning national pay bargaining and insisting that Scottish unions negotiate on the basis of local productivity.

In October 1924 the Conservatives won a landslide election victory. However, Baldwin, the Prime Minister, recognised that his Party had failed to win majority support on Clydeside and faced the prospect of renewed political and industrial unrest. Baldwin, like Lord Lothian in 1884, decided that his Party required a radical revision of thought towards its Scottish policy. In his election speeches Baldwin had indicated that he accepted Scotland faced particular difficulties, but felt that much of the blame was the result of the failure of Scottish institutions to appreciate post-war conditions and the greater competition in international trade. To him the real danger lay in the Scottish people giving up 'hope' and believing that a revolutionary dictatorship (communist or fascist) could provide housing, a better environment and jobs (*Times* 1925).

Baldwin's response was twofold. First, in early 1925 he agreed that the Scottish housing programme should be given an additional boost, principally to encourage local authorities to plan and develop their own schemes of houses. Over-ruling Neville Chamberlain, the utilitarian Minister of Health, he approved a £2m subsidy for a Government-sponsored housing association to build 2,500 steel houses. The houses would be manufactured on Clydeside and guarantee jobs for unemployed shipyard workers. Chamberlain's objection was that the proposed system of manufacture was more expensive than ordinary brick houses, but Baldwin believed that the issue demanded an immediate response and the programme's cost was subsidiary to restoring Scottish confidence in Government. 'Eviscerating the slums', he told a meeting in Glasgow, was a pre-requisite to dealing with Scottish 'discontent'. By 1928 local authorities were building over 20,000 houses per annum and it was estimated that the Royal Commission's target of 200,000 houses would be met by the mid-1930s. The Government's decision on steel housing was a watershed in Scotland's relations with Whitehall. What Baldwin had signalled was that if the Scottish Secretary could persuade his Cabinet colleagues of special Scottish conditions, additional grant aid over and above the strict 'Goschen' formula was possible. By the time of the General Election in 1929, Sir John Gilmour, the Scottish Secretary, had secured the continuation of the Wheatley housing grant, despite its withdrawal in England, an additional grant for maternity and TB provision and a special grant to the Poor Law authorities for providing benefits during the 1926 General Strike.

Baldwin also accepted that Scottish Administration was poorly equipped to deal with the more political environment of Government in the 1920s. In 1922 Munro had proposed reducing the membership of the various Boards, largely on the ground that it had proved difficult to agree policy as quickly and effectively as post-war circumstances demanded. The Board of Health, for instance, had six members, met weekly and, on occasion, could not agree a common submission for his considera-tion. The principal activity of the Board, before 1914, had been to monitor the activity of the local authority and ensure that they were implementing the statutes.

After 1919, the Boards were also responsible for agreeing much higher levels of grant with the Treasury and assessing the amount of need claimed by local authorities. Grants covered the provision of housing, school meals, TB hospitals, the Highlands and Islands medical service, the maternity service and the unemployed workmen's scheme. However, Board members were nominated primarily on the basis of representing Scottish opinion. Thus the Board of Health had members drawn from the legal profession, the local authority, the medical profession and the insurance industry. It was also required to appoint at least one woman. None of its members were career civil servants and none, on appointment, had experience of dealing with other Whitehall departments, or with the Cabinet. The Board, like other Boards had no office in London and had no officer specially designated to liaise with the Scottish Secretary in London when issues arose. Frequently, the Scottish Secretary attended Cabinet committee meetings without the support of officials, in contrast to other ministries. The difficulty the Boards faced in liaising with Whitehall was most evident during the retrenchment crisis in 1921. Munro was unaware that the Treasury and the Ministry of Health had agreed to suspend the housing subsidy until he attended the Cabinet.

Some of the difficulties reflected the fact that the Scottish Secretary remained one of the Government's junior ministers. It was accepted that the Scottish Secretary could speak with authority in Cabinet on matters that were purely Scottish, but these tended to be regarded as matters affecting the Highlands and Islands, fisheries, the Church and where Scottish statute differed from English. However, since 1900 successive Governments had established ministries to implement the introduction of services that covered the whole of the UK; for instance, the Ministry of Labour dealt with labour exchanges and unemployment insurance, whilst the Ministry of Transport dealt with the road network, shipping services and the railways. The Scottish Secretary, in effect, was responsible for only a portion of the Government's services in Scotland. Even in areas where responsibility for implementing policy was divided between the Scottish Secretary and other ministers, like Health and Education, it had been accepted, in principle, that the English ministry was the 'lead' ministry for initiating change. The Scottish housing situation had accelerated the Government's involvement in the provision of housing, but once the Royal Commission reported in 1917, it was the English ministry that took over and promoted the 1919 Housing Act. In these areas the Scottish Secretary was essentially a subsidiary minister whose prime task was to implement a common UK policy in Scotland irrespective of Board opinion.

Baldwin recognised the relatively weak constitutional position of the Scottish Secretary in tackling the specifically Scottish dimension to welfare provision. At the same time as agreeing to the special housing subsidy, he told a meeting of the Convention of Royal Burghs that he accepted that the Scottish Secretary should be raised to a Secretary of State, with the status of one of the Government's principal ministers and the automatic right to a seat in the Cabinet. An increase in the Scottish Secretary's power would, he felt, 'keep the people in good heart' (*Scotsman* 1925). Later in 1925 the Cabinet agreed to support an Act to create a Scottish Secretary of

State and in July 1926 Sir John Gilmour became the first Scottish Secretary of State since the Jacobite rebellion (Pottinger 1979).

The raising of the Scottish Secretary's status in Whitehall had an impact on the position of the Boards. Although the Scottish Secretary invariably consulted the Scottish Office's permanent under secretary for advice on matters submitted from the Boards, constitutionally the Scottish Office was not the superior department. In late 1926 Baldwin accepted a proposal from Gilmour to abolish the Boards of Agriculture and Health and establish departments in their place, each headed by a secretary, a career civil servant. As Gilmour later told the Commons, it was important that the Scottish Secretary should be able to reach 'rapid decisions' with the aid of 'highly trained civil servants'. Like other departments, Gilmour also proposed that the re-organisation would enable the 'free interchange' of civil servants between the departments and 'the Head Office in London'. Gilmour wanted a civil service structure similar to other ministries, with the Scottish Office permanent under secretary responsible for ensuring that the departments carried out the Scottish Secretary's political will.

Gilmour's proposals were introduced in a Bill in 1927, but ran into immediate difficulties. The opposition and the press claimed that the Bill would reverse the steady increase in administrative devolution to the Edinburgh Boards. It noted that the SED had been moved from London to Edinburgh in 1914 and that the Boards generally had come to embody the Scottish national identity, Scottish civil servants dealing with Scottish issues in Edinburgh. A number of MPs questioned Gilmour about the possibility of English civil servants being transferred to Scottish posts in Edinburgh.

Like Harcourt in 1883, Gilmour had failed to appreciate Scottish fears of 'absorption' and the Bill was withdrawn. After advice from civil servants the Bill was re-introduced in 1928 with the specific qualification that the headquarters of the new departments would remain in Edinburgh and that it was the Government's intention to 'centralise' all the Scottish Secretary's departments, including the Scottish Office, in the City (see **Document 88**). All reference to the position of the permanent under secretary was removed. Although opposition to the Bill remained, the majority of Conservative MPs and some Liberals approved the measure and in January 1929, the Departments of Agriculture and Health were established.

At the end of the 1920s Scottish Administration had undergone a considerable transformation. The presence of higher unemployment, a lower standard of living and a heightened belief that radical politics could produce material advancement forced Conservative Governments to concede a restructuring of Scotland's relationship with the Cabinet and its right to receive a higher level of collective provision. However, Scottish Administration remained divided between a number of discrete departments located both in Edinburgh and London. The Scottish Office held some responsibility for co-ordination, but in Whitehall its permanent under secretary lacked the status and authority to act officially as the 'mouthpiece' of Scottish opinion.

EXERCISE 3

Outline some of the weaknesses of Scottish Administration in the early 1920s.
What did Baldwin mean when he said that the elevation of the Scottish Secretary
to a Secretary of State would keep 'the people in good heart'? Looking at the
extracts from the 1924 Home Rule debate and the *Glasgow Herald*, why do you
think there was so much opposition to Home Rule?

I won't provide an answer here, except to say that you should bear in mind the
material shift in Scottish economic conditions and renewed Conservative fears over
Scottish radicalism. Remember to re-read the associated documents!

4. ST ANDREW'S HOUSE AND LABOUR UNIONISM, 1931–50

The rise of mass unemployment and the collapse of the second Labour Government in 1931 brought to an end the Scottish electorate's faith in radical Labour
politics. In the General Election that followed Labour was reduced to a handful
of seats in inner-city Glasgow and the surrounding district. Instead the Labour
Party in Scotland concentrated on building up its power base in municipal
councils, promoting schemes of local authority housing and in campaigning
against the means test. The switch in Labour tactics had some effect and by the
mid-1930s Labour gained control of Glasgow, Dundee, Greenock and a number
of other burghs in west-central Scotland. At the same time unemployment had
fallen to about 15%, about half the level reached in 1932. However, the collapse
of world trade and the imposition of international tariffs greatly affected the
exporting ability of Clydeside industry and, unlike the 1920s, there was a general
acceptance that the traditional industries of coal-mining, steel manufacture and
shipbuilding could no longer sustain Scottish economic development. A more
detailed housing survey published in 1936 indicated that a further 250,000
houses would be required to complete slum clearance and reduce over-crowding.
Labour's failure to retain its radical fervour and its apparent abandonment of
Home Rule led to the establishment of a Scottish National Party, pledged to the
belief that independence would create a new spirit of national identity and
economic regeneration.

Baldwin's National Government accepted that Scottish opinion remained concerned over the link between Scottish administration and Whitehall, despite the
reforms of the 1920s. In 1934, the Treasury agreed to establish a new Scottish Office
division in Edinburgh to deal more directly with the local authorities and their claims
for additional grant-aid. At the same time the Government, after special pleading
from the Scottish Secretary, agreed to establish a separate Scottish Commissioner
under the Special Areas Act. The Act covered the depressed mining areas around
Glasgow and was intended to introduce schemes of public improvement to rejuve-
nate the environment and make Clydeside attractive to English industry. Two years
later Baldwin fulfilled the pledge given by Gilmour in 1928 and established a
Committee to inquire into Scottish administration and its possible concentration in

35 The Scottish Office, St Andrews House, Edinburgh, established 1939. Crown Copyright: *Royal Commission on the Ancient and Historical Monuments of Scotland.*

Edinburgh. The Scottish Office told Baldwin that the Committee would help 'dampen the spirit for nationalism' (Scottish Office 1935).

The Committee reported in 1938 and recommended that the existing division of responsibility between Edinburgh departments and the London-based Scottish Office be broken up (Mitchell 1989). In its place, four Scottish departments would be established with their headquarters in the new St Andrew's House being built in Edinburgh. The Departments would cover Agriculture, Health, Education and Home Affairs, the functions of the latter being drawn from the existing Scottish Office in London. London would continue to have Scottish Office representation, but it would be known as the Office of the Scottish Secretary and house his permanent under secretary and other officials engaged in liaison work. The permanent under secretary's function was to provide advice to the Scottish Secretary where there was a difference of opinion between Departments, co-ordinate their activities in Scotland, and generally promote the Scottish interest in Whitehall.

At one level the re-organisation appeared to support an increase in administrative devolution, giving additional power to those in Edinburgh to meet and deal with Scottish institutions 'on the spot'. However, it also increased the power of the Scottish Secretary and his permanent under secretary to speak in London as the head of a unified ministry, equal in status to other large departments, like the Ministry of Health and the Board of Trade. The Second World War interrupted the developments, but by 1943 the Coalition Government began to consider the issue of post-war reconstruction. Tom Johnston, the Scottish Secretary, who had supported the 1924 Home Rule Bill, pressed the Government to transfer additional responsibilities to the Scottish Office and was successful in securing control of town and country planning (from the Ministry of Planning) and the development of the North of Scotland Hydro-electricity Board (from the Ministry of Fuel and Power). However, the Treasury refused to accept that administrative devolution in economic affairs could benefit Scotland (Scottish Office 1943). An official wrote:

> Towards the end of the nineteenth century when the advances of Government policy lay mainly in the field of education and other social services and the development of local government, and hardly at all in the field of commerce and economics, it was natural that almost all new Government powers should be granted as respects Scotland to the Scottish Secretary. At that time, moreover, Scotland's population bore a respectable relationship to England's, and with the booming of the heavy industries round the Clyde, which created so much of Scotland's wealth, Scotland was not much dependent economically on England. But now, when Scotland's population has dwindled relatively to England's (it is now little more than half the population of London), when Scotland's heavy industries have suffered severe depression, and when most important of all, the Government has widely extended its activities in the economic and industrial spheres and is preparing to an increasing extent to plan the allocation and development of the human and material resources of the country as a whole, the

case for separate administration in Scotland has in many respects grown weaker rather than stronger.

(Treasury 1943)

Johnston was forced to accept the logic of the Treasury's argument and concede that British 'economics' ministries should act to encourage the introduction of new industry. 'Whitehall securities', as he called it, provided the UK with its principal source of capital. Aided by Government grants, the Board of Trade would 'steer' industry from the over-crowded South-East, the Ministry of Civil Aviation would maintain Scottish air services at the same standard as in England and the Ministry of Fuel and Power would ensure that the mining industry could develop new pits in Ayrshire and the Forth basin. The concentration of economic control was further accelerated with the post-war Labour Government's decision to nationalise the mines, air transport, the railways, electricity supply and the gas industry.

Johnston's response was to agree an internal re-organisation of the Scottish Departments (Levitt 1996). The Scottish Home Department was given an additional division to liaise with London and to press the Scottish case for capital investment. It was also given the responsibility to encourage Scottish institutions such as the Scottish Council (Development and Industry) and the Scottish Tourist Board to prepare reports on the Scottish economy and its special needs. The other Scottish Departments were given additional staff to liaise with the British ministries once the investment had been secured.

The nationalisation of indigenous Scottish industry and the removal of the control of investment to London did not go unnoticed in Scotland. Despite Labour's overwhelming General Election victory in 1945, a campaign began to restore the control of domestic industry to either private enterprise or a separate Scottish Parliament. The Scottish Covenant Movement, a loose coalition of nationalists, liberals and communists, sought to stress that 'national renewal' could be sustained equally by enhancing the power of Scottish institutions. The institutions, it said, were nearer to local needs and had a better understanding of Scottish conditions than the English-dominated Whitehall ministries. The first campaign petered to a halt in 1948 when the Government agreed to extend the functions of the Scottish Grand Committee to consider Scottish estimates (which, in Parliamentary terms, meant the annual reports of the Scottish Departments) and the Second Reading of Scottish Bills. An internal review of the co-ordination of Government ministries in Scotland was also promised (Levitt 1998).

The campaign was renewed the following year with considerably more vigour and with apparently greater public support. This time the Government took the matter more seriously and began a discrete counter-campaign to outline the benefits of the Union and Scotland's link with Whitehall. Apart from the alleged additional cost of a separate Scottish Parliament, the campaign outlined the impact of economic 'disengagement' on trade and industry (see **Document 89**). By early 1950 the attitude of Scottish institutions changed from mild support of devolution to outright opposition. The Scottish miners, who feared that Scottish coal would not be sold in

England, re-affirmed their support for a British National Coal Board. The Scottish Council (Development and Industry) published a report on the extent of inward investment and the Lords Provost of Edinburgh and Glasgow stated their concern over a diminished level of Treasury grant-aid. In the autumn the second campaign similarly petered out. As the press reported, the Scottish electorate liked the post-war Welfare State and the low unemployment associated with centralised planning (*Glasgow Herald* 1950). However haphazard the structure of Government Administration in Scotland might appear, Scottish opinion felt comfortable with what the Treasury called 'parallel' administration in the areas of health, education, justice and planning, and 'centripetal' administration in trade and industry. The issue for the future, it recognised, was the ability of the Scottish Secretary to ensure that Whitehall continued to invest in Scotland and recognise its special needs (Treasury 1946).

EXERCISE 4
What do you think is meant by the term 'administrative devolution'? Why do you think Johnston turned his back on Home Rule? Looking at the extract from the Scottish Office briefing, why do you think Scottish business might fear a Scottish Parliament? What do you think is meant by the term 'Labour Unionism'?

In considering these issues it is important to compare and contrast the long-held tradition of protecting the decision-making power of Scottish institutions with new Labour views about nationalism and wider forms of collective provision. You should also make some reference to the concentration of investment in the hands of Government and its implications for economic development. More problematic, the closer we come to the events of say, 1979 and 1997, were the major influences in shifting opinion after the 1950s. **Article 25** and subsequent chapters will provide you with useful leads.

REFERENCES TO BOOKS AND ARTICLES MENTIONED IN THE TEXT

Anderson, RD 1995 *Education and the Scottish People 1750–1918*. Cambridge.
Day, JP 1918 *Public Administration in the Highlands*. London.
*Donnachie, I, Harvie, C and Wood, IS 1989 *Forward! Labour Politics in Scotland, 1888–1988*. Edinburgh.
Dyer, M 1996 *Capable Citizens and Improvident Democrats; the Scottish Electoral System, 1885–1929*. Aberdeen.
*Finlay, RJ 1994 'Scotland in the Twentieth Century: in Defence of Oligarchy?', *Scottish Historical Review* 73, 103–112.
Fry, M 1987 *Patronage and Principle*. Aberdeen.
Gibson, J 1985 *The Thistle and the Crown*. Edinburgh.
*Hanham, HJ 1965 'The creation of the Scottish Office, 1881–87', *Juridical Review* 10, 205–44.
Harvie, C 1993 *No Gods and Precious Few Heroes*. London.
Hunter, J 1976 *The Making of the Crofting Community*. Edinburgh.

*Hutchison, IGC 1986 *A Political History of Modern Scotland, 1832–1924*. Edinburgh.
Jalland, P 1979 'UK Devolution, 1910–14: Political panacea or tactical diversion', *English Historical Review* 94, 757–85.
Kellas, JG 1989 *The Scottish Political System*. Cambridge.
*Levitt, I 1988 *Government and Social Condition in Scotland, 1845–1919*. Edinburgh.
*Levitt, I 1992 *The Scottish Office 1919–59*. Edinburgh.
Levitt, I 1996 'The Origins of the Scottish Development Department, 1943–62', *Scottish Affairs* 14, 44–63.
*Levitt, I 1998 'Britain, the Scottish Covenant Movement and Devolution, 1946–50', *Scottish Affairs* 22, 23–47.
*Lynch, M 1993 *Scotland, 1850–1979: Society, Politics and the Union*. London.
McCrone, D 1992 *Understanding Scotland: the Sociology of a Stateless Nation*. London.
MacKay, D 1996 'The Congested District Boards of Ireland and Scotland', *Northern Scotland* 16, 142–73.
Milne, D 1958 *The Scottish Office*. London.
Mitchell, J 1989 'The Gilmour Report on Scottish Central Administration', *Juridical Review* 34, 173–88.
Mitchell, J 1990 *Conservatives and the Union*. Edinburgh.
Morton, G 1996 'Scottish Rights and 'centralisation' in the mid-nineteenth century', *Nations and Nationalism* 2, 257–79.
Paterson, L 1994 *The Autonomy of Modern Scotland*. Edinburgh.
Pottinger, G 1979 *The Secretaries of State for Scotland, 1926–76*. Glasgow.

FURTHER READING

Those references marked * in the above list are recommended further reading.

REFERENCES TO SOURCE MATERIAL REFERENCED IN THE TEXT

Glasgow Herald (17 and 22 Aug 1883), Leaders.
Glasgow Herald (3 April 1894), Leader.
Glasgow Herald (25 Feb 1950), Leader: 'Stalemate'.
Hansard (27 June 1876), Vol 230, c. 516–22, 'Poor Law (Scotland) Bill'.
Hansard (27 Apr 1894a), Vol 23, c. 1616, 'Local Government (Scotland) Bill'.
Hansard (2 Apr 1894b), Vol 22, c. 1119–21, 'Standing Committee (Scotland) Resolution'.
Hansard (2 Apr 1894c), vol 22, c. 1131, 'Standing Committee (Scotland) Resolution'.
Hansard (30 Apr 1923), vol 163, c. 1027, 'Housing (no 2) Bill Committee'.
W Harcourt (6 April 1883), 'Minister for Scotland'. *Public Record Office* CAB 37/10/30.
House of Lords Debates (13 June 1881), Vol. 262, c. 320–1, 'Minister for Scotland'.
Lord Rosebery (16 and 25 March 1883), 'Minister for Scotland'. *Public Record Office* CAB 37/10/27.
Scotsman (17 Jan 1884), 'Proposed Minister of State for Scotland'.
Scotsman (3 April 1894), Leader.
Scotsman (29 March and 27 April 1919), Leaders.
Scotsman (24 Feb 1925), Leader, 'The Scottish Secretary's Status'.
The Scottish Office (21 Jan 1921): 'Letter to the Treasury on Staff Appointments'. *Public Record Office* T 162/494.

The Scottish Office (28 Nov 1935): 'Letter to S. Baldwin'. *Scottish Record Office* HH 1/896.
The Scottish Office (14 Oct 1943): 'Machinery of Government in Scotland'. *Public Record Office* CAB 87/74 MG(43)10.
The Scottish Office (9 Feb 1948): 'A Review of Government Organisation in Scotland'. *Scottish Record Office* HH 1/1231.
Times (4 Aug 1883), Leader.
Times (6 Oct 1925), Leader: 'Poison and Antidote'.
The Treasury (29 June 1896): 'School Grants, Ireland and Scotland'. *Public Record Office* CAB 37/42.
The Treasury (24 Dec 1943): 'Report of the Committee on the Machinery of Government'. *Public Record Office* CAB 87/72 MGO 36.
The Treasury (June 1946): 'Notes on Regional Organisation'. *Scottish Record Office* HH 1/1231.

PUBLISHED GOVERNMENT REPORTS

Report of the Select Committee on the Poor Laws (Scotland). 1869, London.
Report of the Select Committee on the Poor Laws (Scotland). 1870, London.
Report of the Civil Department (Scotland) Committee. C. 64. 1870, London.
Report of the Royal Commission on the Civil Service (Third Report), Evidence. Cd. 6740. 1913, London.
Report of the Departmental Committee on Scottish Administration Cmd. 5563. 1937, London.
Report of the Royal Commission on Scottish Affairs. Cmd. 9219. 1954, London.

National Identity:
From British Empire
to European Union
Richard J Finlay

INTRODUCTION

In this chapter we will look at Scottish national identity, a phenomenon which has proved to be remarkably resilient. Its seeming long-term imperviousness to the assimilating tendencies of the British state has meant that historians of modern Scotland have been increasingly called upon to explain its historical evolution in the face of a widespread expectation that modernity and progress would ultimately merge the Scottish people into a uniform Britishness. Most Scottish history held that assimilation was the dominant historical trend and consequently looked for those aspects which pointed the way towards integration into the British nation state. Nationalism, on the other hand, was perceived as backward looking and romantic (Finlay 1994a, 127–48; Kidd 1993). Recently, however, demands for some form of self-government have become established as an intrinsic facet of Scottish politics. This has occurred at the same time as Britain is moving towards an integrated Europe with much debate as to the nature of British identity. The issue of Scottish national identity has thus become the focus of much historical enquiry as the nation goes through a period of critical re-evaluation (Broun, Finlay and Lynch 1997).

We will approach this topic under the following headings:

- Issues of identity
- Scotland and the Empire
- Home rule before 1914
- Nationalism in the Inter-War Era
- The growth of the British state in the post-war period
- Scottish nationalism in the 1960s and 1970s: revivals and referendum
- Conclusion

When you have worked your way through this chapter, you should have a grasp of the main ideas and developments which have influenced Scottish perceptions of politics and its role in Britain, the Empire and, more recently, Europe.

1. ISSUES OF IDENTITY

Although Scottish nationalism has been extensively written about, mainly as a result of the electoral break-through of the Scottish National Party (SNP) in the 1970s, the nature of the evolution of Scottish national identity during the nineteenth and twentieth centuries has generally proved to be elusive. In part, this is due to a tendency to concentrate on the nationalist movement itself and equate the development of Scottish nationalism with hostility to the British state (Nairn 1981; Hanham 1969; Webb 1977). However, this is not the case, as for most of the period under review there was no sense of contradiction in being both Scottish and British. In fact, as will be argued below, the Scots willingly donated aspects of their national identity to the manufacture of a British imperial identity. Furthermore, by concentrating on the nationalists as the key to understanding the historical development of Scottish national identity, historians have failed to recognise the emergence of British national identity as the most significant feature of this era. The reason for this is simple. Given the predominance of the assimilationist view of Scottish history, there has been a tendency to regard the development of British identity as natural, while Scottish nationalism has been seen as a rogue phenomenon, reluctant to die out. However, as Scotland now appears to be at a political cross-roads in which national aspirations are accorded an important priority, it may prove to be the case that it is British nationalism in Scotland which is reckoned to be the unnatural development.

To understand the evolution of national identity in Scotland over the last hundred years, we need to examine changing perceptions of both Scotland and Britain. 'Scottishness' and 'Britishness' meant different things to different people at different times. National identity works in conjunction with regional, religious, gender, class, ethnic and other identities. The catholic, highland, male crofter of the late nineteenth century and the lowland, female, protestant lawyer of the late twentieth century would find little in common regarding their national identities other than they would both use the terms Scotland and Britain. Furthermore, home rulers of the late nineteenth century would find little common political ground with contemporary nationalists. Another problem with national identity is that it defies empirical quantification. We can say, for example, how many Scots lived in one-roomed houses in Glasgow in 1881, but we cannot tell how many of them felt more Scottish than British. The historian of national identity has to use a wide variety of sources in the examination of the dominant public perceptions of 'Scottishness' and 'Britishness'. It is this which gives us our clues to the evolution of national identity in Scotland.

> EXERCISE 1
> In the context of our discussion so far, what problems arise in trying to define 'Scottishness'?
>
> Using your own understanding of Scottish national identity today, how important do you think issues such as gender, geography, class and religion are in defining political behaviour?

36 Entry (for 15 January 1865) from the diary of John Sturrock, millwright in Dundee. Sturrock was one of many thousands of Scots who visited and contributed to the cost of erecting the Wallace Monument on Abbey Craig, Stirling. In the eighteenth and nineteenth centuries William Wallace provided a popular and potent rallying point for patriotic Scots, and an enduring symbol of Scottish nationalism. *Dundee University Archives.*

Obviously it is complicated by problems of definition at different points in time and by problems of qualification. Undoubtedly all of the factors mentioned influence political behaviour, some less, some more in the past than they do today.

The Scottish middle class reinvented their national identity in the mid nineteenth century at a time when the traditional Scottish institutions of the law, church and education were buckling under the strain of urbanisation and industrialisation and conspicuously failing in their endeavours to maintain their pivotal role within Scottish society (Phillipson 1990; Anderson 1989; Brown and Fry 1993; Devine 1988). While these professions and institutions were important in the development of a Scottish middle-class, civic identity, they could not provide the cohesion required to bond a unified national identity as Scotland was increasingly divided by religion, class and region (C Brown 1987; Dickson 1980). It was at this time of rapid change that Scots began to adopt Highland symbols as part of their national identity. The Highlands were thought to be a purer Scotland, unsullied by urbanisation (Devine 1994, 84–100). Also, Scottish identity was increasingly portrayed as having certain ideological tenets associated with *laissez-faire* individualism. The cults of William Wallace, the Covenanters and Robert Burns were used to justify the notion that Scotland was a meritocratic society (Finlay 1997a). The 'lad o' pairts' (see Chapters 13 and 24) became one of the most pervasive of all Scottish myths because it reinforced the belief that talent and individual ability was the key to success (McCrone 1992). The dominance of this ideology was reflected in Scottish politics by the power of the Liberal Party which enjoyed a virtual hegemony up to 1918 (Fry 1987, 88–119). Paradoxically, the arena in which the Scots believed best showed off national characteristics was not the nation itself, but overseas in pursuit of the imperial mission.

2. SCOTLAND AND THE EMPIRE

The Scottish role in the creation of the British Empire has undoubtedly been the biggest factor in the making of modern Scottish national identity. Indeed, most of the more obvious symbols of Scottish nationality owe their existence to the imperial past (Morris 1990). In the nineteenth and early twentieth centuries the Scots prided themselves on being a race of empire builders. The language of Scottish politics was replete with imperialist terminology: England was the sister nation of the Empire, Westminster was the imperial parliament and the Union was the imperial partnership. Militarism, colonialism, external economic expansion, racism, the missionary impulse and all the other conventional facets of nineteenth century British imperialism each had distinctive Scottish components (Finlay 1997b; MacKenzie 1993). For the Scots, the British Empire was as much a Scottish creation as an English one. As indignant nationalists pointed out in the 1890s:

> Who built up the Empire? What was its condition at the time of the Union? Save
> a few islands in the West Indies and the plantations in North America . . . there
> were few possessions. The rise of the Empire dates from the Union.
>
> ('A Protest against the Mis Use of the term 'England')

After all, it was claimed, it was Scots who undertook a great deal of the imperial
administration, it was Scottish regiments which had taken a prominent part in its
conquest and defence and it was Scottish settlers who founded large parts of the
white dominion colonies of Australia, New Zealand, Canada and South Africa
(MacKenzie 1993; Finlay 1997b). According to conventional late nineteenth
century European nationalism, the Empire vindicated all those romantic ideals
concerning national virility and military prowess. With kilted Highland regiments
and a host of illustrious generals, the Scots proved themselves a martial race.
David Livingstone and Alexander Duff exemplified missionary zeal and courage,
as well as showing the humanitarian face of 'God's Country', while Glasgow
rejoiced in its self-proclaimed title as 'second city of the Empire', and its economic
basin was ample testimony to the notion that Scotland was the 'workshop of the
Empire'. Indeed, even their English co-imperialists acknowledged the perceived
Scottish talent for empire building and their ability to retain and foster their
distinctive characteristics within the Empire. As the Calcutta *Englishman* of 26
November 1904 put it:

> The Scottish race has two virtues which are not soon likely to forsake it. It is
> intensely patriotic; and it is fraternal to the point at which sentiment ceases to be
> such, and becomes almost a religion. The Scottish have a national idea which the
> English have lost or never attained.

In such ways, Scottish national self-esteem was raised to heights, in a truly popular
sense, never before experienced. The idea of an imperial partnership was enthusiastically endorsed by most Scots by the late nineteenth century.

What is remarkable about Scottish imperial identity is the extent to which it
pervaded all walks of life. Queen Victoria's love affair with the northern kingdom
undoubtedly reinforced notions that the Scots occupied a unique and special role in
the imperial set-up (Duff 1980). The sanctity of the Empire was beyond question and
commanded an almost unique political consensus among Scots. The Liberal church-
man, John Ker, talked about 'Providence having given to Britain the position she has
among the nations . . . and the elastic power of expansion' (Ker 1887, 213). In 1900,
Lord Rosebery told students at Glasgow university that 'an Empire such as our
requires as its first condition an imperial race; a race vigorous and industrious and
intrepid'. Radical Liberals, such as Thomas Shaw and Alexander Hunter, were
likewise convinced of the efficacy of Britain's imperial mission (Finlay 1997c,
Chapter 1). As one might expect, Scottish Tories believed that service to the Empire
was the highest principle to which any Scot could aspire (Craik 1901, 18). Even on
the political left, there was support in Scotland for Britain's civilising mission.

According to Keir Hardie, it was only right and just that the British flag flew in so many parts of the globe (Reid 1978, 124).

This enthusiasm was fuelled by the conviction that the Scots were making a unique and valuable contribution to British imperial prowess. Side by side with statements on British imperial grandeur, one finds the glorification of Scottish characteristics which made the creation and survival of the Empire possible. John Ker, for example, claimed that the Scots had:

> made the British Empire richer by all the contributions of literature and social character that a separate history has enabled Scotland to give. It has been a barrier to the spread of that system of centralisation which is not only dangerous to liberty, but detrimental to healthy progress, and yet it has not weakened the United Kingdom by any divided allegiance. A great people is stronger, and more permanently fertile from the variety of its component parts, and from the friendly play of the electric currents that have their origin in a diversity that is held in friendship.
>
> (Ker 1878, 213)

Rosebery always made reference to Scottish characteristics such as the quality of education and respect for learning, loyalty and trustworthiness, self-reliance and self-discipline, as well as the reputation for being formidable soldiers. All these features of the Scottish character made the Scots ideal empire builders, as Rosebery explained to students in Edinburgh University in 1898:

> We in Scotland wish to continue to mould the Empire as we have in the past . . . From the time of Dundas, who almost populated India with Scotsmen, that has always been the function of Scotland.
>
> ('The Service of the State')

EXERCISE 2
Look back at the quotation from the *Calcutta Englishman*, together with **Document 90a**, and consider whether they reflect similar or different views of the Scots as imperialists. Do you detect a lack of confidence in **Document 90b**? Do you think that the idea of the imperial mission is confined to the middle class?

It is worth noting that the English were as much influenced by Scottish propaganda promoting the innate imperial qualities of the Scots, as the Scots were themselves.

The Scots were excellent at self-promotion and were well known for their clannishness in the Empire. The myth of the 'enterprising' Scot was manufactured by the Scots themselves and its success can be seen by the way in which so many believed in it, including the English. Scots seldom concentrated on the many who failed to make their fortune in the Empire. **Document 90b** shows how concerns over the condition of the working-class were a source for concern. If the population was not healthy and educated, then Britain would be unable to retain the Empire in the face of growing military and economic competition. This ideological combination of imperialism and social policy was known as social imperialism.

Keir Hardie was likewise able to draw on perceived Scottish traditions of liberty and democracy in formulating his political outlook (MacLean 1975, 5–27). The Conservatives presented the values of a martial race as one of the nation's greatest attributes. The noble, but misguided, loyalty of the Jacobites fighting against impossible odds was presented as a quintessential characteristic which was now put to good use in the service of the Empire, as General Gordon was to prove at Khartoum. What remains striking, however, is the ability of different types of Scots, each with their own vision of Scottish character and identity, to integrate it into a wider British imperial ethos. Consequently the Union with England and the Imperial Partnership encouraged a sense of Scottishness and Britishness which reinforced one another.

When Anglo-Scottish tensions surfaced prior to 1914 it was usually a result of the Scots feeling that their contribution to the imperial ethos was not being properly acknowledged. The use of 'England' and 'English' instead of 'Britain' and 'British' was a favourite target for wounded Scottish sensitivity.

EXERCISE 3
Examine **Document 91**. Does it reflect a pride in the Scottish contribution to the achievements of the British state and Empire? Why do you think that the use of 'England' instead of 'Britain' irritated so many Scots?

The answer is self-evident and it is not dissimilar to today when England is used instead of Britain or vice versa. Think of the reaction to 'British' football hooligans.

Even prominent Tories were compelled to remind their English colleagues that Scotland was 'an integral part of the Empire' (Balfour 1924, 89–95). The decision of Queen Victoria's successor to style himself Edward VII was taken as an insult to the Scottish nation as it ignored the fact that the Scots had never had a King Edward. Numerous complaints were raised as to the provision of Scotland's national libraries, parks, museums and galleries, which, when compared to those in England, were perceived as second class (Finlay 1997c, Chapter 2). So although hostility to England emerged from time to time, it had little to do with hostility to the British ideal and was more a result of injured pride. Such blatant reminders that the Scots were the junior partners in the imperial venture were hard to stomach.

3. HOME RULE BEFORE 1914

The issue of Irish home rule instigated a fundamental re-assessment of the imperial ethos in Scotland as contemporaries debated the future political structure of the

Empire. At first the Scots were suspicious that the Irish would receive preferential treatment, usurping the Scots from a special niche in the British political structure. Furthermore, the Irish were perceived as being rewarded for terrorist activities, while the Scots, who were model imperial partners, were in danger of being relegated into second place. Even among those Scots who supported Irish home rule, it was recognised that a similar measure would be necessary to keep things equal and maintain the integrity of the British Empire. Imperial federation was seen as the ideal solution because it offered a remedy for the problems of parliamentary over-work by allowing Dominion and national assemblies to concentrate on domestic legislation, leaving Westminster free to pursue the more important issues of foreign and imperial policy (Kendle 1997).

Imperial federation was seen by its supporters as a way of strengthening the unity of the Empire. It was claimed that it would provide a cohesive bond necessary to maintain loyalty to the abstract notion of the British imperial ideal. Scottish supporters of 'home rule all round', as it was alternatively known, stressed their devotion to the British ideal and far from being a challenge to the British imperial ethos, the Scottish home rule movement was founded on the premise that it would help bond the elements of the Empire more closely. Indeed, in 1888 it was claimed that Scottish home rulers were the real Unionists because they had the best interests of the Empire at heart, while Unionists, by their uncompromising attitude, were separatists because their actions were endangering imperial unity.

> EXERCISE 4
> Examine **Document 92**. In what ways would the creation of a Scottish parliament make the working of the Westminster parliament more efficient? You may like to consider the difficulties of parliamentary over-work and congestion in your response.

The answer is not very different from the current reasons for the setting up of a Scottish parliament. It was believed that it would enable the Scots to make their own decisions on important matters of domestic policy, without being hindered by a lack of parliamentary time, indifference or ignorance about Scottish affairs.

For most historians, Scottish home rule before 1914 has to be interpreted as an uninteresting by-product of the Irish issue, taken on board either to stall Irish home rule or to make it more palatable to the Scottish electorate (Jalland 1979). The debate about the constitutional realignment of the Empire, however, coincided with the gradual emergence of mass democracy and the changing emphasis this occasioned on the political agenda. In 1884, the Third Reform Bill ensured that the working class constituted a clear majority of the electorate. Also, it increased the representation of the 'Celtic Fringe' in the House of Commons. Due to this simple fact of political life, the interests of the working class and the Celtic Fringe would become more prominent in British politics. While Scottish home rule was pursued mainly by enthusiasts before 1910, after this date its significance became paramount in Scottish politics as Scottish national identity, reflecting the interests of an increasing working-class electorate, became more focused on the inward reality of Scotland, rather than the external projection of Scotland to the Empire.

Central to this development were the activities of the Young Scots, a radical ginger group which operated in conjunction with the Liberal Party. The Young Scots were blooded in the general elections of 1906 and 1910 and their contribution was openly acknowledged as critical to the fortunes of the 'splendid triumph of progressivism in Scotland'. By 1913 the Young Scots may have had as many as 10,000 activists in 50 branches in Scotland and their aggressive targeting of key and marginal seats had won them the admiration of friend and foe (Finlay 1997c, Chapter 2). They made extensive use of modern electioneering techniques and had within their ranks an impressive number of some 20 Liberal MPs and a further handful of prospective candidates. Progressivism, as the new liberalism was called in Scotland, was their clarion call and it was the linking of demands for improvement in social welfare legislation and the creation of a Scottish parliament that gave Scottish national identity and its relationship with the Union a new and vital dimension in the period just before the First World War.

After the December election of 1910, the Young Scots made Scottish home rule its immediate priority and prepared to ensure the full compliance of the Liberal Party:

> The Society . . . (demands) Scottish home rule during the present parliament and pledged itself, if necessary, to enforce this demand by running its own candidates.
> (*Young Scots Handbook 1911*, 13)

Indeed, the Young Scots were able to force the Liberal Party to replace its original candidates for the Tradeston and Ross and Cromarty by-elections in 1911 with others thought to be more sympathetic to the national cause. Sitting Liberals were scrutinised to ensure that they supported Scottish home rule in the House of Commons, and future campaigning work for MPs was dependent on their record. Furthermore, it is worth pointing out that in at least one of the three Labour parliamentary successes in Scotland before 1914, the candidate in Blackfriars (Glasgow) had approval from the Young Scots as the sitting Liberal was thought to be lukewarm on social reform and home rule.

EXERCISE 5
Using this section and **Document 93**, briefly outline the key objectives of the Young Scots Society in this period.

Evidence that Scottish home rule was gaining an unprecedented momentum can be found in the reaction of the Conservative and Unionist Party:

> Every Scottish radical member and candidate is pledged to Scottish home rule, many of them emphatically and directly, and the machine driven radical associations throughout the country are, officially at least, eager in its support,

and if returned at a general election, they would declare that they had a mandate
for Scottish home rule.

(Finlay 1997c, 50)

The issue gained in prominence primarily because of its connection with social
reform. According to one Liberal campaigner, JM Hogge, 'the key to all further
legislative progress in Scotland was Scottish home rule'. Westminster was blamed
for indifference to Scottish issues and it was claimed that English conservatism was
blocking Scottish temperance, housing, land and education reform. As one Liberal
parliamentarian put it in 1911, 'there is not one single item in the whole
programme of Radicalism or social reform today, which, if Scotland had powers
to pass laws, would not have been carried out a quarter of a century ago'. Social
reform was the *raison d'être* of the home rule cause: 'We submit . . . home rule . . .
as a means to land reform and general social reform on national lines . . . We urge
all Scottish progressives to cease to cherish vain hopes of Scottish reform from
London' (*Mr Lloyd George and land reform* 1914). By tying Scottish home rule
into the package of new liberalism, its supporters brought a new social and
political dimension to the question of Scottish national identity. Whereas middle-
class Scotland had looked outwards to the Empire and backwards to a cosy
romantic vision of the Scottish past for its sense of national identity, the emergence
of class-based politics increasingly focused national identity upon the inward
reality of contemporary Scotland.

The debate on Scottish home rule also brought into question some of the long held
tenets of Unionism and the relationship with England. Cracks began to emerge in the
national consensus as different political parties laid different stress on different
aspects of Scotland's perceived role in the British constitutional arrangement and its
empire. Radicals within the Liberal Party were moving close to modern Scottish
nationalism and demanded:

> A pledge from every candidate for a Scottish constituency to insist upon the
> granting of Scottish home rule . . . Only by the formation of a strong Scottish
> Nationalist Party can Scotland hope to secure adequate recognition of her needs.
> (*Manifesto and Appeal to the Scottish People on Scottish Home Rule,* 1911)

Furthermore, most Liberals rejected any notion of British homogeneity; Britain
was made up of the sum of her different parts and this, they argued, gave the
Empire its strength. Liberal Unionists were more inclined towards notions of
British uniformity and regularly churned out pleas for British loyalty to defend
their fellow countrymen in Ulster. The Conservatives appreciated the duality of
Scottish and British identity but wanted 'the fine worth and patriotic importance
of Scottish national sentiment . . . directed into legitimate channels'. For them
Scottish nationalism had to be directed away from social and constitutional reform
back into the Empire:

take up a positive, and if need be, aggressive policy and point to the important part which *Scottish National patriotism* has played and must still play *in the wider patriotism of the whole British Empire.*

(Scottish Unionist Party, 'Confidential Memorandum:
Scottish Home Rule', 1914)

Conservatives and Liberal Unionists, who merged in 1912 to form the Scottish Unionist party, rejected Scottish home rule on the grounds that it would be costly and inefficient. Perhaps of greater importance, however, was their fear that any loosening of the imperial bonds would cost Scotland its special role within the British Empire. As one Unionist put it:

> To revive in Scotland or Ireland National Legislators (sic) is to debase and degrade both these countries from the fine position they now hold as equal partners in the imperial government and make them tenth rate, wretched, one horse tributary states.
>
> (*Scottish Review*, 1889)

Even before the outbreak of the First World War, tensions were emerging about Scottish self-perception and its relationship with the imperial structure. The grandiose ideals of a unique role in the creation and maintenance of the British Empire were no longer enough to satisfy the increasing demand for social reform and improvement at home. By 1914 Scottish national identity was turning its attention from the Empire to domestic issues. In 1913 Sir Henry Cowan's Bill for Scottish home rule passed its second reading in the Commons and many assumed that the Scots, like the Irish, would soon have their own parliament. The outbreak of war disappointed the home rule aspirations of both nations.

4. NATIONALISM BETWEEN THE WARS

During the war, Scotland did her bit and more, probably suffering a greater proportion of casualties than any other nation in the United Kingdom. Scottish society was not immune from the jingoism which greeted the outbreak of war and even the strikers of Red Clydeside had their patriotism acknowledged by Winston Churchill (Kirkwood 1935). Arguably, a number of factors should have turned the tide against Scottish home rule. Firstly, there was the collective experience of war which pulled the British national community closer together. Secondly, the key proponent of home rule, the Liberal Party, split and embarked on a torturous process of self-disintegration. Finally, there was the unfortunate example of Ireland where demands for home rule had ended in military occupation and civil war. Yet, in spite of these adverse factors, demands for Scottish home rule became more persistent during the War and its immediate aftermath. Given the strong pre-war correlation between home rule and social reform, it should come as no surprise to find that it was led by the Scottish Trade Union Congress and the Labour Party.

EXERCISE 6

Look at **Document 94**. Why did the Labour Party support the establishment of a Scottish parliament? Do you think that the proposals had been seriously thought out?

The Labour Party was following a traditional line of radical argument. Keir Hardie had long been a committed home ruler, as were most members of the early Scottish Labour Party. As Labour's proposals were more or less the same as the Liberal Party, it is clear that they had not thought long and hard about the subject.

Labour, which emerged as the largest party in Scotland at the general election of 1922, was initially more emphatic and enthusiastic in its commitment to Scottish home rule than the Liberal Party (Finlay 1994b, Chapter 1). Thousands attended mass rallies in the early 1920s, 50 out of Scotland's 74 MPs indicated their support in 1923 and in 1924 when a home rule bill was talked out in the House of Commons, it led to scenes of parliamentary disruption. The tide in the Empire seemed to be going the home rulers' way and many believed that the trend towards self-government in the Dominions would also encompass Scotland. However, by 1927, the euphoria had died on its feet, with the Labour Party blowing cold on any notion of Scottish devolution.

The reason for this *volte face* is simple. Labour may have had an emotional commitment to Scottish home rule, but there is little evidence of an intellectual commitment. Home rule was adopted as part of the Scottish radical tradition. At a time of ideological poverty, when Labour's philosophy was emerging from the melting pot of gradualism and revolution, home rule provided a much needed semblance of coherence. It masked the differences of the Left and Right and its reductionist message that it was all the fault of the English had popular appeal. When the problems of post-war dislocation were addressed in the mid 1920s, however, the solution of centralised British state planning rendered home rule redundant at a stroke (Howell 1986, 229–65; Finlay 1992a, 274–97). One of the key features behind support for a Scottish parliament was the belief that it would have powers of economic and social regeneration, so the fact that these powers would be exercised by Westminster left the proposed Scottish parliament with a much reduced role. Furthermore, the ideological tide was swinging away from nationalism in Labour circles. It was denounced as bourgeois, especially after the appearance of an independent national party in 1928, and thought to have no real relevance to the working-class (Finlay 1992a).

The Unionist position regarding Scottish national identity also underwent fundamental revision in the inter-war era. The popular appeal of imperial sentiment lost its grip in the face of economic depression (Finlay 1994c, 242–59). Scotland was no longer the 'workshop of the Empire', emigration was seen as a sign of poverty at home, with memories of the horrors of the Great War still fresh in many minds. Militarism was no longer held in high esteem and the Empire itself was seen to be drifting apart, especially after the Treaty of Westminster in 1931 which conferred an independent foreign policy upon the Dominion nations. The empire-building days were over, creating a vacuum in national identity as the Scots found that their previous prosperity had been based on economic foundations since destroyed by the Great War. Indeed, the Glasgow Empire Exhibition of 1938 was an attempt to rekindle imperial sentiment with economic growth, revealing just how inter-twined these two concepts were in the Scottish psyche.

The attitude of Unionism to Scottish national identity is revealed upon examining its response to Scottish nationalism in this period. In the 1920s, when the home rule cause was led by the Left, Unionists paid little attention to it believing it to be the intellectual property of republicanism and the working-class. However, in the 1930s, as the depression hit many traditional sections of the Scottish middle-class, nationalism was increasingly articulated by the Right. Whereas Unionism in the pre-war era was confident and aggressive, founded on notions that the Scots were a race of empire builders, in the inter-war period it became defensive and negative.

EXERCISE 7

Examine the speech made by John Buchan in the House of Commons in November 1932 (**Document 95**) and **Article 26**. Does Buchan appear anxious that Scottish nationalism will emerge as a serious force in Scottish politics? What reasons does he give for this sense of unease in Scotland? You should consider the effect of the depression.

Buchan was concerned about the type of people who were turning to Scottish nationalism because he believed them to be 'normal' and thinking Scots. He also made the point that if not stopped, it could grow into a serious political force. Buchan thought that the situation was especially serious because nationalist grievances were largely justified. Like many others, Buchan believed that nationalism was being fuelled by the effects of the depression.

Industrialists predicted that the Scottish economy would not survive without the English connection. Politicians argued that a home rule or independent Scotland would be unable to pay dole money to its unemployed. Unwittingly, perhaps, Unionists established with the Labour Party an inter-war consensus that Scotland needed England for its economic survival. To underline this, Unionists created a message which was a curious mix of a sentimental yearning for the halcyon days of the imperial past and a concentration on the perceived flaws of the Scottish national character. The resultant image was self-contradictory and confused. Side by side with boasts that it was the Scots who ran all the important functions of the Empire were statements claiming that it was well known that the Scots were incapable of running themselves. Sir John Cargill asked readers of the *Scotsman* in June 1934: 'Could they imagine what a Scottish Parliament would look like? He could and would not like to dwell upon it.' Outwith the Union, according to Bob Boothby, the Conservative MP for Aberdeenshire, the Scots would degenerate to a 'pack of miserable savages, adding nothing to world civilisation' (*Nation*, March 1929).

Perhaps the clearest evidence of the confusion which surrounded Scottish national identity in the inter-war era is to be found in the lack of consensus within the ranks of the nationalist movement itself. Broadly speaking, there were three groups which each had competing and contradictory visions of Scottish identity (Finlay 1992b): Scottish British imperialists who wanted to utilise Scottish nationalism to regenerate the imperial ethos; moderate devolutionists who wanted a constitutional realignment within the United Kingdom which would give a Scottish parliament powers over domestic legislation; and separatists who wanted outright independence. The history of the Scottish nationalist movement in the inter-war years is a sorry catalogue of internal party feuds, expulsions and ideological and political vacillation. If anything, the nationalist movement reflected the deeper confusion which surrounded Scottish national identity in the inter-war era.

Given the vacuum into which Scottish national identity plunged in this period, it is no surprise to find that much of the literary and artistic talent endeavoured to recreate a different type of national identity (see Chapter 26). The Scottish renaissance has been hailed as one of the high points of modern Scottish cultural achievement. Yet, the reality, as contemporaries saw it, was one of deep cultural pessimism. Most Scottish critics were obsessed with the death of Scottish culture. Indeed, Hugh MacDiarmid's effort to recreate the Scottish language was interpreted as a sort of cultural artificial respiration, pointless if the language was already dead. Traditional Scottish middle-class institutions also took a hammering during the period: the Church saw its power and influence diminish; the press was subject, along with other businesses, to southern take-overs; the local government reforms of 1929 wiped out the traditional burgh administration; education was increasingly anglicised; and new cultural institutions such as the BBC made few concessions to Scottish national identity. The absorption and destruction of the distinctiveness of the Scottish middle class left the working class as the true heirs to authentic Scottish traditions, particularly in the field of popular culture and sport.

5. THE GROWTH OF THE BRITISH STATE IN THE POST-WAR PERIOD

The Second World War was a major catalyst in forcing the rate of Scottish assimilation to the British state. War-time propaganda projected the myth of an island race, the image of the 'people' working for victory was promoted, mass conscription brought together people from different classes, nations and regions, and the often tragic experience of a society at war all helped to bring about an unprecedented degree of cultural integration. The advent of corporatism and centralised state planning was enthusiastically endorsed in Scotland as it seemed to offer a way out of the impasse of the endemic social and economic problems of the inter-war years. Just as Scottish home rule was being mooted as a serious possibility for post-war reconstruction, Scottish politicians came alive to the opportunities offered by British corporatism. Tom Johnston, the Scottish Secretary of State, was able to show that by effectively putting the Scottish case in the Cabinet, it was possible to wring powerful concessions from Westminster (Walker 1988, 151–62). Johnston's effective stewardship of Scottish government during the war showed that the Union could be revitalised to deliver the goods of economic and social regeneration.

The advent of the Welfare State intensified a greater belief in the efficacy of the British state. The notion that the war had been fought on condition that it would lead to a more just and caring society caught the imagination of many Scots. In cultural terms, the significance of the Welfare State was more profound in Scotland than was the case in England because there was more of an active role for the state to play north of the Border. Given the preponderance of the coal, transport, electric and steel industries in the Scottish economy, nationalisation had a much more profound effect. Put simply in terms of economic well being, the Scots had to look to the Union and the British state for much of their post-war prosperity. Also, there was more for the state to do in terms of addressing Scotland's chronic health and housing problems. Notions of the planned economy fitted in with the growth of a corporatist ideology in Scotland in the 1930s (Harvie 1981; Campbell 1980). The Scottish Council for Industry and Development, the numerous reports into the Scottish economy, the Clyde Valley Plan, the devolution of administration to the Scottish Office in Edinburgh and Tom Johnstone's war-time Committee of the ex-Secretaries of State for Scotland all dove-tailed with post-war developments in corporatist ideology (Campbell 1981). As standards of living rose in the late 1940s and 1950s, any notion that home rule would bring any practical benefits was virtually killed off.

In spite of the apparent success of the 'new Britain', nationalist sentiment grumbled on. The Covenant movement of the late 1940s and early 1950s gathered over two million signatures in favour of a Scottish parliament, the Stone of Destiny was removed from Westminster Abbey by nationalist activists, there was a furore over Queen Elizabeth's use of the 'Second' at her coronation, (to add insult to injury Her Majesty turned up to Scotland for her inauguration in a suit and clutching a handbag), and the Balfour Commission made an unfortunate gaffe by referring to Scotland as a region. The Conservatives did well in the general election of 1955, largely due to their attack on Labour's policies of nationalisation, which it was claimed, meant de-nationalisation for Scotland as the control of key industries moved to London:

> Because centralisation is an essential part of the socialist belief there will be increasingly less recognition of Scotland while socialism lasts . . . (the solution lies) in the recognition of Scotland not as a region but as a nation, in free, but not subordinate partnership with England.
>
> (*Scottish Control: Scottish Affairs: Unionist Policy*, 1949)

EXERCISE 8

Look at **Document 96** and the above extract. Do you think that anti-socialism, rather than Scottish nationalism, was more important in the Unionist message of the early 1950s?

Both were important and both reinforced one another.

The Unionists also used a great deal of Scottish national sentiment in the election campaigns of the 1950s and used the Saltire flag as the party's symbol. Although the Unionists 'played the Scottish card', at no time did the party advocate political devolution (Mitchell 1996a). Instead, it was decided that wherever practical, the role of government in Scotland should be carried out by the Scottish Office (Hutchison 1996b).

None of this presented a challenge to the Union, given that economic prosperity and social well-being lay with centralised planning. Furthermore, while memories of the hungry inter-war era were close at hand, nationalism had nothing more than sentimental appeal. For most Scots, the Union now meant the Welfare State and full employment.

6. SCOTTISH NATIONALISM IN THE 1960S AND 1970S

The 1960s stood witness to the growth of interest in Scottish identity, in spite of the claims of social scientists that Britain was one of the most homogenous industrial societies in the world. Folk music, Scottish television and radio, the popularisation of Scottish history and the continuing support for Scottish sport, all combined to provide a separate Scottish dimension to British identity. The continuing decline of the old imperial markets for Scottish goods, the retreat from empire, leading to the threatened disbandment of the Argyll and Sutherland Highlanders (which caused a storm of protest), and a persistent lagging behind in standards of living, all helped to create an impression that Scotland was not being treated fairly. Regional planning, increasingly used as a remedy, had the effect of further tying in Scottish economic aspirations with British state planning (Fry 1988, 223–51; Hutchison 1996). However, it was the failure of British politicians to keep their promise of consensus politics which spurred on the first nationalist electoral tide in the late 1960s. The Hamilton by-election of 1967 was dominated by popular discontent at the Labour government's economic policies. The success of the SNP taught the Scottish electorate the valuable lesson that a nationalist victory was a very effective way to make London government take notice of Scottish grievances. The response of both main political parties was to revise Scottish policy. In 1968 the Conservatives, under the leadership of Edward Heath, came out in favour of devolution. This decision was imposed on an unwilling Scottish party and most Conservatives outside Scotland paid little attention to it. In any case, after the 1970 election returned the Conservatives, devolution was quietly dropped. The SNP failed to make any headway in the election and only won one seat, leading many commentators to conclude that the nationalist threat had passed. The response of the Labour government was to set up a commission (Crowther, later Kilbrandon) on the constitution. The objective of this was to buy time, and Labour remained hostile to home rule throughout the 1960s and early 1970s (Mitchell 1996b, 35–65).

37 Hugh McDiarmid, Trafalgar Square, anti-Polaris base rally, 1961. *Michael Peto Collection, Dundee University Archives.*

The discovery of North Sea oil arguably destroyed the fundamental pillar of the unionist argument of Scottish economic dependency. The SNP embarked on campaigns of 'It's Scotland's Oil' in the early 1970s and claimed that an independent Scotland would be one of the wealthiest nations in Europe. The roles were reversed in the 1974 elections as the unionist parties made sentimental appeals to history and tradition and urged the Scots not to break the partnership with England while the nationalists displayed a hard-headed pragmatism as it gave the voters the choice of 'rich Scots or poor Britons'. The debate was given a sense of urgency due to the economic crisis. Britain was experiencing growing unemployment, rising inflation, major industrial disputes and a deepening financial crisis. In the October 1974 election, the SNP made considerable progress, winning almost 30% of the vote and 11 seats. The response of the unionist parties was to offer devolution as a palliative which would hopefully diffuse the nationalist challenge. The attitudes of both the Labour and Conservative parties to this issue were driven by electoral pragmatism, rather than principle. Although the SNP achieved an impressive electoral performance in both elections in 1974, its voters, as the opinion polls of the time show, were not motivated by a desire for independence (Miller 1981). Rather, voting for the SNP was seen as the most effective way to put Scotland on the British political agenda and highlight the nation's economic grievances. Paradoxically, the upsurge in nationalist support was driven by a desire to realise the aims and ideals of corporate Britain. All this was borne out in the devolution debate of 1978–79 when the Scots, full of introspection and self-doubt and lacking political will, proved themselves unequal to achieving even the limited form of self-government on offer. The subsequent swing back to the Labour Party at the general election of 1979 showed quite clearly that a substantial proportion of the SNP's vote was indeed a protest at the failure to maintain the corporate vision of Britain.

In many ways, the key to understanding the failure of the devolution referendum in 1979 can be explained by reference to prevailing notions of Scottish national identity. The images which abounded were totally negative. Historians were wheeled out to show that the Scots had never been good at ruling themselves in the past. Scots were portrayed as drunken, common and vulgar with special proclivities towards football hooliganism. The thrusting, ambitious, heard headed, middle-class 'Unspeakable Scot' of the nineteenth century was replaced in the late twentieth century by the working-class 'inarticulate Scot' in popular stereotypes. Given such negative views of their national identity, it is hardly surprising that the middle class set itself against devolution. Furthermore, the prospect of a Scottish parliament was accompanied by the residual fear that it would be dominated by the socialist central belt. Although there was a 40% clause which denied the majority who voted their assembly, it was by no means a ringing endorsement of the principle of home rule. All in all, the devolution fiasco was a reflection of the crisis in Scottish national identity. The consensus era was collapsing, betraying all the aspirations of the post-war generation, and it left the Scots in a cultural and political vacuum. Just as the Empire had provided an outlet for the Scottish vision of Britain, so too had the corporatist Welfare State of the consensus era. Unfortunately, the English electorate took it off the agenda in 1979 when it returned a government committed to rolling back the state and instead endorsing the principles of the free market.

CONCLUSIONS

The Empire and the Welfare State allowed the Scots to be both Scottish and British, and although the situation was always fluid, the Scots believed that they were getting something out of Britain. The Scottish vision of Britain has always been fuelled by a strong sense of pragmatism. The Thatcher and Major governments, however, did much to undermine the Scots' belief in the efficacy of the Union by persistently dismantling and attacking the corporatist agencies and ethos in Scotland. This ethos and the institutions of council housing, comprehensive education, the health service, the Scottish Development Agency and others, were the creations of a post-war British identity and were fundamental in transmitting this sense of British identity in Scotland. In many ways, the upsurge in Scottish nationalism since the 1980s has been a result of the English political nation's rejection of what were seen in Scotland as core British values. Furthermore, the Scottish political community, with the exception of the Tories, have now reinterpreted these values as being fundamentally Scottish and as a consequence, the Tory attack on the 'nanny state' has been seen as an attack on Scottish political traditions. Also, the ethos of Thatcherism which argued that uneconomic concerns would have to sink or swim and that they could not expect support from the state, had a traumatic effect on the Scottish economy in the early 1980s. Arguments that Scotland was being subsidised by England at a time when deindustrialisation was ripping the heart out of the industrial central belt did not make many Scots feel that they were getting a good deal. If the Union did not have any benefits, what was the point in staying in it? It could also be sardonically noted that the Thatcher experiment of the early 1980s could not have taken place without the revenues of North Sea Oil.

As the corporatist vision of Britain was no longer an option for the Scots, it seems as if the last decade has witnessed another reconstruction of Scottish identity which is by no means complete. The European Union is an option that many Scots are considering and their experience of the British Union has arguably left them better prepared for this than their English neighbours. It can be argued that the Scots, because of their experience of British Union, are used to issues of national identity and the dangers posed to it by larger and more powerful countries. As this chapter has shown, definition and redefinition of national identity have been important to the Scottish historical experience. Consequently, perhaps, there is less fear about European Union in Scotland. Also, it has shown that Britain is no more that the sum total of its component parts and that the English habit of equating Britain with England is a gross over simplification. Indeed, it might even be said that there is an even greater need for a study of the English dimension to British national identity. As to the Scottish Union with Britain, pragmatism has been a key feature of Anglo-Scottish relations since 1707 and it is likely to be the same in the future. The creation of a Scottish parliament may mark another chapter in the evolution of the Union since its inception three hundred years ago. However, that story must be left to another historian in the future.

EXERCISE 9

Has this chapter enhanced your current understanding of the political debate about devolution? In view of the way that the Union has evolved over the last hundred years or so, do you think that the creation of a parliament in Edinburgh is a radical break with the past, or the latest chapter in the continuing process of modernisation?

There is no real answer to this. Good cases can be made for both arguments.

REFERENCES TO BOOKS AND ARTICLES IN THE TEXT

Anderson, RD 1989 *Education and Opportunity in Victorian Scotland*. Edinburgh.
Lady Francis Balfour 1924 *Lord Balfour of Burleigh*.
*Broun, D, Finlay, RJ and Lynch M (eds) 1998 *Image and Identity: The Making and Remaking of Scotland Through the Ages*. Edinburgh.
Brown CM 1987 *A Social History of Religion in Scotland Since 1730*. London.
Brown, SJ and Fry, M 1993 (eds) *Scotland in the Age of Disruption*. Edinburgh.
Campbell, RH 1980 'The Economic Case for Nationalism: Scotland', *in* Mitchison, R (ed), *The Roots of Nationalism: Studies in Northern Europe*, Edinburgh, 143–58.
Campbell, RH 1981 'The Committee of Ex-Secretaries of State for Scotland and Industrial Policy 1941–45', *Scottish Industrial History* 2, 3–10.
Craik, Sir Henry 1901 *A Century of Scottish History*, vol I. Edinburgh.
Devine, TM 1988 'Introduction', *in* Devine, TM & Mitchison, R *People and Society in Scotland. Volume I 1760–1830*, Edinburgh, 1–8.
Devine, TM 1994 *Clanship to Crofters' War: The Social Transformation of the Scottish Highlands*. Manchester.
Dickson, T 1980 (ed), *Scottish Capitalism*. London.
Duff, D 1980 (ed) *Queen Victoria's Highland Journals*. Exeter.
Finlay, RJ 1992a 'Pressure Group or Political Party?: The Nationalist Impact on Scottish Politics, 1928–1945', *Twentieth Century British History* 3, 274–97.
Finlay, RJ 1992b 'For or Against? Scottish nationalists and the British Empire, 1919–1939', *Scottish Historical Review* 71, 45–67.
Finlay, RJ 1994a 'Controlling the Past: Scottish Historiography and Scottish Identity in the 19th and 20th Centuries', *Scottish Affairs* 6, 127–48.
Finlay, RJ 1994b *Independent and Free: Scottish Politics and the Origins of the Scottish National Party, 1918–1945*. Edinburgh.
Finlay, RJ 1994c 'National Identity in Crisis: Politicians, Intellectuals and the 'End of Scotland', 1919–39', *History* 79, 242–59.
Finlay, RJ 1997a 'Myths, Heroes and Anniversaries in Modern Scotland', *Scottish Affairs* 18, 108–26.
*Finlay, RJ 1997b 'The Rise and Fall of Popular Imperialism in Scotland, 1850–1950', *Scottish Geographical Magazine* 113, 13–21.
*Finlay, RJ 1997c *A Partnership for Good?: Scottish Politics and the Union Since 1880*. Edinburgh.

*Fry M 1987 *Patronage and Principle: A Political History of Modern Scotland*. Aberdeen.
*Hanham, HJ 1969 *Scottish Nationalism*. London.
*Harvie, C 1981 'Labour and Scottish Government: The Age of Tom Johnston', *Bulletin of Scottish Politics*, Spring 1981, 1–20.
Howell, D 1986 *A Lost Left: Three Studies in Socialism and Nationalism*. Manchester.
Hutchison, IGC 1996 'Government', *in* Devine, TM and Finlay, RJ *Scotland in the Twentieth Century*, Edinburgh, 46–64.
Jalland, P 1979 'United Kingdom Devolution, 1910–14: Political Panacea or Tactical Diversion', *English Historical Review* 94, 757–85.
Kendle, J 1997 *Devolution and British Politics*. London.
Ker, J 1887 *Scottish Nationality and Other Papers*. Edinburgh.
Kidd, C 1993 *Subverting Scotland's Past: Scottish Whig Historians and the Creation of an Anglo British Identity, 1690–c. 1830*. Cambridge.
Kirkwood, D 1935 *My Life of Revolt*, foreword by Winston Churchill, London.
MacLean, I 1975 *Keir Hardie*. London.
*McCrone, D 1992 *Understanding Scotland: The Sociology of a Stateless Nation*. London.
*MacKenzie, JM 1993 'Essay and Reflection: Scotland and the British Empire', *International History Review* 4 (November 1993), 714–39.
Miller, WL 1981 *The End of British Politics?: Scots and English political Behaviour in the Seventies*. Oxford.
Mitchell, J 1996a 'Scotland in the Union, 1945–95: The Changing Nature of the Union State' *in* Devine, TM & Finlay, RJ (ed), *Scotland in the Twentieth Century*, Edinburgh, 85–102.
*Mitchell, J 1996b *Strategies for Self Government: the Campaign for a Scottish Parliament*. Edinburgh.
Morris, RJ 1990 'Scotland, 1830–1914: The Making of a Nation Within a Nation', *in* Fraser, WH and Morris, RJ (eds), *People and Society in Scotland. Volume II, 1830–1914*, Edinburgh, 1–7.
Nairn, T 1981 *The Break-Up of Britain*. London. (Second Edition).
Phillipson, N 1990 *The Scottish Whigs and the Reform of the Court of Session 1785–1830*. Edinburgh.
Reid, F 1978 *Keir Hardie: The Making of a Socialist*. London.
* Walker, G 1988 *Thomas Johnston*. Manchester.
Webb, K 1977 *The Growth of Nationalism in Scotland*. Glasgow.

FURTHER READING

Those references marked * in the above list are recommended further reading, along with the following:

Colley, L 1992 *Britons: Forging the Nation, 1707–1837*. Yale.
Harvie, C 1994 *Scotland and Nationalism: Scottish Politics and Society Since 1707*. London.
Hutchinson, IGC 1986 *A Political History of Scotland, 1832–1924: Parties, Elections and Issues*. Edinburgh.
Keating, M and Bleiman, D 1979 *Labour and Scottish Nationalism*. London.
McCrone, G 1965 *Scotland's Economic Progress 1951–1960: A Study in Regional Accounting*. London.

MacKenzie, JM 1984 *Propaganda and Empire: The Manipulation of British Public Opinion, 1880–1960*. Manchester.

Paterson, L 1994 *The Autonomy of Modern Scotland*. Edinburgh.

Robbins, K 1989 *Nineteenth Century Britain; England, Scotland and Wales: The Making of a Nation*. Oxford.

Scottish Historical Review, Special Edition 'Whither Scottish History', 196 (Spring 1994) 2.

PRIMARY SOURCES

'A Protest Against the Mis Use of the Terms 'England' and 'English' for 'Britain', its Empire, its Peoples and its Institutions'. 1890 Edinburgh.

Lord Rosebery, 'An Address as Lord Rector to the Students of the University of Glasgow, 16 November, 1900'.

Lord Rosebery, 'The Service of the State: Presidential Address to the Associated Societies of the University of Edinburgh, 25 October, 1898'.

The Scottish Unionist Association *1950 Scottish Control, Scottish Affairs: Unionist Policy*. Edinburgh.

Shaw, T 1903 *Patriotism and the Empire*. Edinburgh.

The Highlands since 1850
— Ewen A Cameron

INTRODUCTION

The mid-nineteenth century forms a good starting point for consideration of the recent history of the Scottish Highlands. The population of the region, which had been rising steadily since the 18th century, peaked, in most areas, at this time (Table 1). Further, Highland society was just emerging from the trauma of the Great Famine which had been precipitated by the failure of the potato crop in 1846 (see Macinnes, volume 1, Chapter 9). The famine did not 'end' until the mid-1850s, and it unleashed a new cycle of clearance and emigration.

There are three major points which must be borne in mind in any consideration of the more recent history of the Highlands. Firstly, the 'Highlands' are not a region of uniform conditions. The physical, social and economic features of the region are diverse. Perhaps the most important basic division is that between the coastal region north of the Ardnamurchan peninsula and the islands, and the inland areas in the central and eastern Highlands. The maritime and insular region was the heartland of the crofting communities created by the first phase of the clearances in the eighteenth and early nineteenth centuries. Secondly, the Highlands should not be thought of as entirely separate from the Lowlands. Certainly, there were important distinctions, but the links between the two regions were vital. Thirdly, the fact that the Highland population had been falling, due to outmigration since the mid-nineteenth century, while the Scottish population had been rising, was a conundrum which sustained the interest of governments in the post-1886 period. These demographic trends seem to have been reversed in the 1980s.

This chapter is divided into four sections, the first three being divided chronologically, while the final section considers cultural themes:

- Post famine adjustment, 1850–1880
- Securing the crofting community, 1882–1930
- Dealing with diversity since 1939
- Culture

It is hoped that when you have worked through this chapter, and the associated articles and documents, you will have gained a good understanding of the complexities of the issues involved in the history of the Highlands in this period. You might begin by reading Smout (1986), Chapter 3.

TABLE 1: PERCENTAGE POPULATION CHANGE IN THE CROFTING COUNTIES 1841–1911

	41–51	51–61	61–71	71–81	81–91	91–01	01–11
Shetland	1.7	1.9	−0.2	−6.0	−3.3	−1.9	−0.9
Orkney	3.1	3.0	−3.5	2.5	−5.0	−5.8	−9.8
Caithness	6.5	6.2	−2.7	−2.8	−4.3	−8.9	−5.4
Sutherland	4.1	−2.1	−3.7	−3.9	−6.3	−2.1	−5.9
Ross	5.1	−1.6	−0.6	−3.0	−0.9	−1.7	1.2
Inverness	−1.3	−7.9	−1.5	3.3	−1.3	0.9	−3.1
Argyll	−8.3	−10.7	−5.1	1.0	−1.9	−1.8	−3.7

Source: Census of Scotland 1841–1911

1. POST FAMINE ADJUSTMENT, 1850–1880

Clearance and emigration in this period were rooted in landlord insecurity engendered by the famine. Although some landowners, such as the Duke of Sutherland or James Matheson of Lewis, had sufficient external income to absorb the collapse of their Highland estate finances, many others were not so well off. Casualties of this period included Campbell of Islay and the two major Skye landowners, MacLeod of Dunvegan and Lord MacDonald. Many estates went into receivership and were administered by trustees in the 1850s. In these circumstances the profitability of the estate was the sole consideration and this resulted in many clearances. Even among the landowners who survived there was a great sense of insecurity. A major factor contributing to this was the reform of the Poor Law in 1845, and the fear that further reforms would see the indigent, but able bodied, afforded relief from revenue which was largely provided by landowners. The prospect of such a financial burden was a further variable in the equation which had clearance as its solution (Devine 1988, 171–191). 1851 saw the publication of Sir John M'Neill's report to the Board of Supervision (the body which administered the new Scottish poor law). This important document gave official endorsement to emigration as a way of dealing with Highland poverty.

EXERCISE 1
After reading **Document 98**, an extract from M'Neill's report, comment on its importance in government thinking about the Highlands. Consider to what extent his views were a departure from earlier official thinking about the Highlands.

Your response should consider the fact that the report was an official document from a civil servant who had been closely involved in the famine relief operation. It should also consider the concern which the government had demonstrated throughout the famine relief operation not to demoralise the population by intervention in the normal course of economic or social relations. This was bound to inform

M'Neill's approach and his conclusions. Further, given the long history of emigration from the Highlands, the importance of M'Neill's report was that it advocated large scale assisted emigration as a solution to the problems of the Highlands. This was a sharp break from the past as during the first phase of the clearances governments and landlords were opposed to emigration. Famine and economic and social insecurity had produced a change of view. M'Neill's statement that there was unanimous support for the option of emigration should be considered carefully.

In this period, clearance differed from the earlier phases in several ways. Prior to c. 1815, clearance was an exercise in social engineering, an attempt to release land for profitable pastoral farming alongside the creation of crofting communities to house the relocated population. Such communities were deliberately starved of land in an attempt to create a captive labour force for industries which would provide further profit to the landowner. The best known of these is the kelp industry, but fishing, and even military recruiting, can be included. This economy was severely weakened by the collapse of the kelp industry and wider economic depression in the aftermath of the Napoleonic wars. Indeed, the entire structure teetered on the edge of collapse from 1815 to 1846, with especially in crisis years such as 1816 and 1836–7 (Macinnes 1988a). The famine years destroyed the basis of the economic structure and resulted in a determination that its vulnerability should not be reproduced. Thus, the first phase of clearance was motivated by a desire to relocate a potentially productive population and landlords were active in their opposition to emigration prior to 1820. The post 1815 phase of clearance was driven by a necessity to expel a population which was in danger of becoming a dangerous incubus upon landowners. These factors resulted in a series of clearances in the period from 1849 to 1857. The relationship between clearance and emigration was strongest in the late 1840s and 1850s.

The clearances of this period were concentrated in the West and the Hebrides. On the mainland the most extensive clearances took place in Knoydart and Ardnamurchan. Almost every Hebridean island was subjected to clearance, with especially thorough exercises being carried out in Mull, Barra, Lewis and Skye (Richards 1982, Chapters 13 and 14). The clearances of this period were carried out in a blaze of publicity created by pamphleteers such as Donald Ross and journalists such as Thomas Mulock of the *Inverness Advertiser*. Many of the worst clearances took place on estates under Trusteeship, for example, on Islay and throughout Skye and North Uist. The famine clearances produced emigrants and migrants in large numbers. It is impossible to quantify the numbers who left the Highlands in this period: the numbers leaving Scottish ports for North America and Australia were swelled by large numbers of Irish also *en route* to these destinations.

The bulk of emigrants from Scotland in the nineteenth century were of the skilled urban working class seeking opportunities in the industrial economy of North America. The poverty stricken Highland emigrants were not typical of the Scottish emigrants of the period. Although there was much unassisted emigration, there were three important sources of assistance available to Highland emigrants in the 1850s;

landowners, the Highlands and Islands Emigration Society and the Colonial Lands and Emigration Commission. Landowners funded emigration through money made available to them by the Emigration Advances Act of 1851. Many of the landowners who took advantage of these facilities were those who had been bankrupted, or nearly so, by the famine. Many of the more wealthy landowners, such as the Duke of Sutherland, the Duke of Argyll, Baillie of Dochfour, and Colonel John Gordon of Cluny, assisted emigrants from their own resources. The Highlands and Islands Emigration Society was funded from philanthropic sources, but Sir John M'Neill and the Chief Secretary to the Treasury, Sir Charles Trevelyan, carefully controlled the operations of the Society (Devine 1988, 192–211).

Emigration was thought of as a solution to the Highland problem. It would eradicate congestion and society would be put on a sound footing and would nôt require further external intervention. The end of the clearances in the 1850s did not mean the end of landlord coercion. Very strict estate rules in many areas meant that tenants were not allowed to divide their holdings to accommodate their families. In effect this meant that the supply of land was cut off, marriage was effectively controlled and congestion prevented. In some areas, such as Lewis or the Southern Hebrides, the estate management did not exercise such strict control and a large class of landless cottars, squatters on common land and sub tenants remained (*ibid*, Chapter 12).

The rise of commercialised sport and the continuing problems of the sheep farming industry were the most important structural changes in the Highland economy in this period. It is a profound irony that the sheep farming economy, which had been the catalyst for the creation of the crofting communities, did not manage to retain its profitability beyond the 1860s (Hunter 1973). There were many reasons for this; a collapse in wool prices, a growing preference for lamb among consumers, the flooding of the market with chilled meat from abroad, and the complex system of valuation which made it difficult to sell an interest in grazing land. The result was a growing tendency to move from pastoralism to commercialised sport. This had a number of knock-on effects for the Highland economy. The widespread creation of deer forests resulted in the spread of a highly exclusive form of land use. The deer forest was marketed as a place of solitude. Many forests were advertised to potential tenants with the declaration that they had 'no crofters'. Whilst sheep farming had never been labour intensive, there were peaks of demand for labour at certain points in the year: deer forests had almost no labour requirements. Shooting tenants appeared to make few contributions to the local economy and did not increase the valuation of land for rating purposes. Few crofters actually lost land to deer forests, which largely occupied non-agricultural land at high altitude. However, the existence of this highly exclusive, leisure based, form of land use, alongside continued poverty and land hunger, ensured that deer forests would become a much criticised feature of estate management when the Highland land issue boiled over in the 1880s (Orr 1982).

In the famine years the problems caused by the potato failure were exacerbated by a failure of the industrial economy. Ever since the creation of the crofting communities, the Highland population had been compelled to seek part of their income from temporary migration to the Lowlands to work in agriculture and industry (Devine 1979). The post-famine years saw a recovery of the Lowland industrial economy and a renewed resort to temporary migration in search of work. An optimistic view of this period would stress the increasing cash income from temporary migration, the fishing industry and remittances from permanent migrants and emigrants. This, it is held, permitted a move from a subsistence based economy and a greater reliance on purchased foodstuffs (Hunter 1976, Chapter 7). A pessimistic view would stress the clearances of the 1850s and the continuation of landlord coercion by other means, principally the strict control of subdivision (Devine 1988, Chapter 12). Even if there was no economic crisis to match that in rural Ireland in the early 1860s, or the earlier crises in the Highlands, these were not years entirely free of economic problems, especially in the North-West.

The optimistic view of these years stresses the idea that the outbreak of the crofters' agitation in the 1880s was the result of a revolution of rising expectations (Hunter 1976, 132). The pessimistic version is problematic in view of the events of the 1880s. This view stresses continued coercion by landowners and does not fully explain why the demoralised population rebelled in the early 1880s. One response to these questions would be to point to the longevity of a tradition of simmering protest stretching back to the late 18th century (Richards 1973), with protest increasing in frequency in the period after the famine. Certainly, there were incidents of protest, at Sollas in North Uist in 1854, at Coigach in Wester Ross in 1853, and at Bernera in 1874, but these were isolated incidents, stemming from local grievances, and do not add up to a tradition of protest.

A series of events in the 1870s must also be considered in explaining the increasing unrest. John Murdoch, a former exciseman and unorthodox radical, began his pro-crofter newspaper, *The Highlander,* in Inverness in 1873:

> We this day place in the hands of Highlanders a journal that they may call their own. This we do with the distinct view of stimulating them to develop their own industrial resources and of encouraging them to assert their nationality, and maintaining that position in the country to which their numbers, their traditions, and their character entitle them.
>
> (*The Highlander,* 16 May 1873)

Charles Fraser Mackintosh was elected MP for the Inverness Burghs in 1874 and initiated a challenge to the landlord domination of Highland politics. A greater sense of cultural self-confidence can also be detected in this decade, manifested in the successful campaign to endow a chair of Celtic in the University of Edinburgh and the establishment of a series of Gaelic and Highland societies, most importantly the Gaelic Society of Inverness, founded in 1871. These bodies came together to demand greater recognition of Gaelic in the Scottish education system, which had been recast in 1872, and to form the Federation of Celtic Societies in 1877. Most of these developments were divorced from the material concerns of the crofters, however, and, largely, had their origins in urban areas (MacPhail 1989, Chapter 1), so only partly explain the increasing unrest.

2. SECURING THE CROFTING COMMUNITY, 1882–1930

Most attempts to explain the outbreak of the Crofters' Wars emphasise contingent factors. Considerable importance is given to a renewed economic crisis which peaked in 1881. The previous five years had seen a number of exceptionally bad seasons; tenants were afflicted by falling prices for their stock, potato disease and the baleful results of severe storms in the early part of 1881. The latter destroyed crops and fishing gear in many areas of the North and West. To compound these problems migrants returned from the East Coast fishing with much reduced earnings. The factor on the Earl of Cromartie's Coigach estate in Wester Ross said of the crisis; 'There has been nothing like it for the last forty years or more' (Richards 1994, 284). Other factors include the effect of Irish land agitation on the Highlands. These events, although geographically remote from the West Highlands, had an impact there for a number of reasons. Firstly, newspapers such as John Murdoch's *Highlander,* carried copious reports of the Irish agitation. Secondly, some High-landers came into contact with Irish tenants whilst fishing off the Irish coast. Thirdly, itinerant speakers, such as Edward McHugh, brought the issues of the Irish agitation home to the crofting communities (Hunter 1976, Chapter 8).

EXERCISE 2
After comparing what you know about the famine of the 1840s and the crisis of the early 1880s, consider why the responses of the crofting community were so different.

Your response should demonstrate an awareness of the background to the two decades. The 1840s were a decade of economic distress, both in the Highlands and beyond, and had come after a generation of economic insecurity. Although some assertiveness had been demonstrated in the Disruption of 1843 the message preached by the new Free Church was not one of political activity. The 1880s were informed by many new political ideas coming from urban areas and, specifically on the land issue, from Ireland. Although the period since the famine was not one of unalloyed prosperity it did not match the 1820s and 1830s for economic insecurity and although the early 1880s were difficult years they did not match the complete economic and social collapse of the famine years.

The early incidents of the agitation were concentrated in the Isle of Skye. On the Kilmuir estate in the north of the island, owned by Colonel William Fraser, tenants in the township of Valtos began a rent strike in 1881. In the Braes district, near Portree, a long running dispute over access to grazing land on Ben Lee boiled over in April 1882. The third early incident of land agitation on Skye in this period occurred in Glendale in the west of the island (MacPhail 1989, Chapter 2).

38 John Murdoch, 'The Highlanders Friend'. *Scottish National Portrait Gallery.*

A number of points can be made about these early flashpoints of the Crofters' War. Firstly, although rent strikes were used in two of the cases, rent was not really the issue at stake: the Kilmuir estate was exceptional in this respect. The principal grievance was about access to land which estates had leased out to sheep farmers and which crofters felt to be rightfully theirs. The crofters' claims were based on the argument that they had a historic title to the land, grounded in their use of it over many generations prior to it being turned over to pastoralism. Secondly, these events were important in bringing the cause of the crofters to wider public attention. The newspaper coverage of the Braes incident, in particular, was widespread (Hanham 1969).

The agitation on the ground and the press publicity were vital in the development of the political aspect of the Crofters' Movement. The significant point to note here is that the movement was largely composed of urban activists rather than crofters. There had been considerable organisation of Highlanders in urban areas in the 1870s and the publicity given to the crofters' cause in 1882 drew it to the attention of urban radicals who had no former connection with the Highlands. Thus, the localised grievances of Braes, Kilmuir or Glendale were now being translated into a wider political message about the iniquity of the system of land tenure in the Highlands. Contact was made with a small group of MPs who tried their best to advocate the cause of the crofters in Parliament. These included Dr Charles Cameron, a Glasgow MP and proprietor of the *North British Daily Mail*, which gave considerable publicity to the crofters cause; Donald Macfarlane, MP for the Irish constituency of Carlow; and Charles Fraser Mackintosh, MP for Inverness Burghs since 1874 (Hunter 1974). This small group focused their attention on pressurising the government into granting a Royal Commission to examine the grievances of the crofters. They were successful and a Commission was appointed in March 1883 under the Chairmanship of Lord Napier and Ettrick, a Border laird retired from a long career in the Diplomatic Service.

EXERCISE 3
Read **Article 27**. In your opinion, which were the most important influences in creating the political movement which campaigned on behalf of the crofters.

There were many influences which produced the new political movement which campaigned on behalf of the crofters. The agitation in Ireland, which had begun in earnest in the late 1870s, was important. However, although there were links between the Highlands and Ireland it should be questioned whether they were of sufficient extent to produce direct results. Other important influences would include the growing climate of anti-landlordism in Scotland stimulated by important political controversies such as that over the game laws in the 1860s. The growing links between the Highlands and urban areas are also relevant: new political ideas were transmitted and contact between activists was possible. The effect of the Napier Commission should also be carefully considered as it brought the views of crofters to centre stage for the first time. Compare, for example, the tone of M'Neill's Report

39 The Napier Commission at Glasgow, 1883. *Quiz* 1884.

with that of the Napier Commission. The demand and ultimate implementation of electoral reform was important in creating the conditions whereby crofters' votes could have a direct political result, important in elections from 1885 onwards.

In the second half of 1883 the Commissioners toured the Highlands, taking evidence, much of it in Gaelic, and almost all of it from crofters or their representatives. The Commission gave a considerable fillip to the Crofters' Movement which impressed upon crofters the importance of appearing before the Commission to give evidence. The whole exercise gave the movement the opportunity to put down deeper roots in the crofting community. Several important features emerged from the evidence of the crofters. In many areas the crofters expressed the fear that they would be victimised by estate managements for coming forward to give evidence. This is a clear demonstration of the fact that, although there had been no clearances since the late 1850s, landlord coercion remained a real fear of many crofters. Throughout, the evidence is a clear presentation of the view that clearance and emigration had forcibly broken up a contented society and that the return of ancestral lands would facilitate a reversion to such halcyon days. Such evidence reveals the complex identity of the crofting community at the time, backward looking and defensive, yet positive and assertive (MacPhail 1989, Chapter 3).

As the Commissioners retired to Edinburgh to compile their report, agitation in the Highlands was less in evidence as expectations rose. The report eventually emerged in mid 1884. Although it is a long document containing recommendations on a host of subjects from education to telegraphs, the section on land attracted most attention. It proposed the formal reconstitution of pre-clearance townships. Tenants with land worth more than six pounds were to be given leases setting out strict programmes of agricultural improvement, the implementation of which would be supervised by a township constable. Tenants with less land would be given assistance to emigrate. Napier was determined not to give security of tenure to all tenants and thereby perpetuate congestion and poverty (Royal Commission 1884; **Document 99**).

These recommendations were unacceptable to the Crofters' Movement, who could not concur with the notion of assisted emigration, as it conflicted with their central belief that redistribution of land was the answer to the problems of the crofting community. Neither were the recommendations acceptable to the government, which regarded them as idealistic and impractical. Once the government's rejection became clear, agitation was renewed with a vengeance, and was now much more highly politicised. The Crofters' Movement held conferences at Dingwall in 1884 and in Portree in 1885 where it responded to the government with its own radical programme.

The government turned to new sources of inspiration for the legislation which it now believed to be unavoidable. The landlords had convened their own conference, in Inverness in early 1885, but their voluntary concessions fell well short of what was required. The government sought refuge in applying the principles of the Irish Land Act of 1881 to the Highlands. This act had given the so-called 'Three Fs' to Irish tenants, fair rent, fixity of tenure and freedom of sale. The first two were to be applied to the Highlands. The Liberal government attempted to legislate in 1885 but the bill had not reached the statute book when the government fell in July. The necessary general election could not be held until November and December due to the complex task of drawing up new electoral registers to reflect the enlarged electorate created by the reforms of 1884 and 1885. This political vacuum was filled by a Conservative 'caretaker' government led by the Marquis of Salisbury. The election, when it did take place, resulted in the return of four Crofter candidates, and a new era in Highland politics was inaugurated. When the Liberals returned to power in January 1886 their Irish Home Rule Bill soaked up vast amounts of parliamentary time and split the Party; however, the Crofters Holdings (Scotland) Act received the Royal Assent on June 25 1886, the very day on which the government fell. Unfortunately, these political conditions gave the Crofter MPs little room for manoeuvre. The government pushed the Crofters' Bill through with the minimum of debate and a determined opposition to all amendments tabled by the Crofter MPs. This experience, and the provisions of the Act, ensured that it received a cool reception in the crofting community. The Act endowed the crofting community with the blanket security of tenure, to which Lord Napier was so opposed, and established a Crofters' Commission to adjudicate on fair rents (**Document 100**). There was nothing in the Act, however, to deal with the main grievance of the crofting community, shortage of land (Cameron 1996a, Chapter 1). The 1886 General Election, which followed in July, provided mixed fortunes for the crofter MPs, with one loss in Argyll being balanced by a gain in Sutherland.

EXERCISE 4

Compare the recommendations of the Napier Commission in 1884 and the Crofters' Act of 1886. What are the key differences between them?

The Napier Commission of 1884 recommended security of tenure only for crofters with land worth more than six pounds per year. The report had reforming and improving objectives to increase the average size of crofts to make them economic-ally viable and to improve the agricultural skills of the crofting community. The report had as its basis a complete renovation of the crofting community. The 1886 act, on the other hand, was much more static. It did not propose major tenurial changes, rather it sought to give legislative protection to the existing structure of tenancy. The ethos of improvement, which imbued the Napier Report, was entirely absent. The Act made it very difficult for the structure of holdings to change or for crofters to enlarge their holdings.

These conditions meant that the passage of the Act did not signal an immediate end to the agitation. The focus of the agitation now became the cottar-ridden Island of Lewis, which saw a number of incidents in the period to 1888. There was renewed agitation in Tiree, Skye and Sutherland to which the Conservative Secretary of Scotland, Arthur Balfour, responded with military expeditions. By 1888, however, the agitation had largely died out. This was the result of the beneficial effects of rent reductions awarded by the Crofters' Commission, and improved economic conditions. The important point to bear in mind, however, is that there had been little structural change in the crofting economy. The reliance on income generated from external sources, such as fishing and temporary migration, remained, as did the resultant economic and social vulnerability (Cameron 1996a, Chapters 2 and 3).

The 1890s were a period of relative calm. Economic conditions were, on the whole, more stable and there were few major incidents of protest. The Conservatives were in government for most of the period from 1886 to 1905, with a brief period of Liberal government between 1892 and 1895. They were not keen to tamper with the system of land tenure in the early part of this period. Although they may not have been ideologically in tune with the Crofters' Act, especially in its interference between landlord and tenant, they did not seek to overturn it. Instead, they concentrated on attempting to put the Highland economy on a new footing. As has been stressed, crofting was based on a multiplicity of economic activities, and critics of the system focused on this as its greatest weakness. It meant, they held, that the crofter did not pay enough attention to his land, and that those who were so situated to take advantage of the fishing industry could not do so because they were burdened by the demands of the croft. The initiatives which were attempted in this decade had the rationalisation of the crofting economy as their major objective. A considerable amount of thought was given to extending the railway system, which had reached Strome Ferry and Fort William, to the West Coast, with the objective of providing termini to speed up the transport of fish to the market place. Ultimately, the only railway work which took place was to extend the existing railways to Kyle of Lochalsh and Mallaig. Important, but minor, improvements were made to the infrastructure, with investment in the telegraph network and the facilities for landing fish. The Conservatives also attempted to raise the profile of assisted emigration. An underfunded and badly administered experimental scheme to take crofters from Lewis and Harris to Canada was the only result of their efforts. None of this was sufficient to substantially alter the nature of crofting society, as had been the aim of the policy (Cameron 1996a, Chapter 3).

The principal legacy of this period was the establishment of the Congested Districts Board (CDB) in 1897. This body had as its inspiration the Irish body of the same name which had been established in 1892. The objective of the Scottish Board was to turn the crofters from desultory agriculturalists and fishermen into separate groups of small farmers and dedicated fishermen. This was consistent with Conservative ideas as was the provision of facilities to tempt the crofter to become the owner of his land. Once again, this was an idea which the Conservatives were applying in Ireland. Primarily, the objective was to create a conservative class of owner occupiers and to relieve the landlords of the burden of unremunerative crofting tenants. That the latter was the sincere wish of landlords emerged from their evidence to the Royal Commission which the Liberals had set up in 1892 (Cameron 1994).

The CDB had powers to assist agricultural development and limited powers to buy land for redistribution and sale to crofters. Its overall policy was hampered by lack of money and lack of compulsory powers to purchase land which meant that it could not take a proactive approach. The CDB's major initiative on the land question came in 1904 when two large estates on Skye, Glendale and Kilmuir, came onto the market and the Board was able to purchase both. These estates had seen the heights of the land agitation in the 1880s and both contained politically active crofters. Those at Glendale, however, were able to embrace the idea of owner occupation because portions of the estate afforded the prospect of an economic return. At Kilmuir the Board came up against crofter opposition to the notion of owner occupation. This was partly based on a loyalty to the 1886 Act which gave most of the advantages of ownership, and partly on a calculation that annual payments towards ownership would be higher than current rents, especially when the loss of rating concessions consequent upon crofting tenure was considered. Political considerations also played a part in the failure of the CDB at Kilmuir. In 1905 the divided Conservative party fell from government and was replaced by a Liberal administration which recorded a resounding victory at the General Election of 1906. The Liberals were resolutely opposed to the notion of owner occupation and sought to return to an extended version of the 1886 Act which would be applied throughout Scotland. Their attempts to do so were controversial because of the implications for lowland farming and were held up by the House of Lords until 1911. The CDB was, then, living on borrowed time from 1906 to 1911, and politically aware crofters, such as those in Kilmuir, were well aware of the fact, so its impact was blunted (Cameron 1996a, Chapters 4 and 5).

The years after 1900 saw renewed protest in the Highlands. This was partly due to an economic downturn, accompanied by the fact that the CDB raised the expectations of the landless in the Highlands. Most of the incidents of protest were concentrated in Lewis and the southern islands of South Uist and Barra, where cottars were at their most numerous and land conditions at their most congested. This frustration continued as the limitations of the CDB became more apparent and reached a peak during the years 1906 to 1911 when Liberal land legislation was held up by the House of Lords. Neither was the situation improved with the eventual passage of the Small Landholders Act in 1911. This act had a minimal impact due to its many loopholes and extreme complexity. As a vehicle for dealing with the problem of continuing landlessness in the Highlands it was almost completely useless. The outbreak of war in 1914 cut short the operation of the Act as the Highland land issue went into abeyance for four years (Cameron 1996a, Chapters 6 and 7).

With the facilities provided by an Act passed in 1919, the government effectively nationalised large swathes of Highland land and, in the form of the Board of Agriculture for Scotland, became one of the largest Highland landowners. The 1919 Act was a highly effective piece of legislation which had a major impact on the Highland landscape, especially in the Hebrides where the advent of a sympathetic, educative and supportive landowner was a considerable boon (Leneman 1989; Cameron 1996, Chapter 7).

EXERCISE 5
After thinking about the different approaches to the land issue in the Highlands in the period between 1886 and 1919, present arguments as to which approach was the most successful.

The 1886 and 1911 Acts had as their basis the continuation of a relationship between crofter and landlord, albeit one controlled by legislation. This was held to be closest to the ideals of the crofting community who had no desire to acquire ownership of their land because their ideology already claimed a form of ownership, or stewardship, over the land. The 1897 Act proposed to turn the crofters into owners. This was held to give them a stake in their land and would thereby encourage improvements and social conservatism. Crofters showed no enthusiasm for this idea. The 1919 Act created the conditions whereby the state, in the form of the Board of Agriculture for Scotland, could become the landlord of crofting estates. This was a highly successful reform as crofters on estates so purchased now had a stable and benign landlord with, as a primary function, the development of the crofts on the estate. The disadvantage of such a reform was that not all crofting estates could be purchased by the government and inequalities were created between state and privately owned estates. Further, it could be argued that the holdings created by the land settlement schemes were too small and that the difficult questions asked by the Napier Commission a generation earlier had been ignored since.

The armistice in Europe was the signal for a third phase of land agitation in the Highlands. The principle tactic in this period was the demonstrative invasion of land which crofters felt to be rightfully theirs to use: this has become known as the 'land raid'. Land raids had been evident in earlier periods of Highland land agitation but they reached new levels of sophistication in this period (Robertson 1997; **Article 28** provides more detail on the subject of land raids). On a few occasions they can be seen as determined efforts to reclaim land. Most, however, were public demonstrations designed to draw attention to the general grievances of the crofters and cottars and were combined with skilful rhetoric which amplified the Highland contribution to the war effort. The main concentration of protest in this period was in the outer Hebrides and particularly in Lewis where the problem of congestion was at its height. Other areas of the Highlands, such as Sutherland, had been emptied of population; throughout the Long Island, and especially in Lewis, a large class of landless cottars had multiplied in the decades since the famine (Hunter 1976, Chapter 11; Cameron 1996a, Chapter 8).

During the war Lewis was purchased by the industrialist Lord Leverhulme who had grandiose plans to devote the island to the fish processing industry. Leverhulme had an obsessive distaste for crofting, which he felt would distract his potential workforce:

> In my opinion, this island [Lewis] can be made the most prosperous part of the United Kingdom. The first step to that is the organisation of the land resources of the country on some basis other than that of common grazing rights and

generally the modification of the whole Crofters Land Act so as to provide for a
growing population a growing wealth of the people.

(SRO, Department of Agriculture Files, AF 67/248,
Lord Leverhulme to Robert Munro, 21 Sept 1918)

An epic clash ensued between Leverhulme, who would not release any farms for land
settlement, elements of the crofting population on Lewis, who repeatedly raided
farms, and the government, which was caught between its obligation to implement
the 1919 Act and its unwillingness to see Leverhulme's investment in the island
unfulfilled. The government attempted to reach an agreement with Leverhulme
which involved the suspension of land settlement and a ten year trial period for his
schemes. Growing financial problems in the Leverhulme empire and continued land
raiding meant that this agreement soon foundered and Leverhulme left Lewis with
most of his plans barely beyond the planning stage. Leverhulme's failure to understand the crofting system was profound. His determination to stamp it out ignored
the most salient feature of the system; that it had coexisted with industrial, or semi-
industrial, pursuits ever since its inception (Leneman 1989, Chapter 7; Cameron
1996a, Chapter 8).

The 1919 Act may have transferred the ownership of a great deal of land and
extended the amount of land available to crofters, but it did not reduce the economic
vulnerability of the crofting system. This fact is crucial to any understanding of the
inter-war period in the Highlands. Economic insecurity was the paramount feature
of the period from 1922 to the mid 1930s. The end of the war had been followed by
a brief post-war boom, but by 1922 the economy had slumped and a depressingly
familiar series of events unfolded in the Highlands. In the early 1920s emigration
reached levels not seen since the 1850s. Even in this period, however, this was not
the emigration of the desperate, but the emigration of those seeking new opportunities, the kind of emigration which had been prominent throughout Scotland in the
19th century (Harper 1994). This is an important fact to remember when considering the impact of the world-wide economic crash of 1929 on the Highlands. This
slump cut off prospects for emigration, as industrial North America was no longer a
source of opportunity. In addition, the failures of the industrial economy of Lowland
Scotland impelled many newly unemployed back to the Highlands; the return of the
unemployed was a feature of many rural areas throughout the world during the
slump (Hobsbawm, 1994, 92). An economically disadvantaged population was thus
thrown back onto the resources of the croft. This was a crisis of similar nature to
those of the 19th century. Clearly, the failure of the lowland economy did not
combine with natural disasters of the kind evident in the 1840s, but the perpetuation
of small crofts and reliance on external income resulted in a fragile social and
economic structure.

The dire economic conditions of the 1930s produced new thinking about the
Highlands. In this period there was a move away from a conception of the Highland
'problem' as a land problem. More comprehensive views were taken by such
organisations as the Highland Development League and the Scottish Economic

Committee (Hunter 1991, 41–2). The latter body prepared a report on the state of the Highlands which paid scant regard to the land settlement operation of the immediate post-war period and argued that the Highlands would benefit from a simplification of the administrative machinery. It argued that the appointment of a Highland Development Commissioner and a Central Marketing Agency would help to overcome some of the ingrained problems of the crofting system. This was a serious attempt to consider the ways in which the crofting system could relate to the industrial economy of the Lowlands in a more constructive manner. At this time there was also a noticeable shift in government attitudes to the Highlands. With the huge problems facing governments in industrial areas the Highlands slipped down the political agenda. It was the stricken industrial areas which were endowed with novel administrative structures, in the shape of the Special Areas legislation of the 1930s (Document 101). The government did consider a limited application of the wholesale and expensive programme of intervention recommended by the Scottish Economic Committee's report, but events were overtaken by the outbreak of war in 1939 (Cameron 1996a, 202–4).

EXERCISE 6
Read **Document 102**, an extract from the memoirs of Finlay J Macdonald. Did the crofting system mitigate or exacerbate the effects of economic depression?

Your response should consider the way the depression impacted on the Highlands. The crofters were in an advantageous position in some respects in that they were unlikely to be evicted from their homes and they had access to some means of providing their own food. They were also involved in the production of limited quantities of food which could be turned into ready cash if they could be marketed. Further, the cost of living in the crofting communities was much lower than in urban areas. On the other hand the crofters faced severe problems. Crofting had always relied on earnings from occupations beyond the croft and many of these were no longer available. The production of tweed, a luxury item, was limited by a dearth of demand in time of recession. The economic problems in the lowlands inhibited temporary migration in search of employment and the failure of the wider industrial economy brought about an almost complete halt to emigration. Your response should weigh these various factors in coming to a conclusion.

3. DEALING WITH DIVERSITY SINCE 1939

The basic concern of government in the post-1939 period was to diversify the Highland economy. The over-riding motivation was the continuing, indeed, see-mingly irreversible, process of population decline which dominated the period (Cameron 1996b). As will be noted from the table below, there were isolated points of growth, due to urbanisation and large scale industrial developments.

TABLE 2 : PERCENTAGE POPULATION CHANGE IN THE CROFTING COUNTIES, 1921–1981.

	21–31	31–41	41–51	51–61	61–71	71–81
Shetland	−16.1	−7.0	−3.0	−7.8	−2.8	57.8
Orkney	−8.3	−2.3	−1.4	−12.2	−8.6	11.7
Caithness	−9.2	0	−11.7	20.7	1.5	−1.5
Sutherland	−9.6	−5.0	−10.5	−1.4	−3.0	8.4
Ross	−11.0	−1.3	−2.4	−4.8	1.2	18.5
Inverness	−0.5	−1.2	4.8	−0.7	7.3	24.1
Argyll	−18.1	−1.9	2.6	−6.3	1.0	2.7

The original vehicle for diversification was the North of Scotland Hydro Electric Board, established in 1943. Hydro-electricity had initially been exploited by private industrial concerns in the Highlands. The most notable early schemes were for the aluminium industry, at Foyers on the shore of Loch Ness and at Kinlochleven, in the years before the Great War. The inter-war years were a period of triumph and disaster for those who hoped that hydro-electricity would save the Highland economy. There were engineering triumphs in the exploitation of the waters of Lochs Treig and Laggan for the new smelter at Fort William, and political disasters in the form of repeated failures to get parliamentary sanction for large scale hydro schemes. These schemes were defeated by an alliance of the coal interest, wary of a modern competitor, and Highland landowners, who had acquired a sudden interest in the amenity value of their estates. The Hydro Board was a new departure from these unfulfilled aspirations. It sought to harness cheap electricity to domestic consumers and to provide a ready supply, but not at discount rates, for industrial consumers. The Hydro Board was also given a wider role in its famous 'social clause' which empowered it to collaborate with any relevant bodies to improve economic and social conditions in its area of responsibility: 'It should be an instruction to the new Board to co-operate as fully as possible in the pursuit of its main objectives in all schemes undertaken with official approval for the regeneration of the Highlands, so that the benefits of the new developments may be made available to the fullest possible extent to the Northern area' ('Report of the Committee on Hydro-Electric Development in Scotland', *Parliamentary Papers* 1942–3 IV, 27).

The constructional phase of the Board, from the 1940s to the 1960s, provided much needed employment. The achievement of the Hydro Board has been immense, but it is fair to say that the results have not been all that its creators (chiefly Tom Johnston, Secretary of State for Scotland, 1941–45), had hoped for. The chief beneficiaries have been domestic consumers in all corners of the Highlands, who have received a domestic supply at a flat rate, despite the vast cost of the operation. This, however, is a reflection on the ambitious expectations of those who created it, rather than any failure on the part of those who ran the Hydro Board over the years (Payne 1988).

The second vehicle for widespread change in the Highlands in the post-war period has been regional policy. This can be defined as the provision of special facilities to give certain regions, defined for the most part by high unemployment, favoured status in government expenditure and concessions for the attraction of investment. The first post-war statute was the Distribution of Industry Act of 1945 which scheduled Development Areas for special treatment. In 1948 a large area around Inverness was scheduled in the hope that industry would be attracted. This did not prove to be the case, but it established the idea of trying to concentrate growth in the areas of highest potential in the hope that other areas would benefit. This was the dominant thought behind the establishment of the Highlands and Islands Development Board in 1965. This was the government's major initiative in regional policy for the Highlands. It had long been lobbied for by the STUC, among others, and the idea goes back at least to the 1938 recommendation for a Highland Development Commissioner. Nevertheless, in the mid 1960s the notion of long term economic planning was in vogue and this was the ethos of the Board in its early years. Its membership was dominated by planners (such as its first chairman, Robert Grieve), businessmen and industrialists, rather than those interested in the land issue. It was much criticised for not taking the initiative on the land issue, but this was never the intention of its founders, who did not endow it with powers to do so. Further, its role was never clearly defined: it had to compete with functional bodies, such as the Crofters' Commission, the Forestry Commission, the North of Scotland Hydro Electric Board, and many others. The Board was unable to do very much to influence the Highland economy; as the impact of the oil industry and the European Community was felt in the Highlands, it was overtaken by events. From the mid 1980s, however, the administration of the Board was decentralised and Development Programmes, modelled on European Community initiatives, were implemented in Skye and the north-west of the mainland (Hunter 1991, 167).

One of the major features of the post-war history of the Highlands has been the construction of vast industrial projects which have transformed a number of localities. The aluminium schemes already mentioned were the forerunners of a number of large projects in the post-war period. Perhaps the most novel, because of its modernity and isolation in the local economy, was the building of the Dounreay Experimental Reactor Establishment in Caithness in the mid 1950s. Caithness was chosen as the site for reasons of geology, abundance of water supply, and for the relative lack of population in its immediate environs. The reactor was the principal reason for the County of Caithness becoming an isolated point of population growth among the Highland counties in the 1950s (see Table 1). Large numbers of incoming workers, 'atomics' as they were labelled by the locals, doubled the size of the town of Thurso. There were some knock-on effects as the Atomic Energy Authority moved some of its administrative facilities north; local enterprise provided protective clothing for the workforce, and a technical college was opened in Thurso to cater for the skill requirements of the reactor. By the mid 1960s, however, there was little to disguise the fact that the Caithness economy was dangerously dependant on the reactor establishment.

The second large-scale project, which had a similar impact on its locality, was the establishment, in 1963, of a pulp mill at Corpach, near Fort William. This project was not so economically isolated, as forestry was one of the main industries of the Highlands. The third and final project was the establishment of an aluminium smelter at Invergordon, in Easter Ross, in the late 1960s. This area had long been felt to have the best potential for industrialisation in the Highlands. All three of these projects were the cause of localised surges in population as migrant labour flocked to take advantage of the employment they offered (see Table 1). Critics noted the stress placed on local resources and the dangerous economic dependence which they induced. It was argued by some that the effect of such projects was to exacerbate depopulation in the crofting areas of the west. Similar results were noted when the oil industry impacted on the Highlands in the 1970s and 1980s with the opening of fabrication yards at Nigg and Ardersier in the east and Kishorn in the west.

Although the land issue slipped down the political agenda in the mid 1920s, it was still an issue in the post-war period. The ineluctable fact of the crofting system ensured that. In the immediate post-war period the rigid security of tenure inherent in crofting led to decay in many townships. Many people who inherited crofts did not really want them and/or were in no position to use them properly. A second important fact in this regard was a Court of Session decision in 1917 which decreed that crofters need not reside on their crofts. These two features produced the absentee crofter who, importantly, had all the same rights and security as residents. The legalities of this are not as important as the fact that many crofting townships were left with only an aged resident population and many crofts fell into disuse or into the hands of people who held multiple tenancies or sub-tenancies and who merely used them for grazing, without any regard for draining or fencing. The upshot was widespread decay in the crofting communities. Crofting was not one of the priorities of the post-war Labour Government, but in 1951, just before it demitted office, a Commission of Enquiry was appointed to look into the crofting system:

> In the great majority of cases, the croft by itself was never capable of providing a reasonable living for a man and his family. It had to be supplemented by some other form of work, such as fishing, weaving or knitting. The decline of the crofting system is attributable in great part to the failure of some of these auxiliary industries, notably fishing, coupled with the fact that men and women are no longer content with the modes of life which were acceptable to their ancestors.
>
> (*Report of the Commission of Enquiry into Crofting Conditions*, 1953)

As a result of their recommendations, a new Crofters' Commission was set up in 1955, but without adequate powers to reorganise crofting townships. Little changed until radical proposals were put forward by the Commission in the late 1960s. These aimed to convert the system of tenure into a clear cut system of ownership. It was also proposed to simplify and extend the range of business activities which could be carried out from a croft. These proposals encountered a great deal of opposition within the crofting community and the only result was a Crofting Reform Act in 1976 which gave crofters the right to buy their crofts if they so desired: few have chosen to take up the option. However, the existence of the long established crofting area has allowed the government to take special action without being accused of creating a precedent or arousing expectations in other areas of rural Britain. Crofting has recently enjoyed an improved image, partly due to much better public relations by the crofting lobby, newly and professionally organised by the Scottish Crofters Union (SCU) since the mid 1980s. The SCU was able to capitalise on the notion that crofting was environmentally friendly and in a European context crofting does not appear so anachronistic. It is also held that the existence of the crofting system has prevented wholesale depopulation of the crofting counties. The crofting system continues to operate today, as it has since its inception, in providing a base from which other economic activities can be carried out. This role has been augmented and supported by government in a number of ways. Firstly, since 1955 a system of grants for capital projects, such as housing or other major improvements, has improved the infrastructure of the crofting communities. Concessions for crofters have been maintained throughout the many changes in the methods of raising local authority revenue. It should be noted while crofting is a major part of Highland identity and defines the Highlands geographically in policy terms, it is a minority pursuit in the Highlands (Hunter 1991).

Crofting, however, is not the only controversial aspect of the land issue. A second ineluctable feature of the structure of Highland society is the continuing power of the landowner. This is not to make a moral judgement about the activities of individual landowners, 'good' or 'bad', but to argue that such a distinction cannot really be made given the extent to which a landowner can control the destiny of a particular area. In many ways the crofting community, with a legislative framework to control its tenurial relations, is in a privileged position. There are vast areas of the Highlands which can be bought and sold without any reference to, or concern for, their populations. The problem of the dominance of the large and coercive proprietor has given way to the problem of the faceless and corporate landowner (Wightman 1996; Cramb 1996; MacEwen 1981).

4. CULTURE

Any discussion of Highland culture must take account of the fact that over the last century and a half the linguistic history of the region has moved from being, in places, monoglot Gaelic speaking through bilingualism to, in places, monoglot English speaking. Since 1881 the census has recorded the numbers of Gaelic speakers in Scotland. The statistics are presented in Table 3. The principal feature to note is the decline and dispersal of the language, although some recovery is evident in recent years.

TABLE 3: GAELIC SPEAKERS IN COUNTIES 1881 TO 1971 (% OF POP)

	1881	1891	1901	1911	1921	1931	1951	1961	1971
Argyll	65.2	60.9	54.3	47.1	34.6	33.2	21.7	17.2	13.7
Bute	22.7	20.3	15.7	12.0	4.6	5.2	2.3	1.6	1.9
Caithness	9.5	12.0	9.2	5.6	3.8	2.6	1.3	1.0	1.6
Inverness	76.0	73.2	64.9	59.0	50.1	44.0	30.6	25.9	22.0
Nairn	20.3	27.1	15.3	10.5	6.5	5.2	1.7	1.8	1.6
Perth	21.1	12.0	9.9	7.7	5.3	4.2	1.9	1.5	1.7
Renfrew	2.2	3.2	2.3	1.9	1.3	1.1	0.7	0.6	0.8
Ross	76.6	76.9	71.8	64.0	60.2	57.3	46.0	41.3	35.1
Sutherland	80.4	77.1	71.8	61.8	52.3	44.0	25.3	18.8	14.5
SCOTLAND	6.8	6.8	5.6	4.6	3.5	3.0	2.0	1.6	1.8

Source: Withers 1984

TABLE 4: GAELIC SPEAKERS IN DISTRICTS 1981–1991 (% OF POP)

	1981	1991		1981	1991
Aberdeen	0.6	0.6	*Inverness*	6.8	6.0
Dundee	0.4	0.4	*Lochaber*	16.1	11.1
Edinburgh	0.9	0.9	*Nairn*	1.8	2.1
Glasgow	1.4	1.0	*Perth & K'ross*	1.6	1.3
Renfrew	0.8	0.7	*Ross & C'marty*	7.5	6.2
Argyll & Bute	10.5	7.7	*Skye & L'als*	54.3	42.9
Badenoch	3.8	2.9	*Western Isles*	79.9	69.1
Caithness	1.4	1.2	*Sutherland*	11.3	7.9
SCOTLAND	1.6	1.3			

Source: Rogerson and Gloyer 1995

EXERCISE 7

Examine the statistics in Tables 3 and 4 and present some reasons for the changes in the numbers speaking Gaelic over the years from 1881 to 1991.

Briefly, your answer should consider such factors as the impact of the education system and note that the decline of Gaelic has accelerated despite its growth within the education system. What has been the impact of population movement, both of native speakers moving out of the Highlands and monoglot English speakers moving into formerly Gaelic-speaking areas? Emphasis should be given to the increasing importance of mass media and a more uniform world wide culture imbued with a commercial ethos. Thought should also be given to the attitude of Gaelic speakers to their own language in the face of such developments. Have recent developments, such as Gaelic medium education, failed or merely not had sufficient time to counteract the effects of a long period of decline? The geographical aspects of the history of the language should be considered. Are there any areas where the decline has been less evident and if so, why should this be?

The cultural history of the Scottish Highlands can be discussed by looking at the Gaelic and English literature produced within the region and by noting the fact that the Highlands, and rural Scotland more generally, have been the foremost aspect of Scotland to be presented in cultural forms.

The 18th century saw great achievements in Gaelic culture and the 19th century often suffers by comparison. Gaelic poetry declined into sentimentality in the years before *c.* 1870. The years after 1870 saw a revival which has been sustained into the 20th century. It should not be surprising that these revivals were centred on a small number of significant figures, after all, the language was in decline for much of the period since 1850. Gaelic gained minor footholds in the education system in the 1870s and in legislation of 1908 and 1918, but it is really only since the post 1960s reorganisation of Scottish education that the foothold has become firm (Thomson 1989).

In the 1870s a number of significant poets were at work. The poems of William Livingstone and John Smith were original in their challenging perspective on the changes which had occurred in the 19th century Highlands. Criticism was directed at institutions such as landlordism, commercialised sport and the stultifying influence of Highland Presbyterianism (Macinnes 1988b). Their poetry has been called that of incitement, or *brosnachadh*. This was also a period when strenuous efforts were made to recover the oral tradition of the Highlands, especially through the work of John Francis Campbell and Alexander Carmichael, to name only two of a veritable army of folklorists who devoted attention to the Scottish Highlands in the second half of the 19th century.

The years of political agitation in the 1880s provided subject matter for important figures such as Mary MacPherson (Mhairi Mhor nan Oran) and a host of minor bards who versified on local matters. Nevertheless, one should not over-emphasise the discontinuities with earlier 19th century verse; many of the sentimental themes were sustained, in particular, the emphasis on a 'golden age' prior to the transformation of Highland society and a seeming reluctance to be directly critical of landlords (Meek 1995). In the 20th century Gaelic poetry has become more outward looking and self confident, perhaps best reflected in the work of two major poets, George Campbell Hay and Sorley MacLean. Their work was profoundly influenced by wartime experience and, in MacLean's case, socialist conviction, as well as the Highland past (Black 1987; McCaughey 1987).

The Highlands have been an important theme in wider Scottish culture in the period since 1850. Many Scottish writers in the twentieth century have written about the Highlands. The bulk of Neil Gunn's work is concerned with the Highlands, and some of it, notably *Butchers Broom* (1934) and *The Silver Darlings* (1941), directly concerned with Highland history. Many other writers from outside the Highlands have made the region a major theme in their work. Norman MacCaig's poem, 'A Man in Assynt', or novels by Robin Jenkins such as *The Cone Gatherers,* (1955) or *A Love of Innocence* (1963) are concerned, at least in part, with the Highlands.

There are two important themes in this body of work. The first is the abiding concern with the past, and in particular the clearances. Sorley MacLean's poem 'Hallaig', Neil Gunn's *Butcher's Broom* (1934), Fionn MacColla's *And the Cock Crew* (1945) and Iain Crichton Smith's *Consider the Lilies,* (1968) are all directly concerned with aspects of the clearances. The second important theme is the relationship between the Highlands and the Lowlands. The main characters of Gunn's novel *The Drinking Well* (1946) and of MacColla's *The Albannach* (1932) personally explore this relationship, as do the children adopted by islanders in Jenkins' *A Love of Innocence*. John MacGrath's play, *The Cheviot, The Stag and the Black Black Oil* (1973), which had such an extraordinary impact when it toured the Highlands in the 1970s, encompasses both themes.

CONCLUSION

The last century and a half in Highland history has seen vast changes in the region. In 1850 rural society in the Highlands, in common with many other areas in Western Europe, was recovering from severe famines, and facing a coercive social transformation to ensure that such an event would not recur. The region has become steadily more integrated into wider Scottish and British history but retains important elements of distinctiveness. Two major themes of continuity have been population decline and government intervention, the latter partly in response to the former. It is interesting to note that population decline seems to be reversing in certain areas, as Table 5 shows. This has arisen due to an influx of people to these areas, as can be seen clearly in the case of Skye and Lochalsh.

TABLE 5: POPULATION CHANGE IN HIGHLAND LOCAL AUTHORITY AREAS 1981–1991

	TOTAL CHANGE	NATURAL CHANGE	MIGRATION
Highland Region	6.2	1.0	5.0
Districts			
Badenoch & Strathspey	13.5	−1.7	15.2
Caithness	−3.5	1.3	−4.8
Inverness	11.5	2.6	8.9
Lochaber	−1.1	1.0	−2.1
Ross and Cromarty	7.1	2.5	4.6
Skye & Lochalsh	14.9	−2.8	17.7
Sutherland	−0.8	−4.4	3.6
Argyll & Bute	−1.1	−2.5	1.3
Islands			
Western Isles	−5.7	−3.9	-1.8
Orkney	4.0	−0.5	4.5
Shetland	−3.8	3.2	-7.0

Source: Cameron 1996b

EXERCISE 8

Examine Table 5 and comment on the way it differs from Tables 1 and 2, and suggest some reasons for the differences. You should remember the theme of regional diversity within the Highlands when thinking about these statistics.

The 1980s seem to have witnessed a turnaround in the demographic history of the Highlands. This is emphasised by the fact that this seems to have been caused by the movement of people into the region, whereas the long-term population decline was the result of people moving out of the region. Are these recent changes different from the isolated points of population growth in the period from the 1950s to the 1970s? Are these fundamental changes, or is it too soon to tell? What are some of the likely ways in which a larger population is likely to affect the Highlands. If the Highlands become a more varied community in terms of the background and experiences of its members are the likely results positive or negative for the region? Are technological developments in computing and communications likely to produce a new economic opportunity as demographic patterns change?

Government intervention continues; the Highlands are still regarded as a special case by governmental structures. Indeed, it would seem that this view has been adopted by the European Union which has awarded the Highlands Objective One funding despite the fact that a strict view of the rules would exclude the area from such investment. The beginnings of a population turn-round and a host of examples of cultural assertiveness can be adduced to construct an optimistic view of the current situation. On the other hand, a pessimistic view would stress continuing problems with standards of living and economic performance (see Cameron 1996b).

REFERENCES TO BOOKS AND ARTICLES MENTIONED IN THE TEXT.

Black, RIM 1987 'Thunder, Renaissance and Flowers: Gaelic Poetry in the Twentieth Century', in Craig, C (ed) The History of Scottish Literature, Volume 4, Twentieth Century, Aberdeen, 195–215

Cameron, EA 1994 'The Political Influence of Highland Landowners; a reassessment', Northern Scotland 14, 27–45.

*Cameron, EA 1996a Land for the People? The British Government and the Scottish Highlands, c.1880–1925. East Linton.

*Cameron, EA 1996b, 'The Scottish Highlands: From Congested District to Objective One', in Devine, TM & Finlay, RJ (eds) Scotland in the Twentieth Century, Edinburgh, 153–69.

*Cameron, EA 1997 "They will listen to no remonstrance': Land Raids and Land Raiders in the Scottish Highlands, 1886–1914', Scottish Economic and Social History 17, 43–64.

Cramb, A 1996 Who Owns Scotland Now? Edinburgh.

*Devine, TM 1979 'Temporary Migration and the Scottish Highlands in the Nineteenth Century', Economic History Review 32, 344–59.

*Devine, TM 1988 The Great Highland Famine. Edinburgh.

Hanham, HJ 1969 'The Problem of Highland Discontent, 1880–1885', *Transactions of the Royal Historical Society* 19, 21–65.

Harper, M 1994 'Crofter Colonists in Canada: an experiment in empire settlement in the 1920s', *Northern Scotland* 14, 69–108.

Hobsbawm, E 1994 *Age of Extremes: The Short Twentieth Century, 1914–1991*. London.

Hunter, J 1973 'Sheep and Deer: Highland Sheep Farming 1850–1900', *Northern Scotland* 1, 199–222.

*Hunter J 1974 'The Politics of Highland Land Reform 1873–1895' *Scottish Historical Review* 53, 45–68.

*Hunter J 1976 *The Making of the Crofting Community*. Edinburgh.

Hunter, J 1991 *The Claim of Crofting: The Scottish Highlands, 1930–1990*. Edinburgh.

Leneman, L 1989 *Fit For Heroes? Land Settlement in Scotland After World War One*. Aberdeen.

McCaughey, T 1987 'Somhairle MacGill-eain', *in* Craig, C (ed) *The History of Scottish Literature, Volume 4, The Twentieth Century,* Aberdeen, 147–61.

MacEwen, J 1981 *Who Owns Scotland?* Edinburgh.

*Macinnes, AI 1988a 'Scottish Gaeldom: The First Phase of Clearance', *in* Devine, TM & Mitchison, R, *People and Society in Scotland, Volume 1, 1760–1830,* Edinburgh, 70–90.

Macinnes, J 1988b 'Gaelic Poetry in the Nineteenth Century', *in* Gifford, D (ed) *The History of Scottish Literature, Volume 3, Nineteenth Century,* Aberdeen, 377–96.

*MacPhail, IMM 1989 *The Crofters War*. Stornoway.

Meek DE, 1995 *Tuath is Tighearna: Tenants and Landlords*. Edinburgh.

Orr, W 1982 *Deer Forests Landlords and Crofters*. Edinburgh.

Payne PL 1988 *The Hydro*. Aberdeen.

Richards, E 1973 'How Tame were the Highlanders During the Clearances?', *Scottish Studies* 17, 35–50.

Richards, E 1982 *A History of the Highland Clearances: Agrarian Transformation and the Evictions*. London.

Richards, E 1994 'Poverty and Survival in 19th Century Coigach', *in* Baldwin, JR (ed), *Peoples and Settlement in North West Ross,* Edinburgh, 271–89.

Robertson, I 1997 'Governing the Highlands: The place of popular protest in the Highlands of Scotland after 1918', *Rural History* 8, 109–24.

Rogerson RG & Gloyer, A 1995 'Gaelic Cultural Revival or Language Decline', *Scottish Geographical Magazine* 111, 46–53.

Thomson, D 1989 *An Introduction to Gaelic Poetry* (2nd Edition). Edinburgh.

Wightman, A, 1996 *Who Owns Scotland?* Edinburgh.

Withers, CWJ, 1984 *Gaelic in Scotland*. Edinburgh.

FURTHER READING

Those references marked * in the above list are recommended further reading.

PRIMARY SOURCES

Report to the Board of Supervision By Sir John MacNeill on the Western Highlands and Islands, PP 1851 XXVI.

Report of the Commissioners of Inquiry into the Condition of the Crofters and Cottars in the Highlands and Islands of Scotland, PP 1884 XXXIII-XXXVI.

Report of the Committee on Hydro Electric Development in Scotland, PP 1942–3 IV.

Report of the Commission of Enquiry into Crofting Conditions, PP 1953–54 VII.

Industrialisation
and Industrial Decline
Peter L Payne

INTRODUCTION

In Volume 1 Cooke and Donnachie examined numerous aspects of the Industrial Revolution in Scotland. This chapter seeks to discover 'what came next?' It will be seen that the term 'Industrial Revolution' is capable of conveying an erroneous impression if its use conjures up the idea of the spread of large-scale, factory-based methods of production throughout *all* sectors of manufacturing activity. Nevertheless, such methods *were* largely adopted in certain industries that came to dominate the Scottish economy: cotton textiles, coal, iron and steel and shipbuilding. It was because all of these activities experienced stagnation and decline that unemployment in Scotland was so much higher than the British average throughout much of the twentieth century (Buxton 1980). In this chapter we will examine the development of the staple industries and attempt to explain why other industries, which might have absorbed many of the unemployed, were so slow to emerge in Scotland. We will see too that when, several decades after the end of the Second World War, changes in the structure of Scottish industry did take place, they brought no guarantee of stability.

In short, we will look at several major themes:

- the structure of the industrial sector in the mid-nineteenth century
- the textile industries
- the heavy industries: coal, iron and steel and shipbuilding
- reasons for the slow diversification of the industrial sector
- the changes after the late 1950s
- conclusions

I. THE STRUCTURE OF SCOTTISH INDUSTRY, *c.* 1851

1851 was the year of the Great Exhibition when Britain displayed her predominance in the industrial arts. For an all too brief period Britain was *the* workshop of the world and the material benefits of the industrial revolution trickled belatedly down to the vast majority of the population. The term 'industrial revolution' conveys the idea of manufacturing processes being transformed by the adoption of the factory system. Although cotton was the first to experience this phenomenon, until recently it was implicit – and in some cases, explicit – in most economic histories that

> other branches of industry effected comparable advances, and all these together, mutually reinforcing one another, made possible further gains on an ever-widening front. The abundance and variety of these innovations almost defy compilation, but they may be subsumed under three principles: the substitution of machines – rapid, regular, precise, tireless – for human skill and effort; the substitution of inanimate for animate sources of power, the introduction of engines for converting heat into work thereby opening to more a new and almost unlimited supply of energy; the use of new and far more abundant raw materials, in particular, the substitution of mineral for vegetable or animal substances.
>
> (Landes 1969, 41)

And all this took place in firms that were bigger than those of earlier times and which exhibited a growing scale of operations requiring ever larger capitals.

In the last twenty years, however, it has become increasingly clear that 'the industrial revolution, so far from abridging human labour, created a whole new world of labour intensive jobs' and that in the majority of activities 'it was the workshop rather than the factory which prevailed' (Samuel 1977, 8). Certainly, the fact that a significant proportion of the rising demand of the nineteenth century was met by a proliferation of small producers is evident in mid-Victorian Scotland. The anatomy of Scottish industry in 1851 has been laid bare by Richard Rodger (Rodger 1985; 1988). Utilizing census information, he has shown that the 5,994 urban employers whose returns specified the number of employees engaged a total of 92,656 hands. Of these, 17,306 were women, some 80% of whom were in textiles. The tabulated data (see **Article 29**) reveal the dominance of the small firm: 'Half the firms in mid-Victorian Scotland employed four or fewer workers; more than two-thirds of businesses employed seven or fewer workers and three in every four firms engaged fewer than nine workers. Only 10 per cent of Scottish businesses engaged more than twenty workers' (Rodger 1988, 186). It is apparent that in the mid-nineteenth century many industrial pursuits (for example, cabinetmaking, saddlery, glove and dressmaking, soap and tallow manufacture, non-ferrous metalworking, and even certain branches of textiles) whose total output was cumulatively highly significant, were conducted by small firms.

Yet Rodger also discovered the existence of an industrial dualism in the Scottish economy. By 1851 a number of relatively giant concerns employing hundreds of workers had grown up alongside the workshops of modest size. The 35 largest firms, overwhelmingly in cotton and linen textiles but also in iron, shipbuilding and engineering, hired more than a quarter of the total work force. Rodger's conclusion is that

> by 1851, Scottish firms were already distributed around the twin poles of a fragmented, traditional workshop mode of production or, alternatively, heavily

concentrated on factory production based on labour-intensive unskilled and semiskilled manual inputs . . . The middle range of business organizations – firms with twenty to fifty workers capable of developing a future base for industrial development – formed only 8 per cent of Scottish firms, and almost half of these were in the building and woodworking, textile and clothing sectors, hardly the harbingers of high technology.

(Rodger 1988, 190)

It will be noticed that the size of firms has been measured by the number of hands employed. In the light of those definitions of industrialisation which emphasise the pivotal role played by the substitution of machines for human effort in this process, a better guide to the progress of the supercession of the workshop by the factory would be the capital employed by each enterprise. Such data are currently so fragmentary that this approach is not possible, but this has not prevented economic historians from asserting that the larger firms (as measured by the size of the labour force) were more capital-intensive than their smaller competitors. In other words, the ratio of capital to labour employed in the methods of production adopted by the larger companies grew with the size of the firm. That this was so is almost certainly correct, if for no other reason than that the larger companies in Scotland were in industries such as textiles, iron-making and engineering, in which continued survival in an increasingly competitive market necessitated the diminution of costs by the adoption of factory-based large-scale production. What would be interesting to discover would be the fixed capital employed per worker in mid-Victorian Scottish firms.

It is possible that such data – were they available – would reveal a smaller dispersion around the mean than might be imagined from a superficial comparison of, say, the great ironworks with the village blacksmith or the imposing cotton mill with the handloom weaver. Be that as it may, it is generally recognised that in 1851, and for much of the remainder of the century, all branches of Scottish industry were extremely labour-intensive, not least because the availability of labour at wage rates below those prevailing in Great Britain as a whole (Campbell 1980, 80, 190) provided little incentive for employers to substitute capital for labour.

The relative modesty of their fixed capital needs coupled with the liberal way in which the law of partnership was interpreted in the Scottish courts, partly explains the continued predominance of the small firm in Scottish industry. That there were large companies in Scotland is undeniable. They may even have been bigger than their English counterparts (Payne 1980, 77), but they were far outnumbered by hosts of small firms reliant on skilled artisanal production whose proprietors were more often than not drawn from a single family or from two or more related families. The legacy of this industrial structure and the continuing availability of low-cost labour was, it has been argued (eg Rodger 1988, 189) the retardisation, even the fossilisation, of Scottish industry as early as 1851.

Less controversial is that whatever the diversity of Scottish industry in the mid-nineteenth century, it was dominated by the manufacture of textiles. Of a total non-agricultural labour force approaching 900,000 in 1851, no less than 30% were in textiles, dwarfing every other occupational category, and in three of the four major cities even this figure was exceeded: Glasgow (42%), Dundee (61%) and Aberdeen (35%). Even in Edinburgh, where slightly less than one in six were in 'textiles and clothing', this was still by far the largest source of employment (Rodger 1985, 36–7; Lee 1979, *passim)*. Among the other categories, only in engineering, toolmaking and metal working, building and the preparation of food, drink and tobacco, were more than one in twenty employed in industrial pursuits.

Such statistics, and they are simply representative of the many that might have been cited, have constituted the raw material of much recent analysis and speculation (Lee 1983) on the nature and speed of Scotland's economic growth. It is sufficient here to emphasise that the nineteenth century employment statistics reveal a growing coalescence about a relatively narrow range of activities. There was a thriving coal trade, a buoyant iron industry, the incipient growth of many of the trades associated with these related activities, the germs of later development in the mass production of food and drink for a population increasingly clustered in conurbations and, above all, a textile and clothing industry whose products were exported throughout the world.

EXERCISE I

In analysing mid-Victorian industry, Raphael Samuel (1977) observed that it was 'the workshop rather than the factory which prevailed'. After reading **Article 29** by Rodger (and ideally, some of the sources he has employed), attempt to assess how accurate this description is of Scottish industry at this period.

Rodger puts forward a 'twin pole' model of the Scottish economy, with a small number of large firms, mainly in cotton and linen, employing more than a quarter of the workforce, and a large number of small firms employing far fewer workers.

2. THE TEXTILE INDUSTRIES

Within the textile sector it had been cotton 'with its novel methods of organising work, its rapidly changing technologies and its dynamic growth' (Knox 1995, 1) which had performed a pivotal role in transforming the entire Scottish economy. Yet within two or three decades of 1850, cotton was manifestly declining. The engine of Scotland's industrial revolution had stalled. The reasons for this decline and its chronology have long been debated. Explanations centred on the baneful effects of the disruption of supplies of cotton associated with the American Civil War (Campbell 1965, 110) have given way to more sophisticated arguments (Robertson 1970). These revolve around the nature and composition of the labour force; the attractions of other, more promising, investment and employment opportunities; and a growing – and self-fulfilling – lack of confidence in the long-term future of spinning and weaving that inhibited the capital expenditure necessary for the continued survival of these processes. The most recent and most convincing attempt to explain cotton's decline is by Knox (1995), and even his case might have been strengthened by more detailed comparisons with Lancashire and a greater attention to the marketing of Scottish cotton goods.

It may be, of course, that in permitting cotton to decline while directing their attention to the heavy industries, Scottish entrepreneurs were acting rationally in the employment of scarce resources. Capital and labour could more productively and profitably be used in the manufacture of iron and steel, in heavy engineering and in shipbuilding than in the perpetuation of a branch of industry with lesser growth potential. In a market economy, no region can expect to continue to specialise in those activities on which its past fortunes have been based. Not the least of the lessons to be derived from Scotland's recent economic history is the damaging long-term consequences of politically-inspired attempts to stem structural adaptation to changing economic circumstances.

However, it was not merely a marketing exercise that induced William Knox (or his publisher?) to entitle his exploration into the pre-First World War Scottish cotton industry *Hanging by a Thread,* for it was the manufacture of thread by J & P Coats and their rivals J & J Clark which continued to give Scotland a significant presence in the cotton industry. By concentrating on the manufacture of this apparently simple product, by exploiting the almost insatiable demand created by the rapid global spread of the sewing machine after the 1850s, and by massive capital investment in enhanced capacity and the absorption of lesser competitors both at home and abroad, these two firms had come to dominate the world markets. In 1896 they merged and together with two English companies formed J & P Coats Ltd. With an original capital of £8 million, Coats was perhaps the most efficient and successful of all British nineteenth century industrial combinations. By 1913, driven by the marketing skills of a German, Otto Philippi, Coats were manufacturing thread in ten European countries in addition to Britain, in the United States and Canada, and in Brazil, Mexico and Japan (Payne 1992, 10).

While thread-making prospered, other branches of the cotton industry in Scotland declined. By 1910 the number of spinning firms had decreased to nine compared with the 131 that had survived the trauma of the American Civil War. Employment in the weaving end of the trade, totally fragmented, riven by fierce competition and dependent upon an ill-paid and increasingly demoralised and recalcitrant female labour force, was in 1907 only half that of forty years earlier (Knox 1995, 92). As the central processes of cotton spinning and weaving became, according to Knox (1995, 182), 'the first major casualties in the long historical process of de-industrialisation', their drawn out suffering was inevitably visited upon the related trades of bleaching, printing and dyeing. Some firms simply disappeared. Others, having been swept into the mergers that characterised the latter part of the nineteenth century, lingered on. Only the constituent firms of the United Turkey Red Company – a combination of dyers in the Vale of Leven – retained something of their earlier vigour (Payne 1992, 11).

The decay of cotton, located largely in the west of Scotland, was paralleled by the contraction of linen in the east. As early as the 1850s, some firms, blighted by their dependence on an increasingly costly supply of flax and unable to compete with the superior design, colour and finish of Lancashire cotton, had been forced to specialise. Some sought salvation either in making finer linens, bleached goods, diapers and damasks, as in north Fife, or in heavy linens like osnaburgs, sheeting and dowlais, in the production of which Forfar and Brechin became prominent. But the majority of the great Dundee firms moved into jute. Initially highly profitable – especially during the American Civil War – jute subsequently encountered wildly fluctuating demand, rising continental tariffs and fierce competition from Bengal. By the 1870s the period of 'wonderful prosperity' was at an end. As profit margins fell and technical progress slowed, only the immense accumulated wealth from past operations permitted a handful of the pioneering firms, like Cox Brothers, to survive. By the eve of the First World War, the livelihood of the 40,000 employees depended heavily on the buoyancy of the demand for linoleum, which required jute backing for its manufacture (Lenman, Lythe & Gauldie 1969, 23–40).

Linoleum, devised and continually improved by the innovative Michael Nairn of Kirkaldy and his rivals, among whom Barry, Ostlere & Shepherd and Shepherd & Beveridge were foremost, were able to exploit the demand for floorcovering created by the rising real wages of the lower middle and working classes. Those above them in the social scale preferred and were able to afford rugs and carpeting, a demand met by a host of Scottish firms spawned during the middle decades of the century.

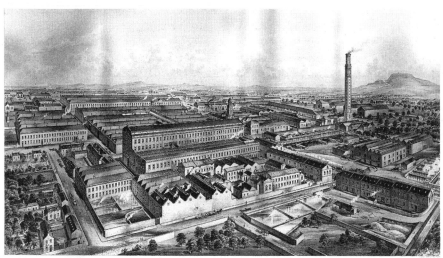

COX BROTHERS LIMITED., CAMPERDOWN WORKS. DUNDEE.
SPINNERS AND MANUFACTURERS
OF
JUTE · FLAX · HEMP &c.

40 Cox Brothers Limited, Camperdown Works, Dundee, perspective view. *Dundee University Archives.*

Foremost of these was Templetons – by 1913 the largest manufacturer of carpets in the UK – but, like the jute makers, the carpet-makers were faced with a capricious demand which only those firms most adept in marketing and in the use of collusive tactics were successfully able to tolerate. Those less fortunate or less skilled – like Gregory, Thompson & Co of Kilmarnock or Alexander Hadden & Sons of Aberdeen – had collapsed by the opening years of the new century, victims of the vagueries of fashion, a refusal or inability to invest or to diversify, and rising continental and American custom barriers (Payne 1992, 13–4).

Similar market conditions confronting the many companies in woollen textiles evoked a more positive response. From making 'coarse inferior homespuns for local country wear and fisherfolk Scottish woollen manufacturing after 1830 evolved into the most aristocratic branch of the British wool-textile industry' (Gulvin 1973, 71, 78). By appealing to that unique blend of nostalgia, snobbery and class consciousness which until recently has retarded the introduction of so many potentially low cost standardised products for mass consumption, the Scottish tweed industry managed to escape the fate of cotton. The manufacture of 'district checks' and largely spurious 'clan tartans', coupled with 'the skilful use of colour, the employment of virgin wool, and uniqueness of texture' was rewarded by the continued existence of those many Scottish firms whose 'names became synonymous with quality': 'Crombies of Aberdeen became renowned for overcoatings, Roberts' of Selkirk for the higher grade tweeds, Wilson's of Bannockburn for military tartan cloths, [and] Johnston's of Elgin for high quality cashmeres, vicunas and alpacas' (Gulvin 1973, 75, 77, 81).

The price for this high degree of specialisation was that the family firms in the trade remained small. Many crowded in to carve out a niche in the market. Expansion was particularly rapid in the Borders, especially in Hawick and Galashiels, in the Hillfoots on the northern side of the upper Forth centred on Alloa, and in the north-east of Scotland in and around Aberdeen. Such success attracted emulation by Yorkshire manufacturers and by overseas competitors, particularly the French and Germans, and when fashion swung away from Scottish tweeds towards light, less durable fabrics, only those possessing considerable entrepreneurial flair survived. Misguidedly moving down-market was suicidal; diversification into worsted yarns and fabrics to satisfy the demands generated by the growing popularity of hand-knitting and sporting and leisure activities, less so. Patons of Alloa adopted the latter tactic and even managed to expand. Fleming, Reid & Co., greatly daring, created the chain of Scotch Hosiery Stores through which to sell their products. Others, notably the Border Knitwear firms, differentiated their products by the skilful use of brand names coupled with surprisingly sophisticated marketing techniques, added jerseys, sweaters, shawls, cardigans, coats and mufflers to their staple products of high quality woollen underwear, and became remarkably sensitive to market opportunities at home and overseas, particularly in the Empire.

Thus it was that the textile industry continued to retain a significant role in the Scottish economy on the eve of the First World War. Some 172,000 or 8.3% of the labour force, far less than in the great days of cotton, were still so employed in 1911. This was no small achievement.

> EXERCISE 2
> From what you have just read, why did the spinning and weaving of cotton in Scotland decline before 1914 while other branches of textiles managed to survive and even prosper?

Fierce competition in cotton forced Scottish entrepreneurs into alternative and more profitable areas of investment such as iron and steel, heavy engineering and shipbuilding. Other branches of textiles, such as linoleum, cotton thread and woollen textiles, survived by specialisation and niche marketing.

3. THE HEAVY INDUSTRIES

3.1 *Coal*

While the numbers employed in textiles were halved, those involved in coal-getting increased fourfold. This huge increase in the labour force was the coalmasters' response to meeting the rising demands of domestic consumers, industrialists (at home and abroad) dependent on coal as their major source of energy, and the voracious appetite for fuel of locomotive and marine engines. This is not to say that the proprietors of many of the Scottish collieries failed to introduce mechanical coal cutters and conveyors, steam driven pumps and fans and all manner of lighting systems and devices involving the use of electricity below ground. Indeed, they were among the most progressive in Great Britain (Buxton 1970, 112; Church 1986, 347). But however ingeneous the new technologies, they served principally to make accessible coal seams hitherto beyond economic reach. Only marginally did they abridge the use of labour. The brutal fact was that even at the close of the nineteenth century, and even beyond, 'at the point of production . . . coal was still [over-whelmingly] excavated by shovel and pick – "tools of the most primitive description, requiring the utmost amount of bodily exertion to render effective".' (quoted in Samuel 1977, 21). And even the most skilled collier required, as the seams became deeper and thinner and the coal face became ever more distant from the winding shaft, the support of increasing numbers of oncost men (reddsmen, brushers, rippers, bottomers, drawers and others who kept the lengthening passageways open, built supporting walls, loaded the coal at the pit bottom and the like [Slaven 1967, 240–41, 248–49]). By 1913, when Scottish coal output reached its peak of 42.5 million tons – or five times the annual level of the early 1850s – no less than 7.5% of the nation's total labour force was engaged in mining and quarrying and the prosperity of the industry, now dominated by huge managerially controlled public companies, especially in the east of Scotland, had become heavily dependent upon the continued rise of domestic and industrial demand and the purchases of overseas consumers.

3.2 Iron and steel

The initial steep upward movement in Scotland's coal output had begun in the 1830s and was related to the contemporaneous expansion of the iron industry. Consuming three to four tons of coal in the production of every ton of pig iron in mid-century, Scotland's iron industry owed its phenomenal growth to the low cost of its product, a function of the enthusiastic adoption of Neilson's hot blast (see **Document 103**) in the 1830s which made possible the smelting of indigenous blackband ironstone which fortuitously lay interbedded with the coal. Within less than two decades, Scotland's share of Britain's iron production had risen from about 5% to 25%. The Bairds of Gartsherrie, Merry & Cunninghame and William Dixon & Co., made vast fortunes by heavy investment in every advance in metallurgical technology, their furnaces fuelled by coal laboriously extracted from the mines which were the original source of their wealth (see **Document 103** for a description). Capital and labour poured into the industry, and if the massive bulk and pyrotechnics of the ever-taller blast furnaces captured the popular imagination, it should never be forgotten that 'from the moment the ironstone is lifted off the trucks, then dropped into the kilns, afterwards taken to the furnace, and then drawn out of it, it has not been handled by any other means than the arms of powerful men, whose strength and vigilance are constantly strained almost to breaking point' (quoted in Samuel 1977, 43). Even as late as the 1920s, the blast furnaces at Gartsherrie and Clyde Iron were, to the incredulity of American consulting engineers, still being hand charged.

So too were the puddling furnaces in which brittle pig iron was converted into ductile, resilient malleable (or wrought) iron. This process was conducted by the puddler whose task was both unimaginably exhausting and highly skilled, since the conversion required him manually to stir the molten pig to facilitate the reduction of unwanted carbon. Exposed to rapid alterations of temperature, half blinded by the light of the furnaces and physically drained by the severity of the toil, the puddler had to judge the precise moment when, guided by its viscosity and colour, the great ball of red hot metal was ready to be dragged from the furnace by men using crude tongs. The further processing of wrought iron was hardly less dangerous and equally labour-intensive. For all the awesome might of huge steam hammers, the initial phase of converting the irregular mass of metal into a shape suitable for rolling involved men positioning and re-positioning it on an anvil during the upward cycle of the hammer head, a task requiring the exercise of great strength and considerable dexterity conducted in an environment of infernal heat attended by the ever present danger of being struck by splashes of molten metal.

Descriptions of the work involved in the metallurgical trades serve to emphasise that in the early stages of industrialisation, the employment of capital, far from diminishing the need for labour and reducing its drudgery, in many instances required for its effective introduction an enlargement of the number of men employed.

In iron-making, the amount of man-handling might have been reduced had the great ironmasters integrated forward into the manufacture of malleable iron. The erection of puddling furnaces and rolling mills adjacent to the blast furnaces, would have reduced the expenditure of both fuel and human energy. Instead, the product of the blast furnaces was allowed to cool into cast pigs which were sold on as the raw material of the foundrymen and wrought iron makers at home and overseas. It must be assumed that the ironmasters believed that their profits would be maximised by concentrating on smelting. However rational at the time, this decision may have had profoundly adverse long-term consequences for the Scottish economy (for the Scottish iron and steel industry, see Payne 1979 and Tolliday 1987).

Nevertheless, by confining themselves to pig iron production, the established ironmasters provided an opportunity to newcomers to venture into the manufacture of wrought iron, the demand for which began rapidly to expand with the development of iron shipbuilding; the continued world-wide construction of railways, the provision of whose permanent ways, locomotives, rolling stock and signalling equipment promised almost inexhaustible markets; and the spread of general and specialist engineering concerns catering to the needs of house, factory and bridge builders, the marine engineers, the suppliers of gasometers and gaswork plant, and the innumerable smaller firms who made tools, fittings and the myriad of useful or bizarre gadgets and decorative ironwork which had so fascinated visitors to the Great Exhibition. In the 1850s numerous small partnerships laid down a series of malleable ironworks, many of them on or near the banks of the Monkland Canal around Coatbridge. In turn, the availability of their high quality product encouraged the establishment of concerns which used wrought iron as their basic raw material: tube works, foundries, tin plate works and bolt and rivet manufacturers.

For a time there were handsome profits to be made, but then came the possibility of bulk steelmaking by the Bessemer process which threatened to undermine the very basis of this cluster of activity. Bessemer steel was more rigid, even more ductile and stronger than wrought iron. Furthermore, it promised to be much cheaper. Intense interest in Bessemer's methods was evinced by the Scottish ironmasters. Many experimented: all failed. What was not appreciated – so little were the chemical reactions involved initially understood – was that the high phosphoric content of 'Scotch pig' rendered it totally unsuitable for use in the converter. Bessemer was denounced as a charlatan: the correctness of the great Scottish ironmasters' concentration on the manufacture of pig iron seemed to be confirmed.

Once again, the way was left open for others to persevere. The most prominent of these were John and Charles Tennant, proprietors of the famous chemical works at St Rollox, whose search for a use for the many thousands of tons of slag, a by-product of their manufacture of sulphuric acid, led to the foundation of the Steel Company of Scotland in 1872 (Gibson 1958). Advised by Sir William Siemens, this heavily capitalised company began to make steel rails by the Siemens open-hearth process but, when the market for rails collapsed shortly after steel production began, the firm swiftly diversified into ship plates, boiler plates, bars, forgings and steel castings, the demand for which grew as the Clyde shipbuilders began to substitute mild steel for wrought iron as the price for steel fell. Between 1879 and 1889 the proportion of steel-built vessels launched on the Clyde rose from 10% to 97.3%.

The expanding demand for shipbuilding steel was *the* critical factor in the growth of the Scottish steel industry. As early as 1880 it became apparent that steel would replace wrought iron throughout the engineering industry. The malleable iron-makers found themselves confronted with the choice of going into steel or going out of business. Several chose steel, among them Beardmores and David Colville & Sons. By 1885, when total production approached a quarter of a million tons, over 40% of the British make of Siemens Steel was being produced by ten Scottish firms. However, with the exception of Merry & Cunninghame, who put down four basic Bessemer converters at Glengarnock in 1885, the old established Scottish iron-masters once again hesitated. They eventually decided that it would be more profitable to stick to smelting and to intensify their activities in coal mining. By the late 1890s, the largest Scottish colliery proprietors were all ironmasters.

The implications of these decisions were soon to become woefully apparent. The structure of the Scottish iron and steel industry had developed in a manner which left it fatally flawed. Essentially, the ironmasters did not make steel and the steelmakers did not make iron, or in the rare cases where they did, they did so at different locations. This weakness was exacerbated by the existence of a number of firms who made *neither* pig iron *nor* steel. They simply purchased steel billets and semi-finished steel for re-rolling. This lack of integration between sequential processes made the lowest possible costs of production unattainable. But this debilitating infirmity was perhaps of lesser significance than steel's overwhelming dependence on the notor-iously fluctuating demands of the shipbuilders. By 1913 no less than 70% of the output of Scottish steel – now nearly 1.3 million tons – was destined for the shipbuilding yards of the Clyde, Belfast and the north-east of England.

EXERCISE 3

How can the failure of the great Scottish ironmasters to involve themselves in the further processing of pig iron be explained? Did this failure have any significant implications for the future of the Scottish iron and steel industry?

One possible explanation is a belief that profits would be maximised by concen-trating on smelting. Reluctance to diversify into puddling furnaces and rolling mills meant that fuel and labour costs remained high. The most serious consequence long-term was the lack of integration in the industry.

3.3 *Shipbuilding*

Yet for the moment there were few inklings of the coming disaster. No Scottish industry appeared more successful than shipbuilding. By 1876 the Clyde had become the world's most important shipbuilding river, building more iron ships than the rest of the world put together. The rapidity with which the steam engine had been adapted for marine propulsion and wood replaced by iron in the construction of hulls explains this transformation. The opportunities inherent in the contem-poraneous expansion of international trade were avidly seized by British shipowners whose demands for carrying capacity were largely satisfied by the firms that established themselves on the Clyde, their slipways jutting out into the river from Old Kilpatrick up to Govan.

The shipbuilders deserved their success. By engineering innovations which made possible higher boiler pressures and greater thermal efficiency; by their primacy in the adoption of steel, and by empirical investigations of hull and propeller configurations, 'Clyde-built' became synonymous with quality (Slaven 1981, 353). And yet the majority of the shipbuilding firms remained curiously small family concerns. Perhaps this was because the sheer volatility of demand for ships inhibited heavy capital investment. Instead, as we have noticed in other sectors of the Scottish economy, the shipbuilders depended on labour-intensive techniques, employing small armies of highly skilled workmen on a largely casual basis, as illustrated in **Document 105**. This enabled them to minimise overheads and to transfer the costs associated with downswings in the shipbuilding cycle to the labour force, the majority of whom could readily be laid off, and to their suppliers, by cancelling their orders for steel plates and more specialised components.

Since individual shipbuilders could do little to stabilise demand, many of them tried to ensure good order books by forming alliances with or even promoting shipping lines (Boyce 1995, 47, 297), a tactic which, it has to be said, sometimes stemmed from the shipowners' propensity to offer shares in their companies rather than to pay cash for their vessels (Moss & Hume 1977, 88–9). There is little question that this close connection between builders and shippers was often beneficial to both parties, and several Clyde builders, such as the Dennys and the Lithgows, discovered that there was more money to be made from operating ships than by building them. But whether or not formal or informal links existed between the shipbuilders and the shipowners, the wellbeing of the former depended ultimately on the shipping companies' reactions to the level of freight rates, the course of which reflected the vicissitudes of international trade. Some shipbuilders could eliminate or reduce this dependency by devoting a major part of their capacity to fulfilling the requirements of the Admiralty. By following this dangerous policy, John Brown's of Clydebank and the Fairfield Shipbuilding & Engineering Co. closely tied themselves to a purchaser the pattern of whose orders was to prove even more erratic than those of the passenger and freight lines (Peebles 1987, 30–89).

Whatever the nature of the markets for which they were intended, the vessels powered by vast reciprocating engines whose performance was governed and measured by the most sophisticated instruments and – in the case of transatlantic lines – luxuriously furnished, were the very symbols of the triumph of nineteenth century Scottish industrialisation. The construction of their hulls, the provision of their engines and their outfitting, involved the assembly of steel components, of all manner of vital and ancillary machines, pumps and equipment, of hand-crafted furniture and furnishings, the majority of which were produced in the west of Scotland. The prosperity of the steel mills, the iron and brass foundaries, the specialist heavy and light engine shops, the factories making precision instruments and tools and, more indirectly, the ironworks and the collieries, all came to depend in varying degrees on the prosperity of shipbuilding, itself conditioned by the fierce competition of similarly oriented regional economies elsewhere, by the course of international passenger and freight rates and by the exigencies of foreign policy.

For all its undoubted technical success and apparent affluence, by the closing years of the century, shipbuilding on the Clyde had become inherently precarious. Examination of the firms' contract files reveals that an increasing proportion of the great vessels, whose elaborate launching ceremonies drew vast and admiring crowds, brought substantial losses to their builders (Campbell 1980, 64–8). These records disclose the symptoms of deep-rooted malaise. Had it been known, this might have occasioned less disquiet if Scotland had possessed a more diversified industrial structure with the capacity for renewed growth. After all, with the earlier decline of cotton, capital and labour had flowed beneficially into iron, shipbuilding and steel. Could not the trick be repeated?

EXERCISE 4
Would you agree that, for all its apparent success, shipbuilding on the Clyde had developed serious weaknesses before the First World War?

The Clyde led the world in shipbuilding and was innovative in the use of steel and engineering design. However, many firms remained small family concerns, used labour-intensive techniques and were vulnerable to fluctuating demand. Look back over the discussions if you did not pick these points up.

41 Welder, John Brown's Shipyard, Clydebank, 1965. *Michael Peto Collection, Dundee University Archives.*

4. SLOW DIVERSIFICATION

Had Scottish industry become less dominated by the great staple trades and had the Great War not intervened, it is plausible to suggest that it might have been. But these permissive conditions did not exist. The war, with its insatiable demands for the products of heavy industry, coal, steel in all of its forms, especially ships and armaments, served not merely to perpetuate the existing industrial imbalance but to exacerbate its inherent weaknesses. For example, while Scottish steelmaking capacity was substantially enlarged, not a single new blast furnace was built in Scotland (Buxton 1976, 108–9). Meanwhile, as the war dragged on, the shipbuilders, many of whom had surrendered to the embrace of the shippers, were taking steps to secure their post-war steel supplies by gaining control of the steelworks. Thus, David Colville & Sons, the largest of the steelmakers, having integrated backwards during the war by purchasing the collieries of Archibald Russell and the limestone quarries of the Carnlough Lime Co., came to be owned by Harland & Wolff; itself part of Lord Pirrie's Royal Mail Steam Packet Co. (Payne 1979, 187). But in building up their ramshackle empires, the shipping companies had became deeply indebted to the holders of their debenture bonds, to their bankers (including the Bank of England), and because of government loans, to the Treasury. When international trade collapsed during the later 1920s, these creditors rushed to protect their own interests, giving rise to such profound internal conflicts that the result was almost total paralysis. The restructuring of Scotland's iron, steel and shipbuilding industries, which might have ensured some degree of regeneration, was rendered impossible (Tolliday 1987, 92-109).

In retrospect, it is arguable that the most serious casualty of this debacle for Scotland's industrial future was the financial collapse of William Beardmore & Co in the mid-1920s. As early as 1905, Sir William Beardmore had acquired a controlling interest in Arrol Johnston, by the eve of the war virtually the only survivor of the fifty or so companies that had been established in Scotland to make motor cars. Beardmore had ambitious plans for Arrol Johnston, which in 1911 had put down extensive new works near Dumfries. During the war these works had turned out aero-engines, a development which had similar long-term potential (Hume & Moss 1979, 51, 160–61, 224; Oliver 1993, 24, 32). But the active pursuit of plans to make cars, taxis, motor cycles and commercial vehicles, and the continued production of aero-engines and even aircraft, was irreparably weakened when in 1928 the entire group of companies with which William Beardmore was associated was brought to the brink of bankruptcy. Control of the parent company, William Beardmore & Co, passed into the hands of the bankers.

With the failure of the car industry and with little or no representation in electrical engineering, pharmaceuticals and man-made fibres, Scottish industry in the interwar years possessed few if any nodes for future development. The sheer depth of the depression inhibited the creation of new pioneering ventures. Nor was help to be looked for south of the Border: a Scottish location had few attractions for those English concerns that owed much of their continued buoyancy to catering to the demands of more affluent consumers in London, the South-East and the West Midlands (Heim 1983, 934). Capital and labour released by the prostration of coal, iron and steel and shipbuilding had nowhere to flow to except to the service sector.

The result was that the industrial structure of Scotland on the eve of the Second World War was almost the same as it had been at the beginning of the century. But whereas the nineteenth century commitment to textiles, coalmining, iron and steel, shipbuilding, marine and heavy engineering had reflected the culmination of half a century of evolving specialisation on sectors in which Scotland enjoyed comparative advantage, between the wars all these activities were stagnating or in decline. This would not have had such disastrous social and economic consequences had Scotland been able to secure a greater share in the 'new' growth industries of the 1930s to take up the slack (Buxton 1980, 549). It was not that this fundamental weakness was unrecognised: repeated enquiries emphasised the need for the greater diversification of Scottish industry (Saville 1985, 13–16), but the very magnitude of the depression inhibited private initiatives, and government intervention was half-hearted and inadequate, not least because the management of economic change was as yet imperfectly understood. Even had this not been the case, it is doubtful whether the process of industrial adaptation would have made much headway. Twenty years was too short a period within which to effect the required degree of structural change, which is 'both slower and more complex than theories of market economics suggest' (Weir 1994, 8). This is particularly so in economies dominated by family firms motivated by survival rather than the maximisation of profit. All too many Scottish companies hung on in the hope that things would get better.

And, with the coming of re-armament in the late 1930s and the Second World War, they did. The demands of war seemed to justify the tenacity of firms in the Scottish heavy industries. Now they were *all* needed. The collusive agreements, the trade associations, the work pooling arrangements designed to temper competition, the refusal to rationalise entire industries by the closure of obsolete plant: all these stultifying policies appeared to be vindicated. And with the outbreak of hostilities and the imposition of schemes whereby government agencies apportioned scarce resources, the structure of Scottish industry was frozen in its early twentieth century mould.

EXERCISE 5
Read **Document 104**. What kind of source is this and what does it convey about the Scottish iron and steel industry in the inter-war period?

This is a private letter accompanying a consultant's report on the iron and steel industry. It identifies the strengths, specially skilled labour, markets and shipping facilities, but also notes inherent weaknesses of inertia especially evident in old poorly located plant and the exhaustion of local fuel and ore supplies. It recommends the development of a new tide water plant on the Clyde estuary.

5. THE CHANGES AFTER THE LATE 1950S

5.1 *The heavy industries*

Not until the late 1950s did the thaw set in. Following the war, such was the pent-up demand that the staple trades enjoyed almost continuous expansion (for the heavy industries in the post-war period, see Payne 1985, 79–113). In coal, the plan adopted by the newly-created National Coal Board envisaged an annual market for the Scottish Division of 30 million tons, a figure that was expected to be attained, despite the phasing out of more than half the existing collieries, by sinking and developing deep and surface drift mines and the modernisation of nearly forty pits in the eastern coalfield. In iron and steel, Colvilles were urged to build a huge integrated tidewater plant on the Upper Clyde of the type first proposed by Brassert & Co in 1929 as being the only way in which the long-term future of the industry could be guaranteed, but Colvilles demurred, believing that the potential effective demand for steel on the scale assumed by the national planners did not exist. Instead, Colvilles pursued the completion of those 'socially responsible and practical schemes' instigated in 1937 which would culminate in the creation of the Raven-scraig complex. Only in shipbuilding was there hesitation. In the years 1946–48, when competition from their principal rivals, Germany and Japan, was temporarily extinguished, Britain once again built and launched just over half the world's tonnage of merchant vessels, some 50% of it coming from the Clyde. Yet the majority of the yards raised neither the capital necessary for fundamental restruc-turing nor did they recruit specialists to senior positions, mainly because both courses of action would have eroded family control and because anything which threatened to disrupt maximum immediate production was to be avoided.

The end of the period of prosperity came with startling swiftness. In the late 1950s, the market for coal collapsed. For some time, the extravagant projections underlying the *Plan for Coal,* published in 1950, had seemed unrealistic. As early as 1951 the Scottish Division was making an operating loss, output per manshift was nearly two cwts less than the British average, and the implementation of reconstruction plans was proving unexpectedly difficult and expensive (Halliday 1990, 180). Such immediate disappointments might have been shrugged off had demand subsequently risen, but quite the reverse occurred as consumers turned increasingly to oil, natural gas and electricity. Had it not been for the reluctant purchases of the state-owned electricity industry, the losses sustained by the collieries would have been even greater. As it was, during the 1960s, the Scottish Division was responsible for almost a half of the total deficits of the National Coal Board. There was no alternative but to embark upon a programme of closures: a labour force of over 83,000 on vesting day was to dwindle to a few hundred when the mines were returned to private enterprise.

Although mistakes were undoubtedly made by the managers of the National Coal Board (Halliday 1990, 173–77), the disappearance of the coal industry was primarily the consequence of changing consumer preferences and intractable geological con-ditions. But what of shipbuilding? Why was it too to shrink almost to insignificance? Here there is greater evidence of human culpability. When Japan and the continental builders were able to re-enter the market in the 1950s, the Clyde builders were simply unable to grapple with the ferocity of international competition. Immediately after the war, they had exploited their advantages to the full, disdaining the opportunity of radical restructuring presented by their short-lived monopoly. But would they have fared much better had they merged, rationalised their productive methods, recruited specialists to senior positions and imposed new work practices on their employees? In fact, following the closure of many famous yards, detailed reports on the parlous state of the industry and the injection of government funds on a profligate scale, they did. But it was too late. Perhaps it was always going to be too late? The fact is that what the world wanted after the war was tankers and bulk-carriers. Far less complex than the traditional products of the Clyde, their essential simplicity made their construction amenable to flow-line methods utilising maximum prefabrication. Offering fewer opportunities for the exercise of craft skills, the tanker gravely diminished the Clyde's most valuable asset. The river's competitive position was further worsened by the evolution of giant vessels, for the construction of which it was manifestly ill-suited. Today, only two yards, Yarrows, now owned by General Electric, who specialise in warships, and Kvearner Govan, owned by a Norwegian company, maintain a precarious existence. The size of the labour force, some 77,000 in 1951, is now too small even to warrant specific inclusion in the *Scottish Digest of Statistics*.

EXERCISE 6
Were the owners of the shipyards or the workers to blame for the collapse of Scottish shipbuilding?

Family firms found it difficult to restructure, recruit specialists into senior positions and impose new work practices on their workers. However the growing demand for tankers and bulk carriers left the Clyde at a disadvantage, with its craft-based methods and shallow water access.

What then of the final member of the heavy triumvirate, iron and steel? If the earlier success of the industry may be explained in terms of a chronological sequence of favourable circumstances, including the use of cheap splint coal and blackband ironstone, rapid technical advance and the appetite of the Clyde for heavy steel plate, then its subsequent decline was inevitable. As supplies of coking coal ran out, as native iron ore deposits were exhausted, the long-term future of the industry in Scotland became dependent upon the creation of an integrated steelworks or a tidewater site and a sufficiently buoyant demand to absorb the products of such a complex. Neither condition applied. Colvilles' decision not to adopt some variant of the Brassert proposals doomed the Scottish steel industry to eventual extinction, as Brassert had predicted, but the speed of its demise was markedly accelerated by the decline of shipbuilding, the failure of demand for the product of the Ravenscraig strip mill, the construction of which had been forced upon Colvilles by government pressure, and the fact that the British Steel Corporation, into which Colvilles had been swept in 1967, could manufacture its products more cheaply at Port Talbot and

Llanwern (Payne 1995). Crude steel output in Scotland reached a peak in the early 1970s, when employment stood at nearly 30,000 men. The final shift at Ravenscraig was worked in June 1992 and at the plate mill at Dalziel two years later.

5.2 Textiles

While coal, iron and steel and shipbuilding were in their death throes, it would have been deeply ironic if textiles had re-emerged as Scotland's leading manufacturing activity. Superficially, several firms – in thread, wool and carpets – seem successfully to have grappled with profound changes in technology, the nature of their markets and the make up of their products. But, essentially, only the *names* have survived. Like the heavy industries, the post-war history of Scottish textiles has been one of decline (Payne 1992, 40–5). The initial defensive strategies of merger between erstwhile competitors, of acquisitions, rationalisation and diversification, were followed by moves of bewildering complexity that culminated in the creation of huge multinational groups. Shrewd marketing tactics have sometimes dictated the retention of highly respected Scottish brand names but the reality is that the majority of the firms who established them have either disappeared or lost their independence. Ultimate ownership and control has passed into the hands of international institutional investors. Furthermore, fierce competition in global markets has led many British-based multinationals to abandon indigenous production altogether and to become mere merchants, buying or having fabrics or garments made to their own specification in India, Malaysia, Hong Kong and Singapore. For example, Coats Viyella, the end-product of a byzantine series of mergers between *c.*1960 and 1986, whose subsidiaries include the once great Scottish firms of J & P Coats and Paton & Baldwins, has long been attempting either to relocate manufacturing capacity to low-cost countries or (in a phrase that sounds as ugly as its implications for Scottish textiles) to 'source from them'. Meanwhile, the Dawson group, the jewel in whose crown is Pringle of Scotland, staggers from crisis to crisis, currently heavily dependent for its survival, it would appear to the outsider, on the continuing success of Nick Faldo on the world's golf courses!

The cumulative effect of the shrinkage of the traditional staples since the mid-1950s has diminished the industrial sector of the Scottish economy and transformed its structure. Whereas in 1951 35% of all employees were engaged in manufacturing, by 1990 the proportion had fallen to but 21%. In four decades nearly 40% of jobs in manufacturing had been lost. Had it not been for a vast influx of foreign capital and enterprise, this figure would have been considerably lower.

5.3 Oil and electronics

The most widely known and most visible manifestation of overseas capital has been associated with 'the coming of North Sea oil', but this dramatic development has created remarkably few jobs in *manufacturing*. The nature of the oil industry is such that it *never* possessed this potential. Certainly, few Scottish firms were able to seize the opportunities created by the manifold demands of the giant multinational companies who from the mid 1960s would search for, discover and exploit the riches beneath the forbidding grey North Sea. The reasons for this failure are complex, but their essence was captured by Ian Wood:

> Such was our Government's haste to get the oil out of the ground as quickly as possible that far too little attention was paid to the build-up of genuine UK oil technology and manufacturing know-how to provide an important new indigenous addition to the UK's falling industrial base
>
> (quoted in Payne 1996, 32)

EXERCISE 7
What impact do you think the discovery and exploitation of North Sea oil had on the Scottish economy?

I won't provide answers here but ask you to reflect on how much the experience of the oil industry differed (if at all) from those of older, more traditional sectors I've described.

Much more success has attended governmentally-inspired initiatives to secure a share in the electronics industry. In marked contrast to the abortive attempts to establish motor manufacture at Bathgate and Linwood and aluminium smelting at Invergordon (Utiger 1995), sustained and costly efforts to transplant electronics into Scotland's industrial belt have been rewarded. Branch factories were established by the major multinationals, IBM, NCR, Burroughs and Honeywell, in the 1950s. These were but the spearhead of an American invasion that boosted employment in an industry virtually unrepresented before the war to about 30,000 by the late 1960s. By the early 1980s, there were nearly 300 companies engaged in the manufacture of electronic products and components, information systems, defence related items and avionics. The Japanese were next to arrive so that by 1993 the estimated share of electronics employment (45,300) in total manufacturing employment had risen to just over 10% (Payne 1996, 24–29).

Yet nagging doubts remain. Multinational companies are inherently footloose, forever seeking to exploit local advantages. When these advantages have been exhausted, they move on to more attractive locations. The anguished clamour of the workers, local and national politicians and church leaders that profit is still to be made by continuing operations, tends to be of little consequence if *greater* profit is to be obtained elsewhere. 'How deeply embedded is "Silicon Glen"?', Turok has asked, and his careful reply is that 'the prospects for self-sustaining internally generated growth of the Scottish electronics industry cannot yet be described as promising' (Turok 1993, 401, 415). This is because the multinationals continue to dominate the critical fields of product design and development and software. Without in any way detracting from their enterprise and energy, the majority of Scottish firms are largely confined to the manufacture of hardware lacking technological content: keyboards, plastic components, cables, sheet metal and packaging and printing materials utilising 'standard machinery and labour-intensive methods'. Of the world's electronic centres Scotland, for all its apparent success, is currently strongest in areas of limited importance to long-term competitiveness. Unless this vital weakness is remedied, and remedied quickly, all that Scotland will possess when the caravan moves on, as many believe it will, to lower cost and better skilled locations in Eastern Europe and Asia, are sites as deserted as that of Ravenscraig.

> EXERCISE 8
> Examine the benefits and disadvantages of the direct investment of overseas companies in Scottish industry.

Multi-nationals have made an important contribution to new employment in Scotland and to the diversification of the Scottish economy. However, the question remains – how long will they stay in Scotland?

6. CONCLUSIONS

Can any conclusions be drawn from this brief survey of Scottish industry since *c.*1850? Perhaps the most important finding is the dynamic nature of industrialisation. There is no stability. The manufacture of cotton, Scotland's first modern industry, was already showing signs of decay at the beginning of our period. The life spans of the heavy industries were destined to be even shorter despite a combination of circumstances, including war and public ownership, which conspired to extend their longevity. Since the Second World War, the pace of change has markedly accelerated. The contribution of industry to Scotland's gross domestic product has fallen; the number of persons gainfully employed in manufacturing has halved. And although over the last five years, aggregate manufacturing output figures reveal that Scotland has outperformed the UK as a whole, this has been almost totally due to the growth of electrical equipment and electronics. If the figures for this most vulnerable sector are stripped out, nearly all the other branches of manufacturing activity – with the exception of whisky distilling – show a deterioration in trend over the past three years. In relation to the UK, the relative positions of transport equipment, including aerospace, mechanical engineering, glass, ceramic and brick making, wood products, rubber, textiles, clothing and footwear, are all declining. In the light of the foregoing discussion, it is frightening that such a well-informed commentator as Chris Baur is able to assert that 'Silicon Glen is keeping the country afloat' *(Sunday Times,* 27 October 1996).

We have also seen that since the war the ownership of the majority of Scottish firms has passed into the hands of powerful international groups, controlled not from Glasgow, Dundee and Aberdeen but from London, New York and Tokyo, and dependent for their continuing survival on the value of their contributions to the global strategy of their owners. With the advent of world-wide information systems, the pace of technical change has accelerated: the possibilities for the substitution of capital equipment for labour – until recently, so painfully slow – now seem boundless.

We have come full circle. Landes's emphasis on the substitution of machines for human skill during the process of industrialisation (quoted at the beginning of this chapter), while patently premature in describing what actually happened before 1939, has now largely come to pass. It is inconceivable that manufacturing industry will ever again employ more than a small proportion of the Scottish labour force.

EXERCISE 9

How far have you, your parents or grandparents been affected by occupational change or migration over the past couple of generations. If you were undertaking a study of working lives, what questions would you ask, and why?

REFERENCES TO BOOKS AND ARTICLES MENTIONED IN THE TEXT

Boyce, GH 1995 *Information, mediation and institutional development. The rise of large-scale enterprise in British shipping, 1870–1919*. Manchester.

Buxton, NK 1970 'Entrepreneurial Efficiency in the British Coal Industry between the Wars', *Economic History Review* 23, 476–97.

Buxton, NK 1976 'Efficiency and organization in Scotland's Iron and Steel Industry during the Interwar Period', *Economic History Review* 29, 107–24.

Buxton, NK 1980 'Economic Growth in Scotland Between the Wars: the role of production structure and rationalisation', *Economic History Review* 33, 538–55.

Campbell, RH 1965 *Scotland since 1707: the rise of an industrial society*. Oxford.

*Campbell, RH 1980 *The Rise and Fall of Scottish Industry 1707–1939*. Edinburgh.

Church, R 1986 *The History of the British Coal Industry. Vol 3: 1830–1913*. Oxford.

Gibson, IF 1958 'The establishment of the Scottish Steel Industry', *Scottish Journal of Political Economy* 5, 22–39.

Gulvin, C 1973 *The Tweedmakers: A History of the Scottish fancy woollen industry 1600–1914*. Newton Abbot.

*Halliday, RS 1990 *The Disappearing Scottish Colliery*. Edinburgh.

*Harvie, C 1994 *Fool's Gold: The Story of North Sea Oil*. London.

Heim, CE 1983 'Industrial Organisation and Regional Development in Inter-War Britain', *Journal of Economic History* 43, 931–52.

Hume, JR and Moss, MS 1979 *Beardmore. The History of a Scottish Industrial Giant*. London.

*Knox, WW 1995 *Hanging By a Thread. The Scottish Cotton Industry c. 1850–1914*. Preston, Lancashire.

Landes, D 1969 *The Unbound Prometheus*. Cambridge.

Lee, CH 1979 *British Regional Employment Statistics 1841–1971*. Cambridge.

*Lee, CH 1983 'Modern Economic Growth and Structural Change in Scotland: the Service Sector Reconsidered', *Scottish Economic and Social History* 3, 5–35.

Lenman, B, Lythe, C & Gauldie, E 1969 *Dundee and its Textile Industry 1850–1914*. Dundee.

Moss, MS & Hume JR 1977 *Workshop of the British Empire. Engineering and Shipbuilding in the West of Scotland*. London.

Oliver, G 1993 *Motor Trials and Tribulations*. Edinburgh.

Payne, PL 1979 *Colvilles and the Scottish Steel Industry*. Oxford.

Payne PL 1980 *The Early Scottish Limited Companies 1856–1895*. Edinburgh.

Payne PL 1985 'The Decline of the Scottish Heavy Industries, 1945–1983', *in* Saville, R (ed) *The Economic Development of Modern Scotland 1950–1980*, Edinburgh, 79–113.

*Payne, PL 1992 *Growth & Contraction. Scottish Industry c. 1860–1990.* Glasgow.

Payne, PL 1995 'The End of Steelmaking in Scotland, c. 1967–1993', *Scottish Economic Social History* 15, 66–84.

*Payne, P L 1996 'The Economy', *in* Devine, TM and Finlay RJ (eds) *Scotland in the 20th Century,* Edinburgh, 13–45.

Peebles, HB 1987 *Warship building on the Clyde: Naval Orders and the Prosperity of the Clyde Shipbuilding Industry, 1889–1939.* Edinburgh.

*Robertson, AJ 1970 'The decline of the Scottish cotton industry 1860–1914', *Business History* 12, 116–28.

Rodger, R 1985 'Employment, Wages and Poverty in the Scottish Cities 1841–1914', *in* Gordon, G (ed), *Perspectives of the Scottish City,* Aberdeen, 25–63.

*Rodger, R 1988 'Concentration and Fragmentation. Capital, Labor, and the Structure of Mid-Victorian Scottish Industry', *Journal of Urban History* 14, 178–213.

Samuel, R 1977 'Workshop of the world: steam power and hand technology in mid-Victorian Britain', *History Workshop* III, 6–72.

*Saville, R 1985 'The Industrial Background to the Post-War Scottish Economy', *in* Saville, R (ed) *The Economic Development of Modern Scotland 1950–1980*, Edinburgh, 1–46.

Slaven, A 1967 'Earnings and Productivity in the Scottish Coalmining Industry during the Nineteenth Century: The Dixon Enterprises', *in* Payne, P L (ed) *Studies in Scottish Business History,* London, 217–49.

Slaven, A 1981 'Shipbuilding', *in* Daiches, D (ed) *Companion to Scottish Culture,* London, 353–5.

Tolliday, S 1987 *Business, Banking, and Politics: The case of British Steel, 1918–1939.* Cambridge, Mass.

Turok, I 1993 'Inward Investment and Local Linkages: How Deeply embedded is "Silicon Glen"?', *Regional Studies* 27, 401–17.

Utiger, RE 1995 *Never Trust an Expert. Nuclear Power, Government and the Tragedy of the Invergordon Aluminium Smelter.* London [Occasional Paper 1 of the Business History Unit of the London School of Economics].

*Weir, R 1994 'Structural Change and the Scottish Economy, 1918–1939', *Refresh* 19, 1–8.

FURTHER READING

Those references marked * in the above list are recommended further reading, along with the following (of which those marked ** contain the reminiscences of working men and women).

Lee, CH 1995 *Scotland and the United Kingdom: the economy and the union in the twentieth century.* Manchester.

**McGeown, P 1967 *Heat the furnace seven times more.* London.

**McKinlay, A 1991 *Making ships Making Men . . . Working for John Brown's – Between the Wars.* Clydebank.

**Pagnamenta, P and Overy, R 1984 *All our working Lives.* London.

Slaven, A 1975 *The development of the West of Scotland, 1750–1960.* London.

Slaven, A and Checkland, S (eds) 1986, 1990 *Dictionary of Scottish Business Biography.* 2 volumes. Aberdeen.

Demography

Bill Kenefick

INTRODUCTION

The materials relating to Scottish demography improve significantly from 1841, both in terms of quantity and quality. As well as enumerators' books and census returns, demographers have access to improved emigration statistics (from 1851) and civil registration of births, deaths and marriages (from 1855) (Flinn *et al* 1977, 21–6). Statistics relating to births, deaths and marriages enable us to understand fertility, nuptuality, mortality, and migration patterns. These help us to identify the main population trends in Scotland, the causes of population growth in the eighteenth and nineteenth centuries, and the growing rate of population decline from the late nineteenth century onward. By closely studying migration, emigration, and immigration, the historian can more accurately plot population movement and distribution, while factors such as fertility, nuptuality and mortality help illustrate how certain forces can both promote and inhibit population growth.

But it is a complex business. When considered together, migration, emigration, mortality rates, or birth and marriage rates, often confuse attempts to analyse population growth or contraction. For example, does population decline because of increased levels of emigration, or are lower birth rates more influential? This chapter will attempt to answer such questions by analysing each of these factors in turn, under the following headings –

- General demographic trends in the nineteenth and early twentieth centuries
- Demographic trends – the regional perspective, 1851–1939
- Population movement in the twentieth century
- Emigration
- Mortality
- Fertility and nuptuality
- Patterns of immigration

By the time you have worked through this chapter and the associated documents and readings, you should have a good understanding of the cause and effect of demographic change and the manner in which fertility, nuptuality, mortality and immigration effected population growth over the period as a whole. You should also understand the main social and economic indicators of change and how they affected population decline by the 1990s.

I. DEMOGRAPHIC TRENDS IN THE NINETEENTH AND EARLY TWENTIETH CENTURIES

By 1850 Scotland was one of the most industrialised and heavily urbanised societies in Europe, a wealthy nation of world importance. One of the major factors associated with industrial development – cited as both a cause and a consequence of economic growth – was sustained and incremental population growth, a growth dependent on such mechanisms as mortality, fertility and the role of marriage. Population growth had helped to create an industrial labour force, and the willingness to move produced the necessary population redistribution for urban and industrial production (Houston 1988, 9; 24).

It was not until the 1870s that the national death rate began a sustained decline. The crude death rate fell from 22.3 per 1,000 to 12.6 per 1,000 between the early 1870s and the second half the 20th century. Scots were, therefore, living longer as the standard of living improved. There were significant regional variations. Death chances varied depending on location and the prevailing social and economic conditions, and birth and marriage rates were similarly effected. For natural increase in a population to occur there has to be an excess of births over deaths as a proportion of the population as a whole. From the 1870s, the natural increase in the population of Scotland was falling. In the 1870s, for example, the average number of children per family was six, but by 1951 was down to 2.5. This trend continued through the second half of the twentieth century. Lower birth rates and lower fertility in marriage were major reasons for the overall decline in Scottish population. Emigration was another factor, particularly as the losses were heaviest among younger, prospective parents.

As Scots left to build new lives overseas, or in England, many foreigners – Irish, Poles, Italians, Lithuanians, Russian, Jews, and increasing numbers of English – came to settle in Scotland. However, their numbers were not great enough to offset the numbers leaving or the decline in the natural increase in Scottish population. Even the great influx of Irish from the 1840s onward was never sufficient to offset the greater outflow of Scots, particularly in those sustained phases of emigration in the 1880s and between 1901 and 1930. After the 1880s, it was natural growth in population numbers, rather than in-migration, that supplied Scotland's labour needs (Flinn 1977, 311). Nevertheless, these immigrant groups played a vital role in Scotland's economy. They also had a dramatic affect on Scottish society, especially the Irish, who brought with them a religion that was alien to much of Scotland and was the cause of considerable tension (Brown 1993; Devine 1991; Maver 1996; Walker 1996).

As Table 1 shows, the population of Scotland was around 2,620,000 in 1841. The following decade it rose to just under 2,900,00 and by 1861 it had reached over 3,000,000 for the first time. From then on population continued to rise and levels only dropped for the first time during the 1920s and early 1930s. By the late 1930s population levels recovered slightly and the population reached over 5,000,000 by the late 1930s; rising marginally each decade to peak at 5,229,000 in 1971. Clearly,

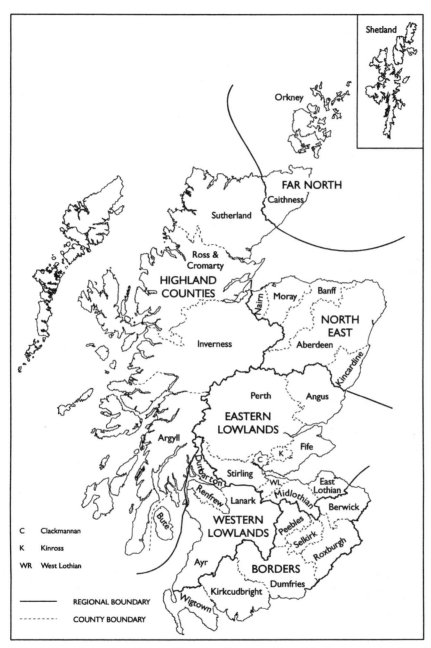

42 Scotland, showing civil counties and regions used in analysis of census and civil registration returns for the nineteenth and twentieth century. From M Flinn (ed) 1977 *Scottish Population History from the 17th century to the 1930s*, (Cambridge University Press), Cambridge.

by the time of the 1931 census population had contracted in real terms for the first time and although there was slight recovery between 1939 and 1971, in general terms stagnated from 1951 onward, and by the 1980s was in decline.

TABLE I: POPULATION OF SCOTLAND 1851 TO 1991 (000S)

Census	TOTAL	INCREASE/DECREASE ON PREVIOUS CENSUS
1841	2,620.2	10.4
1851	2,888.7	10.3
1861	3,062.2	6.0
1871	3,360.3	9.7
1881	3,735.6	11.2
1891	4,025.6	7.8
1901	4,472.1	11.1
1911	4,760.9	6.5
1921	4,882.5	2.6
1931	4,843.0	−0.8
1951**	5,096.4	5.2
1961	5,179.3	1.6
1971	5,228.9	1.0
1981	5,130.7	−1.9
1991	4,962.2	−3.4

* mid-year estimate
**1951 intercesal increase of 5.2 is based on 1931 census figures. If we consider the figures for 1921 (which were higher than 1931) the increase in 1951 is only 4.4%.
Source: Scottish Census

This section will consider two distinctive chronological periods, 1851 to 1939, and 1945 to 1990. The period up to 1939 is almost contiguous, but effects of the First World War and the depression of the interwar years need consideration in their own right – not least because the population contracted for the first time in the 1920s (Anderson 1992 12; 13, fig 1). The years after the Second World War heralded significant economic and social changes, and these reflect the contrasts in demographic trends apparent before and after the war.

1.2 Demographic trends – the regional perspective, 1851 to 1939

Before 1850 the population increased in all parts of Scotland. Thereafter, population growth became regionally uneven, with some regions seeing decline, while others gained (Flinn 1977, 305), summarised in Illustration 42.

Flinn showed that the greatest regional increases in population took place in the Western Lowland counties and that after 1851 this area accounted for the entire net growth of Scotland's population up to 1939. Counties such as Argyll, Kinross and Perth reached their population peak as early as 1831; Inverness in 1841, and by

1851 Kirkcudbright, Ross and Cromarty, Sutherland, and Wigtown had reached their peak also. Berwick, Caithness, Orkney and Roxburgh followed in 1861 and Nairn in 1881, while Banff and Selkirk peaked in 1891. Angus, Aberdeen, and Peebles realised their highest population levels in 1901, 1911, and 1921 respectively (although Aberdeen would see its population rise in the second half of the twentieth century because of the North Sea oil boom) (*ibid* 306). The ten counties comprising the industrial central belt – from Ayr through to Lanark, Midlothian to Fife – saw an increase in population through to 1951 when they recorded their highest ever levels, as did Moray, Kincardine, Dumfries and Bute.

Between 1931 and 1951 the natural increase in the population was proportionately lower than at any time since 1860 and continued to decline from 1951 onward. Up until 1939 we must look to areas such as the Borders and the Far North, and in particular the Highlands, to identify the great bulk of migrant population across this period. Industrial development in the Lowlands pulled in more of the population from other areas. Increased levels of inward migration meant that actual population growth in the Lowlands was far higher than the natural increase would have been – at least up until the 1880s. It is essential, therefore, to consider the complicated relationship between population movement within and outwith a particular region, and the country as a whole, to understand the forces responsible for such population redistribution.

EXERCISE I
Read **Article 30**, an extract from Malcolm Gray's *Scots on the Move.*

What were the main reasons for population movement before 1914? What factors were important when deciding to move from the countryside to the towns and cities, or to leave Scotland altogether? In short, were people being forced (pushed) into leaving, or were they attracted (pulled) towards other locations? Relate this part of the question to the Scottish Highlands. In particular; carefully consider what is meant by the terms 'push' and 'pull' factors.

According to Gray, the decision to leave the countryside and migrate to the town was the result of an amalgam of complex forces, but it was usually a combination of pull to the towns and push from the land. In some cases farm improvements created natural wastage which in effect meant that less labour was needed, or that demand for labour would be more casual and seasonal in nature. In short, patterns of employment were changing and the net result was a gradual reduction in employment opportunities, as occurred in the north-east of Scotland (Gray 1984, 10–23).

The experience of the Highland counties was particularly bad – not least because of the effects of famine (1846 to 1850), and here population pressure was the main problem (Campbell and Devine 1990, 47). There were simply too many people living on too little land, relying almost entirely on the potato for subsistence. When the potato crop failed, due to the attack of the fungus *phytophthora infestans,* there was a catastrophic subsistence crisis (Hunter 1976, 50–89). The famine exposed the poverty of the Highlands, and the lack of alternative employment. The net result was massive permanent migration (many Highlanders chose to emigrate rather than settle in the urban areas of lowland Scotland). For many years before the famine, however, Highlanders had been making the seasonal trek to lowland areas of Scotland to seek employment – a tradition that dated back to the eighteenth century. The Highlands' 'surplus population' simply moved to those areas where there was a demand for labour and during the summer and early autumn months 'huge migrant streams', both male and female, made their way to the Lowlands. Increasingly, the season became more extended. By the second half of the nineteenth century many Highlanders were settling permanently in the Lowlands. Many Highland women went into domestic service. Between 1851 and 1891, for example, 25% of all women engaged in domestic service in Greenock were of Highland origins. Gradually the barriers to permanent out-migration were eroded, particularly among young Highlanders. As a result many turned their backs on their traditional way of life (Devine 1994, 135–45).

The seasonal pattern of migration helped build up information about urban life, often sent to relatives at home. Corridors of communication and migration were established, so temporary migration led in time to permanent settlement. By 1850 there were sizeable communities of Highlanders in Edinburgh and Perth, but the greatest concentration was in Greenock and Glasgow. Between 1851 and 1891, the population of the Highland counties fell by 9%. Between 1891 and 1931 (when the crofter had greater protection by law) it fell by a further 26%. The letter from America or Canada, with offers of financial help and assistance, helped many reach the final decision to emigrate.

The uncertainty caused by changes in employment patterns was one factor which prompted many to leave the land. In the South-West, for example, there was increasing uncertainty of employment. Demand for female labour, particularly dairy-maids, increased (peaking in the 1880s), while the demand for male labour fell. Seasonal work increased, as did temporary Irish labour immigration (Campbell 1984).

According to Smout (1986, 62–4), the proletarianisation of farm work created a growing sense of alienation. In the Borders changes in traditional hiring patterns influenced the decision to leave agricultural labour and seek work elsewhere. The rural experience was far from uniform (Sproat 1984). Agriculture underwent a considerable degree of change, but some traditional patterns of work survived. The 'bondager' system, where a contracted farm employee, known as a 'hind', was obliged to provide a female outworker to work for the hiring farmer without payment, survived through to 1914. Similarly, the 'Hiring Fairs' – a means of engaging farm labour on fixed-term contracts – survived up until the 1930s (Orr 1984). Overall, however, the changing pattern of agricultural employment acted to channel surplus labour off the land and into urban areas. This in turn led to the rural depopulation and a further contraction of the agricultural labour force (Devine 1984, 1–7).

In terms of internal migration the greatest movement of people was towards the west central belt. Glasgow and Edinburgh were the major destinations, the former taking the highest proportion from all regions except the Borders (Flinn 1977, 474–8). Over the same period the numbers engaged in farming in Scotland fell by 18% through to 1891 and in the following 40 years fell by a further 11%. In the Highlands, however, the decreases over the same time-periods were 11% and 30% respectively. In this sense, the Highlands were little different from other rural areas of Scotland. This illustrates the pulling power of the city culture over the more restrictive and narrowly defined culture of the countryside (Smout 1986, 59–60). The process may have been a long one – even more so in the Highlands – but by the early twentieth century 'rural depopulation represented the final victory, in the struggle for the hearts and minds of the people, of the town over the country' (*ibid*, 79–84).

1.3 Population movement in the twentieth Century

EXERCISE 2

Look at Table 2 which shows some of the main regional changes between 1961 and 1991 (use in conjunction with Illustration 43). Identify the regions which experienced population growth between 1961 and 1991.

The Borders, the Highlands, the Western Isles and the Northern Isles (Shetlands and Orkney Isles combined) were losing population up until 1971. Does this trend continue between 1971 and 1991?

Identify the region which lost more of its populations between 1961 and 1991.

TABLE 2: REGIONS OF SCOTLAND AND ISLANDS AREAS 1961 TO 1991 (000S)

Year	1	2	3	4	5	6	7	8	9	10	11	12
1961	102.1	244.6	146.4	320.7	440.3	163.9	710.2	2,584.0	397.8	18.7	17.8	32.6
1971	98.5	263.0	143.2	327.1	438.6	175.5	745.6	2,575.4	397.6	17.0	17.3	29.9
1981	97.3	268.2	141.9	325.1	462.9	187.0	723.2	2,375.0	382.8	18.4	22.8	30.7
1991	101.5	262.0	144.9	333.5	484.7	198.6	703.6	2,189.1	373.8	19.1	22.0	29.0

1 BORDERS REGION 2 CENTRAL REGION 3 DUMFRIES AND GALLOWAY
4 FIFE REGION 5 GRAMPIAN REGION 6 HIGHLAND REGION
7 LOTHIAN 8 STRATHCLYDE 9 TAYSIDE
10 ORKNEY ISLANDS 11 SHETLAND ISLANDS 12 WESTERN ISLES

Source: 1991 Census

Illustration 43 and 44 are based on pre-1996 regional boundaries of Scotland. Clearly, the patterns of change were uneven – even within specific regions. Grampian lost only a small percentage of its population after 1945 when compared

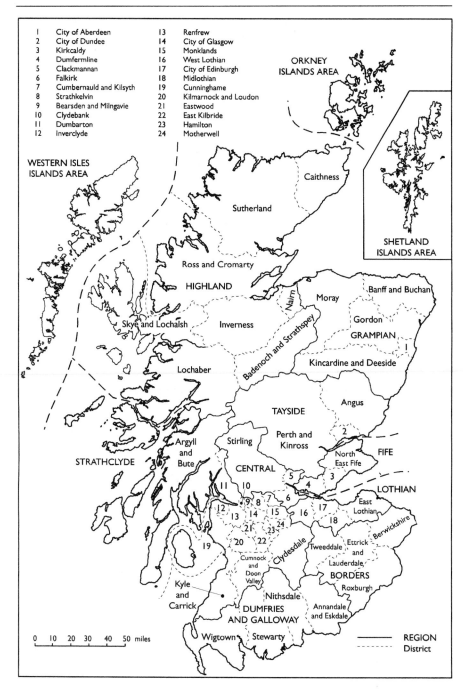

1	City of Aberdeen	13	Renfrew
2	City of Dundee	14	City of Glasgow
3	Kirkcaldy	15	Monklands
4	Dumfermline	16	West Lothian
5	Clackmannan	17	City of Edinburgh
6	Falkirk	18	Midlothian
7	Cumbernauld and Kilsyth	19	Cunninghame
8	Strathkelvin	20	Kilmarnock and Loudon
9	Bearsden and Milngavie	21	Eastwood
10	Clydebank	22	East Kilbride
11	Dumbarton	23	Hamilton
12	Inverclyde	24	Motherwell

43 Administrative Areas. From *1991 Census. Preliminary Report for Scotland*, HMSO. Crown Copyright.

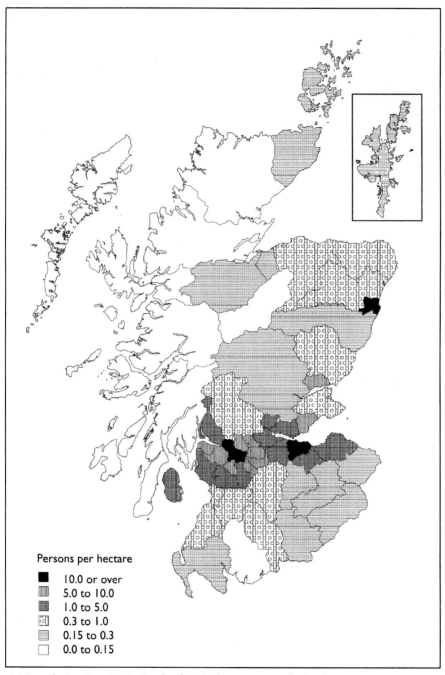

Persons per hectare

■ 10.0 or over
5.0 to 10.0
1.0 to 5.0
0.3 to 1.0
0.15 to 0.3
0.0 to 0.15

44 Population Density in Scotland 1991 by District and Islands Area. From *1991 Census. Preliminary Report for Scotland*, HMSO. Crown Copyright.

to the period up to 1939. These increases were less than they might have been but for economic recession in the oil industry in the 1980s and early 1990s, but were still significantly higher than at any time since the 1920s and 1930s (Anderson 1992, 13, fig 1). In Grampian the population dropped slightly between 1961 and 1971, but increased by over 10.5% between 1971 and 1991. The population of the Borders, the Northern Isles, Highland Region, and the Western Isles fell by over 70,000 between 1911 and 1971 (indeed, the population of the Western Isles was halved over the same period). Between 1971 and 1991, there was little change in the Borders, while in the Western Isles the downward trend continued, with the region losing over 11% of its total population from 1961 to 1991. By contrast, that of the Highland region and Northern Isles increased by over 13% and 16% respectively.

The Central Region, Fife, and the Lothians showed significant population growth by the second half of the twentieth century – an increase of one third, one fifth, and one fifth respectively (*ibid* 12–13). Between 1971 and 1991, however, of these three regions only Fife continued to see its population grow; Central region experienced little change, while the population of Lothians dropped by 42,000 (5.6%). The populations of Dumfries and Galloway and Tayside remained more or less stable throughout the twentieth century, although the population of Tayside dropped by almost 6% between 1971 and 1991. The fall in the population of Lothians and Tayside accounts for no more than 66,000 in total and is not particularly significant when compared to Strathclyde region (formerly the Western Lowlands, including Argyll and Bute). Up until 1961 the population of Strathclyde was growing, but between 1961 and 1991 it fell from 2,584,000 to 2,189,100 – a drop of 15.3%. The population of Strathclyde was therefore lower in 1991 than it was in 1911.

In general terms much of the central belt (except for Central and Fife regions) saw its population contract in the period up to the 1990s. By contrast, the population of the Highlands increased. This was not caused by natural increase, but rather by increased numbers of workers, particularly oil workers, and those commonly referred to as 'white-settlers', largely from England. Highland depopulation was traditionally caused by out-migration. Recent population growth, on the other hand, was due to in-migration, which was far in excess of natural growth. This dynamic also created isolated growth points with areas such as Inverness, Skye and Lochalsh, Badenoch and Strathspey (see Illustrations 43 and 44) having significant population growth (Cameron 1996, 155, Table 1). Thus, the patterns of change are uneven within regional boundaries, but also between regions (Anderson 1992; Cameron 1996).

2 EMIGRATION

The term 'emigrant' refers to those leaving Scotland to settle in England or Wales, and those who settled abroad (the more traditional image of the emigrant Scot). Between 1861 and 1939 over 2,600,000 left Scotland. Up until the 1920s, while many Scots emigrated overseas, large numbers of Scots also crossed the border into England (Flinn 1977, 442). The depression of the 1930s reduced Scottish emigration to a virtual trickle compared with previous decades, 33,595 in total between 1931 and 1938, its lowest level for over a century. At this point, immigration began to exceed emigration – although some of these immigrants included Scots returning from overseas. For much of the period Scotland was losing a higher proportion of its population than many other European countries, and although comparative figures are not available, estimates show that Scotland was perhaps second only to Ireland in terms of total emigration during 1850 to 1939 (*ibid*, 447–8).

EXERCISE 3
Consider Tables 3a, 3b and 3c and **Document 106** which is an extract from the Dominions Royal Commission on Emigration.

What percentage of Scots were moving within the UK when compared to emigration overseas? Look at **Document 106**. How do Scottish emigration figures compare to those of the United Kingdom?

What does Table 3b tell us about the type of person emigrating between 1912 and 1913 and how does this compare with the evidence contained in **Document 106**?

Which were the most popular destinations for emigrant Scots?

Most of these people were drawn from urban areas. Briefly suggest why.

TABLE 3a: ESTIMATED MOVEMENT OF SCOTS TO OTHER PARTS OF THE UK AND TOTAL EMIGRATION OF SCOTS OVERSEAS, 1861–1931

Intercensal Period	UK	OVERSEAS EMIGRATION
1861–1870/1	96,274	148,082
1871–1880/1	98,315	165,651
1881–1890/1	90,711	275,095
1891–1900/1	98,210	185,992
1901–1910/11	68,177	457,419
1911–1920/21	63,069	349,415
1921–1930/31	77,769	446,212
1861–1930/31	592,525	2,027,866

TABLE 3b: OCCUPATIONAL GROUP AND PREFERRED DESTINATION OF THAT GROUP,
EXPRESSED AS A PERCENTAGE OF TOTAL SCOTTISH EMIGRATION 1912–13

Group	% TOTAL	PREFERRED DESTINATION
Skilled trades	47	USA & SOUTH AFRICA
Professional Middle Class	21	SOUTH AFRICA
Labourers (industrial)	23	CANADA & AUSTRALASIA
Labourers (agricultural)	6	CANADA & AUSTRALASIA

TABLE 3C: DESTINATION OF SCOTS AS A PERCENTAGE OF TOTAL SCOTTISH
EMIGRATION FOR SELECTED PERIODS BETWEEN 1850 TO 1939

Period	USA	CANADA	AUSTRALASIA	SOUTH AFRICA
1855–9	33.3	25.2	41.5	–
1865–9	66.0	15.6	18.4	–
1875–9	45.5	11.4	43.4	–
1885–9	71.9	13.0	13.1	2.0
1895–9	63.0	10.1	6.3	20.0
1905–9	43.5	42.7	7.0	6.8
1915–19	33.0	46.7	13.2	7.1
1925–9	33.3	39.0	24.7	3.0
1935–8	14.9	24.4	26.0	34.7

Source for Tables 3a-c: Flinn (1977, tables 6.1.2, 6.1.5 and pp 451–5).

Tables 3a-c give some impression of the destinations of Scots emigrants. Most settled in America and Canada, Nova Scotia being a prime example. Scots also emigrated in substantial numbers to Australia and New Zealand and had done so in ever increasing numbers since the early 1820s (Donnachie 1992, 142–6). These became places where communities of Scots helped generate chain migration and from 1850 to the 1930s a steady stream of Scots emigrated to Australia and New Zealand. Between the 1850s and the 1880s, in terms of the percentage of emigrants leaving Scotland, the numbers moving to Australasia increased. After the 1880s emigration to Australasia slowed down and did not pick up again until the late 1920s. By the late 1930s the percentage emigrating to Australasia increased once more, as it did in the 1940s and 1950s thanks to assisted emigration schemes (Donnachie and Graves 1988, 121–2).

By the latter decades of the nineteenth century many professional and middle-class Scots emigrated to South Africa. After 1904, however, numbers dropped considerably, and only picked up again in the late 1930s. It would seem that life in South Africa did not suit a significant number of Scots and more Scots returned from there than any other location (almost as many returned home as left during that period).

From the 1860s until the early years of the twentieth century, however, most Scots went to America. Canada again became popular for Scots emigrants from around 1905 to 1914, when nearly 170,000 entered the country. By the 1920s Scots were crossing the Atlantic in great numbers, divided fairly evenly between America and Canada. However, many Scots went initially to Canada as a means of gaining entry into the United States, still the favoured destination.

Male emigration was much higher than female for much of this period – males outnumbered females by 2:1 in the 1870s. By 1914, however, there was virtual equality between the sexes. Indeed, between 1911 and 1921 more women than men left Scotland. Between 1921 and 1931 there was an estimated loss of 8.0% of the Scottish population to emigration. Before then the highest recorded loss was 5.8% between 1881 and 1891 and 5.7% between 1901 and 1911. Between 1931 and 1951 the numbers leaving dropped to around 4.5% of the population or 220,000 (Census).

In the early nineteenth century most emigrants came from rural areas, but gradually more were drawn from towns and cities. By the late nineteenth century unemployed Lowland artisans, labourers, and other industrial workers, such as handloom weavers, were more likely to emigrate. Erickson (1972), analysing United States passenger shipping lists for the period 1885–88, estimated that 77% of emigrants were urban, whereas 30 years earlier it was 27%. Economic considerations were paramount in the decision to leave. After a severe depression in the building trade in Aberdeen the late 1880s, for example, nearly every stone mason who could scrape together the fare emigrated to America. In one six-week period alone, during spring 1887, some 2,000 stone masons arrived in New York from Aberdeen (Flinn 1977, 453–5).

By the early twentieth century it was most often the skilled workers who emigrated. Table 3b shows that 47% of the adult males were skilled (55% by the early 1920s) and 21% were drawn from middle-class and business backgrounds in commerce, finance and insurance. Of those who left in 1912–13, 29% were described as labourers, only one in five in agriculture. Most unskilled labourers tended to opt for Canada or Australasia, while the skilled favoured the United States and South Africa. The middle class was particularly attracted to South Africa, but there was little need for the unskilled due to cheap indigenous labour.

EXERCISE 4

Consider **Document 107**, an extract from the Dominions Royal Commission on Emigration. What reasons are offered to explain why Scots did not approach local authorities for financial assistance when emigrating? Compare this information with that contained in Table 3b. Would it strengthen or weaken the argument that emigrants at this time were more likely to be skilled and professional workers and, therefore, needed less financial help.

Occupational structure, place of birth, or the emigrant's last location in Scotland, therefore, varied considerably over time, mirroring specific regional patterns. As previously noted, many thousands left the Highlands and settled permanently abroad rather than following traditional migratory routes to the Western Lowlands. The majority of migrants left because of poor economic and social opportunities at home – economic and social conditions in the south, particularly in the interwar years, were little better. While emigration remained a key feature in Highland depopulation, it dropped during the depression of the 1930s and after the 1960s less Highlanders emigrated as those areas they formerly favoured and settled began to impose restrictions on entry and Scottish emigration levels as a whole dropped considerably (Cameron 1996, 154).

3. MORTALITY

Not until the 1870s did national morality rates begin a sustained decline in Scotland. In the early 1870s the crude death rate average for the years 1870–72 was 22.3 per 1,000, yet ten years before it was only 21.5 per 1,000 living (suggesting that living and working in an urban and industrial setting was detrimental to health). There-after the trend was downward, falling to 19.7 for 1880–82, 17.9 for 1900–02, and 15.2 per 1000 living by 1910–12 – a fall of 29% in fifty years (Anderson and Morse 1990, 23–5). This is indicated in **Document 106**, which is an extract of evidence made to the Dominions Royal Commission, 1912. Indeed, the evidence indicates that by 1910–12, the national death rate in Scotland of 15.2% was actually below the rate of 15.7% estimated for the United Kingdom as a whole. By 1935–8 the death rate had fallen further to 13.3 per 1,000 and between 1946–50 it had fallen again to 12.6 per 1,000. There was no further significant fall in death rate nationally thereafter (Anderson 1992, 19).

There were significant regional variations and differences in death rates (as well as fertility and nuptuality rates) between cities and towns, urban and country areas. In the period 1880–82, for example, the average death rate was 19.7 per 1,000 living. By comparison, the average death rate of the city dweller was 23.3 per 1,000, while in the town it was 20.3 per 1,000 living, and in the countryside it was only 17.3 per 1,000. From the 1880s onward, death rates in all locations fell significantly, although they were still proportionately higher in the cities and towns.

By 1910–12, crude mortality rates in cities had fallen by 41%, by 36% in towns, and by 20% in rural areas. By the 1930–32, however, crude morality levels in the different areas had more or less equalised at around the national average death rate of 13.4 per 1,000 – city regions were now down to 14.1 per 1,000, while town and country regions were under the national average at 13.1 and 12.8 per 1,000 respectively. By the 1950s the crude death rate nationally had fallen to 12.6 per 1,000 and there was no further significant fall thereafter (*ibid*). Clearly, the death rate was falling, indicating improvements in the standard of living. However, analysis of infant morality rates are considered to be a more accurate reflection of living conditions (Cage 1994, 77–92).

TABLE 4: INFANT MORTALITY RATES IN SCOTLAND, 1855 TO THE 1980S (UNDER
AGE ONE, PER 1,000 LIVE BIRTHS)

PERIOD	RATE	PERIOD	RATE
1855–89	120	1920–24	92
1890–94	126	1925–29	87
1895–99	130	1930–34	82
1900–04	122	1935–39	77
1905–09	114	1960s	60
1910–14	109	1970s	40
1915–19	106	1980s	20

Source: Flinn (1977, table 5.5.9.); for 1960s to 1980s see Anderson (1992, fig 4, p 20).

Average Scottish infant mortality rates (under the age of one) between 1855 and 1889 show an annual average rate of around 120 deaths per 1,000 live births. Over the years 1890 to 1894, however, infant mortality rose to 126 per live births, and to 130 between 1895 and 1899. By 1900–4 infant mortality rates had fallen to 122 per 1,000 live births. Thereafter the trend was downwards, and by the late 1930s infant mortality was around 77 deaths per 1,000 live births (as seen in Table 4). Infant mortality continued to decline after the Second World War and in the 1960s, 1970s and 1980s it fell below 60, 40, and 20 deaths per 1,000 live births respectively. Infant mortality before 1900 declined because improved sanitation and cleaner water supplies reduced the incidence of water-borne and diarrhoeal diseases, helped by slum clearance and improved public housing. Widespread city-improvement schemes played a large part, but the effects were limited. Improvements in medicine and health care provisions for women and babies produced further and sustained declines in infant mortality and the establishment of the National Health Service in 1946 led to further improvements thereafter.

There were considerable and significant variations across Scotland and the UK as a whole, not least between urban and rural areas. By 1911, for example, 75% of the Scottish population was living in urban areas numbering 5,000 people or more (1911 Census). In Scotland's 'principal towns', infant mortality fell from 161 live births per 1,000 to 121 live births between 1870–1873 and 1908–1910. By comparison, in the country regions the birth rates rose from 86 to 88 live births. Overall, however, the infant mortality rates in the countryside were significantly more stable. Up until 1910, Scottish cities had lower infant mortality rates than those in England, while average figures for England and Wales were higher than Scotland. The major change took place in the late 1920s, however, when, with the exception of Edinburgh, Scotland's three other cities (Aberdeen, Dundee, and Glasgow), showed higher rates than in England. From this period through to the late 1960s, Glasgow's infant mortality rate was higher than any other urban and industrial centre (Cage 1994, 80). It was not until the 1980s that infant mortality in

Scotland fell to around the English and Welsh levels (Anderson 1992, 22; Cage 1994).

Generally, deaths caused by whooping cough, tuberculosis, and respiratory diseases (among others), were far higher in urban areas than in rural areas, and higher still in city areas when compared to large and small towns. The Western and Eastern Lowlands together accounted for 47% of all infant deaths through whooping cough in Scotland between 1861 and 1870. By 1881–1900 the proportion was 50.4%, rising to 52.4% between 1901–10, and to 56.3% between 1931 and 1939. The incidence of infant deaths by whooping cough declined by over 70% in the same period, but still disproportionately affected the Central Lowlands throughout this period. The effects of tuberculosis were felt everywhere but particularly in the Western Lowlands and the Borders. Deaths caused by respiratory diseases (such as pneumonia) were lower in the Far North and the Highlands (Flinn 1977, Tables 5.6.5 and 5.6.6).

Cage (1994, 82–9) has shown that respiratory diseases were more prevalent in northern Britain than in the south, and in urban areas infectious diseases (such measles) were also more prevalent. He sees overcrowding as the biggest single problem, generating increased child to child contact. Urban housing encouraged such intimate contact, and in Glasgow the problem was even more acute. But within Glasgow there were differences between districts and in all cases those with the highest infant mortality rates were high density working class areas. In short, 'the higher the density per room, the greater the mortality rates' (*ibid* 86). In terms of housing density, concluded Cage, 'Glasgow's was the worst in Britain' and an infant born in Glasgow was less likely to reach its first birthday than one born in any other British city. Improved housing was essential for further improvement in infant mortality rates. Medical advances helped considerably, but only solved part of the problem (*ibid*).

Similar variations in morality rates, although perhaps not of the same order of magnitude, can be observed within other age groups. There were differences in terms in life expectancy between males and females, with females living longer and in greater numbers than males, and women's survival chances improving further after the 1940s. There were also major differences in crude death rates between various city regions and other smaller urban settlements. In the 1860s the death rates were far higher in the cities than many smaller towns. Thereafter, however, Aberdeen, Dundee and Edinburgh began to bring their high death rates under control. Glasgow's record was in line with the other city regions from around the 1880s onward. By that time the problem of high death rates were worse in smaller towns such as Ayr, Dumfries and Stirling (Anderson and Morse 1990, 26–8). Death chances, therefore, varied and depended very much on domicile, gender, and social and economic conditions, as well as age (Anderson 1992, 19).

4 FERTILITY AND NUPTUALITY

Scottish birth rates remained more or less stable, at around 35 per 1,000 of the population, from the 1830s through to the late 1870s, but thereafter began to fall. On average, the national birth rate fell to 25.4 per 1,000 of the population between 1911 and 1915, falling further to 17.7 in the late 1930s, and to 10.4 per 1,000 by the 1980s. There were surges in the birth rate in 1921 and 1947 and again in the 'baby boom' of the mid 1960s, but the overall picture for the period is of a declining birth rate. By the late 1980s, 'there were fewer children alive than there had been at any period since the 1840s' (Anderson 1992, 17–19). What caused this shift towards lower birth rates over this period? Was the Scottish experience any different from other European countries at that time?

EXERCISE 5
Consider **Document 108**, and compare this with **Document 109**, an extract from Royal Commission on Population (1949), and Anderson's chapter on 'Population and Family Life', in *People and Society in Scotland. Volume II, 1830–1914*.

What does **Document 109** consider are the main factors responsible for low family formation and the subsequent fall in the birth rate in Britain?

Does **Document 108** suggest that other factors are responsible for the fall in the birth rate in Scotland?

How does Anderson account for lower births rates in Scotland post 1945?

Legitimate birth rates fell rapidly from the 1870s. Among married couples the birth rate fell by 14%, from 316 to 272 live births per 1,000 between 1860–2 and 1900–2. By 1950–2 this had dropped further to 132 births per 1,000 married women – a fall of 51% from 1900–02. Overall, the legitimate birth rate had decreased by 58% between 1860–2 and 1950–2. The sharpest decline, however, was in the present century (1951 Census) and this trend continued through to the second half of the twentieth century. In 1870, the average number of children per family was six, but by 1951 the number of children was down to 2.5 per family.

After 1945 social attitudes to family formation began to change. There were pronounced regional differences before the Second World War, but these levelled out in the post-war period and in particular by the mid 1950s. Health care improved, as did methods of birth control, which had an effect on birth rates. In terms of births to married parents, after a slight rise during the War, and the ensuing baby boom, there was a brief period where births rose. Between the 1960s and 1990s, however, the trend in the legitimate birth rate was downwards, falling from around 100,000 to 50,000. Married couples increasingly limited the number of children they had. The number of births to unmarried parents, however, increased.

EXERCISE 6
Consider Tables 5a and 5b and and Anderson's chapter, 'Population and Family
Life' in *People and Society in Scotland Volume II*.

What do Tables 5a and 5b tell us about illegitimacy levels in Scotland?

How can we account for lower illegitimacy levels in urban areas of Scotland and
the significantly higher levels of illegitimacy in the North-East?

TABLE 5A: ILLEGITIMATE BIRTHS IN SCOTLAND AS A PERCENTAGE OF ALL BIRTHS
FOR REGIONS, AND SCOTLAND AS A WHOLE, 1860–2 TO 1930–2

	FAR NORTH	HIGHLAND	NORTH-EAST	WESTERN	EASTERN	BORDERS	SCOTLAND
1860–62	5.50	5.61	15.12	7.96	9.37	13.03	9.37
1870–72	6.81	7.07	14.98	8.00	9.22	14.34	9.44
1880–82	7.89	6.86	15.08	6.77	8.00	12.53	8.44
1890–92	7.92	6.48	13.13	5.99	7.46	11.71	7.56
1900–02	7.00	6.42	11.22	5.06	6.19	10.42	6.34
1910–12	8.94	7.67	13.30	6.05	8.49	11.59	7.38
1920–22	9.32	7.79	12.60	5.96	6.80	10.86	7.16
1930–32	9.96	9.48	12.61	6.02	6.88	11.14	7.31

TABLE 5B: ILLEGITIMATE BIRTHS IN SCOTLAND AS A PERCENTAGE OF ALL BIRTHS
FOR CITIES OF ABERDEEN, DUNDEE, EDINBURGH, GLASGOW, TOWNS, URBAN
AREAS, AND SCOTLAND, 1860–62 TO 1930–32.

	ABERDEEN	DUNDEE	EDINBURGH	GLASGOW	TOWNS	URBAN AREAS	SCOTLAND
1860–62	15.34	12.03	9.83	8.71	8.21	9.22	9.37
1870–72	12.27	11.33	8.07	9.31	7.80	8.65	9.441
1880–82	10.99	10.50	7.41	7.76	6.64	7.56	8.44
1890–92	10.27	9.71	7.79	7.72	6.00	7.06	7.56
1900–02	8.09	8.79	6.83	6.40	4.68	5.88	6.34
1910–12	10.42	8.90	7.60	7.34	6.14	7.04	7.38
1920–22	9.37	7.77	7.29	6.47	5.57	6.53	7.16
1930–32	8.18	7.40	6.57	6.20	6.07	6.37	7.31

In terms of illegitimacy, Scotland's record was once one of the worst in Europe, a
situation which improved after 1850. There were significant regional variations
(Tables 5a and 5b) with illegitimacy rates clearly higher in rural areas than the cities
and the towns. Illegitimacy rates in Glasgow were lower than Aberdeen, Dundee,
and Edinburgh (except between 1870 and 1882) and all four compared favourably
with Scottish levels of illegitimacy. By contrast, Aberdeen's illegitimacy levels were

consistently higher when compared to the other cities. As Aberdeen was the main urban conurbation in the North-East and as illegitimacy levels in the North-East were higher than in any other region of Scotland, this is not surprising. As Blaikie (1994, 46, 50) argues, the persistence of certain social practices in the North-East may have been responsible for the high levels of illegitimacy. It can be argued that in the North-East a significantly greater number of unmarried couples cohabited and had children than was socially acceptable elsewhere. Although marriage was the preferred long-term option, a shortage of accommodation meant that many couples with children actually had to live apart (*ibid*).

Illegitimacy levels in rural areas did decrease, but more slowly than in urban areas. In the urban areas as a whole, illegitimate births fell from around 9% to 7.3% of all births during 1850 to 1914. During the 1920s and 1930s the illegitimate birth rate fluctuated between 6% and 8% and by the 1950s had fallen to 4% of the total. From the late 1960s, however, the illegitimate birth rate rose considerably to reach 10% between 1976 and 1980, rising to 24.5% by 1988 (Anderson and Morse 1990, 33). The number of births to married parents, conversely, decreased steadily, and the numbers marrying, as a proportion of the population, also fell. From the 1950s onward more women were having children outside marriage, and from the 1970s all the younger age groups of women increased their propensity to bear children outside of marriage. The result was an 'illegitimacy explosion' (Anderson 1992, 35–7).

Much of Scotland's demographic history differs considerably from that of England and Wales, although more in parallel with the rest of Europe. In terms of the shift from high to low levels of fertility and infant mortality, the general trend in Scotland differed little from most other European nations. Scottish levels of marital fertility, however, were traditionally higher than in England (although marriage chances were significantly lower).

5 PATTERNS OF IMMIGRATION IN SCOTLAND

According to Flinn (1977) there 'were two quite distinctive waves of immigration into Scotland' between *c.* 1850 and 1914. The first was the large influx of Irish, a movement that had already peaked by the 1850s. The second, smaller, wave of immigration emanated from Eastern Europe, mainly Lithuania, Poland and Russia: many of these immigrants were Jewish. There was also a steady influx of English into Scotland from the 1840s onward (*ibid*). Quantifying the extent of Irish immigration is often problematic – particularly when this becomes confused with those visiting Scotland as temporary migrants, mainly, but not exclusively, as seasonal agricultural workers. Some Irish came to Scotland only to emigrate from there to America, while others were returned to Ireland because of the operation of the poor laws.

Between 1841 and 1851 the number of Irish living in Scotland had increased from 126,326 to 207,367 (7.2% of the total Scottish population). During that period, taking into account deaths and departures, the influx of Irish amounted to 110,000 – an increase of almost 90% on the previous decade. Although many more Irish came into Scotland after 1850 (mostly from Ulster), particularly between 1876 to 1884 and 1899 to 1907, the overall rate was much reduced (Pryde 1963, 256). From the 1850s onward, in terms of the proportion of the population of Scotland, Irish numbers decreased. Although by 1881 the number of Irish born in Scotland had risen to almost 219,000, at this juncture they only accounted for 5.9% of total population. By 1901 this fell to just over 205,000 and by 1921 the total number of Irish born in Scotland was just below 160,000 (3.3% of the population). Indeed, estimates show that the numbers of English born in Scotland at this time numbered almost 190,000 – just under 4% of the total Scottish population (1921 Census).

Almost three times as many Irish settled in England and Wales as in Scotland, but the Irish were proportionately more numerous in Scotland. In 1851 the Irish accounted for 7.2% of the Scottish population, but in England and Wales the figure was 2.9%. Table 6 charts the Irish-born population of England, Wales and Scotland over the period 1841 to 1921.

TABLE 6: IRISH BORN IN ENGLAND AND WALES, AND SCOTLAND 1841–1921

Year	ENGLAND AND WALES		SCOTLAND	
	NUMBER	% OF TOTAL POPULATION	NUMBER	% OF TOTAL POPULATION
1841	289,404	1.8	126,321	4.8
1851	519,959	2.9	207,367	7.2
1861	601,634	3.0	204,083	6.7
1871	566,540	2.5	207,770	6.2
1881	562,374	2.2	218,745	5.9
1891	458,315	1.6	194,807	4.8
1901	426,565	1.3	205,064	4.6
1911	375,325	1.0	174,715	3.7
1921	364,747	1.4	159,020	3.3

Source: The Irish in Britain 1815–1914, Roger Swift.

By 1851, almost 70% of all Irish living in Scotland had settled in Lanarkshire, Ayrshire, and Renfrewshire. There were considerable numbers in Glasgow, Paisley and Kilmarnock: 18.2%, 12.7%, and 12.2% of the local population respectively. The Irish also located in Midlothian and Stirling, attracted to the mining and textile districts, and agricultural areas like Wigtownshire. Edinburgh's Irish population was not so substantial, and in 1851 only 6.5% were Irish. The greatest concentration was in Dundee where 18.8% of the population was Irish, by far the largest proportion female. Such settlement patterns remained remarkably constant throughout this period, despite the decline in the numbers of Irish in living Britain (Swift 1990, 11–14).

The Irish were not the only immigrant group, for a second smaller wave came from Eastern Europe, becoming significant in the late 1890s. Before then there were only a few thousand European immigrants, but by 1891 their numbers had doubled. Over the following decade a further 10,000 settled and by 1901 numbered 17,654, rising in 1911 to 25,000. Thereafter, very few new immigrants came into Scotland from Europe. Like the Irish immigrants the great majority of European incomers were men – almost a 2:1 ratio (173.6 to 100). The great majority settled in the cities and towns, with a third in Glasgow alone. The remainder, for the most part, settled in Midlothian (mainly in Edinburgh), Fife and Stirling.

Lithuanian Catholics also arrived in significant numbers, settling mainly in the mining areas of Ayrshire and Lanarkshire (Maitles 1995, 47). Before 1914 there were around 6,000 Jews (mainly Russian and Polish Jews), 4,500 Italians, and around 6,000 Lithuanians (including some Polish Catholics). Between the Wars there was little emigration. By 1951, Scotland was the home of substantial communities of Poles, some 10,600 in total, over 7,000 Americans, 7,000 Germans, 5,700 Russians and 5,300 Italians (Census 1951). There were also smaller communities from Austria, Burma, China, Denmark, Egypt, France and Yugoslavia, among others. During the second half of the twentieth century many more Italians and Lithuanians came to Scotland, as well as greater numbers from Germany, America, Asia, South Asia, South East Asia and Africa (Rodgers 1996).

Only the English increased their numbers in Scotland at each census (Flinn 1997, 111). Between 1841 and 1921 the numbers of English born in Scotland rose from 1.5% to 4% of the Scottish population. By 1921, more English had settled in Scotland than Irish, and the flow of English northward into Scotland only stopped because of economic depression in the 1920s. Well over 60% of English settlers located in the Central Belt; some 20% in the Borders region and almost 14% in the North-East, but only 5% reached the Highlands and Islands. Indeed, four in ten English immigrants lived in Glasgow, Edinburgh, Dundee and Aberdeen. By 1931 the majority remained within these geographical areas, although the proportion living in cities had by then risen to over 47%. Perhaps the major difference at this time, however, was that great majority, almost 9 to 1, were women, mostly domestic servants.

By 1951 the census records that the number of English settlers in Scotland numbered 231,794 (just over 4.5% of total population), whereas the number of Irish had dropped to around 90,000 (1.75% of total population). The number of English settling in Scotland has continued to rise: by the 1991 census the number of English born living in Scotland numbered 345,269 – almost 7% (1991 Census). In 1991, they numbered almost 98,000 out of a total population of 2.2 million (4.5%) in Strathclyde; 29,270 (7.8%) in Tayside; 59,900 (8.5%) in Lothian; 30,789 (9.2%) in Fife; 50,973 (10.5%) in Grampian; 24,255 (12.2%) in Highland; 20,703 (14.3%) in Dumfries and Galloway; 16,489 (16.2%) in Borders, and around 12% of the total population of Orkney and Shetland (1991 Census). Despite the long history of English settlement in Scotland, little has been written about English settlers or their impact on Scottish society: this is one history in need of research.

CONCLUSIONS

According to the 1951 Census, the natural increase in the population of Scotland (resulting from the excess of births over deaths) had been falling in proportion to the population since the 1870s. Between 1871–81 and 1941–51, the natural increase in proportion to total population fell from 14.0% to around 5.8%. In the 1951 Census this was attributed to emigration, in particular of the younger age group of prospective parents. The main cause, however, was the 'long continued and heavy decrease in fertility in marriage' (1951 Census).

Changes in marriage rates and fertility in marriage clearly altered after 1945. Women were having fewer children and the numbers of births in marriage were below 'maximum' fertility levels. Anderson (1992, 29–37) estimates, for example, that in 1911 and 1961 married Scotswomen bore about 57% of the children they were in theory able to produce. By 1961, however, this had fallen to 34%, and was to fall further still. Although marital fertility in Scotland was significantly higher than in England, the net result was the same. Falling births rates accompanied by lower rates of marriage resulted in lower marital fertility rates. Post 1945 we see a reverse of the trend that saw higher levels of illegitimate births in rural areas. In the Western Lowlands, however, the number of illegitimate births increased. Thereafter, the number of illegitimate births registered in urban working-class areas rose considerably (although there were still persistently high levels recorded in the North-East). By the late 1980s, 40% of births to all unmarried parents occurred in the four city districts of Scotland, compared to only 28% of births to married couples. In the cities and manufacturing towns levels of illegitimacy are higher still, and when compared to the levels of illegitimacy in middle class communities the difference is remarkable (*ibid*).

As **Document 109** indicates, the reasons for the changing nature of family formation are indeed complex. Changing social attitudes to child rearing, changing material needs and patterns of leisure, and the economic considerations of producing and maintaining large families, are the most common reasons for lower family formation. Some parents wished to give more quality time to fewer children, particularly when the cost of child rearing was increasing (*ibid* 37–42). Conversely, other couples chose not to have children at all. Improvements in women's health care, health education and birth control have played an important role too.

Population growth in Scotland first went into decline in the 1920s at a time when birth rates and mortality rates were falling. In the preceding decades, as **Document 106** clearly indicates, the level of out-migration from Scotland was significant, and by 1912, for the first time in 100 years, was showing emigration levels well beyond the natural increase in population (Dominions Royal Commission 1912). This was compensated for by immigration, but the net effect was the loss of population. Evidently the Second World War marked a turning point in Scottish demographic trends, due to an increase in mortality rates with, consequently, a significant impact on population growth, although this was offset by a sudden increase in births shortly after the War. When compared to the rest of the UK and other European countries, which experienced a net increase in population by the second half of the twentieth century, Scotland population was declining. Between 1961 and the late 1980s the population in Scotland fell by 1.4%, while the population in Northern Ireland, England and Wales, rose by 10.4%, 8.8% and 7.6% respectively. In other countries within the European union (EEC), Belgium recorded the lowest growth rate of 7.7%. Scotland's economic condition was perhaps the main reason for significant emigration in the 1950s and 1960s (*ibid*, 12–14).

Gray (1990, 35–6) believes it was a combination of both push and pull factors that forced people to emigrate. A major pull factor was better employment opportunities and higher wages offered elsewhere, while a major push factor was the experience of prolonged periods of economic uncertainty at home. When assessing the best chances of personal or family advancement, emigration was seen to be the best option. After 1945 emigration, especially of young people, was to be one of the main reasons for the fall in population; compounded by lower births rates and lower levels of female fertility. Before the 1970s there was heavy emigration in every decade except the 1930s.

During the 1920s around 390,000 more people left than entered Scotland. In the 1950s and 1960s over 500,000 people left Scotland in both decades – half overseas and half to other areas of the United Kingdom. On average 15,000 people per year left Scotland between 1972 and 1986. Emigration and low fertility were at the roots of the decline in Scottish population, which by 1991 was only marginally higher than in 1914.

REFERENCES

*Anderson, M 1992 'Population and family life', *in* Fraser, WH and Morris, RJ (eds) *People and Society in Scotland. Volume II 1830–1914*, Edinburgh, 12–47.

*Anderson, M and Morse, DJ 1990 'The people', *in* Fraser, WH and Morris, RJ (eds) *People and Society in Scotland. Volume II 1830–1914*, Edinburgh, 8–45.

Blaikie, A 1994 'A kind of loving: Illegitimacy, grandparents and the rural economy of North East Scotland, 1750–1900', *Scottish Economic and Social History Review* 14, 41–57.

Brown, C 1993 *People and the pews*. Dundee. (= Studies in Economic and Social History 3)

*Cage, RA 1994 'Infant mortality rates and housing: Twentieth century Glasgow', *Scottish Economic and Social History Review* 14, 77–92.

*Cameron, E 1996 'The Scottish Highlands: From Congested District to Objective One', *in* Devine, TM and Finlay, R (eds) *Scotland in the 20th Century*, Edinburgh, 153–69.

Campbell, RH 1984 'Agricultural labour in the South-West', *in* Devine, TM, *Farm Servants and Labour in Lowland Scotland, 1770–1914*, Edinburgh, 55–70.

Campbell, RH and Devine, TM 1990 'The rural experience', *in* Fraser, WH and Morris, RJ (eds) *People and Society in Scotland. Volume II 1830–1914*, Edinburgh, 46–72.

Devine, TM 1984 'Scottish farm service in the Agricultural Revolution', *in* Devine, TM, *Farm Servants and Labour in Lowland Scotland, 1770–1914*, Edinburgh, 1–8.

Devine, TM (ed) 1991 *Irish immigrants in Scottish society in the nineteenth and twentieth centuries*, Edinburgh.

Devine, TM 1994 *From clanship to Crofters' War: The social transformation of the Scottish Highlands*. Manchester.

Donnachie, I and Graves, A 1988 'Scotland and Australia 1901–1988', *in* Richards, E, Howe, A, Donnachie, I and Graves, A, *That land of exiles. Scots in Australia*, Edinburgh, 121–5.

Donnachie, I 1992 'The Making of 'Scots on the Make': Scottish settlement and enterprise in Australia, 1830–1900', *in* Devine, TM (ed), *Scottish Emigration and Scottish Society*, Edinburgh, 135–53.

Erickson, C 1972 'Who were the English and Scots emigrants to the United States in the late nineteenth century?', *in* Glass, DV and Revelle, R (eds) *Population and Social Change*, London, 360–62.

*Flinn, M 1977 *Scottish Population History from the 17th century to the 1930s*. Cambridge.

Gray, M 1984 'Farm workers in North-East Scotland', *in* Devine, TM (ed) *Farm Servants and Labour in Lowland Scotland, 1770–1914*, Edinburgh, 10–28.

*Gray, M 1990 *Scots on the move: Scots migrants 1750–1914*. Dundee.

*Houston, RA 1988 'The demographic regime', *in* Devine, TM and Mitchison, R (eds) *People and Society in Scotland. Volume I 1760–1830*, Edinburgh, 9–26.

Hunter, J 1976 *The making of the crofting community*. Edinburgh.

Maitles, H 1995 'Attitudes to Jewish immigration in the west of Scotland to 1905', *Scottish Economic and Social History Review* 15, 44–62.

Maver, I 1996 'The Catholic community', *in* Devine, TM and Finlay, R (eds) *Scotland in the 20th Century*, Edinburgh, 269–84.

Orr, A 1984 'Farm servants and farm labour in the Fourth Valley and South-East Lowlands', *in* Devine, TM, *Farm Servants and Labour in Lowland Scotland, 1770–1914*, Edinburgh, 29–54.

Pryde, GS 1963 *Scotland from 1603 to the present day*. London.

Rodgers, M 1996 Contributions in Kay, B (ed) *The complete Odyssey: Voices from Scotland's recent past*, Edinburgh, 1–10, 19–25, 127–135, 227–235.

Smout, TC 1986 *A century of the Scottish people*, 1830–1950. London.

Sprott, G 1984 'The country tradesman', *in* Devine, TM (ed) *Farm Servants and Labour in Lowland Scotland, 1770–1914*, Edinburgh, 143–54.

Swift, R 1990 *The Irish in Britain 1815–1914*, London.

Walker, G 1996 'Varieties of Scottish Protestant identities', *in* Devine, TM and Finlay, R (eds) *Scotland in the 20th Century*, Edinburgh, 250–68.

FURTHER READING

Those references marked * in the above list are recommended further reading.

Urbanisation

—————————————————————— *RJ Morris*

By 1851, Scotland was already a heavily urbanised country, standing second in world rankings only to England (Morris 1990a). The key feature of the Scottish experience was the speed with which Scotland changed between 1750 and 1901. The twentieth century saw a substantial reduction in the overall pace of change (Rodger 1989). Tracing the nature of the change after 1971 is problematic. Recent statistics are offered not in terms of town and country, burgh and landward but in terms of districts, regions, and travel to work areas. The 1991 census report identified a series of 'localities' which included 89% of Scotland's population. These localities were identified as 'continuously built up areas' of 500 or more population and where possible related to the historical identity of old burgh boundaries (Census 1991).

This chapter is split into the following sections –

- Factors influencing change in Scottish towns since 1850
- Housing
- The Police Act, 1862
- The character of urban places
- The post-war period

By the time you have worked your way through this chapter and the associated documents and articles it is hoped that you will have a good understanding of the main issues relating to urbanisation from 1850 to the present.

1. INTRODUCTION

The Scottish urban experience has been dominated throughout this period by the big four – Glasgow, Edinburgh, Dundee and Aberdeen. Each have strikingly different characteristics (Morris 1990a; Rodger 1986) which make generalisation problematic. The task of generalisation, which must be a part of evaluating Scottish urban experience, can be assisted in two ways. Firstly, the big four can be examined in the context of the wide variety of smaller urban places of Scotland. Indicators of occupational structure provide one basis for classification and comparison. Secondly, reflections upon the urban experience of the industrial and commercial world over the last 200 years can be used to pose a number of questions.

To assist in the first task, two sorts of resources are provided with this chapter. The appendix contains some key statistics related to all Scottish burghs of more than 5000 population in 1901. These figures refer to the 75 municipal and police burghs with populations over 5,000. Those who have a spreadsheet available on their computer can enter these figures in about half an hour. Others will want to explore them with a calculator. The major part of the figures refer to selected occupational groups designed to represent the economic character of these towns and cities. They are drawn from the *Census of Scotland* taken in 1901. In many cases the absolute figures matter. Aberdeen, for example, had one of the largest totals of people in fishing. For most purposes of comparison it is best to make some allowance for size. This can be done by taking the total in an occupational group as a percentage of the total population, or by taking it as a percentage of those over the age of ten years of the relevant gender, as this was most likely to be the group from which those occupied would be drawn. The 75 places varied in terms of the gender ratio and the proportion of children in the population. Gender ratios varied from 128 men to every 100 women in Motherwell to 61 men to every 100 women in St Andrews. The proportion of children varied from just under 30% of total population in the rapidly growing mining and metal towns like Cowdenbeath and Motherwell, to under 20% in places like Edinburgh, Galashiels and St Andrews, the latter again an extreme case at 17%. These variations related to the nature of the economy and the speed of recent expansion. The different fortunes of these towns after 1901 are explored in Rodger's chapter on twentieth-century urbanisation in *Scotland in the 20th Century* (1996).

Because the style and resources brought to municipal government were such crucial features of Scottish urban experience, two sets of figures are provided from the *Local Taxation Returns (Scotland), 1900–1901*. These indicate the net rateable value of property in the burgh and the total expenditure made from current income. (The rateable value of property was the basis upon which local taxation, 'the rates', were charged. In theory this valuation reflected the potential annual income of the property). In general the absolute totals relate to the size of the burgh but when the totals are calculated per head some interesting variations appear in the ability and willingness of different places to spend on the provision of services for their inhabitants. Glasgow and Edinburgh emerge as the big spenders both in absolute terms and in spending per head. At the bottom of the table come a variety of fishing and mining burghs – Buckie, Cowdenbeath and Airdrie – where the spending per head was just over 10% that of the leaders.

The second type of evidence provided with this chapter is extracts from the new edition of the *Ordnance Gazetteer of Scotland*, edited by Francis Groom (**Document 110**). The four selected extracts give a snapshot of Coatbridge, Hawick, Motherwell and Selkirk in the 1890s. It is possible to trace the very different material, institutional and social resources used in each town to organise urban life in the late nineteenth century.

Before proceeding it is worth asking why urban experience has merited specific attention both from historians and from the intellectuals and policy makers of the past. The reasons can be derived from two groups of questions which have been directed at the urban place. The sociologist, Louis Wirth, reflecting upon Chicago in the 1930s, saw the defining urban characteristics as size, density and variety. This was not just a description but a base from which 'the urban way of life' could be explained. In the context of the study of Scotland in this period this might be done in simple material terms. Size and density were clearly related to the problems of disease in the nineteenth century and traffic congestion and pollution in the twentieth century. Size, density and variety also created social opportunities and problems (Wirth 1938). The wide variety of associational and institutional life in the cities was another factor. The *Gazetteer* extracts provide some relevant evidence. Some might go further and look for an 'urban personality', more sophisticated and more rational than the 'rural personality' because of exposure to a wider variety of influences and opportunities. For example, city people go shopping, read newspapers and watch sport in enclosed stadia at which they pay entrance money (Barths 1980).

The second set of questions, sometimes associated with the late nineteenth century German sociologist Max Weber, suggest that urban places are linked to specific forms of authority, notably the 'fort and the market' (Weber 1958). Such authority can take the form of specific rules and regulations, special laws applied only to 'urban' places or to the institutions of local government. Examples of all these are evident in Scotland before and after 1850. Such authority was not just a response to urban 'problems' but was also used to promote urban development. Thus in Scotland the royal burgh was used from an early stage as an agent of economic development. In the nineteenth century the police burgh was used to regulate the nature of specific urban places and in the twentieth century, new towns have been built in an attempt to refashion and improve the quality of Scottish society.

2. FACTORS INFLUENCING CHANGE IN SCOTTISH TOWNS SINCE 1850

There were many influences upon the changing nature of Scottish towns in the period since 1850, but three require specific attention. The first is the rapid increase of urban population in the years up to 1911. This varied between towns. Thus Coatbridge increased from 741 people in 1831 to 30,034 in 1891 in a manner characteristic of many of the coal and iron centres. Selkirk moved from 2098 to 7298 in the more sedate manner of many textile towns which tended to grow around existing urban centres. The more rapid the rate of increase the more intense was the problem of housing, feeding and organising the population.

Secondly, these urban centres were influenced by the economic and industrial changes which linked Scotland to the world economy. The new technologies of iron and engineering not only created the economic base of places like Coatbridge and Motherwell but provided the trains and trams, the consumer goods and new construction materials which formed the material fabric of all towns. Economic change has also operated through the growing power of the market not only to structure the relationships of Scottish towns with the rest of the world but also to allocate goods and services, wealth and income within those towns.

Lastly, there were, and are, many features of Scottish towns which can only be explained by inequality, especially economic inequality. In urban terms, inequality showed itself in very material ways in the access to, and control of, space. Thus in nineteenth century Stirling, wealthier residents clearly had the space and means to take care of the sanitation of their own houses whilst poorer inhabitants did not (McKichan 1978). Inequality can also be indicated by general measures such as the varied quality of housing available to residents in different towns and cities (Table 1). The relatively poor quality of housing offered in Glasgow and in the mining and metal towns of Coatbridge and Motherwell was very clear in these figures as is the importance of the large élite houses of Edinburgh.

TABLE 1: PERCENTAGE OF THE POPULATION IN HOUSES WITH STATED NUMBER OF ROOMS

	1	2	3	4	5	6	7+	TOTAL POPULATION
Edinburgh	5.84	30.90	22.75	15.11	6.94	4.10	14.36	305881
Glasgow	13.76	48.68	21.22	7.19	2.91	1.78	4.46	754534
Dundee	9.88	53.17	21.61	6.41	2.66	1.88	4.39	160489
Aberdeen	4.84	33.82	31.98	12.98	3.38	3.31	9.69	158247
Coatbridge	22.37	54.14	13.63	4.00	2.30	1.03	2.54	41599
Motherwell	16.81	53.73	20.25	4.28	1.54	1.06	2.34	39715
Hawick	6.62	32.86	31.01	11.13	8.73	3.68	5.97	16806
Selkirk	7.01	36.45	18.21	15.70	9.75	4.36	8.52	5847

Source: Census of Scotland 1911

These forces were responsible for several distinctive spatial variations in Scottish towns. The market allocated space through property prices and rents. This meant that agencies and individuals with the highest incomes could have first 'pick'. In the early nineteenth century the middle classes took residencies near to their work, sometimes on the same site, and only moved into the country as a form of retirement. By the 1860s and 1870s an increasing number used the train and the tram to live in residential suburbs and thus to escape the environmental and social pressures of the areas in which they worked. At the same time an increasing proportion of the central area of cities was appropriated by a specific group able and willing to pay very high rents, such as banks, department stores, élite places of entertainment and institutions of local government. This was the central business district. Around this area were districts which were increasingly devoted to working class housing often mixed with small industrial premises. Working class housing was also situated near the new industrial zones which grew on the edge of the cities. Many of the larger units of production, like rolling mills and textile factories, needed extensive areas of land and their location was at the edge of towns where rents were low and often related to transport links, such as canal and railway, or to existing village settlements.

The market had a powerful influence on the organisation of space as individuals and agencies tried to get maximum advantage from their income but an account based only on the market, on inequality of income and upon changing preferences, would be too simple. This is because the density and complexity of the town produced important 'externalities' which even those with power and wealth found it impossible to control through the market. Indeed it is part of the definition of an 'externality' that it was and is an advantage or disadvantage that cannot be allocated or requited through the market. Thus when the inhabitants of Stirling came to look for the advantages of paved streets and piped water it was impossible to 'purchase' the advantages they wanted simply by buying in the materials around their own property. The property owners of Stirling needed to co-operate and this required the intervention of local government with tax raising powers. A paved street was something which had to be consumed collectively (McKichan 1978).

The interaction between the problems and opportunities of the urban place and the forms and nature of urban authority emerged in post 1850 Scotland in a number of ways. As labour and capital were drawn to economic opportunities such as those indicated in the four *Gazetteer* extracts (**Document 110**), problems emerged in housing, health, crime and public order. To these were added the perception of the need to create a more positive, civilized social environment. In the early part of the century attention had been given to religion by men like Thomas Chalmers in Glasgow and the evangelical George Bell in Edinburgh. By the 1860s and 1870s amenities such as parks, museums, free libraries and impressive public buildings were also being given attention. All these issues emerged and responses were formed in the context of the particular intensity with which the market operated in the urban place. All aspects of the market, the incomes, wealth and preferences of the decision takers, the costs and qualities of labour, capital and materials as well as the basic laws of property and contract had a powerful influence on many issues. The evidence presented here considers one of those issues, the supply and quality of urban housing, for this was both a universal urban issue and one which reveals many of the specific features of Scottish towns.

> EXERCISE I
> Compare the nature of Scottish urban experience and organisation in the textile towns and the metal producing towns; use **Document 110** and the data base for information and the text of this chapter to help pose questions.

The two textile towns, Selkirk and Hawick, featured here, were long-established towns with their own civic culture and a large number of voluntary organisations. By contrast, the two metal-producing towns, Coatbridge and Motherwell, grew rapidly from insignificant settlements to substantial towns in the space of fifty or sixty years. This rapid growth placed severe strain on housing and Table 1 shows the degree of overcrowding in Coatbridge and Motherwell in 1911 compared to

Hawick and Selkirk. The database at the end of the chapter shows that in both Coatbridge and Motherwell males over the age of ten considerably outnumbered females over that age because of the employment opportunities in heavy industry. The opposite was true in Selkirk and Hawick where female employees outnumbered males in the dominant textile industry.

3. HOUSING

Housing in Scottish towns was dominated by the stone built tenement, characterised by a fairly high quality of construction and, for the majority of the population, a very high level of overcrowding. The information gathered by the 1911 census not only showed the varied quality of Scottish housing but the very high levels of over-crowding which resulted. The distinctive and squalid conditions of the mining and metal towns are even more evident when presented in terms of people per room.

TABLE 2: PERSONS PER ROOM AS A PERCENTAGE OF THE TOTAL POPULATION

	LESS THAN 2 PEOPLE PER ROOM	MORE THAN 2 PER ROOM	MORE THAN 3 PER ROOM	MORE THAN 4 PER ROOM
Edinburgh	67.4	32.6	12.7	4.1
Glasgow	44.3	55.7	27.9	10.7
Dundee	51.8	48.2	20.0	6.1
Aberdeen	62.2	37.8	12.3	2.2
Coatbridge	28.8	71.2	45.0	23.7
Motherwell	31.9	68.1	40.3	19.2
Hawick	66.5	33.5	11.9	3.8
Selkirk	68.4	31.6	12.7	5.0

Source: Census of Scotland 1911

Life in one room was a topic of moral horror for middle class propagandists as they contemplated the mixing of generations and sexes. Even the minimal privacy and organisation of domestic space available in the north of England back-to-back house was impossible in the single room. It was also a space in which disease spread with ease. In these one and two roomed houses, density was not just a theoretical construct. Late nineteenth century Glasgow was unusual in that women suffered as badly as men from TB, a droplet infection that prospered in crowded conditions, an indication that the home rather than the workshop was the most crowded environment (Fraser and Maver 1996).

EXERCISE 2
Examine the influence of size, density and variety upon the Scottish town, consulting **Document 111** and **Article 32**.

Table 2 shows Coatbridge and Motherwell top of the overcrowding league, whilst smaller and older settlements such as Hawick and Selkirk fared relatively well. **Document 111** shows that the relationship between housing and employment was not necessarily straightforward with Partick's shipyard workers, for example, choosing to live centrally in Glasgow where there was more chance of employment for their wives. The human effects of urban overcrowding are highlighted in **Article 32** which describes the links in Edinburgh between housing conditions and death rates from diseases such as cholera, typhoid and typhus.

In Scotland the tenement was a favoured building type for many reasons. The nature of Scottish property law with high land transfer costs involved in the feu was an important factor (Rodger 1979; 1996). The availability of stone rather than the more friable brick influenced a materials choice which allowed high buildings. Climate, tradition and the relatively low levels of real and cash income for Scottish wage earners all contributed. It must be said, however, that in a European context the tenement was the dominant method of housing urban populations and ensuring that the best use could be made of the expensive land near to the markets and workplaces of the city. It is only by reference to the English habit of living in small roomed urban cottages that the Scottish tenement causes such debate.

The manner in which the Scots responded to the nature of their urban housing with its problems of health, morality and public order is illustrated by evidence from the 1885 *Royal Commission on the Housing of the Working Classes*. In the nineteenth century Royal Commissions were a characteristic method by which policy makers and public opinion explored a wide variety of issues. The summary of their Scottish evidence showed a clear preference for using private acts of parliament specific to each city rather than the national acts like Cross's Act which had been made available by the Westminister Parliament. There were two reasons for this. Firstly, because Scotland had its own distinctive property laws, early public health and housing acts had either ignored Scotland or come much later than equivalent English ones, thus leaving action to local initiatives. In most places this related to a long Scottish tradition of strong civic regulation. Secondly, Scotland was fortunate in that the urban industrial centres of the nineteenth century in general, already had an established system of urban government, usually in the form of the Royal Burghs. There were no 'Birminghams' and 'Manchesters' with their assorted systems of parishes and improvement commissions. These Royal Burghs had sustained a powerful tradition of regulation and direction. The Dean of Guild was an old quasi medieval office which rapidly adapted itself to the control and regulation of building. The few exceptions such as Motherwell and Coatbridge were ones which proved the rule. This reliance on the initiative of the locality was responsible for the very wide range of civic provision and consciousness in Scottish cities.

> EXERCISE 3
> Explore the variations in civic spending shown in the figures in the Appendix
> and compare the institutional and civic provisions outlined in the *Gazetteer* case
> studies (**Document 110;** see also **Articles 33 and 34**).

There are large variations in civic spending between the big spenders represented by
the big cities of Edinburgh and Glasgow which spent over £3 per head in 1901 and a
small fishing town such as Buckie which spent 7/- (35p) per head in the same year.
The *Gazetteer* shows that the long-established towns such as Selkirk and Hawick
benefited more from voluntary and charitable contributions to municipal infrastructure than relatively 'new' towns like Coatbridge and Motherwell. They also had
a much longer tradition of civic government to draw on.

Royal Commissions consisted of men chosen by parliament to represent a variety
of interests, thus a direct study of this evidence makes it possible to examine the
housing question with the information and prejudices of some of the leading
policy makers. These men questioned and heard evidence from expert witnesses.
Henry Broadhurst, for example, was a trades union leader and hence represented
'the working classes'. **Document 111** is an extract from his questioning of Sir
William Collins, one of Glasgow's reform-minded Lord Provosts which gives
some indication of the complex decisions working people took when they
decided where to live and the factors which influenced their decisions. Other
evidence contained in the Report includes that of Robert Paterson, the city
valuator and assessor for Edinburgh, who laid his detailed knowledge of
property, its owners and its occupiers before the Commission. All the paradoxes
produced by the market were evident in his evidence – there was considerable
overcrowding but houses were empty with little incentive for more building (RC
1884–85, Qs 18605 to 18635). James Gowans, Lord Dean of Guild gave a
useful account of the manner in which an ancient office from the pre-reform
period had turned into a tough agent of building regulation. Despite his breezy
confidence his evidence showed that the simple intervention of local government
authority together with a limited amount of philanthropy was only a partial
solution which helped some better paid wage earners but not the unskilled (RC
1884–85, Qs 18841 to 18874 and 18917 to 18938). The statistics quoted in
Table 3 were provided by Dr Littlejohn, another Edinburgh witness, appointed
Medical Officer of Health in 1862. He was one of a new type of paid official
who brought his professional skills to the service of a local authority. The use of
statistics, especially those collected by the state through the Census and the
Registrar General of Birth, Deaths and Marriages, were a key feature of the
debates of this period. Without these the policy makers would have operated
blind, guided by prejudice and anecdote. Statistics like this carried increasing
authority in public debate.

TABLE 3: DISTRICT DEATH RATES AND POPULATION DENSITIES, EDINBURGH 1863 AND 1883

District	DEATHS PER 1000		PERSONS PER ACRE	
	1863	1883	1863	1883
Upper New Town	17.4	15.1	90.3	63.4
Lower New Town	15.5	16.2	95.4	87.8
Canongate	31.2	27.5	206.7	178.9
Tron	34.6	28.9	314.5	178.5
St Giles	28.8	22.4	121.8	102.3
Grassmarket	32.5	26.9	237.6	204.4
Nicholson St	29.0	21.1	286.0	301.1
Newington	21.79	17.34	21.1	47.7
Grange	13.78	15.81	7.5	36.7
Morningside	22.5	18.3	4.1	12.6

Source: Evidence of Dr Littlejohn to Royal Commission on the Housing of the Working Classes, PP 1884–85, vol 31.

The changes over time and the contrasts between areas invited the reader to relate the contrast in death rates and their improvement to the nature of the areas and to the 'improvements' carried out under the 1866 Edinburgh Act. They diverted attention from other factors not related to area, such as improvements in nutrition, changes in the nature of disease, better understanding of sick nursing and the use of isolation policies for infectious diseases. The four poorer areas, Canongate, Tron, St Giles and Grassmarket showed clear improvements in death rate and the reduction in density marked the clearances of the Improvement Act (Morris 1992). At the same time there were improvements in almost all other areas. It may be that some of the displaced population found its way into the Lower New Town and the Grange. There were other influences at work. The expansion of the central business district reduced population in both districts of the New Town whilst southward suburban expansion led to population increases in the Grange, Newington and Morningside. In the latter case the middle class tradesmen of Newington and the white collar workers of Morningside were able to increase population density without a rise in the death rate but then their new housing was being built under the watchful eye of the Dean of Guild armed with growing powers under Police and Improvement Acts.

EXERCISE 4

Identify the influences upon the major features of urban authority in Scotland; what aspects of this authority were specifically Scottish?

Scotland had a strong tradition of urban government, usually through royal burghs which had a long tradition of regulations and direction. The quasi-medieval office of

45 The narrow of the Murraygate, looking south-west, 1875. *Dundee University Archives.*

46 Stewart's Court, looking from The Seagate towards Gellatly Street, 1876. *Dundee University Archives.*

Dean of Guild, for example, could be adapted to the control and regulation of building. Only in a few exceptions like Coatbridge and Motherwell was the local government framework missing, unlike the situation in England where many new industrial towns had to cope with a diversity of practices of improvement commissions.

The Commission also took evidence from Sir William Collins, publisher and, in 1877, the first teetotal campaigner to be Lord Provost of Glasgow. With him was JB Russell, Medical Officer of Health in Glasgow between 1872 and 1892, a man especially active in campaigns against poor housing conditions. Two themes emerged from their evidence. The first involved the complex decisions working people made when they chose where to live. The labour market for the whole family, the food market and the provision of services such as education were as relevant as the housing market. It is important to see wage earners treating the whole of Glasgow as the arena for their decisions and not just one district. They were able to do this because of the transport provided by train and tram – products of the industrial technologies which had so transformed the economy of their city. The second issue involved the nature and use of authority within the city. Glasgow had a more ambitious and assertive civic tradition than Edinburgh but both Collins and Gowans were perplexed by the limited success of their attempt to improve housing through the market (RC 1884–85, Q's 19439–19493). In 1885, the policy makers of Glasgow were still fearful of displacing the profit seeking private builder as the provider of better housing (Hart 1982: **Article 33**).

4. THE POLICE ACT OF 1862

In Scottish cities property, wealth and income operated through the market with the support of law and contract. Such market authority was sustained and at times modified by the authority of the urban place. By the mid and late nineteenth century, this authority was based upon a distinctive series of national and local acts of parliament. (Morris 1990a; **Document 112**). The most important was the Police Act of 1862 which enabled relatively small populations, with the approval of the Sheriff of the County, to form themselves into quasi autonomous jurisdictions with powers of taxation and regulation under the Act. Such actions enabled the populations of these police burghs to exclude the regulations and taxation of other urban jurisdictions. Many middle class residential suburban populations which were in functional terms part of a larger whole were able to declare 'independence' in this way. Portobello was separate from Edinburgh and Broughty Ferry from Dundee. Other industrial places, of which a number of fishing burghs like Pulteneytown were the most distinctive, sustained separate existence with low levels of tax and services.

EXERCISE 5
Check the occupational character of some of these places in the Appendix of data for 1901; look at the spending character of these burghs.

Broughty Ferry, a former fishing village, displays a typical middle-class employment pattern by 1901 with men in professional and commercial occupations amounting to some 15% of the male population over the age of ten and unoccupied females accounting for 64% of the female population over that age. Rutherglen displays a very different pattern with some 20% of men employed in metals, compared to 4% in Broughty Ferry. Unoccupied females accounted for some 78% of the female population of Rutherglen. The thrifty citizens of Rutherglen spent a mere 34p a head on burgh expenditure in 1901 which compared with Broughty Ferry's £1.77 a head, although neighbouring Dundee spent £2.25 a head.

The most spectacular result of this legislation was the creation of a 'ring of burghs' around Glasgow, each with distinctive industrial and residential characteristics and regulations, service levels and taxation to match. As the population of Glasgow expanded, its élite began to feel increasingly restricted by, and resentful of, these burghs which were functionally part of Glasgow but separated in terms of authority. From the late 1870s, the case for expansion was guided with considerable skill by Glasgow's town clerk, JD Marwick. The initial result was the City of Glasgow Act implemented in 1891 which brought six of the police burghs and several outlying communities into Glasgow's jurisdiction. Kinning Park joined in 1905 and Govan and Partick in 1912. The case for expansion was examined with great care by the Glasgow Boundaries Commission which reported in 1888 (Fraser and Maver 1996; **Document 112**). The Commission recognised the separate identities and character of many of the areas involved but set out clear reasons why in an urban area these interdependent places should be under one authority. Some areas simply lacked the critical mass to sustain adequate services. Other areas were failing to contribute to services from which their inhabitants benefited both directly and indirectly. There were also some urban functions like river purification and disease control that required unified and coordinated authority. The evidence of the Boundary Commission contained a debate about the nature of urbanism and its proper relationship to urban power.

EXERCISE 6
What were the main issues in the Glasgow boundary extension debate. How far do they have a wider relevance to understanding Scottish urban authority ?

Document 112 clearly shows that the small police burghs surrounding Glasgow were dependent on Glasgow for services such as water supply and tramways but had severe shortcomings in their police and fire services. **Article 33** shows that municipalisation of water, gas, tram and electricity services by a 'progressive' authority like Glasgow could reduce the cost of public services through economies of scale. As urban areas grew and improved transport systems allowed people to live further and further from their work, these were issues that concerned all Scottish cities.

*   *   *

The formidable nature of the power appropriated and thought to be legitimate in the Scottish civic tradition has already been mentioned in terms of building regulations, but this power showed itself in a number of other distinctive ways. In many royal burghs a common good fund had been accumulated from the collection of market tolls and the management of corporation property. This 'common good fund' was often used to promote local projects such as the development of the university in Glasgow. The creative use of power may be contrasted with its more repressive aspects such as the ticketed houses (Morris 1990a). This was the basis of an especially hostile relationship between the poorer sections of urban societies and the authorities. It was yet one more feature which denied privacy and self direction to large numbers of urban working people.

5. THE CHARACTER OF URBAN PLACES

By 1901, the urban places had a distinctive range of spending and ambition as well as distinctive labour markets and social structures. Regulation and social order were much more than the local implementation of state power. Scottish cities produced a rich associational and institutional culture, with even small towns such as Hawick and Selkirk showing considerable variety (**Document 110**). In the metal towns which had seen recent, rapid growth, associational life was sparse and the emphasis was on less open types of organisation. The older centres inherited an active associational life from pre-nineteenth century corporate and craft organisations. Voluntary and quasi autonomous associations both played an active part in developing and experimenting with social relationships, in the formation and expression of social and political interests and in mediating between different social groups. It is significant that Motherwell ended the century with a series of violent strikes and trade disputes which required military intervention, whilst tiny Selkirk produced co-operative forms in both production and retailing (Duncan 1991; Gilbert 1985). The French political analyst Alexis de Tocqueville saw autonomous voluntary associations of this type as characteristic of civil and political culture in Britain and the United States and suggested that they were the basis for a successful and tolerant system of representative government. Scotland had played an active and innovative part in the development of associations, notably in Mechanics Institutions, Temperance Associations and Savings Banks in the early part of the century (Morris 1990b).

Scottish towns were places of consumption as well as production. In Edinburgh, Princes Street, George Street and the Bridges area of the central business district became increasingly elaborate theatres of consumption. When John Reid published his *New Illustrated Guide to Edinburgh* at the end of the century, the new buildings of Messrs Jenner and Co (1893–95) were mentioned along with the hotels, galleries and historical buildings. The visitor was told that it was 'in the free Renaissance style . . . decorated with statuary, the female figures giving symbolical expression to the fact that women have made the business concern a success'. It was a wonderful scrapbook in stone borrowing from Jacobean England, the Loire and the Bodleian

Library Oxford. This was a place for fantasy shopping very different from the earlier simple shops and warehouses of South Bridge. Glasgow had a retail architecture which showed more confidence in the new industrial materials of steel and glass. This retailing infrastructure was not only a matter of theatre and fantasy but also a serious means of informing those with money of the products of industry and trade. It was an education which enabled consumers to select and create their own material worlds. In 1894, there were Highland ornaments and the latest novelties in electro plate from Thomas Smith and Sons in Princes Street or watches and gold teeth plates from BJ Moloney two blocks away. David Foulis at 61 George Street offered the Patent 'A1 Edinburgh Simplex' Convertible Range which promised 'an abundant supply of hot water' when fitted up 'by our own workmen'. That was a local product but Waterston of Frederick Street offered the Hitchcock Mechanical Safety Lamp from Watertown, New York. The smaller towns were also foci for consumption and information about the new material world of trade and industry. By the 1860s, High Street, Hawick was the place to find out about The Alexandra, Pilbeam's Patent Lock Stitch Sewing Machine which 'no family should be without'. No-one in Melrose needed to feel left behind in matters of dress as William Sinclair had just 'secured the services of an EXPERIENCED WEST END CUTTER from London'. In the high streets of the border towns could be found Edinburgh confectionery, pattern books for all makes of wallpaper, information on pen nibs from Birmingham and billiard tables from Edinburgh as well as endless information on fencing and sheep dip (Rutherfurd 1866).

The urban place was a place of interaction. The *Gazetteer* extracts (**Document 110**) detail bank branches which tied local families and business into a national and international economic system. The Post Office, the newspapers and the rail station were part of the same system. Historians tend to read local newspapers for information about the locality in which they were published but the original purchasers used them as a point of access to national and world news. A content analysis of a newspaper like the *Edinburgh Evening Courant* shows that it was as much about the parliament and court in London, about diplomatic activity in Europe and the Empire, about prices in New York and Liverpool as about local events. Water supply, sewage and drainage, telegraph and railway linked towns and the elements of towns. Industrial technology and trade played a crucial part in the physical fabric which was essential to the effective organisation of urban life. Many documents of urban life in Scotland deserve more notice than they get: the man-hole covers cast by some forgotten company in Falkirk or the surviving items of nine-teenth-century sanitary ware from Barrhead get hardly a glance in their daily use (Oglethorpe 1996).

The diary of John Inglis, chief clerk and assistant cashier to an Edinburgh legal firm shows how one man used this complex of locations, flows and opportunities around 1880. Inglis was not a wealthy man but one of the better paid of Edinburgh's growing army of white collar workers. In many ways he used the city as people like him must have done for 200 years. Talk or 'a bit of crack' was important, in the street or with friends who came to tea at the weekend. Inglis walked a great deal, to work and back or for recreation. (As towns grew larger specific public places like Princes Street Gardens and the Arboretum became more important). He used a range of institutional resources that had only become available since the 1820s, such as the Mechanics Library and the Savings Bank. Inglis was able to vote in national and local elections. He attended lectures at the School of Arts and the Oddfellows Hall. Cheap readily available newsprint greatly widened his experience. The *Scotsman* newspaper was important to Inglis. Through it he learnt about the collapse of the City of Glasgow Bank, military disasters in South Africa and the Tay Bridge disaster. He read a wide range of political speeches. Ideas on vegetarianism and rational thought came through the periodical press like the *National Reformer*. The railway was important to Inglis for business trips to North Berwick and Aberdeen. He used the suburban lines for visits to friends in Slateford and to Aunt Lily at Joppa. The North British Railway took the family for holiday at Innerleithen. He does not often mention the town as a place of consumption although he saw a 'skillet' at Grays the ironmongers in George Street, and that 'wringing machine' Teen (his wife) spoke of in the Grassmarket (Vaughan 1984). Inglis learnt French and German and read widely. His Edinburgh was a very Scottish city (he read Ferguson 'for the old Scottish words'), but it was also a world city in which he used his knowledge of languages to answer letters in French and German.

EXERCISE 7
Discuss the claim that Scottish towns and cities must be understood as places of consumption as well as places of production.

By the end of the nineteenth century, a city like Edinburgh could boast of a 'theatre of consumption' like Princes Street and Jenner's new buildings of 1893–5 as the jewel in the crown. Even a smaller place like Melrose could claim 'an experienced West End cutter from London'. **Document 110** shows a working-class town like Motherwell opening a new Co-operative store in 1894.

6. THE POST-WAR PERIOD

After the 1914–18 war, Scotland experienced a considerable slow-down in economic growth, and hence in urban growth. This slow-down varied across different regions and types of urban place (Rodger 1996). The period after 1918 was marked by a long battle to control and direct the urban environment. Whilst housing remained the major urban problem, economic development and regeneration gained increasing importance. Urban policy experienced an increasing struggle between central and local agencies of government. Local authority housing became an increasing element of housing stock but only within a legislative and financial context provided by central government. The various functions of the poor law withered away to be replaced, in general, by agencies directed from the centre. Poor Law payments were supplemented and then replaced. After the 1911 National Insurance Act, unemployment benefit was controlled by the Ministry of Labour in

London but sickness payments were controlled by what became the Department of Health (Scotland) in 1921. In 1934, means tested benefits were directed by the London-based Unemployment Assistance Board, leaving the sick, widows and elderly with the Poor Law until the transfer to the National Assistance Board in 1948. This marked the true end of a poor law controlled by a locally based representative body. By 1947, the poor law hospitals had been transferred to Regional Hospital Boards.

In Scotland, this centre/local tension had a distinctive feature. After 1920, the Scottish Office, created in 1885 and located in Dover House, London, became an increasingly coherent agency, with growing powers and a physical and bureaucratic presence in Edinburgh. As a result Scotland had an integrated urban hierarchy and distinct legal system (unlike Wales) as well as the ability to form a 'view' across the whole range of domestic policy which (unlike England) could be represented as such both in cabinet and in relationships with urban authorities. For urban authorities, the Scottish Office was a formidable agency which not only mediated between the locality and Westminster but also formed a focus of initiative and policy within Scotland. This was demonstrated by the Scottish Special Housing Association (SSHA), formed in 1937, which became an active agency of the Scottish Office in the face of considerable local authority hostility. This hostility was most evident in the tension between Glasgow Corporation and the Scottish Office around the policy recommendations of the Clyde Valley Report of 1946 (Abercrombie and Matthew 1949) which urged the dispersal of over half million people from Glasgow as a solution to housing shortage and overcrowding. Evidence of Glasgow's reluctance to lose population appeared in the many tower blocks built within the city in the 1960s. The Scottish Office countered this with the attractions of a number of new towns: East Kilbride (1947), Cumbernauld (1955) and Irvine (1966). The SSHA was active with scattered and often small scale housing development, one of the most important being 1,500 houses built around Linwood in support of the new Rootes/Crystler car factory. In 1965, the Highlands and Islands Development Board (HIDB) initiated its growth centre policies (Butt and Gordon 1985). In 1975 the Scottish Development Agency (SDA) created a series of urban regeneration projects such as the Glasgow East End Renewal scheme. Like the New Town Corporations and the SSHA, these bodies were agents of the Scottish Office and drove urban policies from a national, that is a Scottish perspective, rather than from a local or civic perspective (Donnison 1987). Since 1970 centre/local tension has appeared in the reform and re-reform of local government which has often had the desire to curb the power of Glasgow (Gordon 1985; Keating and Midwinter 1983).

The same challenges to local identity and control can be seen in the less pressured environment of Selkirk. In 1964 the SSHA started to build 226 houses with the national architect Sir Basil Spence. The local gas works closed in 1953 and were replaced by the national grid. The Selkirk Picture House (cinema) closed to be replaced by the home-based consumption, but national production (UK and Scotland), of television entertainment. Economics and technology, as well as government structures, all detracted from local control and identity (Gilbert 1985).

The twentieth century also saw the introduction of a variety of new ways of thinking about, and responding to, urbanism. Scotland not only adopted ideas available from the networks and flows of western industrial capitalist society but also made innovatory contributions. Patrick Geddes, the Edinburgh-based natural scientist and intellectual, became a cult figure for a national and international town planning movement (Meller 1990). His thinking is perhaps best represented by the material on Edinburgh which he prepared for his influential Cities and Town Planning Exhibition in 1910. He saw cities as carriers of cultures and civilisation which could only be understood by a study of the city in the context of its region and history. Social relationships and physical fabric had been deeply damaged by the unregulated pursuit of profit during industrialisation. The 'problems' thus created could be solved in an evolutionary way by the intervention of professionals – the planners. Geddes' methods of survey and his holistic plan which was concerned with social relations, with the quality of cultural life and with physical conditions, were important for a generation of planners like Patrick Abercrombie (see below). His almost mystical insistence on the importance of trees and gardens and upon the evolutionary link between a city and its past was too easily forgotten.

Charles Rennie Macintosh was a designer and architect associated with the Glasgow style, a distinctive part of a wider European movement often identified with Vienna (Kaplan 1996). Perhaps in retrospect it was not the flowing lines and sparing use of ornamentation which were important but his assertive ambition to provide his clients with a total integrated package of house, furniture and decoration, his 'style'. Equally significant was a relationship which dominated urban patterns of consumption. Macintosh appropriated and contributed to national and international streams of taste and style whilst producing something linked to a specific place in a distinctive way. It was a clear case of the Irn Bru versus the Coca Cola relationship in urban experience.

The Civic Survey and Plan for Edinburgh prepared by Sir Patrick Abercrombie in 1949 shared many of the characteristics of the total area plans prepared for Scottish cities in the years after the 1939–45 war. The inspirational guidance of Geddes had been replaced by a more stark, more practical, but still highly moralised, confidence that the scientific analysis of the problem could produce solutions. Issues tackled included the importance of the motor car as well as of housing, the use of classification and separation of function (zoning), the faith in modern technology and architecture, and the very equivocal and limited appreciation of historical architecture (Abercrombie and Plumstead 1949). The plan was driven by the principles of dispersion of the population from densely built areas in the inner city and containment by the green belt. Over the next thirty years the general aims of the planners were subverted by a population increase above prediction, a failure to anticipate the impact of mass car ownership in terms of pollution and congestion, the poor quality of much modern building and architecture and a major change in popular taste towards a wider appreciation of the buildings of the past.

There were others who did not seek to control and direct the city but endeavoured to express the nature of the urban experience in a variety of ways. In the 1950s and

1960s, Oscar Marzaroli, a Glasgow photographer, and his friend, the painter Joan
Eardley, worked to capture brief moments of beauty and humanity in the squalid
conditions of Glasgow (Oliver 1988). In their pictures people became actors rather
than victims waiting to be planned into a problem free life. In their photographs and
paintings, working class people enjoy themselves, shout, smile or simply exist in
streets awaiting demolition or tower blocks which have not yet become targets of
social criticism. The 1970s and 1980s belonged more to the novelists. Some were a
type of *roman noir d'écosse*, notably in the work of William McIlvanney (1983).
One of the most outstanding was *Lanark*, by Alasdair Gray, a complex surrealist
tale of the incoherent, fragmented, dislocated nature of urban experience. The most
extreme account of urban chaos and loss of control is Irvine Welsh's Edinburgh
novel *Trainspotting*. Its drug culture status should not hide its importance for
expressing a particular sort of Scottish urban experience.

The increasingly chaotic and aggressive nature of urban representation in Scotland is one reflection of the fundamental changes affecting Scottish towns. These
changes were heralded by local government re-organisation in the mid 1970s which
deliberately created districts and regions designed to unite urban and rural areas in
single functional units spreading the costs of services in a more effective and
equitable manner. Urban projects were rapidly overwhelmed by changes in the
world economy leading to the de-industrialisation of many areas and culminating in

47 Sketch of Princes Street Bypass Scheme. From P Abercrombie and D Plumstead
1949 *A Civic Survey and Plan for the City and Royal Burgh of Edinburgh*, (Oliver
& Boyd), Edinburgh.

the closure of the Ravenscraig Steel works near Motherwell in the early 1990s. Government initiatives to provide re-training and to ameliorate environmental deterioration could do little to halt this trend. Outward migration by Scottish people and inward investment by international firms seeking appropriate labour and investment grant conditions were the major responses. By the mid 1980s changes in communications and consumption patterns were turning many cities inside out. The Scottish version of 'edge city' was established. These areas were already notable for massive local authority housing schemes and were marked by many indicators of urban deprivation such as unemployment, juvenile crime and perinatal mortality. They were joined on the urban outskirts by the motorway by-pass, by manufacturing plants and in the 1990s by the shopping mall and company office. The latter depended more on proximity to the motorway and airport than to the railway station and central business district. In successful cities, central locations have been gentrified with abandoned offices, factories and warehouses being converted to dwelling places. Cities have competed to attract cultural events, festivals, museums and leisure facilities, often using historical cultural identities as pawns in a bitter contest for prestige and investment. This process is by no means over.

ACKNOWLEDGEMENTS

My thanks to Richard Rodger and Ian Levitt for help and advice with this chapter.

REFERENCES TO BOOKS AND ARTICLES MENTIONED IN THE TEXT

Barth, G 1980 *City People. The Rise of Modern City Culture in nineteenth century America*. Oxford.

Butt, J and Gordon, G (eds) 1985 *Strathclyde. Changing Horizons*. Edinburgh.

Donnison, D and Middleton A (eds) 1987 *Regenerating the Inner City. Glasgow's Experience*. London.

Duncan, R 1991 *Steelopolis. The Making of Motherwell, c. 1750–1939*. Motherwell District Council.

Fraser, WH and Maver, I 1996 *Glasgow, Vol II: 1830 to 1912*. Manchester.

Gilbert, JM (ed) 1985 *Flower of the Forest, Selkirk: a new history*. Selkirk Common Good Fund.

*Gordon, G (ed) 1985 *Perspectives of the Scottish City*. Aberdeen.

Gray, A 1982 *Lanark. A life in 4 Books*. London.

Kaplan, W 1996 *Charles Rennie Mackintosh*. Glasgow and London.

Keating, M and Midwinter, A 1983 *The Government of Scotland*. Edinburgh.

McIlvanney, W 1983 *The Papers of Tony Veitch*. London.

McKichan 1978 'A burgh's response to the problems of urban growth: Stirling, 1780–1880', *Scottish Historical Review* 57, 68–86.

Meller, H 1990 *Patrick Geddes. Social Evolutionist and City Planner*. London.

*Morris, RJ 1990a 'Urbanisation and Scotland', *in* Fraser, WH and Morris, RJ (eds), *People and Society in Scotland, vol II, 1830–1914*, Edinburgh, 73–102.

Morris, RJ 1990b 'Associations', *in* Thompson, FML (ed), *The Cambridge Social History of Britain, 1750–1950*, vol 3, Cambridge, 395–443.

Morris, RJ 1992 'Death, Chambers Street and Edinburgh Corporation', *History Teaching Review, The Yearbook of the Scottish Association of Teachers in History* 6, 10–15.

Oglethorpe, M 1996 'The Bathroom and the Water Closet', *in* Carruthers, A (ed), *The Scottish Home*, Edinburgh, 203–21.

Oliver, C 1988 *Joan Eardley, RSA*. Edinburgh.

Rodger, R 1979 'The Law and Urban Change', *Urban History Yearbook*.

*Rodger, R 1996 'Urbanisation in Twentieth-Century Scotland', *in* Devine, TM and Finlay, RJ (eds), *Scotland in the 20th Century*, Edinburgh, 123–52.

Rodger, R (ed) 1989 *Scottish Housing in the Twentieth Century*. Edinburgh.

Weber, M 1958 *The City* (edited and translated by D Martindale and G Neuwith from text of 1921). New York and London.

Welsh, I 1993 *Trainspotting*. London.

Wirth, L 1938 'Urbanism as a way of life', *in* Reiss, AJ (ed), *Louis Wirth. On Cities and Social Life*, Chicago, 60–83.

FURTHER READING

Those references marked * in the above list are recommended further reading.

PRIMARY SOURCES MENTIONED IN THE TEXT

Abercrombie, P and Matthew, R 1949 *The Clyde Valley Regional Plan*. Edinburgh.

Abercrombie, P and Plumstead, D 1949 *A Civic Survey and Plan for the City and Royal Burgh of Edinburgh*. Edinburgh.

Census of Scotland, 1911, British Parliamentary Papers 1912–13, vol 109.

Census report for Scotland, General Register Office for Scotland, 1991.

Inglis, J 1984 *A Victorian Edinburgh Diary* (edited by Ena Vaughan). Edinburgh.

Local Taxation Returns (Scotland), 1900–1901. British Parliamentary Papers, 1903, vol 59.

Royal Commission on the Housing of the Working Classes, British Parliamentary Papers, 1884–85, vol 31.

Rutherfurd, J and JH 1866 *The Southern Counties Register and Directory with the Counties of Roxburgh, Berwick and Selkirk* (Reprint 1990). Borders Regional Library, Selkirk.

APPENDIX

Key statistics relating to all Scottish burghs of more than 5000 population in 1901

burgh	POPULATION	MALES 10+	FEMALES 10+	PROFESSIONAL MALE	DOMESTIC FEMALE	COMMERCIAL MALE	TEXTILE MALE	TEXTILE FEMALE	FISHING MALE	MINES AND QUARRIES MALE	METALS MALE	BUILDING MALE	UNOCCUPIED MALE	UNOCCUPIED FEMALES	EXPENDITURE £	NET VALUATION £
Aberdeen	153503	52822	64634	1653	5597	2671	1466	3960	976	2477	4948	5291		42798	375366	771093
Airdrie	22288	8433	7759	156	538	283	152	504	0	1580	2179	721		5764	10832	64089
Alloa	11421	4160	4588	125	348	188	299	524	15	43	953	316		3083	24803	52305
Arbroath	22398	7445	10238	222	551	266	1250	2384	210	25	953	609		6015	33995	83829
Ardrossan	6077	2305	2278	46	242	112	14	20	0	21	305	164		1703	1156	29209
Ayr	28697	10269	12056	374	1491	490	265	545	27	199	791	1403		7999	49810	167609
Barrhead	9855	3659	3681	47	330	140	440	490	1	46	758	462		2416	5547	28708
Bathgate	6786	2677	2311	56	214	62	30	62	0	781	252	233		1725	3356	17392
Borrowstounness	9306	3669	3199	70	240	109	16	20	3	517	602	223		2307	12382	34879
Brechin	8941	2895	4268	98	282	83	658	1340	0	56	135	334		2182	9591	31618
Broughty Ferry	10484	3386	4940	158	987	345	226	143	130	29	154	305		3178	18621	58421
Buckhaven	8000	2953	2753	43	105	33	59	300	183	1247	82	153		2087	4352	18312
Buckie	6549	2194	2643	51	235	22	52	73	658	3	105	189		2030	2297	13633
Campbeltown	8286	2938	3301	76	390	90	35	49	318	17	321	334		2448	11291	37930
Carnoustie	5204	1744	2372	71	166	110	130	263	15	5	150	179		1627	4207	23808
Clydebank	18670	7505	6096	47	201	137	32	44	7	22	4271	669		4655	1825	84620
Coatbridge	36991	15205	11960	217	922	416	80	90	0	1654	6699	917		9530	21486	165497
Cowdenbeath	7457	2842	2399	33	72	27	46	20	0	1638	52	158		1787	3013	13538
Crieff	5208	1747	2443	97	467	50	40	309	0	24	67	254		1572	3978	31287
Dalkeith	6753	2479	2790	85	327	120	125	189	0	258	120	260		1889	4778	29699
Denny/Dunipace	5158	1863	1771	25	103	32	9	5	0	609	327	108		1300	5133	11348
Dumbarton	19985	7748	7235	134	551	188	63	426	4	27	3994	583		5346	22869	72375
Dumfries	13092	4549	5580	217	723	167	354	564	1	60	236	433		3388	30701	74551
Dundee	161173	53677	72723	1177	3007	2618	12117	27655	19	474	6662	4409		35156	363005	788643
Dunfermline	25250	8737	10992	233	519	301	1169	2979	0	1535	589	797		6517	41899	88205
Dunoon	6779	2226	3323	111	479	124	41	49	13	25	159	368		2353	18389	62640
Edinburgh	317459	113982	142231	6755	22823	8173	1257	1495	13	25	7911	13614		88573	989954	2519609
Elgin	8407	2792	3909	167	634	128	156	187	0	47	156	405		2555	15789	39335
Falkirk	29280	11867	9917	266	785	575	70	49	0	288	4711	970		7764	47318	105191
Forfar	11397	3678	5219	122	293	136	838	1702	0	36	193	377		2699	18324	41695

Place														
Fraserburgh	9105	3200	3485	57	446	81	56	39	391	19	175	166	2363	5299	33157
Galashiels	13615	4822	6174	111	397	178	1681	1670	1	25	290	344	3360	10349	62360
Glasgow	761709	288039	303143	6875	24094	20708	9169	18386	14	3640	53382	25538	191671	2804738	4627392
Grangemouth	8386	3554	2781	45	191	182	25	18	4	89	409	245	2244	8375	50213
Greenock	68142	26477	26012	524	1850	1213	269	1880	1	107	8211	2068	18595	157601	318883
Gourock	5244	1787	2393	81	326	168	28	27	1	66	173	166	1709	11056	39425
Govan	82174	29646	27569	324	1200	1265	347	864	8	130	11931	2673	19843	84284	341709
Hamilton	32775	13143	10815	249	712	355	117	215	0	5696	539	934	8466	56937	107198
Hawick														17143	67595
Helensburgh	8554	5842	8117	112	671	235	33	26	4	26	262	466	2843	18913	68275
Inverness	21238	7735	4199	325	713	212	192	128	11	31	156	405	6331	38746	111753
Irvine	9618	3524	3614	102	342	421	38	122	18	53	704	956	2641	12512	28531
Johnstone	10503	3722	4255	45	140	111	549	1153	0	396	504	417	2554	14922	36696
Kilmarnock	34165	12824	13251	266	919	426	501	1300	1	759	3479	1292	8952	57313	140798
Kilsyth	7292	2790	2438	42	129	46	37	94	0	1353	62	131	1931	6427	16278
Kinning park	13852	5156	5091	40	246	180	51	152	0	38	1488	421	3510	9808	62493
Kirkcaldy	34079	12391	14211	251	759	393	823	2642	12	783	1153	1245	8971	33488	139961
Kirkin-tilloch	10502	3933	3948	73	381	215	119	333	0	701	916	334	2805	15121	34252
Lanark	5084	1815	2188	70	211	47	71	192	2	181	64	246	1433	4549	18124
Leith	77439	29597	29834	614	2696	1647	376	789	267	121	3585	2457	20679	145599	471197
Leven	5577	2036	2148	57	168	60	95	219	0	510	192	183	1506	2763	17615
Lockgelly	5472	2107	1748	28	75	29	14	107	0	1257	48	130	1400	2167	9755
Maxwell-town	5796	1971	2596	89	272	64	270	322	3	18	18	236	1613	2138	22409
Maybole	5892	2107	2182	40	117	75	17	10	0	7	110	105	1432	3070	15008
Montrose	12427	4450	5674	132	611	126	375	995	64	14	239	369	3460	11153	54305
Motherwell	30418	12290	9622	123	391	317	68	165	0	2083	4188	735	8189	12685	109280
Musselburgh	11711	4227	4723	123	419	152	70	336	181	553	194	412	3171	12039	43692
Oban	5427	1956	2383	84	467	77	30	77	46	82	82	261	1535	7598	42737
Paisley	79363	27903	32912	596	1868	1326	2947	8279	3	413	4960	3027	19267	180267	328235
Partick	54298	20165	21216	574	2218	1578	286	280	6	139	6864	2115	15060	40985	265050
Peebles	5266	1847	2459	79	231	69	359	457	0	16	83	235	1505	9426	25944
Perth	32873	11908	14422	456	1295	576	1198	1999	18	62	790	1327	8646	86297	175702
Peterhead	11794	3866	4780	86	585	99	95	123	512	54	225	308	3322	13259	42234
Pollokshaws	11183	3897	4572	75	503	261	332	679	0	190	506	442	2841	5530	38922
Port Glasgow	16857	6448	6145	69	205	131	214	1196	6	16	3660	430	4240	22377	58046
Pulteneytoun	5137	1830	2040	50	136	47	63	20	359	9	76	121	1602	1772	13356
Renfrew	9296	3545	3304	45	144	88	15	359	2	11	1976	239	2408	13124	31018
Rothesay	9378	3061	4437	141	648	165	45	69	31	33	134	395	2919	22049	69425
Rutherglen	16185	5788	6086	81	311	230	217	831	0	886	1032	487	4131	9268	47467
St Andrews	7621	2402	3913	184	944	62	29	15	91	20	70	318	2364	8858	56194
Saltcoats	8120	2696	3310	85	317	126	33	69	25	250	207	372	2397	5480	33112
Selkirk	5486	1921	2582	57	157	55	663	762	0	11	104	183	1424	7739	27048
Stirling	18403	6608	7814	246	1030	291	214	329	7	173	506	815	5090	24571	96727
Stranraer	6036	2139	2590	74	342	71	50	15	52	6	124	210	1789	3876	24096
Wishaw	20873	8284	6853	119	434	173	59	64	0	1734	2575	585	5515	21111	55891

Religion

Callum G Brown

The period since 1850 is one of enormous contrasts in the role of religion in Scottish life. The changes experienced were very similar to those felt in other developed countries such as England and Wales, the United States and parts of continental western Europe. In Scotland, as in these places, religion in the Victorian and Edwardian periods was immensely important in civil life, and in the first half of the twentieth century religious affairs remained extremely significant in both public affairs and in individuals' lives. From the late 1950s, however, dramatic and profound change occurred in the role of religion in people's lives, creating an ongoing crisis in the churches from which – in the late 1990s – there appears to be no easing. From a high point in church-going in the mid Victorian period and a high point of church connection in the first decade of this century, religion has, during the last four decades of the millennium, been slipping relentlessly from social significance.

This chapter takes the following major themes to investigate this transformation in religion in Scottish life:

- The changing church structure
- Religion in the cities; the churches and social policy
- The social experience of religion
- Catholics, assimilation and sectarianism

This builds upon the earlier chapter on the period between 1700 and 1850 in Volume 1. By the time you have completed these chapters, you should have a clear understanding of the changing role of religion in Scottish society since 1707.

I. THE CHANGING CHURCH STRUCTURE

In 1850 Scottish religion was in the midst of great change. The Free Church formed in 1843 had taken 37% of the clergy and upwards of 40% of the adherents of the Established Church of Scotland, adding to the substantial numbers of Protestants who had joined dissenting presbyterian churches in the previous hundred years. In 1847, the majority of 'old' presbyterian dissenters – those in the Secession and Relief churches – had come together in the United Presbyterian Church, constituting a prospering urban denomination with great local strength, notably in Glasgow where it was the largest single denomination in 1851. The potato famine brought tens of thousands of Irish immigrants, mostly Catholic and very poor, to Scotland in search of work and a living wage. The vast majority settled in Glasgow and its environs where the Catholic Church started to enjoy a surge in numbers. In addition, the 'hungry forties' had generated enormous diversification and experimentation in political, religious and ideological values amongst the Scottish working class, throwing up new social movements such as teeotalism and Chartism, and new churches, many of a highly evangelical character, such as the short-lived Chartist Church, the Church of the Latter Day Saints (the Mormons) and the Evangelical Union. From the cauldron of economic and demographic dislocation in the 1840s, there emerged new economic structures (notably the rise of heavy industry based on Clydeside shipbuilding and locomotive manufacture), new occupational and social groups (like the artisans of the so-called 'labour aristocracy'), 'respectable' working-class occupations like railway staff and policemen, and the 'new' middle class of commerce who peopled many of the new suburbs of the mid nineteenth century.

These changes to ecclesiastical, economic and social structures established a new context for organised religion in Scotland. The meaning of religion in Scottish civil society had changed dramatically since the eighteenth century. No longer was the state church, the Established Church of Scotland, the only church in a parish. As late as the mid 1830s, the Church of Scotland still had a strong grasp of worshipping Scots: even in Glasgow and Edinburgh, where the Church was weakest within Scotland, it retained the attendance of almost half of the churchgoers and the nominal adherence of many more. But by 1851, it was severely weakened. Only 32% of all those who went to church came through its doors, and less than a fifth of the population as a whole. In some parts of Scotland, the Established Church could not, after 1850, be described as a significant participant institution; in large cities like Glasgow and Edinburgh, and in most of the Highlands and Hebrides, less than 10% of the people worshipped in it. Though the establishment status of the Church of Scotland was to survive until the 1920s, by 1850 it was already a shadow of its former self.

One consequence was that the kirk session system of parish supervision finally fell apart in most of Scotland in the 1840s and 1850s. The parish minister and his elders no longer took an interest in the moral behaviour of parishioners as a whole, only taking an interest in those who were members and adherents. The Church of Scotland followed the example of the dissenters – the U.P. and Free churches – by concentrating increasingly on Victorian moral concerns: especially the drinking habits of members, and bringing to book any who might 'bring a scandal upon the body'. Churches were becoming private clubs – very large clubs – which embodied the ideals of Victorian society as a whole, and in so doing the kirk session systems of the presbyterian churches became concerned with the 'respectability' of the congregation rather than the moral state of all parishioners.

In other ways, the parish state was disintegrating. Already in 1845, the poor-relief system had been modified to reduce Church of Scotland control. Then in 1872, after a long fight, the dissenting presbyterian churches got their wish to abolish the parish schools of the Established Church and to create a national system of education under directly-elected school boards: one school board was created for every large city and for every other parish. Dissenting churchmen came to dominate these, standing as candidates for their own denomination, and even with the arrival of Labour representatives in the 1890s the school-board system preserved the influence of the churches under the school boards until 1919 and under their replacement, the County Education Authorities, until 1929. It was only at the beginning of the 1930s that the churches ceased their effective control of state education in toto. At the same time, however, the Roman Catholic Church in Scotland maintained separate schools for Catholic children. These were given the status of state schools from 1919. As a consequence of all this, the Protestant churches were, in the 1920s and 1930s, becoming extremely worried about the growing status of the Catholic Church whilst their own status was diminishing.

In effect, after 1845 the Church of Scotland was being subjected to a process of disestablishment. Its status as the state church had always rested on a mixture of powers and functions. These were whittled away by the legislative changes enacted by Parliament largely at the instigation of the powerful Free and U.P. churches. The Victorian period was the heyday of Protestant dissent in Scotland as it was in England and Wales. As Table 1 shows, the Church of Scotland was numerically overwhelmed by the adherents of other churches, especially the presbyterian dissenters in the Free and U.P. churches. The mid-Victorian years (between 1850 and 1875) witnessed spectacular growth in church connection, apparent in the

48 Alexander Penrose Forbes, Bishop of Brechin c. 1860. *Dundee University Archives.*

building of large numbers of churches in both urban and country areas of Scotland. New congregations were formed and older churches were replaced with new ones at a pace not seen before or since. However, from the 1870s onwards church growth slowed down appreciably, especially amongst the dissenters, and in 1900 the Free and U.P. churches amalgamated to form the United Free Church which then entered immediate negotiations for reunion with the Church of Scotland. That final major realignment in Scottish presbyterianism required the removal of virtually all the main forms of establishment from the Church of Scotland, and with that accomplished by parliamentary legislation in 1921 and 1925, the bulk of the U.F. Church was reabsorbed in the Church of Scotland in 1929. In the main, the church structure has remained unchanged from then until the present.

EXERCISE I
How did the civil status of the Church of Scotland change between 1850 and the present?

Briefly, the Church of Scotland found its civil functions in welfare and education eroded as the dissenters called upon the state to democratise these areas of society. Initially, the effect was to reinforce religious influence in the civil affairs, but in the early twentieth century the trend has been toward a truly 'secular' control of society's institutions.

The religious affiliations of the Scottish people have also shown significant

49 Free Church General Assembly, Inverness, 1888. *Dundee University Archives.*

changes between 1850 and the present – partly as a product of these modifications to the church structure. Table 1 summarises statistics of church adherence in Scotland between 1850 and 1990.

TABLE I CHURCH ADHERENCE IN SCOTLAND 1850–1994[1]

	CH. OF SCOT.	FREE CH. U.F. CHURCH[2]	U.P. CHURCH	OTHER PROT.[3]	R.C. CHURCH	OTHERS[4]	TOTAL AS %AGE OF POPULATION[5]
1850	271,902	198,570	128,571	68,449	169,059	2,998	26.5
1875	475,846	275,442	170,298	105,510	305,334	4,984	34.1
1900	661,629	492,964		187,083	446,733	10,539	38.9
1925	762,774	536,407		232,987	602,334	17,014	41.6
1950	1,271,247[2]	24,556		193,795	745,125	26,613	38.6
1975	1,041,772	14,198		146,851	813,000	44,568	33.3
1994	715,571	7,218		123,407	742,750	55,400	25.9

Notes:
1. This table shows actual, extrapolated or estimated figures for church communicants, members, adherents or 'claimed' population. Linear extrapolations have been used for 1850 (subject to weighting by data in the Religious Census 1851) and between datapoints. Estimations (partly based on marriage data) have been used notably for Jews, Muslims and 'New Religions'.
2. The vast bulk of the Free and U.P. churches amalgamated in 1900 to form the United Free (U.F.) Church, and the bulk of its members united with the Church of Scotland in 1929.
3. 'Other Protestant' includes the Free Church (post-1900), the Free Presbyterian and Associated Presbyterian churches, the Scottish Episcopal Church, all branches of the Methodist Church, the Congregationalists and the Baptists.
4. 'Others' includes Jews (which make up about 70% of the figures until 1950), Muslims (which makes up half the growth in this category after 1950), and the Church of the Latter Days Saints, Jehovah's Witnesses and other 'new religions' (which together make up the other half of the growth after 1950).
5. Total church adherence, excluding Sunday-school rolls, expressed as a percentage of total Scottish population.

Sources: These figures were drawn from the author's running dataset on annual Scottish church adherence, which is compiled and calculated from a wide variety of sources, the most important being R Currie, A Gilbert and L Horsley 1977 *Churches and Churchgoers: Church Growth in the British Isles since 1700*, Oxford, 128–221; J Highet 1960 *The Scottish Churches*, London, 54–69; and yearbooks and directories of the various denominations.

> EXERCISE 2
> Study Table 1 closely and comment on what it shows about (a) changes in the relative strength of the different churches between 1850 and 1994, and (b) changes in the level of religious connection amongst Scots as a whole over the same period.

Briefly, the figures in Table 1 show that the Church of Scotland suffered from vigorous growth by the Free, U.P. and other Protestant churches in the Victorian period, especially during 1850–75, but that it recovered in the twentieth century from the reclamation of the majority of presbyterian dissenters. Other Protestant churches – such as the Baptists and the Congregationalists – continued to grow strongly until the 1930s, whilst the Catholic Church enjoyed sustained growth until 1975. Meanwhile, other churches grew steadily – primarily the Jews from the late 1880s until the 1940s and Muslims and 'New Religions' after 1950. The column on the right-hand side of Table 1 shows a steady growth in the percentage of Scottish adults who were church adherents until 1925, and a decline thereafter – a decline that steepened between 1975 and 1994. All the Protestant churches showed a decline in numbers from 1950 to the present, whilst the decline in numbers in the Catholic Church began later, after 1975. With the rapid fall in church connection in 1975–94, only newer churches (notably Islam and the 'New Religions'), have bucked the trend of decline in organised religion in late twentieth century Scotland.

2. RELIGION IN THE CITIES: THE CHURCHES AND SOCIAL POLICY

We saw in Volume 1, Chapter 4, how the growth of industrial and commercial cities was perceived in the early nineteenth century as posing a problem for the churches. Thomas Chalmers, the doyen of Scottish presbyterian ministers, had been especially influential in raising concern amongst the rising urban middle classes as to the alienation of the working classes and the poor from church influence and control, and the resulting accumulation of 'so many masses of practical heathenism' in large towns. Though he died in 1847, his concern became, in the second half of the nineteenth century, the keystone of the 'home mission' to the working classes.

In 1851, Rev Robert Buchanan of the Free Tron Church in Glasgow told the Free Church general assembly:

> By far the greatest part of all the ministerial and pastoral work at present going on in our great towns is conducted on what we have learned, from the vocabulary of the great master of Church extension [Thomas Chalmers], to call the *attractive*, in contradistinction to the *aggressive* system. According to the attractive system, the place of worship is built, and the minister preaches to those who come to hear him, and with more or less fidelity watches over them, as one that must give account . . . [But] the attractive system leaves multitudes in all our great towns in a state of total estrangement from the house and ordinances of God . . . Whether men will believe it or no, there are elements of mischief gathering deep down in these dark and dismal recesses of the city that will spread havoc around them, if any social or political convulsion should stir them into life, and give them even a momentary triumph. Those demon-like figures that were seen mounting the barricades in Paris [in 1848], and shedding blood like water at the late revolution, few had ever beheld them before . . . I have often shuddered in traversing the wynds of Glasgow to think that we have there in abundance the very materials with which the St. Antoines and the St. Marceaux of Paris have, again and again, fed the flames of its frequent

revolutionary conflagrations . . . Surely, however, humanity and religion do not need such an argument to summon them into the field.

(Buchanan 1851, 6, 9)

This type of appeal for churches and schools to be built in Glasgow and other Scottish cities became a hallmark of Victorian evangelical religion, summoning the prospering businessmen and industrialists to magnanimous philanthropy and the middle and working classes to voluntary effort in dozens of types of 'aggressive' agencies of evangelisation. At the base of these agencies was the Sunday school, which emerged after 1850 – and remains to this day – as the primary organisation of youth recruitment to the Protestant churches. In 1851, there were 240,614 children enrolled in Sunday schools of the three main presbyterian churches alone and, by 1900, 458,668 – which represented 45% of all Scottish children aged five to fourteen years. After 1850, the Sunday school was joined by many other agencies of evangelisation: for older children Bible classes, young men's and women's prayer groups, Christian Endeavour, Gospel Temperance meetings, the Bands of Hope, the Good Templars, the Foundry Boys' and Girls' Religious Society, the Boys Brigades; and for adults, mill girls' prayer meetings, Mothers' Kitchen Meetings, and many more.

EXERCISE 3
Read **Document 113** and describe the nature and social impact of the 'aggressive system' of evangelisation in the middle of the nineteenth century.

Briefly, home missions combined different agencies of evangelisation in 'aggressive' visiting of the poor and working classes in their homes, through targeting of occupational and age groups, and through street preaching. Working-class neigh-bourhoods were bombarded by home-mission workers so that a powerful though diffusive religious culture was maintained in urban society.

The nature of home mission work changed in the early 1870s with the advent of urban revivalism, spawned especially by the American revivalists Moody and Sankey. Their visit to Scotland in 1874 turned evangelisation into very big business, replete with a show-business style of promotion and stage management, and an emphasis on 'revivalist' religious services with short duration, with the audience whipped-up to a restrained emotional high-pitch at which point 'inquirers' were invited to step forward to answer the 'call' to be 'saved'.

In the late Victorian and Edwardian periods (c. 1880 – c. 1914), the role of the churches in social policy entered a crisis. This was in part a product of a crisis in evangelicalism, in which members of the middle classes lost faith in the power of individualism to reform the working classes, and in part it was a product of the rise of alternative forms of social policy – emanating in particular from the labour movement. Though Christian socialism of the 1890–1914 period offered a see-mingly viable compromise with a new social morality led by the Labour Movement, the leaders of the Church of Scotland and the United Free Church adopted a right-wing anti-Labour and anti-Catholic stance in the 1920s and 1930s, creating a damaging ideological gulf between presbyterianism and the bulk of Scots (C Brown 1997, Chapter 6; SJ Brown 1990; 1991a; 1991b; 1994).

Since 1945, the Scottish churches have undergone slow but significant changes in their political position. The experiences of the Second World War, the welfare state in the post-war years, and Scotland's immense social and economic problems (notably the need for massive slum clearance and council housing, and the collapse of heavy industry), educated a new generation of clergy to greater sympathy with consensual social democracy and – for many – even socialism. When Margaret Thatcher came to power in 1979, the Scottish churches – both Protestant and Catholic – united in an informal opposition to the tenets of free-market economics which her Conservative Government espoused. This led most famously to a hostile reception to Mrs Thatcher's so-called 'Sermon on the Mound' in 1988 when she defended the scriptural foundations for her government's hostility to welfarism and state intervention before the general assembly of the Church of Scotland. Indeed, many clergy and church workers found a new role at parish level during the 1970s and 1980s as organisers of campaigns against industrial closures, but it did little to stem the declining social significance of the churches, as by then a wider de-Christianisation of the Scots was well under way.

3. THE SOCIAL EXPERIENCE OF RELIGION

Despite the massive changes in the political ideology and the structure of the Scottish churches between 1850 and 1945, there was much slower and less dramatic change in the social experience of organised religion. Christian beliefs, values and practises remained strong amongst people of all social classes.

In the second half of the nineteenth century, the religiosity of the middle classes was widely acknowledged. Individualism became widely accepted as the core theme of these values, setting store by the ability of each person to control their own destiny through hard work, a marked religiosity, and 'respectable' behaviour which reflected attachment to a rising number of moral values: sobriety, thrift, sexual correctness, probity in business, liberality in philanthropy, regular (usually weekly) church attendance, and voluntary endeavour in religious, temperance or charitable organisations. There is much evidence of the punishing schedule of religious and philanthropic work undertaken by the middle and upper-middle classes. One entry from the diary of Michael Connal (1817–93), a wealthy merchant and prominent educational philanthropist who ran his own Spoutmouth Bible Institute for the working-class youths of Glasgow's east end, gives a flavour of the concerns of the evangelical social reformer:

August 1872

January 17. – Wrote to-day to London about out-door pensioners of the Royal Asylum for Incurables. The [finance] bond over Stirling's [charitable] Library shown to me cancelled. Things are getting into shape there. The [Glasgow] Technical College programme agreed upon. I dined at the Dean of Guild's yesterday – an official dinner. Sat for a little in the dining-room with [Rev] Dr. Norman Macleod [of Barony Church, Glasgow], who recommended Elliot Nicol's Bible lessons. He appeared to think that sceptical opinions of the present day should be met by young men who are teachers being called together in conference. Think often with pleasure of the "Spout" progressing. Surely it will do good to young men.

(Gibson (ed) 1895, 145)

Religion also played an important part in the lives of the upper working classes in the mid-Victorian period. In the era of steam-power and heavy industry, skilled artisans became an important section of Scottish society – a group conscious of their own economic power and of their own identity as a social group. These 'aristocrats of labour' were by no means all alike, but amongst many of them was to be found a strong culture of religious respectability. John Sturrock, a millwright in Dundee, started a diary when he moved to Dundee in his mid-twenties so that 'I may be able to form an estimate of how I have spent my leisure time, whether I have been trifling it away or turning it to any particular advantage'. He recounts in daily entries the life of a fastidious, hard-working and (mostly) teetotal bachelor, given to church attendance usually twice every Sunday, and entertainment from 'crack' with friends, walks around Dundee and discrete courting of his future wife. Leisure time, by his own standards, had to be 'to advantage' which he got from reading *The English Mechanic* and attending drawing classes and religious lectures. At the time of writing his diary, he was 'sermon-tasting' widely amongst Dundee Free Church congregations, trying to decide which to join:

February 1865

Sat. 4. Spent the afternoon at the newspapers. Went in the town at half past six and got home again a little past eight. Then wrote a little and read a little at Scott's *Poems* before going to bed.

Sun. 5. Lay till nine o'clock as usual and went to Free St. Andrews in the forenoon and afternoon. Happened to see an old acquaintance, Bythinia Emers, at church in the forenoon, with whom I went along the Nethergate a bit. Went and heard the Rev. George Gilfillan's monthly lecture in the evening on the religious aspect of Ireland. Got home about eight o'clock and read a while at the *Sunday Magazine* before going to bed.

Mon. 6. Working till ten o'clock tonight and will be for all the week.

Sat. 11. Got off at two o'clock and spent the afternoon at the newspapers. Then went in the town and happened to meet Elizabeth Packman, with whom I went along to her mother's and stopped till about ten o'clock. Then took a look at Crabbe's *Poems* which I bought tonight and also a Valentine for somebody. Got to bed about twelve o'clock.

Sun. 12. Got up at half past eight, half an hour earlier than usual. Went to

Free St. Andrews forenoon and afternoon, and heard a sermon in the evening by
the Rev. Dr. McGavin on behalf of the Young Men's Christian Association on
'Young men – their Obligations and Blessings', and which the Rev. Doctor
handled in a very eloquent and impressive manner. Happened to meet Helen
Wright as I was coming home, with whom I turned and went a short way in the
Nethergate. Got home a little before nine. Read a chapter and psalm and went to
bed about ten.

Tues. 14. Took this evening to myself and went to the Scottish Reformation
Society's annual festival or soiree, where I enjoyed myself nicely and was so
highly pleased with the proceedings and object of the society that I intend to join
it the first opportunity. Got home about eleven o'clock.

(quoted in Whatley (ed) 1996, 29, 51–2)

Sturrock is the exemplification of the respectable Victorian artisan, frugal and
thrifty, for whom Sabbath sermons were stimulants to personal reflection and,
occasionally, self-remonstrance. Piety and churchgoing were pivotal in his life and
culture, and in October 1865 he finally joined Free St Enoch's Church.

For women, there was special pressure to conform to a strict personal code of
behaviour, derived from, and underpinned by, Christian ethics. This could be just as
powerful in the lives of lower-working-class women as it was for the male merchant
and artisan.

EXERCISE 4

Document 114 is an extract from the private memoir of Christian Watt, a
fisherwoman from the Moray Firth coast. After reading it, consider Christian's
approach to personal morality in the 1850s, to public perception of her
'respectability', and to the Church of Scotland's kirk session. Then compare and
contrast the role of religious matters in her perceptions and behaviour, as
revealed in her memoir, with that of Michael Connal and John Sturrock as
revealed in their diary entries quoted above.

Briefly, Christian had an acute sense of her personal morality, and though full of
bravado towards both her neighbours and the kirk session, she was worried about
moral condemnation in the community. In the personal accounts of Connal,
Sturrock and Watt, there is to be seen a common Christian culture and ethical
code which crossed the very different economic experiences of these three individuals.

Perhaps the most striking feature of religious experience between 1850 and 1950
was the extent of children's connections with religious organisations. In a survey of
76 protestant women asked about their membership of youth organisations between
the 1890s and 1939, 68% had attended Sunday school, 36% the Band of Hope (and
a further 9% other temperance organisations like the White Ribboners and the
Good Templars), 13% had belonged to the Brownies, Girl Guides, Girls' Guildry or

Girls Association, and 14% had been in church choirs (C Brown and Stephenson 1992, 100–1). For boys, the Scouting movement and the Boys' Brigades were extremely important, and mostly congregational-based, organisations. Scottish membership of the BBs rose from 12,796 in 1900 to 26,575 in 1910 and to 35,922 in 1934, with the greatest concentration in working-class areas of west-central Scotland, whilst the Cubs and Scouts had a more middle-class, suburban and east of Scotland image (C Brown 1996, 217). Temperance organisations were also important until the 1930s: the Bands of Hope for children, the Good Templars for older teenagers and young adults, and the League of the Cross for Catholics both young and old. When asked about their religious experience, those who were children or young people in the first half of this century recall an incredibly intense connection with church life. Mrs N.2 (b 1906) was brought up in Glasgow, her father a tram conductor. Asked to recall how she spent Sundays as a child, she said:

> Sundays we were at church a lot. Church and the Sunday school. Then when I got older, the Bible class it was. But there was a lot of the church. And Monday was the Band of Hope (Laughs); I always remember that – the Band of Hope. Tuesday was the Girl Guides. You know it seemed to be all church things.
>
> (quoted in C Brown 1997, 149)

In Larkhall in Lanarkshire in the 1920s, the same intense Protestant Sunday was apparent; Mrs W.2 (b 1916) went to Sunday school during the day and 'at nights the Hebron Hall or any, you know, any meeting houses at night time.' Mrs Q2 (b 1912) lived in a pit village in Stirlingshire where, during the week, she attended the Brownies, the Guides and the Rechabites for concerts and pantomimes, whilst on Sundays:

> You went to church and then you came home, had something to eat and you went to the Brethren in the afternoon – Sunday school, they let you go in there. You got these tickets, you know, verses on them and that, you know to learn, and maybe a cup of tea and a cake. I think it was the cake we went for [Laughs]. And then to the Evangelistic Meeting at night. That was really all we had, all our pastime you know . . .

With little variation, respondents tend to recall one church service and typically two Sunday-school sessions – frequently with different denominations. Sunday was still the Sabbath in Lowland as well as Highland Scotland in the first half of the twentieth century. Mrs 0.2 (b 1899) from Montrose remembered:

> Q   So you could play in the [Sunday] afternoons? Were you allowed to?
> A   No, no. All boots and shoes were cleaned the night before and of course the dishes and that were all washed . . . every Sunday night she [mother] held a small service on her own, singing hymns and read out of the Bible and everything like that . . . Just the family.

Molly Weir recalls of inter-war Glasgow that as well as 'the big Church, where we went to Sunday School and Bible Class, and had our church parades of Girl Guides and the Boys' Brigade, we had the excitement in summertime of tent missions coming to Springburn to convert us'. She, like many, attended religious services of Protestant, Catholic or Methodist churches for 'the sheer enjoyment' and 'just because one gave tattie scones, the next sausage rolls and the other gave pies'(Weir 1972, 69–71).

In adulthood, church connection tended to be less intense, but nonetheless very profound. Although the Victorian practice of attending church twice on Sundays was falling away after 1900, weekly attendance was still very common. One oral-history survey suggested that, in the first half of the century, amongst Scottish parents, 27% attended church weekly, 40% went 'regularly', 20% that only father or mother attended either weekly or regularly, and only 13% never attended church (C Brown and Stephenson 1992, 100). Many women recalled meeting their husbands at the parish church. Mrs K3 (b 1906) recalled 'a superintendent in the primary who prided herself in getting young couples together, you know . . . And I was the pianist, in the primary Sunday school, and she was a great one for making matches. And that was where I met my husband when we were seventeen.'(quoted in C Brown 1997, 153–4).

The weight of corroborative oral and autobiographical evidence – together with the statistical evidence summarised in Table 1 – makes it difficult to avoid the conclusion that the Scottish people stayed in remarkably close contact with church agencies until the 1950s. Periodic religious revivals occurred in places and periods of social stress: in fishing villages struck by a poor herring season in 1921, in striking mining families in 1921 and 1926, and on the island of Lewis in 1949 during economic readjustment in the crofting counties. The Catholic Church, too, found the first seventy years of the century one of growth in its constituency, and assimilation as an institution of Scottish civil society. The number of Catholics rose from 343,000 in 1892 to 614,469 in 1939, and continued to rise to an all-time peak of 828,300 in 1980. With economic depressions in the 1920s and 1930s having no adverse impact on long-term religious adherence, and despite the right-wing swing of presbyterian leadership, the people seemed to remain in relatively close connection with their churches on the eve of the Second World War.

EXERCISE 5
From what you have just read, describe the impact of religion on the lives of young people in the first half of the twentieth century.

Briefly, most young people were brought up in a family and social environment dominated by Sunday churchgoing and week-day religious organisations. The social function of the churches was important, laying the foundations for adult church connection.

The trends of the inter-war period seemed to continue in the years 1945 to 1956. In the midst of post-war austerity, there was a strong Protestant growth in Scotland

marked by evangelistic campaigns by the Church of Scotland and smaller denominations, culminating in the 'All Scotland Crusade' led by Rev Billy Graham in 1955.
Graham preached to large audiences in Glasgow's Kelvin Hall, and to almost a
hundred thousand at Hampden Park and further large numbers at Edinburgh's
Tynecastle Stadium. His visit to Scotland seemed to reflect the reassertion of
puritanism in Scottish civil life, evident in the continuing strict controls of drinking,
local censorship of cinema films, and regulation of Sunday activities (including the
tying-up of children's swings in public parks). Yet, from 1956 church membership,
church-going, Sunday-school enrolment and other indicators of religious connections started to fall dramatically, accelerated in the mid 1960s with the dawn of
modern youth culture. Young people started to abandon the churches and even
organised religion entirely for western mysticism, political activism or – most often –
for no direct substitute.

Sociologists in the 1960s and early 1970s conducting research into church decline
concentrated their energies on issues of social-class analysis. Strongly influenced by
the same conceptual frameworks which influenced historians who were at the same
time studying Victorian churchgoing (Volume 1, Chapter 4), researchers were
convinced that it was the working classes who were leading the haemorrhage of
the churches. One investigation of the Prestonfield area of Edinburgh in 1965
produced two conclusions:

> [First] The widely perceived lack of 'communal' characteristics in the Church of
> Scotland, and the formalized and 'associational' patterns that obtains with her,
> may make her particularly uncongenial to working-class persons. Working-class
> life style, with its basis in informal structures of inter-personal relations and its
> 'immediacy' of content, is perhaps largely incompatible with the major
> institutional forms of religion. Secondly, the accurate conception of the Church
> as middle-class in orientation, composition and leadership may serve as another
> basis of working-class estrangement from the Church.
>
> (D Robertson 1968, 27–8)

A further larger study of Falkirk in the late 1960s concluded that 'the membership of
the churches is heavily weighted in favour of the middle classes (Sissons 1973, 284).
This was an extremely influential judgement within the Church of Scotland on
whose behalf the Falkirk study was undertaken, and it has remained something of an
axiom within that denomination (Wolfe and Pickford 1980, 94; A Robertson 1987,
189). However, both the Prestonfield and Falkirk studies are open to challenge. In
the Falkirk case particularly, the investigator chose to characterise only unskilled
workers as 'the traditional working-classes' (Sissons 1973, 60), failing to highlight
that skilled, partly-skilled and unskilled manual workers collectively made up 60%
of Church of Scotland affiliation in the burgh, and that partly-skilled and unskilled
churchgoers claimed by far the highest level of weekly churchgoing (see retabulation
of Sissons' evidence in C Brown 1992, 63). Moreover, other work (including a study
of Alloa by Panton [1973]) tended to indicate that levels of upper working-class

church affiliation and practice were the highest in society, and that the social composition of presbyterian congregations in the 1960s was very similar to that found by Hillis in the mid-nineteenth century (see **Article 6**, Volume 3).

Class analysis of church decline since the 1960s has, with time, receded to give greater importance to age and cultural analysis. Understanding the youth evacuation of the churches has been a topic to which churchmen and sociologists have returned again and again. Between 1956 and 1980, the crucial trend towards the religious alienation of youth was established, and religious sociologists sought to advise the Church of Scotland on what was happening amongst young people.

> EXERCISE 6
> Read **Documents 115 and 116**. Comment on the emerging perceptions of the youth crisis in the churches during the later 1950s and the 1960s.

Briefly, the churches were stunned by the change in young people's religious attitudes that was becoming apparent by 1960, and closer analysis in 1969 suggested a loss amongst both middle- and working-class children, founded upon a failure in the family support for church connection.

The crisis intensified in the 1970s and 1980s as those children who left the churches in the later 1950s and 1960s got married (with a growing inclination to avoid church weddings), brought up children whom they did not send to Sunday school or church, and who in turn by the 1980s and 1990s were having families which were one or even two generations removed from church life or an active Christian family environment. With Catholic families starting to follow the same trends from the later 1970s (and with increasing intensity in the later 1980s and 1990s), the Scottish people became rapidly dechristianised in the last quarter of the twentieth century (C Brown 1997, Chapter 7).

4. CATHOLICS, ASSIMILATION AND SECTARIANISM

In Chapter 4 (Volume 1) we noted briefly how the growth of Irish Catholic immigration in the late eighteenth and early nineteenth centuries increased presbyterian hostility to Catholicism. This section returns to this theme for the period since 1850.

We have seen from Section 1 how the Catholic Church became the fastest growing major denomination in Scotland between 1850 and 1975. The main concentration of Catholics from Ireland was in the Glasgow region, but smaller concentrations were also evident in Edinburgh, Dundee and small industrial and mining communities of the central belt. But in the twentieth century, and especially after 1945, Catholics have spread out throughout the Lowlands, including into more rural districts. After difficulties in church building in the period 1800 to 1850, the Church was better able to construct churches in the twentieth century. The Church had been officially allowed to re-establish the Scottish hierarchy of dioceses and archdioceses abolished at the Reformation only in 1878, nearly thirty years after it had occurred in England and Wales. The Roman Catholic Church had also to struggle in the provision of schooling for children of Catholic parents, and whilst virtually all Protestant schools were absorbed into the state system in 1873, Catholic schools only started to be subsumed within the state sector from 1919 (Treble 1980). And legal penalties against the Catholic faith have been slow to fall: it was only in 1926, after a police confrontation associated with the opening of the Carfin shrine in Lanarkshire, that the Host could be legally processed on the highway (McGhee 1965).

If institutional assimilation was a long and hard process for the Catholic Church, it has been even longer for Catholics themselves. An older tradition in Catholic historiography was to approach the experience of Irish Catholics in Scotland as dominated by the anti-assimilationist tendencies of, firstly, Catholic poverty and, secondly, Protestant hostility and discrimination. For the nineteenth century, the poverty, low-skilled job access in Scotland, and the political disenfranchisement suffered has been the context in which much of the understanding of Catholic assimilation has been presented (Handley 1945; Treble 1979, 121–2; McCaffrey 1970, 36). The early studies of the twentieth century continued to focus on persecution and the poverty of the Catholic community (Handley 1947, 302–27). In more recent work, some studies have continued to follow this line of interpretation, emphasising the formation of a 'fortress mentality' by the Catholic Church in an attempt to quarantine its adherents from native Protestantism. From the mid nineteenth century until perhaps the mid twentieth century the Church sought not only to keep Catholics in touch with religious observance, but also to nurture them within a 'cradle-to-grave community' centred on the Catholic Church: a community of religious voluntary organisations like the Catholic Young Men's Association, church-inspired football clubs, the temperance organisation the League of the Cross and a Catholic business community (Aspinwall 1982, 47, 53). But this very perception of a growing and maturing 'fortress' of Catholic leisure, commerce and welfare shows the evidence of a maturing Catholic community and increasing economic mobility within Scottish society. The charitable Saint Vincent de Paul Society was, according to one study of Glasgow, the mechanism by which, between 1848 and 1920, leading Catholic male laity were 'enabled to transmit, albeit unwittingly, the significant values of the host society to their co-religionist: thrift, sobriety, self-help, and community', whilst to 'the poor they offered the riches of a superior, older ethnic culture' (Aspinwall 1986, 448, 454). In Dundee, another historian stressed the role of the Church in utilising its institutions and voluntary organisations in encouraging assimilation of Catholics to the values of urban and industrial society (WM Walker 1972, 663). Though the combined effects of economic depression and Protestant discrimination for scarce jobs may have created 'a crisis of the work ethic' amongst Catholics (Aspinwall 1987, 394), many historians have pinpointed the key role of Catholics in the Scottish Labour Movement – including the Labour Party – as the most significant indication of assimilation of Catholicism as a whole within modern Scottish society (Woods 1980; Gilley

1980; Gallagher 1987a; 1991). Since the 1960s, though, assimilation has been increasingly the product of rising prosperity amongst Catholics, a sharing of the benefits of improved housing, health educational opportunity and leisure opportunities. An initial consequence of this has been the Catholic Church's perplexity at the failure to sustain its adherents within a distinctive mentalité of organisations and religious values (including the increasing breakdown in the 1980s and 1990s of the willingness of Catholic parents to consider exclusive Catholic schooling for their children). A more far-reaching consequence has been one shared with Catholics in most European countries – the widespread rejection by the young of traditional Catholic doctrines on birth control and marriage only to Catholics. As with Protestant churches, the Catholic Church's greatest challenge has been to preserve the faith amongst the young, and the most recent evidence is that Catholic marriage, mass attendance and even faith is crumbling rapidly in the final decade of the millennium.

EXERCISE 7
Discuss the factors ascribed to the assimilation of the Irish-derived Catholic community in Scotland between 1850 and the present.

Historians have suggested that the Catholic Church encouraged an insular social and religious environment for adherents around the Church and its approved voluntary organisations and schools from the mid-nineteenth century. Though this continued into the twentieth century, the Labour Movement and, latterly, economic prosperity, are seen as contributing to a levelling of Catholic and Protestant experience, making way for a common decline in religiosity towards the end of the period.

The arrival of both Protestant and Catholic Irish in Scotland in the nineteenth century transformed Scottish sectarianism into the mould created in the north of Ireland. The Orange Order became established in Scotland largely as a result of Irish Protestants (McFarland 1990), and other anti-Catholic 'missions' were set up – notably in Glasgow – to challenge 'Romanists' and seek converts. In the second half of the nineteenth century, Protestant-Catholic antagonism in Scotland was common within industrial society, though it was becoming increasing the preserve of working-class communities. Though major cities like Glasgow did not experience the same level of Catholic-Protestant segregation and political sectarianism as in Liverpool (Gallagher 1985), there was significant occupational and residential segregation of Catholics and Protestants in smaller industrial communities. From the 1850s, the iron and coal industries in Monklands were heavily segregated with skilled jobs dominated by Protestants and unskilled jobs dominated by Catholics; in addition, the community was residentially segregated between predominantly Protestant Airdrie and predominantly Catholic Coatbridge. This situation, it has been suggested, was the product of deliberate employer policy to encourage Protestant skilled and unionised workers to identity with the Protestant employers, thus keeping the Catholics un-unionised and less likely to result in the formation of a united labour movement (A Campbell 1979, 193–5, 223). Many lesser examples of anti-Catholic discrimination by employers were to be found in the depression of the inter-war years, and in certain industries – such as Clydeside shipbuilding and engineering – skilled jobs and preferment lay in the hands of 'Orange' foremen.

The inter-war years witnessed a different form of sectarianism – arguably the most public anti-Catholicism since the seventeenth century. In the late 1920s and early 1930s, anti-Catholic political parties emerged in Glasgow and Edinburgh. In Glasgow, Alexander Radcliffe led the Scottish Protestant League which reached a peak of electoral support at municipal elections in 1933 with a third of the vote. Meanwhile, in Edinburgh, a more demagogic leader, John Cormack, took Protestant Action to the forefront of street campaigning and local politics, ending up as a councillor for Leith until the 1960s.

EXERCISE 8
Read **Article 35** by Tom Gallagher. Assess the factors behind the growth and decline of sectarianism in Scotland in the 1930s.

The economic slump of the inter-war period, combined with Protestant insecurity with Catholic advance in education and other spheres, contributed to the emergence of anti-Catholic political movements in the early 1930s. These lost most of their momentum as a result of economic recovery in the later 1930s and the outbreak of war.

The most prominent venue in Scotland since the 1890s for Protestant-Catholic antagonism has been football. Whilst respectively Edinburgh's Hibernian and Heart of Midlothian clubs, and Dundee's Hibernians (since 1923 United) and Dundee clubs, emerged in the 1860s and 1870s as Catholic and Protestant identified clubs, it has been Glasgow's 'Old Firm' of Celtic and Rangers football clubs which developed as the most intense and enduring sporting symbol of sectarian rivalry in not only Scottish but western European society as a whole. Parkhead and Ibrox football stadia have been, throughout the twentieth century, the focus for a religious-political divide, drawing on the heritage of the divided north of Ireland, with the Irish tricolour flying above the former and the Union Jack and the Red Hand of Ulster acting as common banners of the Protestant Loyalism of the Ibrox faithful. Old Firm matches have invariably been tense confrontations, occasionally punctuated by crowd trouble. Though in the late 1980s and 1990s the acquisition of English and overseas players, anti-bigotry campaigns by the Clubs, all-seater stadia and improved crowd control, have all helped to reduce tensions, the symbols remain. Indeed, recent research suggests that the religious-political alignments of Northern Ireland still have a profound impact upon perceptions of identity for fans of these clubs, and with the gap between the status of these two clubs and other Scottish football clubs widening, they are acting as foci of identity for Catholics and Protestants in many parts of Scotland (Bradley 1995; see Lambert, this volume, Chapter 26).

The whole nature of the impact of Northern Ireland upon Scotland – its Protestant as well as its Catholic heritages – has only recently been opened up to study by historians (G Walker 1995). It links into wider debates concerning religion and national identities in Scotland – British, Scottish and Irish (see Finlay, this volume, Chapter 15).

REFERENCES TO BOOKS AND ARTICLES MENTIONED IN THE TEXT

Aspinwall, B 1982 'The formation of the Catholic community in the west of Scotland: some preliminary outlines' *Innes Review* 33, 44–57.

Aspinwall, B 1986 'The welfare state within the state: the Saint Vincent de Paul Society in Glasgow, 1848–1920', *in* Sheils WJ and Woods D (eds), *Voluntary Religion,* Oxford, 445–59.

Aspinwall, B 1987 'Broadfield revisited: some Scottish Catholic responses to wealth 1918–40', *in* Sheils WJ and Wood D (eds), *The Church and Wealth,* Oxford, 393–406.

Bradley, JM 1995 *Ethnic and Religious Identity in Modern Scotland: Culture, Politics and Football.* Aldershot.

*Brown, CG 1992 'Religion and secularisation', *in* Dickson, T and Treble, JH (eds), *People and Society in Scotland vol III 1914–1990,* Edinburgh, 48–79.

Brown, CG 1996 'Popular culture and the continuing struggle for rational recreation', *in* Devine, TM and Finlay, RJ (eds), *Scotland in the Twentieth Century,* Edinburgh, 210–29.

*Brown, CG 1997 *Religion and Society in Scotland since 1707.* Edinburgh.

Brown, CG and Stephenson, JD 1992, '"Sprouting Wings"? Women and religion in Scotland c.1890–1950', *in* Breitenbach, E and Gordon, E (eds), *Out of Bounds: Women in Scottish Society 1800–1945,* Edinburgh, 95–120.

*Brown, SJ 1990 'The social vision of Scottish presbyterianism and the Union of 1929', *Records of the Scottish Church hIstory Society* 24, 77–96.

*Brown, SJ 1991a '"A Vision for God": the Scottish presbyterian churches and the General Strike of 1926', *Journal of Ecclesiastical History* 42, 596–617.

*Brown, SJ 1991b '"Outside the Covenant": the Scottish presbyterian churches and Irish immigration, 1922–1938', *Innes Review* 42, 19–45.

Brown, SJ 1994 '"A Solemn Purification by Fire": responses to the Great War in the Scottish presbyterian churches, 1914–19', *Journal of Ecclesiastical History* 45, 82–104.

Buchanan, Robert 1851 *Spiritual Destitution of the Masses in Glasgow.* Edinburgh.

Campbell, A 1979, *The Lanarkshire Miners 1775–1874.* Edinburgh.

*Gallagher, T 1985 'Protestant extremism in urban Scotland 1930–39: its growth and contraction', *Scottish Historical Review* 64, 143–67.

*Gallagher,T 1987a *Glasgow: The Uneasy Peace: Religious Tension in Modern Scotland.* Manchester.

*Gallagher, T 1987b *Edinburgh Divided: John Cormack and No Popery in the 1930s.* Edinburgh.

Gallagher, T 1991 'The Catholic Irish in Scotland: in search of identity', *in* Devine, TM (ed), *Irish Immigrants and Scottish Society in the Nineteenth and Twentieth Centuries,* Edinburgh, 19–43.

Gibson, JC (ed) 1895 *Diary of Sir Michael Connal 1835 to 1893.* Glasgow.

Gilley, S 1980 'Catholics and socialists in Glasgow, 1906–12', *in* Lunn, K (ed), *Hosts, Immigrants and Minorities,* Folkestone, 160–200.

Handley, JE 1945 *The Irish in Scotland 1798–1845*. Cork.

Handley, JE 1947 *The Irish in Modern Scotland*. Cork.

McCaffrey, J 1970 'The Irish vote in Glasgow in the later nineteenth century' *Innes Review* 21, 30–6.

McFarland, EW 1990 *Protestants First: Orangeism in Nineteenth Century Scotland*. Edinburgh.

McGhee, S 1965 'Carfin and the Roman Catholic Relief Act of 1926' *Innes Review* 16, 56–78.

Panton, KJ 1973, 'The Church in the community: a study of patterns of religious adherence in a Scottish burgh', *in* Hill, M (ed), *A Sociological Yearbook of Religion in Britain, no. 6*, London, 183–205.

Robertson, A 1987 *Lifestyle Survey*. Edinburgh.

*Robertson, D 1968, 'The relationship of church and class in Scotland', *in* Martin, D, *A Sociological Yearbook of Religion in Britain*, London, 11–31.

Sissons, PL 1973 *The social significance of Church membership in the Burgh of Falkirk*. Edinburgh.

Treble, JH 1979 'The market for unskilled labour in Glasgow, 1891–1914, *in* MacDougall, I (ed), *Essays in Scottish Labour History*, Edinburgh, 115–42.

Treble, JH 1980 'The working of the 1918 Education Act in Glasgow Archdiocese', *Innes Review* 31, 27–44.

*Walker, G 1995 *Intimate Strangers: Political and Cultural Interaction between Scotland and Ulster in Modern Times*. Edinburgh.

Walker, WM 1972 'Irish immigrants in Scotland: their priests, politics and parochial life', *Historical Journal* 15, 649–67.

Weir, M 1972 *Best Foot Forward*. London.

Whatley, C (ed) 1996 *The Diary of John Sturrock, Millwright, Dundee 1864–5*. East Linton.

Wolfe, JN and Pickford, M 1980 *The Church of Scotland: An Economic Survey*. London.

Woods, IS 1980 'John Wheatley, the Irish and the Labour Movement in Scotland', *Innes Review* 31, 71–85.

FURTHER READING

Those references marked * in the above list are recommended further reading.

Women and
Gender Relations

Arthur McIvor

Scotland in the mid-nineteenth century can be portrayed as an intensely patriarchal society, where women lived acutely prescribed lives and were commonly regarded as inferior, second-class citizens. A regime of gender apartheid prevailed, articulated by one prominent Scottish trade union leader who pontificated that a woman's 'natural sphere is the home' (STUC, AR, 1919, 84). Clearly, this situation changed through the twentieth century and gender inequalities within Scottish society have been eroded. However, the dynamics of this process have yet to be adequately analysed, whilst historians and other commentators disagree as to the timing, the causes and the extent of this transformation. Thus there is a need to overview the existing body of knowledge and take stock. This chapter attempts to do just that.

The task of providing an overview is difficult, because research on women's history in Scotland is less well developed than in England – we lack the critical mass of empirical research and the expert syntheses of historians such as Jane Lewis (1984; 1992). Recent research has, however, produced a series of path-breaking articles, edited collections and monographs (Gordon 1990; 1991; Gordon and Breitenbach 1990; Breitenbach and Gordon 1992; Reynolds 1989; Corr 1983; King 1993; Leneman, 1991). This has extended knowledge and raised the visibility of women in the historical record. Much of the best of this work, notably that of Gordon and Breitenbach, has moved us significantly from the notion of women as passive victims, whilst questioning the view that a 'quiet revolution' has occurred in women's social, economic and political status (Young 1985; Glasgow Women's Studies Group 1983). Even with this work, there remain significant gaps in our understanding of the changing patterns and continuities in Scottish women's lives. Accordingly, this chapter draws on some of the vast body of oral evidence and the rich seams of official documentation, as well as the secondary literature. The potential of oral evidence in opening a window into Scottish women's lives has been demonstrated by Jamieson (1986), Faley (1990), Brown and Stephenson (1990) and Stephenson and Brown (1992). My argument will be that whilst inequalities based on sex, like social class divisions, have undoubtedly dissipated over the course of the last 150 years, gender inequalities in the socio-economic sphere have remained doggedly persistent and continue to characterise modern-day Scotland. I also want to try to sustain and develop somewhat the argument that Scotland had a more patriarchal society than England, particularly prior to World War Two.

The chapter is divided into three main sections:

- Women and gender relations in Victorian Scotland
- Home and family: the 'private' sphere since *c.* 1900
- Work and politics: the 'public' sphere since *c.* 1900

To adequately assess continuities and change over time, a benchmark is needed, so I will start by discussing the position of Scottish women within Victorian society.

> EXERCISE 1
>
> Make a list of the potential primary sources that you could exploit to research the history of women and gender relations in Scotland since 1850. Why do you think the documentary sources are so poor prior to World War Two?

Your list might include government papers and enquiries, such as the decennial census, the factory inspectors' reports and Royal Commissions (for example on Equal Pay in 1944); oral testimony; newspapers and magazines; autobiographies and diaries; film; and the surviving records of political and work-based organisations where women participated (for example the suffrage movement, the trade unions and the co-operative movement). For a useful guide, see Beddoe (1988). You will have your own views on the second part of the question, however, one interpretation is that the paucity of documentary sources prior to World War Two is connected with the exclusion of women from the 'public' arena – from involvement in positions of influence and power – itself the product of an intensely chauvinist society where women were widely regarded as inferior.

I. WOMEN AND GENDER RELATIONS IN VICTORIAN SCOTLAND

In most areas of life in Victorian Scotland, women were subordinate to men. They were less free, less independent, less valued and more constrained due to the prevailing patriarchal legal system and the dominant chauvinist values and attitudes of the day. There were, however, important differences in women's experience depending upon social class and locality and some not insignificant changes in gender relations over the second half of the nineteenth century. The first point to make is that legally women were not deemed worthy of independent ownership of property. On marriage a woman's belongings were ceded to her husband: movables became his property (until 1881) and he became the legal administrator of his wife's heritable wealth on marriage, his consent being necessary for any disposal of wealth (Marshall 1983, 274, 278). This power was not finally stripped away until the Married Women's Property Act, Scotland, 1920. Divorce was costly and divorce law favoured the husband, including the issue of custody of the children. Hence many women remained trapped in loveless marriages, indeed, there were only 142 individuals suing for divorce in Scotland as late as 1900 (Marshall 1983, 301). Typically, marriages were only dissolved on the death of one partner. Within the middle and upper classes even the choice of marriage partner was severely constrained by parental prejudice and the social conventions which dictated conjugal union with a partner of roughly comparable property.

Women's status as citizens was also severely prescribed. Women only gained limited access (married and property-owning) to the franchise in local elections from 1871, and they were denied the right to vote in national elections. This was despite the fact, as suffragists pointed out, that many women were ratepayers: hence the slogan 'no taxation without representation'.

Gender discrimination also operated acutely within education, training and the trade unions in the mid-Victorian period. Corr (1983a) and Moore (1992) have shown how school curricula continued to emphasise a domestic training – 'housewifery' – for girls and technical skills for boys. In working class families, daughters were usually removed from school before sons and, not surprisingly, literacy levels were lower amongst women than men in mid-nineteenth century Scotland. Higher education in Scotland remained strictly a male-only domain, at least until the late nineteenth century, when some courses in some universities were opened up to women. Access remained severely restricted, however, until after World War One. Similarly, working class women found it difficult to get entry to and training for skilled, craft work. This was partly the product of patriarchal prejudice by employers who rationalised that women would leave employment on marriage and hence were not worth the trouble and expense of training. However, as Gordon's research (1991, 101) has shown, trade unions also played a key role through their exclusionary tactics, their stranglehold over recruitment into some skilled occupations and their rules forbidding the employment of women in their trades. Thus, 'trade union practices reproduced and reinforced the sexual divisions of labour in both the home and the workplace'. As trade unions became more powerful, gender discriminatory tactics could become more effective, as the example of the Edinburgh printing trade demonstrates (Reynolds 1989).

Clearly, a well-defined sexual division of labour characterised Scottish society in the Victorian period, with men occupying the public arena of paid work, politics and trade unions whilst women were confined predominantly to the home and family. Social convention within the middle and upper classes dictated that within a family, the wife and daughters should remain at home, servicing the needs of the husband, providing succour and stability, and not engaging in paid work. Some sought relief from such a prescribed, ornamental existence through engagement in philanthropic endeavours – such as workhouse, hospital and prison work, or aid through the Magdelene institutions to the prostitutes of the major Scottish cities (Mahood 1992, 42–64). Whilst more research is required to flesh out the strength of attitudes and social mores, it is likely that most women of this class conformed to convention, remaining the proverbial 'angel in the home'.

There was less sexual constraint further down the social scale, more illegitimate births and irregular marriages (including co-habitation). Nevertheless, middle class ideals permeated downwards as the Victorian period progressed, reforming elements of plebian, rough culture. Gray (1976) has demonstrated how a non-working wife was deemed a vital element of the lifestyle of the Edinburgh 'labour aristocrat' – that is a craft artisan, or someone who matched a craftsman in earnings. Domesticity may have been limiting, but within the world view of Victorian society it denoted respectability and status. Critically, for working class women in Victorian Scotland, marriage invariably meant a reorientation of their lives, from paid employment in the formal economy, in factories, sweatshops and in domestic service – to unpaid labour within the confined isolation of the home and family. In this sense marriage was much more of a watershed than it is today. Moreover, according to the decennial Census, before the First World War significantly fewer married Scottish women were engaged in paid work outside the home (around 5%) compared with their English counterparts (around 10%). While this may reflect economic imperatives – the lack of job opportunities in Scotland – it seems possible that this demonstrates the more intensely patriarchal nature of Scottish society.

Around this prevailing pattern, there were significant local and regional variations. According to the Census, about a quarter of married women continued in paid employment in Dundee, largely in the jute mills, whilst less than one in twenty married women were in paid work in Glasgow in 1911. Gender relations in the two cities were thus somewhat different, with women in Dundee enjoying more economic independence and developing a distinctive and quite radical factory culture (Gordon 1991, 137–211). Here, according to popular mythology, men were the 'kettle-boilers'. Matriarchal power was also evident in some of the fishing communities of the North-East where many women were involved in the industry as equal partners with men, owning property with the right to sell fish from a creel being passed down the female line (Livingstone 1994, 15). Such examples suggest that the prevailing and somewhat abstract notion of patriarchal dominance needs to be qualified with a recognition of the rich mosaic of experience across a variety of different communities, labour markets and traditions.

Cyclical and seasonal unemployment and underemployment, as well as low male earnings (notably amongst unskilled rural and urban labourers) invariably drew married women into the formal economy to maintain family income and ensure survival, and much of this, on the fringes of the 'black economy' – for example childminding, washing, mending, sewing, knitting and the taking in of lodgers – was unrecorded. It is important to re-emphasise that the main primary source used to evaluate occupational structure and change – the decennial census – significantly underestimated female involvement in paid employment, largely due to the gender bias which saturated its recording methodology. Much of women's activity within the home had economic value, so it is wrong to postulate that married Victorian women did not work.

The work of a married woman within the home in the Victorian period was extremely labour intensive and invariably debilitating and included a wide range of physically gruelling tasks, performed seven days a week: nursing, caring, feeding and minding children; washing and ironing laundry; frequent shopping; food preparation, cooking and washing-up; scrubbing, sweeping, polishing and blackleading the house, the stair, the yard and the household equipment and utensils (such as the iron and chrome kitchen range); sewing, knitting, making and mending clothes, as well as responsibility for financial budgeting and management. Most of this was done by hand, without the aid of any sophisticated equipment. Washing, often undertaken in the communal tenement washroom, could take more than a full day. In addition, given the size of families and female life expectancy of forty-four years in the mid-Victorian period, few women would have experienced life without dependent children under the age of twelve in the home. Indeed, more than a half of a woman's life was taken up in producing, nursing and nurturing children. Victorian notions of the sexual division of labour dictated that child rearing and household tasks were unequivocally defined as 'women's work'. Daughters were expected to help with household chores and child-minding very early in life, whilst sons and fathers were usually exempt from all but a few specialised tasks, such as decorating and shoe repair. For daughters, housework invariably continued even after entering full-time employment. All this was bound up with deeply entrenched notions of masculinity and femininity.

The sanctity of marriage and family was reinforced by the existence of formal and informal marriage bars operating across the economy. Such discrimination meant that full-time paid employment in the Victorian period was largely undertaken by younger women. Occupational choice was severely constrained. Whilst the decen-nial census, as already noted, under-represents female participation in the formal economy, it still provides a guide as to the occupational profile. According to the 1851 Census, 90% of all working women in Scotland were engaged in just four industries: textile manufacture (26%); agriculture (25%); indoor domestic service (23%); and clothing manufacture (16%). Gender segregation – both horizontal and vertical – in occupations was probably at its height in the mid-Victorian period. At this point, the work women did (with only a few exceptions) was synonymous with low status, monotony and little tangible rewards. Few women in Scotland had penetrated either teaching or clerical work. Corr (1990, 303) has shown how the feminisation of teaching as a profession was much slower in Scotland than England where in 1851 62% of teachers were women compared to 35% in Scotland.

A clear expression of the subalternation of women within Scottish society is provided in a comparison of the earnings of male and female workers. Women's labour power was seriously undervalued in the Victorian economy, women earning, on average, around half that of men. The first systematic government wages survey in 1906 shows that the average weekly earnings of the Scottish adult woman were 65 pence compared to £1.43 pence for an adult man, a gender wage differential of 45.2%. This average, however, masked a range of experience. Significantly, even in textile manufacture, one of the most highly paid female occupations, women earned only 54% of the male average. 'Sweated' work, for example seamstressing, was amongst the lowest paid. Moreover, in the relatively rare cases where women did the same work as men, they were still paid considerably less than their male counter-parts (Gordon 1991, 30–33).

Gender wage differentials reflected the prevalent chauvinist attitudes of Victorian employers and the state, the ghettoisation of women into lesser skilled occupations and the social exclusion of women from much craft artisanal work. Work performed by women was invariably labelled as unskilled, irrespective of objective elements, such as task range, discretionary content and training period. Thus, whilst some trade unions managed to socially construct 'skill' – and hence maintain high earnings and status – the opposite occurred for the work women performed, with social destruction of genuinely skilled work, such as working with the needle in seamstressing. The Victorian period also saw the linked notions of the 'family wage' and 'supplementary earnings' become firmly entrenched. It was almost universally accepted (including by the trade unions) that the male wage should reflect the idea that he was supporting a family, whilst the female wage duly reflected economic dependence. This custom had serious implications for women in general and independent unmarried working women (over half a million in Scotland in 1911) in particular. The state also played a role in such undervaluation by interventionist legislation, such as the Factory Acts, which limited the employment of female labour within certain hours (excluding women, for example, from night work) and, hence, diminished their market value.

The dominance of domestic ideology and the structural subordination of women in Victorian Scotland did not, however, go unchallenged. King (1993) and Leneman (1991) have outlined how middle-class Scottish women pioneered the campaign for women's suffrage in the third quarter of the nineteenth century and Gordon (1991), Young (1985) and Knox (1995) have demonstrated how Scottish working class women were actively involved in strikes and other forms of collective action (including food riots and demonstrations). This threw up some strong female leaders and role models, such as Margaret Irwin and Mary MacArthur in the trade union movement, Eunice Murray and Lavinia Laing Malcolm in the suffrage campaign and Marion Gilchrist, Elsie Maud Inglis and Anne Louise McIlroy who were among the first female graduate doctors to qualify in Scotland (Livingstone 1994, 17, 19, 22–4, 38–9). Such challenges to patriarchy intensified as the Victorian period progressed and there were some limited successes, such as the (albeit restricted) extension of the local/municipal franchise to women and the (albeit limited) opening up of higher education. Textile factory workers, including those in Dundee and Glasgow, were amongst those who demonstrated a sharp sense of collective consciousness and a willingness to actively resist the worse excesses of exploitative capitalism, expressed through a high strike rate in the late-Victorian and Edwardian years. Significantly, however, such activities tended to be spontaneous, arising organically from below, invariably taking place outside the formal channels of the male-dominated trade union movement, which continued to neglect women's interests and ignore them as potential members. Separate, gender-specific organisations emerged to represent women's political aspirations and trade union concerns, such as the Women's Social and Political Union and the National Federation of Women Workers. Thus, Scottish women were an active agency in this process, rather than passive recipients of a male-centred culture and patriarchal control (Gordon 1991).

However, it remained difficult to break down generations of socialisation and acculturation. Sporadic and periodic evidence of female activity, resistance and organisation thus needs to be kept in perspective. I suspect that the vast majority of Scottish women in the Victorian period internalised and rarely, if ever, questioned their inferiority and second class citizenship – the lack of rights, job segregation, undervaluation and structural subordination which characterised this intensely patriarchal society. Gender apartheid was part of the 'natural' order of things in Victorian Scotland. Oral evidence for the late nineteenth and early twentieth centuries tends to support such a conclusion. How then did this scenario change during the course of the twentieth century? Why, and to what degree, have gender inequalities within Scottish society been eroded since the Victorian period?

EXERCISE 2

The ongoing process of industrialisation in the nineteenth century enabled Britain to incubate the most powerful trade union movement in the world. Read the extracts from Gordon and Renolds (**Articles 36 and 37**) and comment on the prevailing attitudes of the Scottish trade unions towards women in the period before World War One.

You will have come to your own conclusions as to whether the trade unions were part of the 'problem'. However, it seems to me that the evidence strongly supports the view that the trade unions in pre-World War One Scotland largely accepted the status quo and did little in an active fashion either to recruit women to the trade union movement or to incorporate issues and campaigns (such as equal pay or job discrimination) which would attract female members and to which women workers could relate. In this sense the trade unions were effectively restricting their own sphere of influence and, at the extreme, contributing to the maintenance of gender inequalities and apartheid within Scottish society.

2. HOME AND FAMILY: THE 'PRIVATE' DOMAIN

Women's lives were intimately bound up with the family and the household and this 'private sphere', in turn, impacted critically upon women's involvement in the 'public sphere' of paid work and politics. During the twentieth century significant changes have taken place within the private sphere in Scotland, though commentators are divided as to how much emphasis to place upon these changes and to what extent this affected the everyday experience of women's lives.

Undoubtedly, the critical change was the control women achieved over their fertility (Table 1). From the 1870s to 1900 there was a modest fall in Scottish fertility rates, notably amongst the middle classes. Whilst large variations continued to exist in family size between different social groups, the average family size came down to six by 1900 (Gordon 1990, 216–7). The trend continued downwards until World War Two, with a rise thereafter linked to a fall in the mean age of marriage (Table 2). From the 1960s, fertility rates fell drastically again, though the downward trend slowed markedly in the 1980s. This is linked to the widespread availability of the birth control pill from the late 1960s and to delayed marriages from the late 1970s. What is important to recognise, though, is that the decline in family size is clearly a long-term phenomenon which pre-dates 'the pill' and is linked to other modes of contraception, including the condom and abstention. What 'the pill' did was to usher in an unprecedented period of sexual freedom and give women personal control over fertility. Control over family size must rank as one of the most fundamental transformations in women's lives. Critically, the maternal care period – producing and nurturing children – contracted from around 50% of an average woman's life span in 1850 to constitute only around 15% of a woman's life span by the 1990s, given the average number of children per family at two and female life expectancy of seventy-seven years.

TABLE 1: GENERAL FERTILITY RATE (PER 1,000 WOMEN AGED 15–44)

	SCOTLAND	ENGLAND AND WALES
1870–2	149.4	153.0
1880–2	145.5	148.0
1890–2	132.5	129.0
1900–2	120.6	114.7
1910–2	107.4	98.6
1920–2	105.9	91.1
1930–2	78.8	64.4
1940–2	73.7	61.3
1950–2	81.4	72.1
1960–2	97.8	88.9
1970–2	83.3	81.4
1980–2	62.2	61.8
1990–2	59.3	63.8
1994	55.9	61.9

Sources: 96th Annual Report of the Registrar General for Scotland, 1950 (1953); Central Statistical Office, Annual Abstract of Statistics, no 130, 1994; no 132 (1996); Office of Population Censuses, Birth Statistics, 1837–1983, Historical Series, England and Wales (1987)

TABLE 2: MEAN AGE AT MARRIAGE IN SCOTLAND: FEMALES

1861–70	25.6
1871–80	25.6
1881–90	25.7
1891–1900	26.2
1901–10	26.2
1911–20	26.7
1921–30	26.5
1931–40	26.4
1941–50	26.0
1951–60	25.1
1961–70	24.1
1971–80	24.7
1981–90	26.6
1991	28.5
1992	29.1

Source: Central Statistical Office, Scottish Abstract of Statistics, no 22 (1994)

One comparative point is worth making: the fall in fertility initially occurred more rapidly in England than Scotland. Thus Scottish families remained substantially larger than English families in the first half of the twentieth century (Flinn 1977, 346–7). Class structure is of primary importance in explaining such differentials – Scotland had a smaller middle class than England and, as Table 3 indicates, social class continued to be a major determinant of family size. Religion may also have played a part, because Scotland had a larger proportion of Catholics than England in the first half of the twentieth century. Moreover, the birth control campaign experienced more opposition in Scotland than in England. There were just twenty voluntary birth control clinics in Scotland prior to 1930. King (1993, 144) has exposed the severe problems of birth control campaigners in inter-war Glasgow and argued that the city was particularly permeated with hostile attitudes. On the whole the Scottish labour movement between the wars had a regressive attitude towards birth control, an attitude partly driven by a fear of alienating the Catholic vote. Prominent members of the Independent Labour Party, including John Wheatley, Stephen Campbell and James Maxton, were amongst those who voted and campaigned against the extension of public information and medical advice on contraception (Young 1985, 137–9). On the other hand, the Scottish Co-operative Women's Guild helped to disseminate birth control information, publishing leaflets and speaking on the issue at meetings.

TABLE 3: FERTILITY RATE AND FAMILY SIZE IN SCOTLAND BY SOCIAL CLASS, 1950

Social class	FERTILITY RATE	AVERAGE FAMILY SIZE	% WITH NO CHILDREN
I	86	1.48	24.6%
II	83	1.72	22.3%
III	108	1.90	19.7%
IV	121	2.33	17.0%
V	124	2.58	16.2%

Source: Census of Scotland, 1951, volume III (1954).

The demographic gap between Scotland and England narrowed through the twentieth century. In both family size and female economic activity, Scotland was little different to England by the 1990s. Regional variations within Scotland had also narrowed (Flinn 1977, 326–7). The second half of the twentieth century has also seen change in family structures, including significant erosion of married family life in Scotland. Between 1971 and 1991 the marriage rate (including re-marriages) fell by 16%, a larger proportion of marriages have broken up, and there has been a sharp rise in births outside marriage (Regional Trends 1975, 48; 1993, 47). Divorce and co-habitation rates have risen sharply. In 1960 there were less than 2,000 divorces in Scotland. In 1994 there were 13,133 and around 75% of these cases were initiated by women (Equal Opportunities Commission 1995, 76). The liberalisation of divorce law through the twentieth century provided women trapped in bad marriages with the opportunity to escape. Double standards in divorce law were removed in the 1920s, making it possible for women to divorce men on the same grounds. The Divorce (Scotland) Act of 1938 introduced a wider range of grounds for divorce, including cruelty. The provision of legal aid to women in divorce cases in 1949, 'no-fault' divorce law reforms in the late 1960s and 1970s, and the passage of the Family Law (Scotland) Act in 1985 have had particularly beneficial results – the latter providing for a somewhat fairer distribution of family resources and property upon marital breakdown (EOC, 77, 89; Breitenbach 1989, 179). Marital and partnership breakdowns have led to a rapid growth in single parent families – now around one in five Scottish families. Not least because of the continuing undervaluation of female labour, this situation has exacerbated the problem of poverty amongst single parent families (90% of which are headed by women) which is now a major at-risk group (Glendinning and Millar 1992, 3–10; 42–4).

It can reasonably be argued that the decline in the practice of live-in relatives, less children, artificial contraception, the diffusion down the social scale of labour saving household gadgets, rising housing standards and improved health and longevity combined to have positive effects upon Scottish women's lives through the twentieth century. Such substantive changes went some way to emancipate women from the stultifying drudgery that characterised housework and family responsibilities at the end of the nineteenth century, and provided women with more freedom and autonomy, not least in sexual behaviour. Anderson emphasises such positive amelioration in his evaluation of changing family life in twentieth century Scotland (Anderson 1992). But is this too sanguine an interpretation? Did relationships, the distribution of resources within families and the sexual division of labour within the Scottish home undergo a radical transformation in the twentieth century?

Oral testimony from 1900 to 1950 suggests a relatively unchanging pattern of activity and experience within the private sphere of the home and family (Jamieson 1986, 66–7). In this sense, political emancipation via the franchise had little impact upon the everyday socio-economic experience of women prior to World War Two. Girls continued to be prepared carefully for a life of servicing the male 'breadwinner'. In response to the question 'did your father help your mother with any jobs in the house?' one Stirlingshire woman commented: 'No. No. No, my father was very well looked after in the house, even to the fact that his tea was poured out for him, and everything was just there for him to sit down. He was the worker o' the house' (Stirling Transcript, G1). Long habituation and socialisation meant that such sex stereotyping of roles within the working class family continued to be accepted without question. An Edinburgh woman recalled life for her mother in the 1930s thus: 'She was always working, she never got out anywhere. That was her life'. She continued: 'I had six brothers and four sisters. As we got older we did more work. My brothers were treated like gentlemen. That was general. I was second youngest but the ones before me got a lot to do. We didn't mind; that was our life' (Pentland and Calton 1987, 10; see also Faley 1990, 58–60). Domestic tasks continued to be performed with the minimum of mechanical aids – the domestic technological revolution was an incremental process, but few working-class families even had access to electricity before the 1930s. Thus the domestic labour process remained physically debilitating up to World War Two – doubly so where poorer women engaged in paid work to supplement family income.

Whilst oral testimonies have begun to redress a serious gap in our knowledge, the internal life of the Scottish family in the twentieth century is still in need of more systematic research. We know very little about how, when, and to what degree relationships, resource distribution and the sexual division of labour within Scottish families changed. A recurrent theme that emerges in the literature, however, is domestic violence. Wife-beating was common within Scottish working class homes in the late nineteenth century and this was evidently still prevalent in Glasgow in the twentieth century (Young 1985, 141; McIntyre 1980). One historian has recently argued – using oral evidence – that relatively high levels of domestic violence on Clydeside between the wars was intimately linked to a crisis of male identity brought on by the collapse of male employment in the traditional heavy industries and resultant changing patterns of recreation (Hughes 1996, 9–19; 46–7). On the basis of research in Glasgow police records, Dobash and Dobash (1979) argue that the state in the 1970s legitimised domestic violence by refusing to consistently prosecute offenders. Clearly, domestic violence remains a persistent feature of relationships at the end of the century. Witness the Zero Tolerance campaign and the fact that, in 1996, 150,000 people across Britain phoned the domestic violence helpline.

Three final points are worth making, all important caveats to the 'quiet revolution' thesis which hypothesises that a cluster of reforms and changes through the twentieth century conferred full rights of citizenship upon women (Marshall 1983). Firstly, it has been persuasively argued that despite the so-called 'revolution' in domestic technology there has been little fall in the number of working hours spent by full-time housewives on housework and childrearing (Hardyment 1988; Davidson 1982; Cowan 1989). This apparent paradox has been explained by the fact that standards in all areas of the domestic labour process – childcare; cleaning; cooking; laundry etc – have increased commensurately. Nevertheless, labour-saving domestic technology has been emancipatory in its impact in the sense of providing more choice over the allocation of time within the general context of household and childcare work. What appears to have happened is that childcare and socialisation have become more important within the family (Davidoff 1976, 147).

Secondly, much has been made of the emergence in recent years of a more equitable system of unpaid domestic work distribution within the home, a transformation popularly eulogised in the notion of 'the new man'. Change in this respect, however, is more limited than the hype suggests and appears to have gone furthest in professional, middle-class families. Segregated roles and sex-typing in domestic labour clearly remains the norm, even where both partners are working full-time. According to one quite comprehensive time-budget study, British women averaged 26 hours per week more than men on housework in 1961, whereas by 1983–4 women averaged 16 hours more (Gershuny 1986, 13–39). The same survey found that where both partners were in full employment, women did around twice as much domestic labour as men in the mid-1980s (Joshi 1989, 160–1). Unfortunately, no such time budget research appears to exist for Scotland and Gershuny's work is not broken down by region. However, Howard Kahn's recent study of the domestic labour of a hundred wives in Edinburgh reveals high levels of monotony, fatigue and stress and marginal involvement of men in the running of the home and family (Kahn 1994). The available evidence suggests that continuity prevails and that a fundamental transformation in the sexual division of labour within the home has still not occurred.

Thirdly, it appears that unequal distribution of resources within the home continued through the twentieth century. Oral and other evidence indicates that before the Second World War married men typically kept a portion of their income as personal pocket money (for drink, tobacco, newspapers etc), thus enhancing their access to regenerative and diversionary recreational activities such as football, betting and the pub (Jamieson 1986, 66–7). Unfortunately, there appears to have been no recent work on resource distribution within families specifically relating to Scotland. However, Vogler's study of 1,200 British households in the 1980s shows that only around one in five used more egalitarian financial/income pooling systems, such as joint bank accounts (Vogler 1989; also Glendinning and Millar 1992). In the majority of households men almost certainly continued to have access to larger quantities of personal spending money than women. Moreover, economic dependence on the husband's higher wage increased women's vulnerability to future poverty in cases of marital breakdown. This was part of a vicious circle. The undervaluation of female labour in the formal economy could be used to rationalise an unequal sexual division of labour within the home, with women designated the lion's share of housework and child-rearing, on the grounds of maximising family income. The time spent on such unpaid work in the home in turn disadvantaged women (in the sense of loss of accrued employment experience) in the formal labour market. This conundrum demonstrates the continued strength of patriarchal values, which remain deeply embedded within the Scottish family.

To sum up so far, it remains difficult to come to any firm conclusions on the changing role of women within the family in Scotland. However, the pivotal ameliorative change was control over fertility, which proved far more emancipatory in its impact than any political or legislative developments. Clearly, much of the context in which women were operating within the family has altered since c. 1850. However, what is important is that the pace of change was extremely slow before World War Two and that there were wide variations in experience amongst women, dependent upon social class, religion and location. Nevertheless, a variety of factors have radically altered the women's environment, resulting in a considerably less prescribed and more independent existence. Women have chosen different patterns: delaying marriage until almost thirty; leaving the family home earlier to co-habit with a partner; divorcing rather than tolerating unsatisfactory partners; more frequently combining paid with unpaid domestic labour.

However, to say this is not to imply that gender inequalities within the home and family have disappeared. On the contrary, change in the private sphere of the home and family appears to have lagged behind ameliorative changes in the public sphere. Despite some tangible movement towards the more symmetrical household, particularly amongst middle-class, professional groups, 'the new man' remains a distant ideal, rather than the reality within contemporary Scottish society. Female subordination and economic dependency within the home, the persistence of a marked sexual division of labour, the maldistribution of resources within the family and the survival of chauvinist attitudes and patriarchal values continues to characterise the Scottish family. Thus the notion of a *radical* transformation, or 'quiet revolution', in women's position and role within the family in Scotland during the twentieth century is hardly supported by the evidence. At the very least such an hypothesis has to be used very cautiously, and hedged with an array of caveats and qualifications. Can the same be said about women in the public sphere of politics and the workplace?

EXERCISE 3
Oral testimony has been utilised to good effect to destroy the myth of female inactivity in the economic sphere and to shed insight into other areas of women's lives and gender relations. Read over the extracts from oral testimonies (**Document 117**). What are the strengths and weaknesses of oral history methodology in relation to the history of women and gender relations? What do the extracts tell us about the patterns of women's lives and gender relations before World War Two?

Again, you will have come to your own conclusions on the utility of oral history. There are potential difficulties to be overcome with such a subjective source, such as the fallibility of memory (often respondents are being asked to recall events and experiences from a very long time ago), conscious and unconscious distortion (time alters perceptions), the representativeness of the experience (sampling). However, using best practice techniques, experience and judgement such problems can be minimised. Moreover, all sources include some bias and need to be treated critically and sensitively. Given the potential of oral history to open up. areas of experience which have not been documented, such as the inner world of family life, the advantages far outweigh the weaknesses. On the second part of the question, my view (though you may well disagree) is that such testimony suggests much continuity in the basic patterns of women's lives, supporting the hypothesis that the First World War and the vote made little difference to the everyday experience of Scottish women up to the 1940s.

3. WORK AND POLITICS: THE 'PUBLIC' DOMAIN

After a long struggle, women achieved equality of citizenship, gaining the franchise on equal terms with men in 1928. Trade unions have also been opened up to women, whilst labour markets have been transformed with significant changes in women's experience of waged work in Scotland. Important developments in the twentieth century have been the movement of married women from the home into paid employment; an erosion in occupational segregation by gender; rising real wages and declining gender wage differentials; and the legal banning of gender-specific discriminatory employment practices. However, regional and class differences in experience have remained significant and gender inequalities in the public sphere have continued, albeit in a somewhat diluted form. In other words, progress towards equal opportunity in politics and employment has been made but the process is by no means complete. What is most striking is the persistence throughout the twentieth century of structural inequalities and discrimination against women in the 'public' arena. This is most evident, perhaps, in employment.

Taking the basic measurement of economic activity rates (that is, the proportion of the population participating in paid employment according to the Census), the period 1900–1930s witnessed relatively little change. From the 1930s, however, female economic activity rates rose sharply. In the period 1901–1931 around 35% of women between school leaving age and retirement were officially classified as economically active. By 1991 the figure was 67%. Before World War Two marriage and childbirth drew most women back into the domestic sphere. What had changed by the end of the twentieth century was that female economic activity invariably took place outside *as well as* inside the home. Moreover, paid employment was also concentrated into a shorter time span with proportionately fewer younger (under 18) and older (over 60) women working, partly the product of the raising of the school leaving age, the expansion of higher education and the provision of state pensions – including a widows pension introduced in the 1930s.

50 Trade Union Committee, Stanley Mills, Perthshire, 1915.

TABLE 4: FEMALE EMPLOYMENT IN SCOTLAND, BY MARITAL STATUS, 1911–1991
(EXPRESSED AS A PERCENTAGE OF TOTAL FEMALES EMPLOYED)

	MARRIED	*SINGLE
1911	5.3	94.7
1921	6.3	93.7
1931	8.5	91.5
1951	23.4	76.6
1961	38.7	61.3
1971	57.8	42.2
1981	62.0	38.0
1991	60.4	39.6

Source: Census of Scotland, 1911–1991.
* *Includes those widowed and divorced.*

Before World War Two strong social and institutional pressures existed to keep
married women out of the formal economy. The heightened participation of women
during the 1914–18 war had little long-term effect, with few holding down wartime
jobs thereafter due to trade union opposition, legislation (the Restoration of Pre-
War Practices Act) and a barrage of newspaper and magazine propaganda post-war
which resuscitated the Victorian domestic ideal. Such 'masculine madness', as one

51 Glasgow Clippies, *c.* 1915. *Springburn Museum Trust.*

Scottish feminist (Eleanor Stewart) called it, meant that discrimination, especially against married and older women in the labour market, abounded in the interwar period (Young 1989, 181; 183–4). The marriage bar remained firmly in place in teaching and the civil service and many other occupations exercised an informal bar and, indeed, preference for younger, unmarried workers (STUC 1931, 69–71; 1934, 73). Moreover, a stigma was clearly attached to those married women who continued to work in the formal economy. One Edinburgh shop assistant recalled:

> If you were allowed back to work after marriage they would have said 'what a shame she's got to go and work'. So even if you were hard up, the last thing was to go back to work. It was not the done thing – Oh no! In those days the man was supposed to be the provider.
>
> (Pentland 1987, 19–20)

Things evidently began to change in the 1930s, and at an accelerated pace after the Second World War. Full employment after 1945 provided more job opportunities whilst the pool of single women in the labour market shrank because of the rising school leaving age and longer periods spent in full-time education. The enhanced labour market participation by married women has been facilitated by smaller family size, rising real wages and growing expectations fuelled by the revived feminist movement of the 1960s and 1970s. However, a crucial causal factor has been the expansion of part-time job opportunities outside the home. Between 1951 and 1981 the proportion of total female jobs in Scotland that were part-time (ie defined as a working week of under 30 hours) rose from less than 5% to 41%. Significantly, at the latter point, only around 7% of all male Scottish employees worked part-time. Hence, whilst job experience ranged widely, the 'bi-modal' or M-shaped profile of female employment became more prevalent in Scotland during the course of the twentieth century. Typically this meant an initial eight to ten year period of work outside the home until reaching the mid to late twenties, followed by a period of several years of unpaid work within the home, rearing and nursing children, and capped off by a return to work in the formal economy on a full or part-time basis until retirement (Joseph 1983, 163–4).

The overall pattern of female employment in Scotland is very similar to developments within the British economy as a whole. At the very broadest level, there has been a marked shift from manual, industrial, primary employment towards tertiary, clerical, service and distributive work. Agriculture in Scotland, for example, employed at least 126,000 women in 1851 (this is almost certainly an under-estimate), around 40,000 women in 1901 and only 4,300 in 1991 (see Sprott, this volume). Whilst only two female commercial clerks were recorded in the 1861 Census, by 1991 there were over 110,000 women in public administration, banking and insurance, the vast majority of which were clerical workers. Indeed, the major employment growth area for Scottish women has been the non-manual, services sector – insurance, banking, business services, public administration, local government, teaching, nursing and shopwork. 75% of all Scottish women employed in the formal economy were clustered in these occupations by 1991, compared to less than 20% in 1901. Thus the twentieth century has witnessed a transformation with the gradual feminisation of clerical work in Scotland.

Female employment in the manufacturing sector in Scotland has also undergone considerable change. The traditional sectors of textiles and clothing suffered catastrophic contraction as foreign competition eroded markets, forcing closures and rationalisation. In 1991, less than 25,000 women were employed in textiles and clothing, around 1% of the total Scottish female labour force. On the other hand, the process of technological change, new mass-production assembly-line techniques, deskilling and more sophisticated division of labour led to a substantial increase in the proportion of females employed in light engineering, food and drink processing and transport and communications. Much of this expansion has stagnated since the late 1960s. For example, female employment in engineering rose from around 3,000 in 1901 to over 60,000 in 1971, thereafter dropping back to 32,000 in 1991.

Perhaps the most significant change in the occupational profile of women workers in Scotland in the twentieth century has been the virtual extinction of the indoor domestic servant, the largest single occupation for women before World War Two, accounting for some 20% of the total female labour force. However, counter-balancing this has been rising job opportunities in the low-paid personal services sector with the expansion of private and state sector employment, including institutional cleaners and caterers. Shop work also became more common, with women employed in distribution rising from 54,000 in 1901 to peak at 157,000 in 1971. However, job opportunities in this sector have levelled out in the last quarter of the twentieth century, partly as a consequence of the growth of giant stores and the penetration of labour-saving micro-chip technology (McIvor 1992, 138–44).

The evidence from the Census therefore supports the notion of significant erosion over the course of the twentieth century in horizontal occupational segregation. A much wider range of job opportunities was opened up to women. Gender inequalities have, however, persisted and a distinct sexual division of labour has continued to characterise the employment market. In 1991 around 70% of women workers were clustered in just four (personal services; clerical; professions; distribution) out of 16 broadly classified occupational orders (Joshi 1989, 159). Moreover, it was predominantly women who performed the lesser paid, lower status part-time jobs. Indeed, around 90% of all part-time workers (around 500,000) in Scotland in the early 1990s were women. The position of part-time female workers perhaps best reflects the continuing undervaluation, degradation and discrimination exercised against women in the post-war labour market in Scotland. They have remained amongst the least organised and most exploited sections of the post-war Scottish labour force – low paid; low status; often working unsocial hours; with few of the employment rights enjoyed by full-timers.

Gender segregation in employment was undoubtedly less prevalent in the 1990s compared to the mid-nineteenth century, but it remained pervasive nonetheless. Many areas of manual employment continued to be monopolised by male workers. Within 'newer' occupations, women tended to be ghettoised into the lowest status, poorest paid, menial jobs, with male workers in the most skilled, responsible and best paid jobs. Breaking the employment profile down by socio-economic status reveals the dogged persistence of vertical occupational segregation and gender apartheid in job opportunities.

TABLE 5: VERTICAL SEGREGATION: SCOTTISH WORKERS BY SOCIO-ECONOMIC GROUP, 1961 – 1991 (AS A PERCENTAGE OF TOTAL WORKFORCE BY GENDER)

Group	1961		1991	
	MALE	FEMALE	MALE	FEMALE
Employers	3.1	1.5	3.7	1.7
Managers & administrators	4.7	2.1	12.1	7.0
Self-employed professionals	1.0	0.1	1.2	0.3
Professional employees	2.3	0.6	5.7	1.7
Intermediate non-manual	3.5	10.7	10.0	0.1
Junior non-manual	2.3	38.7	9.2	35.6
Personal service	0.9	11.7	1.8	8.3
Foremen/women & supervisors (manual)	3.4	0.4	3.6	0.8
Skilled manual	36.2	9.4	23.5	2.8
Semi-skilled manual	12.8	14.6	12.7	8.4
Unskilled manual	8.8	7.3	4.9	9.7
Own account workers	2.0	1.2	5.7	1.9
Farmers (employers & managers)	1.9	0.3	0.8	0.1
Farmers – own account	1.1	0.2	1.1	0.3
Agricultural workers	4.0	0.9	1.6	0.4
Armed forces	1.4	0.1	1.4	0.1
Total (thousands)	1504	712	1143	930

Source: S Kendrick (1961) 'Occupational Change in Modern Scotland', *Scottish Government Yearbook*, 1986, 246–7; *Census of Scotland*, 1991.

Upward social mobility into the top status jobs is evident over 1961–1991 for both male and female workers (Table 6). However, in relative terms the position changed little over these years. What remains persistent is the over-representation of women in subordinate grade jobs and obdurate under-representation in the employing, managerial and professional categories (Table 5). Hakim (1994) has argued a similar case for Britain as a whole. The proportion of women in the lowest status jobs has hardly changed, whilst a larger proportion of male workers have experienced upward mobility. Significantly, the unskilled manual group has become considerably more feminised. Such data tend to support those who have argued that women have a separate class status to men and should not be subsumed within the class position of the male breadwinner (Marshall, Newby, Rose and Vogler 1988, 63–84). These figures also support the notion that upward social mobility for women in Scotland has not been any faster than for men over the past three decades. One important reason for this has been the characteristic degradation in job status achieved by women on re-entering the labour market after an absence rearing children. Deskilling through the characteristically truncated female work cycle occurred, exacerbated by the fact that married women and single mothers were more geographically immobile. One survey has estimated that around 30% of women returning to work after having children experience a fall in previous job status (Joshi 1989, 169–70).

TABLE 6: VERTICAL SEGREGATION: JOB DISTRIBUTION IN SCOTLAND BY GENDER (EXPRESSED AS A PERCENTAGE OF TOTAL WORKFORCE BY SEX), 1961 AND 1991.

	1961		1991	
	MALE	FEMALE	MALE	FEMALE
*Proportion of workers in highest status jobs**	13.0	4.6	23.5	10.8
*Proportion of workers in lowest jobs***	22.0	57.7	15.9	53.6

* *Represents the grouping of categories 1–4 and 13 in table 5.*
** *Represents the grouping of categories 6,7 and 11 in table 5.*

EXERCISE 4

What do you think are the main strengths and weaknesses of the decennial census as a source for researching patterns of female employment since 1850?

Statistics can give a false impression of certainty. It is important to evaluate such data critically and with a dose of healthy scepticism. There are problems with changing criteria, especially relating to the recording of occupations, which makes it difficult to strictly compare the 'profile' offered by the census over long periods of time. In particular, the early censuses seriously under-recorded the economic activity of women and because of prevailing attitudes exaggerated the number of women working as domestic servants in the Victorian period. Nevertheless, after making such allowances, the census still provides a fairly accurate snapshot of the labour market (especially after World War One for women) and can be usefully exploited to demonstrate changing patterns of discrimination based on gender in the workplace. Indeed, there is considerable potential for a serious quantitative analysis of occupational segregation by gender in Scotland, along the lines of Hakim's (1994) work south of the Border.

Part of the ameliorationist/'quiet revolution' argument is premised upon the notion of growing economic independence for women through the twentieth century as real earnings and the real value of state welfare benefits rose. However, the under-valuation of female labour has remained an enduring feature of Scottish society. The differential between male and female earnings changed little over 1900–1939 and eroded only slowly over the period 1939–70. As late as 1970 Scottish women averaged only 54% of male earnings. Thereafter, as a consequence of equal rights legislation, the gap narrowed sharply, though gender wage differentials remain a marked feature of the Scottish economy in the 1990s, as Table 7 indicates.

TABLE 7: GENDER WAGE DIFFERENTIALS: SCOTLAND AND ENGLAND COMPARED, 1906 AND 1992

	I. ADULT MALE EARNINGS (WEEKLY)	II. ADULT FEMALE EARNINGS (WEEKLY)	% COL II TO COL I
Scotland 1906	£1.43	£0.65	45.2%
England 1906	£1.51	£0.69	45.3%
Scotland 1992	£324.60	£221.90	68.4%
England 1992	£343.60	£244.20	71.1%

Sources: 1906: Board of Trade Earnings and Hours Inquiry (September 1906); 1992: Dept of Employment, New Earnings Survey (1992), Part E, Tables E110.1, E113.1.

The 1906 figures represent averages derived from 22 industries where information is consistently provided on both male and female full-time earnings in the Board of Trade Labour Department wages survey. The 1992 figures are average gross weekly earnings of full-time workers on adult wage rates. The gender wage differential is even greater if earnings over a lifetime are considered, because of the child-rearing employment gap and (until recently) women retired five years earlier than men and there has been a greater tendency for women in their fifties to reduce their involvement in paid work, whereas men have been much more likely to continue full-time employment to the official retirement age.

A major cause of this persistent gender wage differential has been (and continues to be) the economic penalty women pay for withdrawal from the labour market to have and rear children. Joshi (1989) has calculated that women taking eight years out of employment potentially reduce their lifetime earnings by 46% in comparison with a woman who remains childless. Moreover, equal pay has been difficult to achieve because of the persistence of sexual discrimination working at a number of levels, including skills acquisition, normal hours worked and access to overtime. Child care facilities dismantled after World War Two remain inadequate. Moreover, the post-1945 state-initiated formal incomes policies restrained wage rises which penalised service sector workers (where overtime and bonus payments were rare) compared to blue collar workers. Employers have proven to be persistently reluctant to promote women or to train women for skilled and responsible positions. An example would be higher education, where very few women achieve entry into senior lectureships, readerships or chairs. During the equal pay debates in the 1970s many trade unions recognised that this was the crucial issue: 'Without equal opportunities, equal pay is only a partial success' commented the Scottish Schoolmasters' Association.

For much of the twentieth century, gender differentials in educational attainment were also a pivotal cause of undervaluation in the labour market. Sex-typing in education eroded painfully slowly, contributing to sustaining inequalities and constraining women's chances of upward social mobility. Double standards in educational provision for girls and boys persisted into the post-Second World War period, including a greater chance of young men gaining qualifications through higher education than women. Until recently, progress in Scotland in this respect had been slower than in England (*Regional Trends* 1993, table 5.11). There continue to be marked gender differentials in the type of degree courses undertaken, though by 1990 the gender balance in access to degree level courses in Scotland was roughly equal. Current debates within the secondary (ages eleven to eighteen) school system suggest that the wheel has turned full circle, with girls in Scotland achieving significantly better grades than boys at both Standard and Higher levels and, hence, performing better than male candidates in the mid-late 1990s in gaining entry into higher education. In this sense, equality became a reality in Scotland by the 1990s.

TABLE 8: PROPORTION OF FEMALES TO TOTAL POPULATION EDUCATED TO DEGREE LEVEL IN SCOTLAND: BY AGE COHORT, 1991

	% FEMALE
Aged 18–29	49.7
Aged 30–44	40.6
Aged 45–59	27.1

Source: Census of Scotland, 1991

Trade unions have played a vital role in protecting Scottish workers' interests against rapacious employers and the vagaries of volatile labour markets. A positive correlation exists between high wage industries and levels of trade union density. It follows, therefore, that participation in such collective organisations by women would enhance their living standards and contribute to economic independence as well as having spin-offs in terms of better contractual conditions and a more conducive work environment. However, whilst collective protest and industrial action by women were not unknown before World War One, women were largely excluded from the male-dominated world of the Scottish trade unions (Gordon 1988; 1991; Reynolds 1989; Knox 1995; Glasgow Labour History Workshop 1989; Kenefick and McIvor 1996). For much of the twentieth century Scottish trade unions continued to absorb and reflect the dominant sexist values of the day, rather than championing the cause of gender equality. Female union membership levels were lower (proportionately) than in England and whilst there were a number of actively involved women prior to the Second World War, representation in decision-making positions within the union hierarchy was marginal (McIvor 1992, 155; Breitenbach 1982).

From the 1930s Scottish female trade union membership accelerated, rising from around 50,000 to over 350,000 by 1979. Women were drawn more systematically into the institutions of the Scottish labour movement and, as members, reaped some of the benefits of collective organisation for mutual protection. From being a relatively poorly organised region of Britain in the early twentieth century, Scottish women were amongst the most well-unionised at the end of the century. 38.4% of Scottish women were members of trade unions in 1992, compared to 30.9% in England (*Employment Gazette* 1993, 686; *Regional Trends*, no 28, 1993, 98; McIvor 1996, 204).

Male chauvinism within the Scottish trade unions has undoubtedly declined through the twentieth century, but very slowly. It was not until the 1970s that trade unions in Scotland became more sensitive to the needs and aspirations of their female membership. This was partly in response to the revived civil rights and feminist movements and to growing female membership of unions and the crisis trade unionism in Scotland suffered as a result of the erosion of their traditional membership base as coal and heavy industry contracted. Thus in the 1970s many unions initiated positive action programmes to facilitate change, attempted to improve female representation, created Women's Committees and special conferences and changed recruitment policy, for example, with reduced subscription rates for part-time workers and maternity. Moreover, issues particularly pertinent to women workers were increasingly taken up, such as childcare, sexual harassment, employment rights of part-time workers, health issues, access to education, parental leave and equal pay. Women, however, remained seriously under-represented within the largest Scottish unions recruiting women (McIvor 1992, 166; McIvor 1996, 204–5). But there have been significant improvements in the access of women to decision-making positions within the STUC, the result, partly at least, of recently-adopted policies of positive discrimination. In 1980 there was only one female member of the 21 strong STUC General Council and of 580 delegates to the STUC Congress only 39 (or 7.1%) were women. In 1994 there were 12 women on an expanded General Council of 37 and of 503 delegates to the STUC Congress, 118 (23%) were women. So, whilst patriarchal values proved persistent, there are tangible signs that the overbearing male chauvinism of the Scottish trade union movement is being dismantled and that gender equality in the workplace is at last being prioritised on the trade unions's policy agenda.

The same might be said for politics, though such a generalisation requires serious qualification. The fundamental change has been the extension of the right to vote in elections to women; initially locally – women voted on equal terms with men from 1881 – and then nationally with initial enfranchisement in 1918 under an age and property qualification, followed ten years later with full enfranchisement of women aged 21 and over. From 1901 women had the right to be elected as local councillors and in 1918 Eunice Murray, a moderate suffragist, became the first Scottish woman to stand (unsuccessfully) for Parliament. It was not until 1923 that Scotland's first woman MP, Katherine Marjory, Duchess of Atholl, was elected to the House of Commons. The first woman to enter the House of Lords was not until 1958.

It continued, in reality, to be extremely difficult for women to become actively involved in parliamentary politics, not least because of the location of the work, the unsociable hours and innate male opposition from many quarters. Nevertheless, some strong female political figures emerged in Scotland in the first half of the twentieth century, including Helen Crawfurd, Rose Kerrigan, Marion Henery, Agnes Hardie, Clarice McNab Shaw, Jennie Lee, Jean Mann, Margaret Herbison and Agnes Dollan (Burness 1992, 156–70; Melling 1983).

Numbers of activists increased after 1945, but quantitatively women continued to be seriously under-represented in Parliament. In the early 1980s, only 13.7% (compared to over 18% for the UK as a whole) of Scotland's 1,639 local councillors were female whilst in the mid-1990s, only 7% of Scottish MPs (compared to 9% of British MPs) were women (Abercrombie and Warde 1990, 239). This scenario was improved with the landslide Labour victory in the 1997 General Election, when 12 women won seats out of Scotland's 72 constituencies. Even this dramatic change needs to be kept in perspective. 1997 saw female representation in the House of Commons increase to about 20% of the total. Whether a devolved Scottish Parliament radically alters this situation remains to be seen.

EXERCISE 5
Comment on some of the ways that social class, race and locality have affected women's experience and gender relations in Scotland since c. 1850?

One of the main weaknesses in such a chapter as this is the impression it gives of an homogeneous experience based upon gender. Whilst the nature of patriarchy was a critical influence, and has been emphasised here, it needs to be recognised that the realities of women's lives were extremely varied and that women themselves were active players capable of mediating prevailing circumstances through strategic choices and their own popular culture. Race, locality and social class were all important variables. Occupational choice was constrained for Irish women in the late nineteenth century and Asian women located in Scotland in the late twentieth century. Opportunities and cultural norms varied across Scotland, with the experience of women in the Highlands and Islands differing greatly from that of the more cosmopolitan lowland town dwellers. Particular communities, such as Dundee and the North-East coast fishing ports, incubated a more matriarchal environment. Social class, moreover, remained a key determinant of life changes, creating a vast gulf in the experience of upper and middle class women – the proverbial 'angel in the house' and the female proletariat. This is reflected, for example, in jobs, family size, consumption, education and standards of health.

CONCLUSION

My main conclusion is that the notion of a 'quiet revolution' in Scottish women's lives since 1850 should be employed cautiously. A degree of economic independence came soonest to urban middle class and professional women and latest to poorer urban and rural women. That is not to deny that women in Scotland at the end of the twentieth century have a higher status and more respect as citizens, and enjoy more autonomy, more choices and a less prescribed existence than their Victorian counterparts. That is clearly the case as the gender inequalities which were such a central feature of Victorian society have diminished. In this respect political and legal reforms have been important, as well as widening job opportunities and access to the protective matrix offered by the trade unions. Perhaps control over fertility has been the critical change which has undeniably had an ameliorative impact upon the everyday lives of Scottish women.

The key point I would emphasise is that whilst gender inequalities within Scottish society, like class divisions, have been eroded through the twentieth century, they have by no means been eradicated. What has occurred through the course of the twentieth century has been the conferring of more independence and autonomy to women across all social classes. What has not happened is any significant shift in labour distribution within the home, nor are women valued equally within the Scottish labour market, whilst women's access to positions of power and decision-making within society remain sharply circumscribed. The ability to vote and open access to the institutions of power (eg local and national government) have not been translated into anything like near equal representation of women. Despite the provision of a more level playing field, women continue to be disadvantaged. Indeed, occupational segregation, the undervaluation of female labour and a distinctive sexual division of labour within the home and family have remained three persistent features of Scottish women's lives since c. 1850. Improving general living standards have masked the disparity and inequality of opportunities, disguising the fact that the economic dependency of women upon men has continued, albeit in modified forms. The enduring structures of family and home life are of particular importance in this respect because a basic prerequisite for real equality of opportunity and full participation by women within the public sphere on equal terms with men is a more equitable distribution of domestic work and family responsibilities within the private sphere of the home.

Finally, whilst hard and conclusive data is illusive, the evidence supports the view that Scottish society was more patriarchal than English society, at least up to World War Two. Occupational segregation appears to have been more marked; Scottish families were larger and a significantly smaller proportion of married women worked in Scotland before Second World War than in England. Moreover, until recently, gender differentials in educational attainment were wider in Scotland than England and before 1939 there were also proportionately fewer women in trade unions in Scotland than in England. Scottish women were (and remain) under-represented in Parliament and local government – even more so than English women. However, it must be emphasised that the literature remains extremely thin on such issues and more systematic research is necessary. There is much scope for a comprehensive age-cohort oral history project and for developing comparisons with other European countries. Dismantling the surviving and not inconsiderable vestiges of gender apartheid within contemporary Scottish society also remains on the policy agenda for the new millennium.

REFERENCES TO BOOKS, ARTICLES AND SOURCES MENTIONED IN THE TEXT

Abercrombie, N and Warde, A 1990 *Contemporary British Society*. Cambridge.
Anderson, M 1992 'Population and Family Life', *in* Dickson, A and Treble, JH (eds), *People and Society in Scotland. Volume III 1914–1990*, Edinburgh, 12–47.
Beddoe, D 1988 *Discovering Women's History*. London.
Breitenbach, E 1982 *Women Workers in Scotland*. Edinburgh.
Breitenbach, E 1989 'The Impact of Thatcherism on Women in Scotland', *Scottish Government Yearbook*. Edinburgh.
*Breitenbach, E and Gordon, E (eds) 1992 *Out of Bounds*. Edinburgh.
Brown, C and Stephenson, JD 1992 '"Sprouting Wings"? Women and Religion in Scotland, c1890–1950', *in* Breitenbach, E and Gordon, E (eds), *Out of Bounds*, Edinburgh, 95–120.
Burness, C 1992 'The Long Slow March: Scottish Women MPs, 1918–45', *in* Breitenbach, E and Gordon, E, *Out of Bounds*, Edinburgh, 151–73.
Corr, H 1983a 'The Schoolgirls Curriculum and the Ideology of the Home, 1870–1914', *in* Glasgow Women's Studies Group, *Uncharted Lives*, Glasgow, 74–97.
Corr, H 1983b 'The Sexual Division of Labour in the Scottish Teaching Profession, 1872–1914', *in* Humes, WM and Paterson, HM (eds), *Scottish Culture and Scottish Education, 1800–1980,* Edinburgh, 137–50.
Corr, H 1990 'An Exploration into Scottish Education', *in* Fraser, WH and Morris, RJ, *People and Society in Scotland. Volume II 1830–1914*, Edinburgh, 290–309.
Cowan, RS 1989 *More Work for Mother*. London.
Davidoff, L 1976 'Rationalisation', *in* Barker, DL and Allen, S (eds), *Dependence and Exploitation in Work and Marriage*, London, 121–51.
Davidson, C 1982 *A Woman's Work is Never Done*. London.
Dobash, RE and Dobash, R 1979 *Violence Against Wives*. London.
Equal Opportunities Commission (EOC) 1995 *Equality Issues in Scotland*.
Employment Gazette, January 1993
Faley, J 1990 *Up Oor Close: Memories of Domestic Life in Glasgow Tenements, 1910–1945*. Glasgow.
Flinn, MW (ed) 1977 *Scottish Population History*. London.
Gershuny, J, Miles, I, Jones, S, Mullings, C, Thomas, G and Wyatt, S 1986 'Time Budgets', *Quarterly Journal of Social Affairs*, 2, 13–39.
Glasgow Labour History Workshop 1989 *The Singer Strike, Clydebank, 1911*. Glasgow.
Glasgow Women's Studies Group 1983 *Uncharted Lives. Extracts from Scottish Women's Experiences, 1850–1982*. Glasgow.
Glendinning, C and Millar, J (eds) 1992 *Women and Poverty in Britain: the 1990s*. London.
Gordon, E 1988 'The Scottish Trade Union Movement, Class and Gender, 1850–1914', *Scottish Labour History Society Journal*, 23, Glasgow, 30–44.
*Gordon, E 1991 *Women and the Labour Movement in Scotland, 1850–1914*. Oxford.

*Gordon, E 1990 'Women's Spheres', *in* Fraser, WH and Morris, RJ, *People and Society in Scotland. Volume II 1830–1914*, Edinburgh, 206–35.

* Gordon, E and Breitenbach, E (eds) 1990 *The World is Ill-Divided*. Edinburgh.

Gray, R 1976 *The Labour Aristocracy in Victorian Edinburgh*. Oxford.

Hakim, C 1994 'A Century of Change in Occupational Segregation, 1891–1991', *Journal of Historical Sociology* 7, 435–54.

Hardyment, C 1988 *From Mangle to Microwave: The Mechanisation of Housework*. London.

Hughes, AM 1996 *Popular Pastimes and Wife Assault in Interwar Glasgow*. Honours Dissertation, University of Strathclyde.

*Jamieson, L 1986 'Limited Resources and Limiting Conventions: Working Class Mothers and Daughters in Urban Scotland, c1890–1925', *in* Lewis, J (ed), *Labour and Love: Women's Experience of Home and Family, 1850–1940*, London, 49–69.

Joseph, G 1983 *Women at Work: The British Experience*. London.

Joshi, H (ed) 1989 *The Changing Population of Britain*. London.

Kahn, H *Scotland on Sunday*, 27.11.94.

Kenefick, W and McIvor, A 1996 *Roots of Red Clydeside, 1910–14?* Edinburgh.

*King, E 1993 *The Hidden History of Glasgow's Women*. Edinburgh.

Knox, WW 1995 *Hanging By a Thread: The Scottish Cotton Industry, c1850–1914*. Preston.

*Leneman, L 1991 *A Guid Cause: The Women's Suffrage Movement in Scotland*. Aberdeen.

Lewis, J 1984 *Women in England, 1870–1950*. Brighton.

Lewis, J 1992 *Women in Britain since 1945*. London.

*Livingstone, S 1994 *Bonnie Fechters*. Motherwell.

Mahood, L 1992 'Family Ties: Lady Child Savers and Girls of the Street, 1850–1925', *in* Breitenbach, E and Gordon, E (eds), *Out of Bounds*, Edinburgh, 42–64.

Marshall, G, Newby, H, Rose, D and Vogler, C 1988 *Social Class in Modern Britain*. London.

Marshall, R 1983 *Virgins and Viragos: A History of Women in Scotland from 1080 to 1980*. London.

McIntyre, S 1980 *Little Moscows*. London.

McIvor, A 1992 'Women and Work in Twentieth Century Scotland', *in* Dickson, A and Treble, JH (eds), *People and Society in Scotland. Volume III 1914–1990*, Edinburgh, 138–73.

McIvor, A 1996 'Gender Apartheid?', *in* Devine, TM and Finlay, RF (eds), *Scotland in the Twentieth Century*, Edinburgh, 188–209.

Melling, J 1983 *Rent Strikes*. Edinburgh.

Moore, L 1992 'Educating for the 'Women's Sphere'', *in* Breitenbach, E and Gordon, E (eds), *Out of Bounds*, Edinburgh, 10–41.

Pentland and Calton Reminiscence Group 1987 *Friday Night was Brasso Night*. Edinburgh.

Regional Trends 1975–1995.

Reynolds, S 1989 *Britannica's Typesetters*. Edinburgh.

STUC, AR = Scottish Trade Union Congress, *Annual Reports*.

STUC = Scottish Trade Union Congress, *Women's Advisory Committee Agenda and Report*, 18 November 1972.

Smout, TC 1986 *A Century of the Scottish People 1830–1950*. London.

*Stephenson, JD and Brown, CG 1990 'The View from the Workplace', *in* Gordon, E and Breitenbach, E, *The World is Ill-Divided*, Edinburgh, 7–28.

Stirling Women's History Project, *Transcripts*. Smith Library, Stirling.

Vogler, C 1989 'Labour Market Change and Patterns of Financial Allocation within Households', Working Paper 2, *ESRC Social Change and Economic Life Project*. London.

Young, JD 1985 *Women and Popular Struggles: A History of Scottish and English Working Women, 1500–1984*. Edinburgh.

Young, JD 1989 *Socialism and the English Working Class*. Brighton.

FURTHER READING

Those references marked * in the above list are recommended further reading.

ACKNOWLEDGEMENTS

I would like to acknowledge a debt to the following, who provided comments on the text and/or help with information, sources and references: Margot McCuaig, Audrey Canning, Ronnie MacDonald, Anne-Marie Hughes, Helen Corr, Pat Thane, Callum Brown, Neil Rafeek, Eleanor Gordon, Jan Gershuny and the late Jane Stephenson.

Lowland Agriculture and Society

Gavin Sprott

This is a considerable, yet in many ways an under-developed, subject area. Much has been written on the economic and social history, but without integrating that with the evidence of material culture and technological change. This has led to a failure to grasp one essential. In Volume 1, Ian Whyte considered the Agricultural Revolution. Was there one or not? Whatever happened and whatever your conclusion, the process was still unfinished business in the mid-nineteenth century, and remained so until after the Second World War.

This arose from one simple fact peculiar to the nature of farming, which was the technological difficulty of achieving complete industrialisation. By the late eighteenth century it was possible to concentrate and part-industrialise some processing, including jobs such as threshing and milling, but the primary production remained on the face of the land, and industrialising that was a long, piece-meal and drawn-out process. Many aspects of cultivation and harvesting remained labour-intensive and essentially pre-industrial until the coming of tractors with hydraulics and combine harvesters. By the same token we are often dealing with a hybrid society, where the labour relations were industrialised, but the ethos retained much of the old pre-industrial peasant Scotland. And dominating the middle of this period is what might be called the Thirty One Years War, with agriculture an essential element in the Home Front. It is these paradoxes and cross-currents that give this period its richness and fascination.

We will consider the topic under the following framework:

- High Farming: 1840s to 1870s
- Depression and War: 1880s to 1945
- The Revolution Complete: 1940s to 1970s
- Europe – 1973 onwards

The six documents (**Documents 118 to 123**) and three illustrations will provide sample source material for exploring various themes which will emerge from what is basically a narrative history.

1. HIGH FARMING: 1840S TO 1870S

In the mid-nineteenth century the contrast between the Lowlands and the Highlands and Islands could not have been more stark. In the latter, much that had been familiar was in ruins, and the level of personal distress must have been appalling. The Lowlands, on the other hand, were enjoying a period that would be looked back to with fond nostalgia. Change there was, but of a highly productive nature.

This ethos is caught in Henry Stephens' *Book of the Farm*. First published in 1844, it was so successful that a second and enlarged edition came out in 1851. In this Stephens laid out his credentials with a modesty bred of total self-confidence. He mentioned his 'liberal education' (for which read 'civilised') at Dundee High School and Edinburgh University. He then went to learn about agriculture from George Brown, a well known farmer at Whitsome Hill, 600 acres in Berwickshire. Most unusual for the time, Stephens recounts how 'I laboured with my own hands at every species of work which the ploughman, the field worker, and the shepherd must perform in the field, or the steward and the cattle-man at the steading: even in the dairy and poultry house part of my time was spent'. Unusual, not just in that the young academic got his hands dirty, and stuck at it for two years, but in the last two functions he engaged in what was then regarded as women's work. After a year as steward, he then went on a year's tour of continental Europe, which had just been opened up after the long years of the Napoleonic Wars, studying various farming regimes. From this combination of education, practicality and a natural curiosity, Stephens produced his 'standard' work, that would be usefully read by farmers all over the British Isles as a kind of text book (Stephens 1851, ix). It is unlikely that you will have access to this book, except through a library, but the important point to note is the extent to which lowland agriculture became 'industrialised'.

> EXERCISE 1
> Read **Document 118** and try to identify the main features of harvest work in the mid-nineteenth century.

What stands out is the heavy dependence on animal power and human effort. Mechanisation, however, was in evidence, indeed, what appears in general is that in the middle of the century so many things were coming together. There was a national agricultural press in the *North British Agriculturalist* and the penny post to send for goods and machinery advertised, and despite the occasional disaster, an efficient system of credit and credit transfer to pay for them. By the late 1850s all the major and most minor Lowland burghs were rail-connected, so the means were there to transport both manufactured goods and the raw materials to make them. There was thus a national and even international market on an unprecedented scale. This comes out strongly in **Document 119**.

In technical terms, the mid-1850s set the stage for a century. There would be numerous developments during that period, but the basic framework would be the

same. The average skills and level of technology employed by many Lowland
farmers and workers then would not have been out of place in the 1940s.

Farm buildings are a form of working plant. There crops are processed and stored,
the livestock is handled and some of it housed, and a base for the field machinery, the
farmer and the workers is provided. This period saw a considerable re-building and
enlargement of these buildings, and their careful conception and grand scale can still
be seen in some that survive for instance in the shadow of modern farm buildings in
East Lothian, and in the abstract, in Stephen's *Book of Farm Buildings* (Stephen and
Burn 1861). They reflect a massive investment in a business partnership, where the
estate provided the fixed plant, and the farmer provided the stock and working
capital. The other major but less visible investment was below the ground, in the
form of thorough field drainage. This had been developed by James Smith of
Deanston and was steadily applied to the more productive ground, existing and
potential, by breaking up the hard pan beneath the top-soil by sub-soil ploughing.
Combined with cheap industrially-produced clay *tiles* or pipes, this allowed the
surface water to reach the drains. It enabled the cultivation of many previously
difficult but rich carselands, and the doing away with the corrugated surface of the
rigs or cultivation ridges. These had been the main obstacle to the widespread
adoption of Patrick Bell's reaper (1828). Now the road was open for McCormick's
and Hussey's light American reapers popularised in the Great Exhibition in 1851.
Field machinery would diversify into numerous developments over the next half-
century. Most important would be the binder, which not only cut the crop, but

52 At Morphie, St Cyrus, Montrose, 1903. Horse-worked agriculture was very labour-
intensive. This picture includes the greive (top left), the horsemen, cattleman, women
outworkers, domestic servants in the farmhouse and the shepherd and his dog (right).
National Museums of Scotland, Scottish Life Archive (Mr Playfair, Abbey Mains).

threw the sheaves off ready-bound. Others would include for instance potato diggers, better seed-drills, hay-making machinery and so on. As most of the Lowland countryside was never far from developing urban industry, this labour-saving investment would enable farming to survive better than it would have done otherwise in the lean years to come.

In contrast, the social structure remained, and was dominated by the estate. This domination is revealed by the statistics of land-ownership. In 1878, 95% of Scotland was owned by 1,758 people. Many of the estates were very large, to the extent that 68 of the above landowners possessed nearly half of the country (M'Neel Caird 1878, 122–26). This was partly the legacy of the 1685 law of entail, which was very strict, and subsequent modifications which were very slow to effect any significant break-up of the large estates. The pattern was largely the following:

Laird
Professional: Factor
Tenants: Farmers – Tradesmen
Small Independents: Tradesmen – Semi-skilled workers
Servants: Farm workers – Estate workers – Domestic servants

Within this spectrum there was a vast variation of emphasis. Lairds varied from great noblemen to out-at-the-elbow minor gentry, although the above statistic underlines the fact that there were few of the latter. There was the occasional 'bunnet laird' or owner-occupier, in character more like a middling tenant farmer. Professionals could range from ministers, lawyers and doctors, some of whom might be 'well connected' landless gentry, to the *dominie* or an emergent professional such as a vet, who had risen by dint of education and ability. Tenants varied from the substantial men of business of the Lothians and Tweeddale to the peasant 'guidman' of old who employed a minimum of servants and followed his own plough. The mainline trades such as miller, smith and joiner usually tenanted their premises. But there were many tradesmen who had feued their ground, particularly in villages which had started as planned ones, which gave them an independence. Villages and small towns were a base for travelling merchants with their spring carts, carriers, and tradesmen who often travelled, such as tailors. Tradesmen might also be based on smallholdings – crofts (in the Lowland sense) or *pendicles*. There were also occupations such as dyking, ditching, rabbit and mole-catching which demanded no trade apprenticeship and sustained many people.

Those who were employed included the bulk of the population, *servants* in the terminology and mind-set of the time. A considerable proportion of the servant population was employed by the tenants, as farm-workers or domestic servants. Servants were often highly and sometimes fiercely differentiated into a hierarchy of status. The gulf between an experienced shepherd and a 'bondager' or woman outworker, between a head keeper and a stable boy, between the butler and the chamber maid, was vast.

Then outwith the servant population were unfeed workers who might get odd seasonal work, labour to tradesmen, or road work, not to mention the various rural industries such as quarrying and saw-milling. And beyond that was the mobile population of seasonal workers from Ireland or the Highlands, itinerant peddlars, the travelling people, and the odd and often eccentric vagrant.

Nineteenth-century country society was thus varied enough to contain a considerable range of sub-cultures. Tolerance or rejection of the *status quo* depended on where you were in the social spectrum. Aberdeenshire can illustrate some of the options. There was the occasional growl, as expressed by William Alexander, through his hero Johnny Gibb's contemptuous dismissal of the lairds as 'a set o' reivin' scoonrels' (Alexander 1881, clvi). But overall, if there was a happy land, for the bulk of the population that lay not in reforming the existing one, but in carving out an independent existence elsewhere. That could take the form of a kind of internal frontier, such as breaking in a croft on the bare windy hillsides of Buchan. The croft was often a heart-break, overtaken by the depression in the 1870s and nothing to show for it. For the younger man, a move to the bothies of Kincardineshire or Angus might bring companionship and a greater personal freedom, before moving on to something else in the towns or abroad. To the eve of the Great War, Buchan was one of the main recruiting areas for the Canadian Pacific Railway seeking emigrants to populate the virgin lands that flanked the rails. Against the extraordinary frost-bitten hardship of a prairie winter was set the prize of independence.

The estate as a social organism was itself changing. The era of high farming, heavy investment and fat rents was accompanied by a widespread rebuilding of many *big hooses*, and in the shadow of that, the houses of the bigger tenants, and with this went greater social differentiation and the erosion of feudal familiarity. This accelerated towards the end of the century as grandees from industry, mining and shipping established themselves in rural splendour.

Traditionally, the estate was a private property with a public face. The strain of this duality was put to the test in the case of the Hopes of Fenton Barns, where well respected and long established tenants were refused a renewal of their *tack* or lease because they had publicly expressed political opinions that differed from those of the laird. But the public uproar was that this was an abuse of the system, of the same mentality as allowing game to consume the farmer's crops with no redress. It was felt to be unfair play, not a cause for revolutionary change. Davitt's and Parnell's Irish Land League, which did so much to create modern rural Ireland, had no counterpart in Lowland Scotland. In older rural Scots terminology, the personal description of 'an auld liberal' described someone of a paradoxically anti-establishment conviction yet of a bullet-proof personal conservatism, and Hell mend anything out of its appointed place. This was the spirit which supported the Free Kirk (which at its inception *was* liberal: see Volume 1, Chapter 4), and sought to chain 'landlordism' to standards of decency and the common weal, not to abolish it.

EXERCISE 2
Investigate a pre-1914 estate as a social entity. This may be explored in various physical aspects. The following could, for example, be considered: the siting of

the Free Kirk (off estate ground); the siting and dedication of schools; the alignment of railway lines; the rebuilding and configuration of the *big hoose* reflecting the relationship of the master (and mistress) and servant, and the shadow reflection of this in the bigger farmhouse.

2. DEPRESSION AND WAR: 1880S TO 1945

The end of the American Civil War (1865) signalled the great break-out into the heart of the continent, largely empty but for the unfortunate native peoples and buffalo. Once the productive capacity began to be realised, European farming was plunged into crisis. To the grain of the Mid-West was added that of the Canadian prairie, besides a sizeable cheese production. There was beef from the South American pampas, wheat and wool from Australia, and the dairy products and mutton from New Zealand. Refrigeration, the compound steam engine and the Suez Canal (1869) all assisted this process. In mainland Europe, railways were opening up the eastern steppe lands, and the dumping of cheap Russian grain became another threat.

Germany and France put up the shutters of protection. Thirled to Empire and the slogan of Free Trade, Britain did not. There were also other imperatives at work. Britain (not Ireland) now had as many town as country dwellers. By 1911, 60% of Scotland's population lived in settlements of over 5,000, and 50% in burghs of 20,000 or more (Rodger 1996, 124). 'The Great Depression' also included depressed prices and relatively cheap food. No government was going to risk otherwise, but to the farming interest, it was 'The Great Betrayal'. There was however the counter-vailing increase in purchasing power, when large sections of Europe's urban population could for the first time afford such luxuries as butter, eggs and flesh. Food processing as we understand it today was born in 1869 with Hippolyte Mège Mouriès' invention of margarine. Most people throughout Europe were on the edge of nutritional sufficiency, and besides the increasing productivity of farming, such developments were an additional response (Hoffmann 1989, 9–13).

The effect on a more exposed British market was thus towards a degree of specialisation. It was now more difficult for farmers to unload their primary product – grain – on the market. The result was what might now be called 'downsizing'. In Scotland, 10% of the best land went out of crop production. In the big cornlands of south-central and eastern England, the devastation was much worse, with up to 25% prime arable being put down to grass. But Lowland agriculture was developing that vital integration with its markets which would enable it to survive better than its southern neighbour. The South-West and West Central Lowlands provided fresh dairy products for the numerous small towns which made the central industrial conurbation. Years of high investment had given the cropping areas of the Lothians and Eastern Borders high enough productivity to at least hold their own against imported grain. Besides, the staple of Scotland had in the past been oats ('corn' in Scots), still widely grown but displaced from its prime position by the potato, and a main crop in the Lothians, and an important one in Ayrshire, Fife, East Perthshire and Angus. The international triumph of the Aberdeen Angus cattle breed at the Paris Show in 1878 confirmed a quality of meat that imported Argentinian beef could not touch, and that has its place at Smithfield to the present day. Nor was any area of the Lowlands (except perhaps the extreme South-West, the Laich of Moray, Easter Ross and Caithness) far from the town, and a market for fresh produce.

The other factor was professionalism. This had its roots in the 'Improving' mentality of the previous century, with its attempt to marry theory with best practice. That included what came to be known as the 'Scotch' rotation, in which only a third or even a quarter of the ground was under cultivation at one time. Come the depression, this rotation could be stretched, and the ground under crop would produce a higher yield from the benefit of what was in effect more fallow. In the South, the tendency was to contract and maintain the arable in a central core, with no resulting productivity gain.

The professionalism of Scots farmers was reinforced – and in a way recognised – by the foundation of the West of Scotland Agricultural College in 1899, and similar colleges in 1901 and 1904 in Edinburgh and Aberdeen respectively. These were practical institutions concerned with producing effective farmers, and behind them lay the labours of Patrick Wright, himself of an Ayrshire farming family, who had provided lectures on agriculture from 1887 in the Glasgow Technical College.

In 1891 Wright was appointed professor in charge of a newly formed Department of Agriculture. This was partly the result of the Local Taxation (Customs and Excise) Act of 1890. Horrified by the vast number of licensed premises, the government sought to reduce them by offering license holders compensation for giving up, but found that many were brewers and distillers. There was a public outcry that they and not the people put out of work should receive compensation, so the money was diverted, some of it to help 'technical instruction'. Some of this 'whisky money', which was administered by the city and county councils, went direct to the Technical College, and indirectly through the hiring of lecturers by several of the south-western counties. It was the perception of the benefits of scientific knowledge among the farming population that built the momentum that led to the 'West College' (at Auchincruive) as it became known (Martin 1994, 2–4).

Wright united intelligent experiment, interpretation of agricultural statistics (he was the first to gather them on a scale that rendered them useful), and a knowledge of work in the field of agricultural science in other parts of Europe that made him unique in the UK at the time.

Nor was professionalism the sole province of the farmer. The ploughing matches that the improvers had started towards the end of the previous century had become part of popular culture, and the focus of a fearsome work ethic, where the charge of 'nae pyin attention' was a mortifying one. The bothy men might affect a disregard for kirk and virginity (in fact the bothy districts produced no more illegitimacy than the norm), but their songs praised skill and knowledge at work. The man who could drive a good *fur* or furrow, turn out a smart *pair o' horse*, or thatch and rope the handsomest corn ruck in the district was king.

And in practical terms, competence mattered. When it came to what on the East

Coast was known as *speakin time*, that period before the end of the *fee* or contract, the farmer might ask a man if he would *bide* or stay on for another term. If the farmer 'didna speak', then the contract was at an end. If and when people did move on, it was usually within a district, and there was a fair degree of knowledge about who was a good farmer to work for, and who were able or indifferent workers, and this would be reflected in the bargain struck at the *Feein Market* or hiring fair.

Although obviously wages mattered, other things were taken into account. There was a dislike of working for incompetent farmers, and conversely, the farmer who had invested in modern machinery and was 'up-to-date' would be a draw. There was the obvious point that overall a good farmer would be easier to work for, but the fierceness of the work ethic encouraged this as well. It also meant the primacy of the man's interest where in fact there was a shared one in those areas where married farm workers were the norm, as in southern and much of central Scotland, and this related to housing. This rather than wages was the perennial grouse of the Scottish Farm Servants' Union formed in 1912. 'Tied' houses were provided as part of the work contract, and were the universal accommodation for farm workers. Despite periodic and desultory attempts to improve them, they were frequently riddled with damp and lacking in a reliable water supply, let alone sanitary facilities. Yet here the women had to bring up what were frequently large families. Lowland rural housing was often as wretched as the urban housing, but with none of the systematic plans to come to terms with it that were being hatched in the cities of late Victorian Scotland. More than wages or working conditions, housing was the worst aspect of life in Scotland, then and still now. In the countryside this situation would continue with only a creeping improvement until the drastic changes that followed World War Two (Sprott 1996, 172–4).

Nor was poor housing all, for the women were also an indispensable part of the labour force in the South-East and the West and South-West. In Mid and East Lothian, it was difficult for a man to get a 'single fee', that is one where his wife or daughters or a substitute were not a part of the bargain. Root-crops and market-garden products such as cabbages and carrots are demanding of constant attention. Such was the imperative to work the land that the eldest daughter could find herself periodically carrying the youngest child out to the fields to be suckled by the mother. In the dairying West and South-West the women were heavily involved in the work of milking, and often of butter and cheese-making. Milking machines – a part-Scottish invention – were available from the early twentieth century, but they were of limited effectiveness, and only became widespread with the coming of electricity to the countryside in the middle of the century. The memories of these times are by no means uniform. One side recalls a struggle against the competing demands of housework and outwork, another the camaraderie of being part of a workforce, even if in the East the women were often overseen by the *wumman gaffer*, who was of course a man.

Life was thus dominated by work. At the turn of the century it was a six-day week and between a ten and twelve hour day, depending on district and how much daylight there was to sustain work. That work could start at five with the grooming and feeding of the horses, *brakfest*, then *yokin-time* at six. The *mid-yokin* of one to two hours was as much for the ease of horse as of man. Work could go on until six, with the horses still to attend to, and in time of harvest it could go on into the evening. It did not go unnoticed that for four months in the year farm servants would scarce see their homes in daylight except on a Sunday, and this occasionally prompted philanthropic calls for a half-day on Saturday, for instance by cutting out the mid-yokin and sending the men home early at three, making for a seven-hour day. Thus the public appeal by Sir Andrew Agnew of Lochnaw in 1859. In the event, the half-day would only creep in in the Lothians between the wars, and get official recognition in 1937.

Sundays and New Years Day were the only occasions that formally escaped this pervasiveness of work. A day off to attend an agricultural show or the feeing market related to work, although both would as often as not end with the *guid crack* of the beer-tent or pub. Removal from one fee to another might get the concession of a day off *tae pit the gairden in*, and would necessitate a day for the *flittin*, with usually two carts from the new farm being the maximum required (or provided) to contain all a family's gear. *The Kirn* or *Meal an' ale* at the end of harvest celebrated the end of the main season's work. Ploughing matches were about the skills of work, but often leavened by fun, such as prizes for the most handsome horseman. Horsemen's societies were essentially work-centred. Bothy songs were for the most part about farming life. When the Scottish Women's Rural Institutes started in 1917, the focus was (and often still is) on food and home products of women's domestic work. Gardening and bee-keeping were, and are, an extension of food production. Even at a basic level, a Sunday afternoon's walk would as often as not include an appraisal of the neatness of the stacks in neighbouring cornyards, or the straightness of the *dreils* in the neighbouring *parks* or fields.

The pre-Great War countryside was not some Arcadia of independent working men, and much of it would appear to modern sensibilities as a pretty *roch* and unromantic place. Before 1914 might appear as halcyon days compared with what was to come, but they were in fact ones of bitter political division and industrial strife. The 'Turra Coo' incident (a riot over Lloyd George's plans for National Insurance) which has passed into the folk-lore of the North-East was a comical uproar, and was very minor compared to the tensions caused by trades union rights, women's suffrage or Irish Home Rule, but was a sign of the times. The emigration already mentioned also reached its peak at this point. When war was declared, country people enlisted with the same alacrity as townsfolk, perhaps as unsettled by the mood of that era as much as by any military fervour. The benefits of the subsequent war-time economy for the countryside have overshadowed the sad fact that the competition of the New World had all but done its worst, and that by 1912 the rural economy was improving.

EXERCISE 3

The photograph taken at Morphie shows the staff of a horse-worked farm. Using **Documents 120 and 121** assess the conditions of farm workers in Scotland.

What assessment can you make of the work ethic, and how was it expressed? What attitudes can you discern towards established authority, religion, politics, etc, and does that conform to expectations. The interest of this is to get under the skin of the attitudes of a different age, and not to intercept the past in terms of the present.

However you have responded you should be alert to the existence of significant regional variations. In this respect there is still ample room for the contribution of local historians!

In August 1914 the most acute military pundit could have been forgiven for assuming the war would be a rapid one of cut and thrust, followed by a decisive show-down, such as at Sadowa or Sedan. The French army had been re-trained in a sprit of sub-fanatical *élan*, and where possible the Germans moved their troops by express train. Not that the thought of a strategic threat to the UK's food supplies had not been considered seriously by a parliamentary committee at the turn of the century. But even then, it was considered that the Royal Navy would prove adequate to protecting what now accounted for 75% of the UK's food supply.

Only in the late spring of 1915 did it dawn that the war might continue beyond the harvest of 1916. A committee was appointed under Eugene Wason to look into agricultural production in Scotland, and made suitable noises about the break-up of more grass-land, more 'motor tillage' and an increase in productivity, but nothing practical was done. This was because the focus was still on the military side of the war. The countryside (and indeed Scotland as a whole) already had an immediate involvement derived from its enthusiasm for the Rifle Volunteers movement dating from 1859. The Volunteers represented a kind of citizen army, which was affiliated to regular parent regiments in 1881, and absorbed into the Territorial Forces in 1908. In the countryside the Volunteers included the more settled populations of the villages and small towns, where there was what approximated to a steady and respectable 'yeomanry' to fill the ranks. For the pleasant diversions of competitions in marksmanship and annual camps, these organisations now exchanged warfare. Next followed the farm workers. The whole process was assisted by the post-Crimea army reorganisation which had 'repatriated' regiments to local bases and training areas, and established that local loyalty to a particular regiment that persists to this day. The recruits were not slow in coming. Although it is difficult to establish precise figures, it appears that about a third of the eligible male rural population of Scotland went to war.

It took the spectre of catastrophe to drive change. Stalemate in the land war provoked the clash of the British and German fleets at Jutland in May 1916. Despite the greater British losses, the German fleet had to run, much of it floating wreckage. Throughout the remainder of 1916 Germany steadily intensified her submarine warfare as an alternative. Meanwhile, the Somme campaign, which had started with such high hopes, incurred a hideous loss of life and ended with the new volunteer armies in tatters. British industry could not even supply reliable ammunition before, yet now that industry was being throttled. To add to these woes, the harvest of 1916 was terrible. The crop was half that of 1914, and for potatoes, a yield of only four tons to the acre was common. When the U-boat war became unrestricted and reached a crescendo early in 1917, there was a real possibility that Britain would starve of food and supplies, and lose the war. This was the crisis that galvanised the UK into the creation of a 'home front' which set a pattern that would be revived by the threat of Hitler, and would inform government attitudes to farming for decades after the war.

Drastic action was taken. The Board of Agriculture was given power to direct the use of land and alter tenancies. In the spring of 1917 local Agricultural Executive Committees were at work, assessing every possibility for increasing production and organising a massive sowing programme. A brake was put on rural recruitment to the armed forces, and all available labour was mobilised, including older men, and the early release of youths from school. The Womens Land Army was created, and countrywomen were encouraged to stay on the land by improving their wages relative to those of men, instead of being drawn off into the munitions and armaments industries in the Central Belt. The Corn Production Act guaranteed minimum prices for oats and wheat, and also minimum wages, which were agreed between representatives between the still young Farmers' and Farm Servants' unions.

It worked. There was a drive to produce root crops which would feed more people, a drastic reduction in meat consumption (which is a wasteful way to produce food) and a swing back to the traditional fare of oatmeal and potatoes. Thus stock-levels were maintained, but even so milk production had dropped by 40% by the end of the war. The effort to mobilise labour reduced the shortfall in the workforce to 15%, but in the following two years the acreage under grain increased by 20%. And in the end, even the German submarines were beaten. By the end of 1917, the supply of foreign wheat had been restored to pre-war levels. The converse was true for the civilians of Germany. Such was the level of malnutrition by 1918 that Spanish Flu cut through the population like a knife, and the loss of children in particular would be a cause of lasting resentment against the British and their blockade in the post-war years.

The Great War produced little technological change in the countryside. 'Motor tillage' brought the Fordson tractor, but in practical terms, powered mechanisation had little effect. In that field, the consequence of the war was to divert UK agricultural machinery productive capacity to arms, and hand the market to US producers, so that when hostilities ended, they were in a dominant position. This reinforced what was already a huge lead. For instance, by 1886, 10% of the grain production in California (by then the biggest wheat-grower in the Union) was being harvested by combine (Quick and Buchele 1978, 93). Attempts were made to turn swords into ploughshares, as with the *Glasgow* tractor, made initially in Mother-well. It was technically far ahead of the Fordson, but at £375 it was over three times the price, and with the additional handicap of poor marketing, it was doomed. Between 1921 and 1938, not one British tractor maker was in permanent production (Sprott 1978, 6). The only area where tractors caught on was in Buchan, because of the endemic horse-sickness that had developed after the war. This gave it for a few years the distinction of being the most mechanised part of the UK.

Overall, these early tractors were of limited use. For cultivation they required a new design of trailing plough. The tractor's brute strength was useful for working binders during the harvest, the heaviest work that horses had to do at a time of year when they were least fit to begin with. But yoking a tractor to sawn-off and adapted horse machinery was of little economic advantage. The first combine in Scotland – a Massey Harris – was tried at Hedderwick Hill in East Lothian about 1930 but was not persevered with. The Clayton-Shuttleworth at neighbouring Whittinghame and Cairn-dinnis was successful in 1932, but would remain a lone experiment for many years.

The structural changes that followed the Great War were far-reaching. The most obvious was the start of the break-up of the estate system that had dominated the Scottish countryside hitherto. Immediately following the war, land prices had been buoyant, but the repeal of the corn Production Act in 1921 and renewed depression had a shock effect. Land prices tumbled, until by 1930 they were a third of what they had been a decade before, with ground changing hands for as little as £10 per acre. This was driven by other factors besides depression. Many estates were encumbered by accumulated debt, sometimes added to by the death of the laird in the war, and the consequent death duties.

In this process, many tenants became owner-occupiers. Before the Great War owner-occupation was insignificant. By 1930 it had trebled to two fifths, and the proportion would grow continuously until by 1991 two thirds of farms were owner-occupied. This has been the biggest upheaval in land-holding in lowland Scotland since the great abbeys frittered away their land in the sixteenth century. For many estates which had profited or even been created by that earlier upheaval, it was now the end of the road.

The spectacular success of the Scottish Women's Rural Institutes points to the hunger for something different. Started in 1917 at Macmerry in East Lothian as a war-time morale-booster, the organisation spread rapidly through Scotland and to the rest of the UK. For the first time it offered women activity that was their own – and not supervised by the *wumman gaffer*. At the outset the movement was the subject of male sniping, a perverse measure of its worth.

A major victim of the U-boats had been what remained of the native forests, because timber was a vital war material. The Forestry Commission was created in 1919, one of the main proponents being Sir John Stirling Maxwell. In the Lowlands, this deliberate creation of forest had a marked effect in the South-West and the central Borders. There were visionary expectations, with bleak hillsides and meagre populations superseded by 'beautiful waving woodland . . . giving health and shelter to the denizens of the colonies of workers, with crops and grazings interspersed . . . Add to this the effect of the subsidiary industries which will spring up in the wake of the forests . . . the home of a population such as has not been seen for the past century and longer' (Boyd 1920, 144). One way or another, forestry would always fall short of expectations.

53 Advertisement for the Ferguson-Brown tractor and system, *c.* 1937. Harry
Ferguson was an evangelical salesman, and used advertisements to educate. This
tractor design was followed by the Ford Ferguson, then the Standard Ferguson, the
latter remembered as 'the wee grey Fergie'. *National Museums of Scotland, Scottish
Life Archive.*

There was an effort to import some of the organisational frameworks that had so benefited farmers in the Netherlands and Denmark in the form of co-operative marketing boards. The idea was not new to Scotland (centralised creameries in the South-West, egg producers in the North-East and Orkney), and was just one of the hopeful developments whose spread had been stunted by the war. Periodic glut and a fragmentation of the market now drove milk and potato producers towards the creation of their respective marketing boards by 1931, but not without a rear-guard battle by individually minded farmers (a not unfamiliar phenomenon). More government-backed intervention would follow the nadir of 1929–30.

The other major development of the post-war decade was in the field of research. There was a desperate need for it. Casual surveys showed that the potato crop alone was riddled with disease, and that chaos attended the classification of individual strains. The great breeders of the previous century had a swarm of charlatans at their tails, who would market seed potato under a new name just to sell it. This field alone demanded solid research to bring order out of chaos. The Rowett, Morden and Macaulay research institutes were the direct result of government support, and the investment would yield unexpected results sooner than people expected. The first director of the Rowett Institute was John Boyd Orr. People had long made the crude approximation that you are what you eat, but Boyd Orr set about examining this in a scientific way, first in animals, then in humans. His findings were partly responsible for the introduction of the milk in schools scheme in 1934, and formed the basis of rationing in the coming war. This produced the healthiest generation of youngsters that Britain had seen. He was the father of our modern obsession with diet.

A particular friend of Boyd Orr was Walter Elliot, one of a well known family of Lanarkshire auctioneers, farmer at Bonchester Bridge in Roxburghshire, and Conservative politician. The Wall Street Crash had brought renewed depression, and a mood of near despair in what was now talked of as the agricultural industry. It was to this situation that he came as the UK Minister of Agriculture in 1932, and where his predecessors had merely wrung their hands, Elliot took action. The Wheat Act of that year guaranteed prices simply by taxing imports. The resentment in Scotland at a measure that benefited mostly English farmers produced a temporary subsidy for beef and some restriction on South American imports.

There were other fundamental matters to which government turned its attention. The state of the land was one. Much of it had seen little drainage or lime since the 1880s, and starting in 1930 there was a series of schemes to bring it into better heart. Milk was recognised as a major potential source of infection, and from 1935 a drastic clean-up of the dairy herd started with tuberculin testing. There were schemes to encourage the cultivation of land that had lain in grass for seven years and more.

EXERCISE 4
Read **Article 38** and consider the factors which produced change in the agricultural labour market in Scotland.

In formal terms, the government recognised the need for a framework of employ-ment. The legislation on agricultural wages in 1937 may look impressive, but it was tinkering at the edge of a creaking system. Housing, not wages, continued to be the big issue. When wages had been fixed during the war, Joe Duncan, of the Scottish Farm Servants' Union, was quick to point that out. The creeping (but still unim-pressive) improvement in housing was perhaps reflected in the spread of the weekly wage in southern Scotland, and with that a lesser inclination to seek a new place at the term. But it would take another war and its aftermath to effect any radical change.

When war returned, the organisational pattern of the previous round was revived, with various adaptations and additions. Forty district Agricultural Executive Committees or 'Warags' were in action immediately. Conscription was used to maintain labour in vital war industries as much as supply the armed forces, and the 'Stand Still' act of 1941 stopped men moving to new fees, and hastened the demise of old habits. Only 12%, or a third, of the previous proportion of Scottish country people joined the armed forces. After initial difficulties, the Women's Land Army and the smaller Women's Timber Corps became useful organisations (10,000 by 1943). The Polish forces did much to secure the harvest in the east of Scotland in 1940. At the end of the war, there were 19,000 prisoners of war on Scottish farms.

The contrast with 1914 was the energy and thoroughness shown right from the outset. It was desperately needed. Following the fall of France in 1940, the supply situation was potentially far worse than in the previous war. The Nazis were free to raid UK supplies from bases between the North Cape and the Spanish border. As the war spread out from Europe, shipping was needed to supply the military in Africa and Asia. Therefore the full scale of the achievement is seen in the average rises in production taken over the whole conflict: oats 33%; wheat 32%; barley 72%; and potatoes 57%.

Changing technology began to have an effect. War had cut off cheap supplies of animal feed, but since 1918 the horse population had declined by about a quarter, nor was there the same shadow army of military horses. Besides maintaining hay production, there was now a drive to spread the making of silage. Powered mechanisation was now more than a curiosity of propaganda value. In Scotland the Government Tractor Service (which by the end of the war included a fleet of balers, binders, threshing mills and even eleven combines) was used as a flying squad to fill the shortfalls where they were identified by the Warags. Although that arrangement left ample margin for muddle, the work got done.

The same Warags allocated the nearly 4,000 tractors and 170 combines that reached the Clyde through Lend-Lease. They came in crates 'CKD' – 'Completely Knocked Down' – and had to be resurrected. The modest machinery dealerships which had grown during the inter-war years now had to develop a vastly expanded servicing capacity. Furthermore, servicemen would return from a war conducted by tanks, trucks, jeeps and aircraft. For the first time there would be a substantial technical organisation and expertise in the countryside.

3. THE REVOLUTION COMPLETE: 1940S TO 1970S

The agricultural war effort was reinforced by an unwritten understanding that when the dust settled, there would be no return to the bad old days of neglect and depression. What the farming community got was the Agriculture Act in 1947, the Agriculture (Scotland) Act in 1948, and an annual price review which looked to the likely levels of support at least eighteen months ahead, and enabled farmers to plan. Support was provided through a system of 'deficiency payments', that is, the difference between the costs of production and world market prices. Agriculture would differ greatly from the newly nationalised industries in having a framework of government support that encouraged and rewarded private investment. After a recovery from the devastating winter that started in January 1947, this is what happened.

The Ferguson System provided something to invest in. This had been developed by Harry Ferguson since 1933. At the heart of it was a three-point hydraulically-controlled mounting which made tractor and implement into one integrated unit controlled by one man (see illustration 54). The design went through various incarnations until Ferguson combined with the Standard Motor Company in 1947 to produce half a million tractors in the coming decade. Combine design also matured rapidly, with recognisably modern self-propelled models becoming common in the 1950s (Sprott 1996, 180–220).

The result was that after an initial dip at the end of hostilities, during the 1950s production started to climb above war-time levels, and by the end of the decade it

54 Claas Super combining barley at East Pinkerton, East Lothian, 25 September 1954. This new generation of self-propelled machines cut an average of two acres per hour and, together with the Ferguson system tractor, rapidly replaced horse working. *National Museums of Scotland, Scottish Life Archive (Ian Fleming, Edinburgh).*

stood at 60% higher than before the war (Symon 1959, 269). Added to the productive capacity of modern machinery were the increasing dividends of agricultural science in increasing yields, both in animal husbandry and the containment of crop disease through plant breeding (*Agriculture in Scotland*, DOAS, 1951, 11). A startling example of change is the increase in yield from the already high-yielding Friesian cow. A lactation is the time the beast is in milk after the birth of a calf. In the UK, in 1955 this averaged 532 litres. In 1967 it was 3673 litres, in the 1970s it was above 3750 litres, and continued to climb (Robinson 1988, 167). The use of new herbicides also increased yields, and would provide grounds for the coming generation to question the apparently manic march towards ever-increasing production at the expense of the environment.

All this was achieved with a diminishing work force. The core of regular war-time farm-workers remained stable, but not all the country people who had gone to the war returned. More drastic, the Women's Land Army was disbanded, the POWs left, and the war-time squads of specially recruited labour came no more. At a rough estimate, this amounted to a cut of nearly a quarter of the labour force. Despite the fact that farmers could recoup pay-rises through subsidies being related to the cost of production, town wages now out-stripped those of farm workers. The only new labour was a trickle of unfortunates with no home to go to on the war-ravaged continent.

For those that did remain, housing *began,* for the first time, to reach a reasonable standard – internal sanitation and hot water supply, a second bedroom, and a war on that old enemy, damp. What decades of pious recommendation and the offer of public subsidy had failed to achieve was now driven by the farmers' requirement to retain a labour force.

The first casualties of mechanisation were the old-fashioned country tradesmen. There were few threshing mills to maintain, a fast dwindling stock of horses to shoe and provide with harness and carts. Farm buildings adapted to the new machinery and bulk-handling, and old ones were replaced with portal-framed sheds prefabricated in the town and erected in a few days. Some tradesmen adapted to become agricultural engineers, fabrication contractors or to run garages, but their numbers were fewer.

However, the shortage in farm workers fuelled a drive for productivity, and a fundamental depopulation of the countryside set in. In the decade 1970–80 the total employment in agriculture fell from 47,000 to just over 40,000. Underlying this total was a more drastic trend, because there was an increase in part-time and casual work. The total of full-time jobs fell from 37,000 to 28,000 (Ingham and Love 1983, 75).

Country schools closed, village shops dwindled, and the buses that had robbed the railway branch lines of their passengers in the 1920s were now reduced. This process has continued to the point that farming people are actually now a minority in the countryside, and the labour force is still contacting at 2% a year (*Scottish Rural Profile*, HMSO 1991).

EXERCISE 5

The Ferguson tractor advertisement, the photograph of the combine harvester and **Document 122** illustrate both the expectations and technology of post-war agriculture. What was the rationale for continuing government intervention in agriculture after 1945?.

The years after Hitler's war were harder for some than others. Germany had been through it before with the terrible *Steckrübenwinter* – the winter of the 'neeps – in 1918–19. Now came the *Trümmerjahre* – the years of trouble. France was not so badly effected as Germany, yet the continuing *années de rationnement* were severe enough in the cities for the authorities to fear a Communist takeover. Rationing also continued in the UK, but it was the inconvenience of unexciting choice, 'austerity' as it would be known, nothing like the desperate hunger that affected most of continental Europe. For many slum-dwellers in the UK, rationing had brought the first experience of a balanced diet. Of all the combatants, the UK was the only one not to have been ransacked or destroyed. For the others, war spelt terrible hunger. The original Coal and Steel Community was formed by the Six in 1951, with the intention of so interlocking the production of basic commodities that war would be impossible. This was followed by the setting up of the EEC in 1957, which stipulated the development of a common agricultural policy, reflecting a policy decision already reached in 1955. Article 39 of the Treaty of Rome detailed the objectives of increasing productivity, a fair standard of living for the agricultural community, stable markets and supplies, and reasonable prices. The Stresa Conference which followed in 1958 foresaw that to increase farm incomes would require a transfer of cash from the non-agricultural population through a price support policy, but also that rural industrialisation should be developed to provide alternative employment. Nevertheless, the conference committed itself to the preservation of the family farm. Underlying this was the recognition that creating rural industries was easier said than done, and that a destabilisation of the family farms that comprised the vast bulk of the Community's holdings would create a serious social problem.

The Common Agricultural Policy – CAP – finally came into being in 1962. There were to be three 'fundamental' principles: market unity through the harmonisation of prices, a preference for Community produce through tariff protection, and a funding of the system from community and not individual state funds. The last two principles have been adhered to. The first would be widely flouted through individual states manipulating the 'green money' system, first to cushion the swings of currency values on their farmers, and then to continue individual state agricultural policies through the back door.

The hand of the CAP was exercised mostly by intervention buying, that is by purchasing products once they reach a base price. The idea was that produce would be taken into store when harvests were good and the price low, and released onto the market when prices rose, as in the Seven Ill Years, and thus iron out short-term market fluctuations. But the post-war bounds in productivity and continuation of high intervention prices led to production constantly outstripping demand, hence the fabled wine lakes and butter mountains. The intention was that the other hand of the CAP should be shown through the 'structural' policy, proposed in the Mansholt Plan of 1968. This recognised that fiddling with price mechanisms was only part of the answer, and that in the longer term Community rural society required a degree of reconstruction. This was attempted in 1972 with 'social-structure directives' which sought to invest in agricultural modernisation, training and early retirement, but as subsequent history would show, structural policy would be totally overshadowed by pricing control.

4. EUROPE – 1973 ONWARDS

In 1973, the UK finally managed to scramble aboard the EEC. It joined an organisation that had developed an ethos and *modus operandi* that it had not had a hand in creating. This was reflected in that the majority of Community regulations concerned the various *regimes* governing the pricing and control of agriculture, and by the end of our period, this was where 67% of the Community budget went also (Ingram and Love 1983, 248). In agricultural circles UK entry was greeted with an optimism bordering on euphoria, reflected in the rise in land prices. The Community took over the mantle of price support at the point where the UK post-war settlement was coming in for serious questioning. In 1975 came CAP regional measures, which included compensatory allowances for cattle and sheep in 'less favoured areas'. That included the hill farms of Scotland.

When the UK joined, the money spent on structural matters was only 5% of that spent on price control, which continued to rise (*Consumers and the Agricultural Policy* 1988, 20). In 1987 the Community was headed for bankruptcy, and in effect imposed a financial freeze, and an extension of recently introduced quotas on production to bring the CAP under control. But the party had been over for Scottish farmers for over a decade. After reaching a peak in 1975, prices dropped sharply, in the following years recovering only marginally for livestock but more sharply for crops. The growth in output was not enough to balance the rises in costs.

This process had far-reaching effects. There was a slide away from the traditional mixed farming of Lowland Scotland with a move to more cereal production on the East Coast in particular, marked in areas such as Buchan which had been traditionally dominated by beef cattle. This had been accompanied by increased investment in machinery to replace labour in a drive to contain costs, and the creation of machinery rings and the development of contracting for specific operations (Sprott 1996, 183).

Between 1977 and 1981 the Scottish banks increased their loans to farmers by 200%, ostensibly to finance investment (Ingham and Love 1983, 81). For some the gamble did not pay off, because money went on current costs such as wages and overheads. Where the lurch to cereal production and the associated capital expenditure had been marked, coupled with the pinch in costs and compounded by inflation and high bank charges, it was the end of the road for some. And once the move to cereals has been made, it is difficult to backtrack to livestock, because the return on investment is longer and the skills not so easy to re-acquire. Thus an area such as Buchan, which was a very heartland of Lowland rural culture, with its attractive Doric tongue, experienced an unprecedented influx of strangers farming in a different way, and the regional character was dealt a severe blow.

In human terms the result has been the steady diminution of agricultural workers as a group to the point of being overshadowed in numbers by the farmers themselves. Farms are no longer the substantial communities that they were, but family-run 'production units', often worked by a man and a boy. Half the farms of Scotland now use only family labour. By way of contrast, in the earlier half of this century, an East Lothian farm of 500 acres might support the farmer, a grieve, seven or eight *hinds* or ploughmen, an *odd boy* (the *orra loun* further north), a cattleman and assistant, shepherd, and equal if not more numbers of women workers, some drawn from the families of the hinds, supplemented by various seasonal squads such as bands of Irish workers to lift potatoes. Together with the children, this could make a community of over 50 people. By 1965 that number would have more than halved (Coppock 1976, 25), and by the 1980s the figure would be halved again, with the same ground worked by three or less people, making a local group of perhaps between nine and a dozen.

This loss of community would lead to a marked bout of introspection among farming people in the 1980s, and the creation of organisations such as Rural Forum by various rural interests to try and make sense of it. This was fuelled among other things by the rise of suicide among farmers, who may have been good judges of a beast, but who were also poor accountants, and now found themselves to be in a lonely occupation.

By 1980 Lowland Scotland was well on the way to becoming what the post-war planners imagined it ought to be: either a food-factory, a dormitory, or a play-ground. Intensive production had hammered the natural fabric, and planning restrictions had stifled the development of alternative rural industry and housing. In 1960 the Department of Health for Scotland codified this in its circular stating that there should be no new houses built outside existing villages. This is in astonishing contrast to Eire, where in the decade 1970–80 there was an increase of 20% in the rural housing stock, and 90% of this was in dispersed locations, not villages (Jennings 1987, 156). Self-appointed guardians of the countryside may sneer at the 'hacienda style' in rural Eire, but there is life in the place. A journey from even the six counties of Northern Ireland into the not dissimilar Galloway and Dumfries-shire will produce the shock of a comparatively empty countryside. One opinion is that the preservationists have been a menace born of ignorance, with little concep-tion of how completely even the 'wild' landscape of most of Europe has been the creation of man.

EXERCISE 6
The advocate for government support for agriculture makes his point in
Document 123. Considering the triangle of country people, government policy,

and science and technology, consider the contrast of public policy before and after 1973, and – if you are game – the options for altering the CAP with regard to the rural areas of Lowland Scotland.

REFERENCES TO BOOKS AND ARTICLES MENTIONED IN THE TEXT

*Alexander, W 1881 *Johnny Gibb of Gushetneuk in the Parish of Pyketillim*. Edinburgh.
Boyd, J 1920 *The Scottish Farmer Album*. Glasgow.
Consumers and the Common Agricultural Policy 1988. HMSO.
*Coppock, JT 1976 *An Agricultural Atlas of Scotland*. Edinburgh.
Hoffman, WG 1969 '100 years of the margarine industry', *in* Van Stuyvenberg, JH 1969 *Margarine: An Economic, Social and Scientific History, 1869–1969*, Liverpool, 9–13.
Ingham, K and Love, J 1983 *Understanding the Scottish Economy*. Oxford.
Jennings, R 1987 'Rural housing and housing policy in Ireland', *in* MacGregor, BD, Robertson, DS and Shucksmith, M (eds) 1987 *Rural Housing in Scotland*, Aberdeen, 156.
M'Neel Caird, A 1978 *Report on the present state of the agriculture of Scotland*. Edinburgh.
Martin, DJ 1994 *Auchincruive: The History of the West of Scotland Agricultural College*. Edinburgh.
National Consumer Council 1988 *Consumers and the Common Agricultural Policy*. HMSO.
Quick, G and Buchele, W 1978 *The Grain Harvesters*. Michigan.
*Robinson, GM 1988 *Agricultural Change*. Edinburgh.
Rodger, R 1996 'Urbanisation in Twentieth-century Scotland', *in* Devine, TM and Finlay, RJ (eds) 1996 *Scotland in the 20th Century*, Edinburgh, 122–52.
Scottish Rural Profile 1991. HMSO.
*Sprott, G 1978 *The Tractor in Scotland*. Edinburgh.
*Sprott, G 1996 'Lowland country life', *in* Devine, TM and Finlay, RJ (eds) 1996 *Scotland in the 20th Century*, Edinburgh, 122–52.
*Stephens, H 1851 *The Book of the Farm*, 2 Volumes. 2nd Edn., Edinburgh.
*Stephens, H and Burn, RS 1861 *The Book of Farm Buildings*. Edinburgh.
Symon, JA 1959 *Scottish Farming Past and Present*. Edinburgh.

FURTHER READING

Those references marked * in the above list are recommended further reading, along with the following:

Fenton, A 1987 *Country Life in Scotland*. Edinburgh.
Marten, B nd *Harry Ferguson*. Belfast.
Powell, B nd *Scottish Agricultural Implements*. Princes Risborough.
Robertson, BW 1978 'The Scottish farm servant and his union', *in* MacDougall, I, *Essays in Scottish Labour History*, Edinburgh, 90–114.
Sprott, G 1995 *Farming*. Edinburgh.

Class

——————————————————————— J Foster

INTRODUCTION

Almost all historians writing about twentieth century Scotland have placed 'class' near the centre of their analysis. In some cases it has been to make 'class' a mainspring of explanation (Dickson 1989; Fraser 1988; Gray 1975; Melling 1990; Morris 1991; Smith 1984; Smout 1986; Young 1979). In others it has been to contest this centrality (Harvie 1981; McLean 1983; McCrone 1996; Paterson 1994). But either way class has tended to dominate the debate. Most Scots would still define their country's history in terms that refer to class – even if it is sometimes to stress that Scotland is not like that any more. The socialism of the Red Clyde, the industrial dominance of heavy engineering and mining, the impact of male-employing industries on social and sexual values, the power of the Scottish trade union movement and the political supremacy of the Labour Party would all figure in most peoples' personal explanations of what Scotland has been like this century.

As a concept, however, 'class' is apt to play tricks on historians. It is not directly a thing or an event. It is a device for categorising people and relations between them. And, as an analytical device, it has no standard or agreed usage: social scientists quarrel constantly about its definition. To make matters still more complicated, social scientists have to share the term with everyone else. People in society at large use 'class' in various ways to make sense of their society. By doing so, they also define relations and pass judgements – with consequences that impact on history. If enough people share the same 'class' assumptions about how power and wealth are distributed, such convictions can drive political action and become a real life social phenomenon. In this guise 'class' has indeed figured significantly in the history of twentieth century Scotland. On occasion those holding power have felt themselves directly threatened, and for that reason alone the use of the term 'class' has become highly politicised. Asserting or denying its validity is a political as well as a scientific act.

The chapter considers the subject of class since 1850 under the following headings:

- Definitions
- Debates
- Sources
- Episodes
    Pre-1914 inheritance
    The Red Clyde and its aftermath

Class and Trade Union Militancy in the Era of Full Employment
Class and Post-Industrialism

We will begin by examining the range of definitions, then outline the debates that have unfolded around their application to recent Scottish history and consider the sources available to test and illuminate the controversies. Only then will we examine those events in which 'class' may have played a starring role.

I. DEFINITIONS

Two great systems of social science analysis dominate the definition of class. The Marxist approach makes 'class relations' central to the power structures by which a society produces its wealth and distributes it. The Weberian approach stands back from such grand assumptions. Instead Weber presents 'class' more as an analytical tool which can be used alongside 'status' and 'power' to examine the way people categorise themselves. It seeks to identify how far people's perceptions of their place in society are determined economically by their 'class' standing in terms of *market* position, or, conversely by their ranking in terms of *social status* – or, finally, by their relative powerlessness or empowerment in terms of the *political* system (Edgell 1993).

Marx sought to explain the overall process of social development in terms of the struggle between classes. He defined these classes by their dominant or subordinate position within a succession of progressively developing productive relationships:

> It is always the direct relationship of the owners of the conditions of production
> to the direct producers – a relationship always naturally corresponding to a
> definite stage in the development of the methods of labour and thereby its social
> productivity – which reveals the innermost secret, the hidden basis, of the entire
> social structure, and with it the political form of the relation of sovereignty and
> dependence, in short, the corresponding specific form of the state . . .
>
> (Marx, 1959, 791)

This usage of class gives central place to the specific relationship that enables one class to extract the surplus product from the other. Within capitalism Marx saw this relationship as based on the power of the owners of capital over the sellers of labour power – and his definition of labour is a rather special one. Unlike Adam Smith, Marx did not define labour in terms of the manual character of the task. For Marx, labour represented the integration of mental and manual activity and he defined the working class as including *all* those selling their labour power. Moreover this relationship was not simply one between capital and labour. What was critical was the state-endorsement of that relationship in a way that gave capital the power and authority within the workplace to extract *surplus* labour (Westergard 1996).

Marx also made another important distinction in his discussion of class: that between the class-in-itself and the class-for-itself. The class-in-itself referred to the objective position of labour within production relations: how *many* people are employees. The class-for-itself referred to the actual social process by which people become aware that they had interests which were antagonistic to those who extracted 'surplus value' and consequently to the wider state system which sustained and enforced these relationships. Marx saw this development of 'class conscious-ness' as historically contingent and not necessarily continuous or even. But he also saw it as of central importance – because it was such class consciousness alone that had the power to move history forward to the next stage of human development.

All this is quite contrary to the Weberian approach. Weber saw no necessary link between political power and economic processes. The sale of labour was a normal market transaction: the state could not automatically be assumed to be backing one side or the other. Such market transactions did indeed involve a clash of interest between buyer and seller, and there was certainly also a difference in the economic powers of the 'positively' and 'negatively' privileged 'commercial classes'. But there was no systemic conflict.

That said, Weber did see class position, as he defined it, as the 'predominant factor' in determining an individual's life chance in modern society – with classes defined as groups of people who shared a common class situation in terms of:

> The typical chance for the supply of goods, external living conditions and personal life experiences, in so far as this chance is determined by the amount or kind of power, or lack of such, to dispose of goods or skills for the sake of income in a given economic order . . .
>
> (Weber 1961 cited by Edgell 1993, 12)

Weber's emphasis is on 'amounts' and 'kinds'. He is concerned with the 'typical chance for the supply of goods' and its relationship to the 'amount of power' to dispose of goods. This stress leads to a perception of class as a *gradation*. The 'positively privileged' commercial classes would include industrial and agricultural entrepreneurs, merchants, bankers, professionals – but also workers 'with mono-polistic qualifications and skills'. The negatively privileged commercial classes would include 'skilled, semi-skilled and unskilled workers'. In between the two there would be middle classes that would include shopkeepers, liberal professions and also workers with exceptional credentials and/or skills. These analytical categories would in turn be subsumed within wider 'social classes' which would be the entities perceived as social groupings in real life. Weber defined these social classes as 'the totality of those class situations within which individual and inter-generational mobility is easy and typical'.

So for Weber 'class conflict' is indeed possible. It refers to those circumstances, such as moments of economic crisis, in which disagreements between buyers and sellers within a market situation become exacerbated and hence dominate other aspects of life. But these moments are inherently episodic. They do not lead anywhere in particular. The normal situation is that in which people perceive position in society in terms of 'social classes' and status.

Marxists would argue that Weberians have transformed 'class' into a purely descriptive term which maps surface phenomena and fails to penetrate to the 'innermost secret' of society: the process whereby the surplus is extracted by a socially dominant class. Weberians would reply no less sharply. The Marxist position involves unprovable assumptions about the exploitative character of the social system and equally unprovable claims about what people really believe when they become involved in class-based movements.

These, therefore, are some approximate definitions. Historians often choose not to use these definitions very precisely or, if they do use them, not to make their assumptions explicit. But, in sum, the Weberian and Marxist positions do underlie most of the key debates.

EXERCISE I
Read Smout (1986, Introduction and Chapters 10 and 11) and consider what perspective he adopts on this issue.

Smout is not a Marxist, but significant areas of his study (his Introduction, pages 2 and 3 and Chapters 10 and 11) are conducted as dialogues with Marxist positions. Smout seeks to stress in response the very limited purchase of doctrinally Marxist socialism in Scotland, the heterogeneous character of working class culture and a diversity of social causation – which he perceives to be incompatible with Marxism. This is not to devalue Smout's views. Rather it serves to emphasise the variety of interpretations of Scotland's recent history.

2. DEBATES

Inevitably, because of the politicised character of the concept, the history of class in modern Scotland has been sharply contested. Three underlying themes may be identified:

The Scottish angle: whether there is actually any scope for a specifically Scottish dimension for a phenomenon so closely tied to the rise of industrial society and for such an integrated an economy as that of Britain.

The 'class consciousness' question: whether, within the wider conceptual contest between Marxist and Weberian positions, either analysis can be appropriately applied to the episodes of apparently mass class-based political activity from the 1910s onwards.

The 'post-industrial' question: whether the social and economic transformations of the last third of the twentieth century, particularly the decline of heavy industry, have meant the end of class as a significant element in social development – or whether, conversely, proletarianisation in the Marxist sense has intensified.

Before going on to look at sources and actual events, it is useful to examine the structure and assumptions of these debates a little more closely.

The 'Scottishness' debate is in many ways the intellectually richest and most interesting. It was originally a response to accounts of labour history which, since the writings of Sidney and Beatrice Webb in the 1890s, tended to tell the story in terms of a single British movement. More recently the debate has been given added impetus by the work of Kendrick, Bechhofer and McCrone. They have argued that there is little to distinguish Scotland in terms of class structure within the regional diversity of Britain as a whole and that the growth of industrial society produces its own pressures towards greater uniformity.

The debate is important for two reasons. It introduces the issue of culture. And it has centred on relations *between* classes. Because the debate is about national characteristics, its proponents have tended to focus on the special characteristics of Scotland's employers and the impact this had on their relations with their workers. The result has been to root the discussion of class very firmly within specific analyses of Scottish history.

Smout (1986) and Smith (1984) have argued that Scottish uniqueness derived from the strength of the Liberal, Presbyterian and Free Church values among employers and within Scottish society in general. Scottish Chartism had, they claim, been mainly non-revolutionary and Christian in character and helped provide the soil in which a mass-based, Gladstonian Liberal party could grow. This radical but reformist orientation had gained additional strength from the particularly large stratum of skilled tradesmen resulting from the rapid growth of Scotland's engineering and shipbuilding industries. The progressive Liberal paternalism of Scottish employers coloured the perceptions of these privileged and aristocratic workers – values reinforced by the anti-landlordism brought to Scotland's cities by the continuing stream of highland and rural immigrants. The outcome was a trade union movement that kept its Liberal links much later than in England and only surrendered them with the wider break-up of the Liberal Party and the assault on labour conditions during the First World War.

This perspective is challenged by another group of historians also defending Scottish uniqueness. They too focus on relations between classes, but do so in order to claim that Scottish employers were in fact more authoritarian and anti-union than their counterparts south of the Border. Fraser (1988), Melling (1982) and McIvor (1996) have an economic rather than cultural starting point. They highlight the economic vulnerability of Scottish employers, their perceived need for lower wage costs than competitors in England and the existence of relations with organised labour that were far more volatile and, on occasion, violent. Fraser links this to events in the first half of the century. The very fraught industrial climate of the 1820s and 1830s produced legal judgements which precluded the recognition of trade union organisation for a full generation after this had been conceded in England. Hence, the inheritance from the earlier nineteenth century was 'liberal' only in the free market sense. The elaborate structures for collective bargaining characteristic of Victorian England, which did much to sustain traditions of reformist labour politics, had little counterpart in Scotland. The result was a trade union movement which was providing a rich soil for radical and socialist politics by the end of the nineteenth century.

> EXERCISE 2
> Though these two positions may appear to be quite incompatible, they may also – like the blind man and the elephant – be describing different aspects of the same phenomenon. Consider in what ways this might be the case.

Both sides of the debate would probably agree firstly, that most Scottish employers were Free Church Presbyterians who followed the paternalist doctrines of Thomas Chalmers (Smout 1986, 186), and, secondly, that collective bargaining in Scotland was less developed than in England, trade union membership was smaller and the political influence of the Liberal Party was more persistent.

The difference between the two positions is mainly one of causation: whether it was the belief system of the employers which promoted a stress on common values, or whether it was the social frictions arising from the need for lower wages which pushed employers towards stressing common values, hence developing a brand of liberalism which increasingly supported collective (municipal) responsibility for social provision.

Aspects of the 'Scottishness' debate are continued into our next area of dispute: the 'redness' of the Red Clyde and the content of class-based politics in the 1920s and 1930s. This debate focuses much more directly on the relative applicability of Marxist and Weberian models. The key issue is the content of worker consciousness.

Both sides would probably agree on the size and speed of the transformation of political attitudes over the seven years between 1914 and 1921 and the degree to which these years marked the defining moment for the character of labour politics in Scotland. The disagreement is over the cause of the transformation. Did it involve some element of class consciousness in the Marxist sense – a level of mass involvement in a struggle that was perceived to be against capitalism as a social system – or was it a more limited series of tactical battles to improve labour's position within the market?

The Red Clydeside leaders themselves tended to paint the period in revolutionary tones. A number of modern historians have used recently opened government records to vindicate this interpretation. In general these historians root their analysis in the presumption that there was already something special about labour politics in Scotland before the war and, specifically, that collective bargaining structures were weaker and less developed. Hence the explosive character of class relations once the balance of workplace power changed in face of wartime full employment.

The opposing camp also tends to go back to the earlier debate. Authors such as McLean (1983), Reid (1985), Harvie (1981; 1992) and Smout (1986) would argue that what was previously special had been the dominance of the culture and politics of the privileged stratum of skilled workers. The industrial struggles of wartime were in part a sectional defence of these privileges and in part the assertion of an altogether new agenda of issues raised by those unskilled and semi-skilled workers who hitherto had largely lacked trade union organisation. These new issues focused on the concerns of the very poor – housing, health and poor relief – and gave rise to the dominance of a reformist Labour Party firmly rooted in municipal politics.

This Weberian interpretation has one further element that links it into the final area of debate. McLean and Harvie in particular see the war years, 1914–19, as initiating a new type of alliance between Scotland's professional élite and the representatives of the underprivileged. On the one side trade union and labour leaders used the war to highlight the scale of Scotland's urban deprivation. On the other, the wartime requirements for social consensus created an environment in which civil servants could respond creatively. The resulting dialogue took a particularly active form in Scotland precisely because of the inherited liberal and Christian values of the nation's professional élite.

The outcome has been what David McCrone (1992b), following David Marquand, has termed the 'principled society'. The alliance created pressures for significantly higher levels of Scottish social expenditure than those in most other parts of Britain and this, in turn, has produced an increasingly large stratum of professional people involved in combating social deprivation and committed to the values of service to the community. Accordingly, these historians would argue that the late twentieth century rise of a service economy has taken a special form in Scotland.

As the factory-based manual working class has gone into eclipse, these new social values have secured a dominant place in Scottish politics and increasingly defined themselves against the individualism of post-Thatcherite England. This, they argue, explains the rise of both Labour and nationalist political identities in face of a Scottish Conservative tradition that has been unable to sustain its previous 'one nation' image. In good Weberian fashion values and ideology are seen to take a determining hand in fashioning a society in which specific class interests – in terms of position within the labour market – have become much less important but where general concern for the less privileged is more marked than south of the Border.

Marxist commentators take a diametrically opposed position. They argue that the larger scale of social expenditure in Scotland can be related to the vigour of the working class challenge, both in the 1910s and 1920s and later, and that the later twentieth century has witnessed a greater proportion of the population being directly exposed to exploitative class relationships.

The interest of this final debate is that it brings us back to two key areas of contention between the Marxist and Weberian positions. One focuses on the different occupational and economic definitions of class and how these are mapped on to census categories. The other concerns the status of episodes of heightened class activity – such as the industrial militancy of the early 1970s, the miners' strike of 1984–85 or mass civil disobedience associated with the poll tax campaign of 1989–91. For the Weberian viewpoint such episodes are of significance because they are not typical and hence underline the non-systemic character of class-based conflicts.

For Marxists, on the other hand, these moments represent the expression of underlying fissures within society. They are short-lived precisely because the power structures of society penalise the expression of opposition that challenges its fundamental character.

3. SOURCES

The source material for the study of class behaviour is vast. But it is often quite difficult to evaluate as the following examples illustrate.

On the afternoon of Friday, 31 January 1919 a future British war minister was making a tortuous journey through the backstreets of Glasgow. Angry crowds had broken away from the protest demonstration in George Square. There was much police activity. Our hero, constantly fearful of identification, was trying to get back to the Glasgow Trades Council strike headquarters before they were raided. Once there, his first act, successfully completed before he was arrested, was to destroy papers in which the key junction boxes of the Glasgow city electricity supply had been marked out for sabotage. A couple of weeks before he, along with other key leaders of Clydeside labour, had signed the proclamation headed 'A Call to Arms' which urged the workers of Scotland to embark on an indefinite general strike unless their demands for a 15% cut in the working week were met. Fifty years later Lord Shinwell, by then a privy councillor of long standing, wrote his autobiography. He spends some pages discussing the failed general strike of January 1919. His main intent is to demonstrate that his role was to urge moderation. The strike itself was a gesture of 'self-sacrifice by shopstewards and trade unionists to help the workless'. It was the government which had conspired to create confrontation and which was caught up in a 'neurosis about red revolution' (Shinwell 1973).

Historians will never know what options and possibilities flitted through the mind of Lord Shinwell in January 1919. The episode demonstrates the inherent difficulty of finding and using source materials for most types of class mobilisation. It is not just that much relevant material will be destroyed or will never be put on paper in the first place. Key protagonists will quite often change their ideological positions and subsequently reinterpret their actions. This also applies, perhaps with even more force, to those who have not directly sought positions of power and respectability but who have simply seen their aspirations dashed by failure and defeat. Oral history can be immensely illuminating in the recovery of the perceptions of the rank and file. But it can also encounter silence. Episodes like the strikes of 1926 or 1984–85, which for many individuals resulted in loss of employment, family break-up and personal disaster, are ones which people will often not want to remember.

Our second example comes from the other side of the class divide. Early in 1972 the Conservative Government of Edward Heath sharply reversed its hard-line, proto-monetarist economic policies. Members of Heath's government subsequently claimed that this reversal of policy only occurred in face of the most serious threats of social unrest – particularly on the Clyde. Nicholas Ridley said that the government feared the spread of civil violence from Belfast to Glasgow. Peter Walker cited apprehensions that 'unless some action was taken social disorder of a type not seen in this country' would occur in the city. For Jock Bruce-Gardyne, the PPS to the Scottish Secretary of State, the critical moment had been the statement by the Chief Constable of Glasgow that he would need an extra 15,000 men if the government did not intervene to save the four Upper Clyde shipyards (Woolfson 1986).

Yet closer examination of actual events on the Clyde in 1971–72 reveals altogether no threat of direct physical violence. The government's real concerns at the time were, it would seem, of a different order. They were those of managing opinion. Ministers were particularly alarmed at the degree to which a Communist-oriented shop stewards movement was displacing the authority of established trade union leaders and correctly fearful of the impact of this shift in leadership on their wider industrial relations reforms. They were no less anxious about the effects of the closures on small and medium business and on the political cohesion of the Conservative Party in Scotland. Yet such concerns were never publicly voiced. In terms of what ministers actually said, the government appears to have been running scared of ghosts.

All this highlights the more general problem. Moments of class mobilisation are usually short-lived. By nature they tend to challenge existing structures of allegiance. They therefore pose extremely difficult issues for governments. Whether these moments are seen as essentially untypical or structurally significant, responses are almost always carefully guarded. The public admission of a tactical retreat will itself usually be prejudicial to the task of maintaining social control. Very little can be taken at face value – either at the time or, as in the 1970s, when alibis were being constructed after the event.

So, although there is an immense volume of material on class-based movements, what evidence there is cannot be easily assessed, and at key moments it is apt to fall silent. Ian MacDougall's monumental listing of labour records in Scotland reveals the scope available: trade union minutes, pamphlets, newspapers, personal correspondence, autobiographies, novels, oral history recordings, records from central and local government and employers associations. This treasury contains much of use to historians. But, particularly for class-based movements, not every document can be believed on its own terms (MacDougall 1978).

The same goes for the apparent plenitude of statistical data on class structure. The censuses of population and production, medical records from schools and health boards, the Register General's figures on mortality by occupation, the Board of Trade/Ministry of Labour series on strikes and trade union membership are all susceptible to sharply differing interpretations. Even the raw material will often be of uncertain value – and all the original ambiguities will be multiplied at each stage of reclassification.

EXERCISE 3
Consider one example. An old man dies of some kind of respiratory illness in a Glasgow tenement in the 1950s. An overworked doctor has to write the death

certificate. What does he put down as the cause of death – and for the old man's occupation? List the obstacles which will stand in the way of an analytically usable entry.

The doctor is likely to have known little of the life history of the old man. Even if the doctor is told of his last employment, it may not have been his main employment. Many previously semi-skilled workers, such as shipyard rivetters, would rely on labouring or janitorial jobs once their strength failed. Similar problems would arise with the cause of death. To the doctor the cause of the death might appear to be respiratory failure brought on by bronchitis and exacerbated by heavy smoking. The actual cause of death might have been the effects of asbestos exposure experienced while working in a shipyard.

4. EPISODES

The episodes which follow are intended to provide a general descriptive background for the discussion of class in modern Scotland. These summaries are brief and schematic. Moreover, like all such interpretative treatments, their structure and emphases depend on the assumptions of the author.

4.1 *Employers and workers in Scotland before 1914*

Organised labour faced a particularly uphill struggle in later nineteenth-century Scotland. Significantly less workers were unionised than in England. Labour representation in parliament was virtually non-existent. Both Alexander Macdonald, Scottish miners leader in the 1860s and 1870s, and Keir Hardie, Scotland's best known labour politician, had to move south of the Border to secure election.

Demographic, economic and cultural factors all appear to have been at work. Employment tended to be subject to much wider fluctuations than in England – especially in heavy industry. There was more emigration out of Scotland by skilled workers – but also much more immigration into Scotland by unskilled workers fleeing famine in Ireland. In fact without this immigration Scotland's population would have stopped growing from the middle of the nineteenth century. Scottish wages in most industries were between 10% and 15% lower than those in England.

All these trends were, to a greater or lesser extent, interlinked. The plentiful supply of raw, unorganised unskilled labour from Ireland and rural Scotland seems to have been strongly associated with the disproportionate growth of coal, iron and steel. The dependence of the Scottish economy on heavy industry made it particularly vulnerable to trade cycle fluctuations and the long periods of high unemployment led to the emigration of skilled labour who could achieve better wages elsewhere. And there was also a political factor. The law remained far more hostile to trade unions than in England where their legality had been largely conceded by the 1850s.

Correspondingly there was little counterpart to the elaborate systems of collective bargaining which existed in England. Scottish employers relied far more on market forces: making concessions when trade was booming and clawing them back once unemployment had returned. Long-term collective bargaining agreements would have impeded this periodic settling of scores.

Taken together these factors meant that the development of trade unionism in Scotland was significantly out of phase with that in England. Scotland lacked the large and financially stable skilled unions which emerged in England in the 1850s and 60s. For most of the late nineteenth century Scotland's labour movement was made up of its own small and localised craft unions and affiliates of English industrial unions operating in very adverse circumstances. This gave the Scottish movement its own distinct periodisation. Many groups of skilled workers were still struggling for recognition in the late 1880s at a time when unskilled were starting to organise. Correspondingly, the gulf between old (skilled) and new (labouring) unions tended to be somewhat less marked in Scotland.

Organisationally, the counterpart to the weakness among individual trade unions was the importance assumed by the Scottish trades councils, often described as United Trades Councils. Even after 1889 much trade union organisation tended to be short-lived and the trades councils continued to take responsibility for organisation among individual trades and to campaign on a wide range of social as well as industrial issues. The foundation of the Scottish Trade Union Congress in 1897 was symptomatic of this perceived need for a united Scottish focus.

Looking at developments chronologically, the 1850s and 1860s saw the consolidation of the first wave of Scottish Trades Councils (Edinburgh 1849; Glasgow 1858; Dundee 1867; Aberdeen 1868). This was at a time when employers in all Scotland's major industries were either able to exclude the majority of their workforce from trade unions (cotton textiles) or to impose successful lockouts to destroy trade union power (as in coal in 1856 or shipbuilding in 1865). Temporarily high employment between 1870–72 saw a renewed push for unionisation in mines, in heavy engineering and shipbuilding (where a 51 hour week was won) and also among labourers in agriculture and transport. These advances were, however, short-lived. Lock-outs followed in the mines (1874), in the iron industry (1874) and in the shipyards (1877) wiping out the gains in both wages and shorter hours. The labourers' unions almost all disintegrated. After the successive defeats of moves for collective bargaining in shipbuilding (1881–85) and in the mines (1885–87), renewed organisation began in 1888 and continued to 1890 in conditions of near full employment. By 1890 organisation of some kind existed in most trades. But as unemployment returned the shipbuilding unions were once more defeated in 1891 as were the miners in 1894 – though both retained some elements of organisation and continuing recognition. The labouring unions in transport once more disintegrated although those in the docks hung on as part of British-based unions. These years saw the creation of a new wave of trades councils: Motherwell (1889); Govan and Falkirk (1890); Paisley (1891); and Coatbridge (1894).

Politically, the key years for the formation of some form of ideologically-explicit class organisation were the 1880s. The Scottish branches of the Marxist Social Democratic Federation and its break-away sibling, the Socialist League, were formed in 1884. Initially the Socialist League and the SDF had some success in bringing together trade unionist activists, supporters of the Highland Land Restoration League (then involved in the Crofters War) and of Michael Davitt's Land League. Joint rallies 30,000 to 40,000 strong are recorded for 1886 and 1887. Demands included the nationalisation of the railways and of industry in general. In 1888 Keir Hardie established the Scottish Labour Party in order to campaign for parliamentary representation – at a time when the mine-owner dominated Liberal Party in Lanarkshire refused to enter the same type of Lib-Lab pact arrangements that existed in England. The Independent Labour Party, formed in 1893, absorbed what remained of the Scottish Labour Party as well as the few thousand activists who had been mobilised through the wave of trade union organisation between 1888 and 1890.

Independent labour politics in Scotland consequently had its own distinct characteristics in parallel to those in the trade union movement. On the one side, there was no systematic policy of electoral pacts with the Liberals before 1914 and this made electoral success much less frequent. On the other, there was a greater degree of organisational cohesion. The Marxist SDF remained in membership of the Scottish Workers Representation Committee – which from 1900 brought together trades councils, the STUC and socialist societies to secure parliamentary representation.

This said, it should be stressed that prior to 1900 the great majority of male manual workers in Scotland did not vote for Labour or Socialist candidates. If they did vote, and over 40% did not possess the vote, most would have used it to support Liberal or Conservative candidates. Only a minute fraction of clerks, teachers, technicians and foremen would have supported Labour. Religious identities remained important. Perceptions of 'place' within a hierarchy of occupations and wealth dominated personal life.

This conclusion returns us, therefore, to the earlier debate on definitions. This type of social behaviour might seem to conform exactly to the Weberian model. Despite the overall disparities of wealth, it was the perception of relative difference *between* strata of working people that assumed the greatest importance. Against this, the Marxist might point to the uneven but persistent process by which class-based organisation emerged in Scotland during the fifty years before 1914 – to the extent that it had by then visibly eroded the base of the Liberal Party in most industrial centres.

EXERCISE 4
Examine the figures for profits, wage and tonnage for Fairfield Shipyard set out below. What do they tell us about a) the economic environment in which employers had to operate and b) income distribution?

These figures are very interesting and reveal: strong fluctuations in the volume of work; significant fluctuations in the value of the work per ton (largely reflecting the proportion of naval work); extreme fluctuations in the volume of profits – compared with the relative stability of wages per ton constructed. This level of year by year fluctuation would predispose employers to minimise fixed investment and to maximise the degree to which the labour force could be expanded and contracted in line with demand (note, for instance, the drop in the wage bill in 1884–85).

The distribution of income between capital and labour fluctuates strongly. When profits were at their highest, as in 1883, the income to capital (in this case one man, the sole partner in the firm, William Pearce) was 4,000 times greater than the wage of the average worker. The proportion of income going to capital tends to rise between the 1870s and the 1880s.

TABLE 1: FAIRFIELD YARD: PROFITS, WAGES AND VALUE OF WORK IN £000S AND THOUSANDS OF TONS.

	PROFITS	WAGES	VALUE	TONNAGE
1871	3	223	728	21
1872	50	238	800	28
1873	115	207	883	28
1874	92	225	1029	26
1875	49	165	483	24
1876	18	172	436	16
1877	0	166	154	4
1878	0	226	720	20
1879	58	173	950	19
1880	85	224	904	23
1881	45	261	587	26
1882	47	375	1112	32
1883	259	373	1003	33
1884	194	341	1177	29
1885	169	154	188	8
1886	93	237	683	23
1887	76	196	663	13

Source: Strathclyde Record Office: UCS 2/7/15 "Profits Declared, John Elder". Fairfield yard in Govan was the biggest on the Clyde. It had been in operation on that site since the 1850s. At full capacity working, as in 1883, the yard would employ up to 6,000 workers. Up to 1878 the yard was a partnership dominated by the Elder family. From 1879 the yard was owned by a single partner, William Pearce.

Document 124, an extract from the minutes of the Clyde Shipbuilders Association, shows us a great deal about this group of employers to collective bargaining. The period June to November 1882 shows groups of skilled workers sufficiently well organised to take the initiative in pushing for wage increases. Opposition from the Clydeside shipbuilding employers is also well organised. It is, however, interesting to note that the employers were always on the alert to backsliding by individual firms – often anxious to recruit labour in periods of labour scarcity (note comment on John and George Thompson in the minute of 14 September 1882). The decision to recruit strike-breakers from England may reveal the degree to which skilled joinery trades had already secured relatively high levels of unionisation across central Scotland. The specific arrangements for controlling the scabs reveals considerable prior experience. Note in particular the stipulation about employers continuing to control the scabs' tools (which would render any premature departure futile). The length of the dispute shows the strength of organisation on both sides. The employers' attempts to evade arbitration, especially by the Liberal MP and shipowner Sir Donald Currie, demonstrate both their determination to resist any wage increase and an awareness of a wider public opinion. If the Fairfield figures are anything to go by, the defeat of the joiners' claim enabled the employers to sharply increase their share of income in 1883.

The period November 1883 to January 1884, one of sharply declining demand, shows the employers taking the initiative to force down wages. The employers were willing to meet deputations from the boilermakers union who represented iron workers. But they were not willing to depart from their demand for a 10% wage cut. The meeting on 4 January 1884 made concessions to smaller groups of workers such as engineers and joiners – presumably to isolate the ironworkers who represented the biggest single group of workers.

EXERCISE 5

How do Smout (1986, 23–58) and Smyth (**Article 39**) account for the breakdown of Liberal hegemony and the rise of the ILP?

The accounts by Smout and Smyth have much in common, and both note the obstacles to independent labour politics posed by the weakness of the trade union movement in Scotland. But there are also significantly different emphases. While Smout sees Keir Hardie's challenge in 1886 as arising from the 'logic of Liberalism's own progressive ideology', Smyth portrays it more as the product of the intransigence of employer-dominated Liberal caucuses in a society where trade unions remained largely unrecognised. And while Smout stresses the ideological grip of Liberalism as the main factor holding back electoral support, Smyth stresses the impact of the limited, pre-1918 household suffrage in urban Scotland – where the prevalence of rented accommodation and sharp fluctuations in employment led to very frequent changes of address even among skilled workers. Voting figures, for Smyth, are not an adequate reflection of support. In terms of what created the social base for independent labour politics, Smout stresses the degree to which Keir Hardie and the Scottish Labour Party carried forward and drew on the ideas of the radical wing of Scottish Liberalism. Smyth, on the other hand, stresses the importance of class-specific organisation. He notes the increasing skill of socialist organisers in directing their campaigning to practical issues of immediate material interest to different constituencies within the working class: municipal provision, unemployment, poor relief, housing.

4.2 *The Red Clyde and its aftermath*

By 1918, in contrast to this earlier weakness, Scotland's trade unionists were viewed by government and employers alike as the most militant and politically radicalised in Britain.

Already prior to 1914 there were some indications of change. The post-1911 armaments drive produced rising employment levels and a renewed wave of unionisation. Women workers were particularly to the fore, and these years saw significant levels of solidarity action between different groups and grades of workers. Politically, the Independent Labour Party and its Glasgow-based weekly newspaper *Forward* began to create a density of local organisation that in parts of the city became a preponderant part of community life.

The war itself took these changes much further. The first upsurge of unrest occurred in the autumn and winter of 1915–1916. Workers in the munitions factories and in the shipyards initiated illegal strike action to resist the attacks on the previously negotiated conditions for the skilled worker. The resistance was organised at workplace level by unofficial shop stewards' committees and co-ordinated between workplaces by the Clyde Workers' Committee. This industrial unrest coincided with a locality-based struggle on rents and eventually resulted in factory and shipyard walk-outs in support of the rent-strike leaders in November 1915. This wave of unrest was ended by a series of concessions by the government on wages and rents combined with an attempt to isolate the political leadership of

55 Bleachers strike workers marching through Almondbank village, Perthshire, 1920. *Dundee University Archives.*

the movement: the arrest and deportation of the leaders and the temporary suppression of socialist newspapers, including the ILP's *Forward*.

This first upsurge gained considerable prominence – probably because of the precedents it set. But it was in fact dwarfed in scale by the series of strikes which erupted two years later in the autumn and winter of 1917–1918 over bonus payments. On this occasion the strikes engulfed a much wider range of industries, including coal, iron and steel, and spread through central Scotland. The government saw this strike wave as particularly dangerous because it coincided with the October revolution in Russia and was accompanied by further community agitation on prices and food shortages and the appearance of a politically radicalised ex-servicemen's movement. Again the government combined the tactic of substantive concessions with the removal of the political leadership, notably the imprisonment of John Maclean.

The government's fears became even more focused by events twelve months later immediately after the defeat of Germany in November 1918.

On this occasion the strongly politicised socialist leadership of the Clyde Workers' Committee succeeded in winning an alliance which combined most workplaces in the West of Scotland, the Glasgow Trades Council and the Scottish Trades Union Congress. This grouping demanded the enforcement of a forty-hour week. The objective was to maintain wartime levels of full employment and to ensure the absorption of returning soldiers – after the government had conceded fast demo-bilisation in face of troop mutinies in December 1918. In Scotland a significant number of these ex-servicemen were being organised in the socialist-led Discharged Soldiers and Sailors Federation. The resulting industrial action spread from the Clyde through the Lanarkshire coalfield to Fife and coincided with similar action in Belfast. The use of mass pickets, composed of both strikers and discharged service-men, ensured that the strike quickly closed down virtually all workplaces and industrial power supplies.

On Friday, 31 January a mass lobby of the Glasgow City Chambers by over 50,000 strikers and ex-servicemen ended in serious conflicts with the police. The government ordered the military occupation of the city and the arrest of the strike leaders.

On this occasion also the crisis ended with some concessions. Hours were reduced to forty-seven and for the time being there were no sackings or victimisations in the main workplaces. The following twelve months saw a historically high level of strike action in Scotland – especially in the steel industry and coalmining.

Politically, the immediate post-war years saw electoral success for socialist-aligned candidates in most industrial localities on Clydeside and in the coalfields. It also appears to have seen a significant level of mass identification with socialist politics. Members of the anti-war ILP won two seats on Clydeside in 1918 and a further thirteen in 1922. For two years running the Scottish conference of the ILP voted for affiliation to the (Communist) Third International. Members of the newly formed Communist Party won the parliamentary seat in Motherwell and came close to winning in Greenock and Kelvingrove (which then included the shipbuilding and dock area of western Glasgow).

It was the developments of these years, both industrial and electorally, which gave substance to the term 'Red Clydeside'. From late 1920, however, mass unemployment engulfed virtually all sectors of Scottish heavy industry: coal, steel, shipbuilding and heavy engineering. Over the following decade, the trade union movement shrank to half its previous size, socialist shop stewards were removed and within the Labour Party the Left was marginalised. Instead the cautious reformism of municipal politics, sometimes in alliance with the Catholic Church, became the predominant force within the Labour Party. Apart from localised pockets, mainly in the coalfields, and a massive but short-lived upsurge during the 1926 General Strike, those calling for the replacement of the capitalist system found only very limited support.

EXERCISE 6
Read the minutes of the North West Engineers and the Clyde Shipbuilders Association for 30 and 31 January 1919 and intelligence reports to the Cabinet in January and April 1919 (**Documents 125 and 126**). List the tactics considered, respectively, by the Clydeside employers and the Cabinet for controlling the challenge posed by the unofficial strike. Consider what these discussions tell us about the relative priorities of the employers and the government.

Read the 'Call to Arms' (Illustration 56), 'Now is the Hour' (**Document 127**) and the passage from Gallacher's *Revolt on the Clyde* (**Article 40**) alongside the intelligence reports CAB 24/74, MUN 5/18 and AIR 1 586 16/15/41 (**Document 126**). Assess the objectives of the strikers and their leaders.

The documents produced by the strike committee and more specifically by the key socialist activists, such as John Maclean's editorial in the 'Call' for 30 January, show considerable sophistication – as would be expected by a leadership cadre on Clydeside with long experience of the dynamics of mass movements, both before and during the war. They were not seeking a physical confrontation. They had no illusions about the possibility of any immediate challenge to state power (most people, notes Maclean, are not 'of our way of thinking'). Yet they also saw themselves at a key turning point. There existed the possibility of creating an alliance between discharged servicemen and workers in industry by developing a movement to cut hours radically and thereby expand employment. If successful, this would serve to maintain the favourable balance of power on which the mass influence of the shop stewards' movement had rested during the war. It would then provide a platform for more extensive demands. If, on the contrary, this movement was unsuccessful, the return of mass unemployment would quickly decimate the influence of the Left in industry.

The momentum of the strike's spread appears to have taken the strike leaders by surprise. The initial core of support for the strike in the shipyards, the 25% of the workforce willing to ignore union instructions not to strike, probably matches the level of explicit socialist commitment. But there was clearly a wider level of spontaneous support, particularly in some of the mining areas, once the initiative had been taken. The Intelligence Report on John MacLean shows him as seeing the miners as taking the lead. If the government was to be challenged on the control of industry, it should come from this group who could exercise power over the country's only source of energy and whose industry was already *de facto* nationalised. When Gallacher called on the temporarily victorious strikers to march away from the City Chambers, he was clearly also operating on these assumptions and seeking to prevent a conflict which would allow military intervention.

EXERCISE 7
Read Smout *History of the Scottish People* (Chapter 9), Campbell (**Article 41**) and summarise their explanations of the rise and fall of 'class conscious' working class politics over the two decades after 1914.

I too see large-scale unemployment and the exclusion of socialist militants as responsible for the loss of mass influence by the Left and also for the upsurge in sectarian politics. To this extent 'culture' is not seen as something constant and self-sustaining but as itself mediated by the balance of class relations. At the same time I think we should stress the degree to which there was no simple return to the pre-war status quo, and that socialist class politics retained an important focus within many working-class communities.

4.3 *Class and trade union militancy in the era of full employment*

The return to near full employment in wartime Britain brought a speedy resumption in the growth of trade union membership. This continued until the end of the 1970s when over 50% of Scots in employment were trade union members. The Second World War also brought the large-scale re-entry of women into the labour force and into the trade union movement which, though checked at the end of the war, was resumed in the 1960s and 1970s. The post-war period also saw the spread of unionisation among white collar employees in industry, again reaching its peak at the end of the 1970s, and within the public sector.

Politically the post-1945 period also saw a resounding victory for the principle of the planned collective provision of welfare needs – and to a degree for socialised production as well. Many of the demands associated with socialist campaigning since the beginning of the century had been met by the 1960s: the nationalisation of the heart of Scotland's heavy industry, coal, steel, gas, railways, electricity and road transport, the creation of a socialised national health service and the development of public sector housing to a level where it became the majority tenure for all Scots. Yet this did not happen quite as the socialists of Red Clydeside had envisaged. It was very much a governmental implementation from the top down. It did not occur in the context of radical popular mobilisation. Both Labour and Conservative parties shared a broad degree of policy consensus – including support for the maintenance of both the empire and the American-backed NATO alliance. Electorally, the

56 To the Workers - Call to Arms! After the First World War a militant movement developed on the Clyde to campaign for a 15% cut in the working week. A proclamation headed 'A Call to Arms' was drawn up which urged the workers of Scotland to embark on an indefinite general strike unless their demands were met. *The Trustees of the National Library of Scotland.*

Conservative Party was able to secure over 50% of the Scottish popular vote in 1955.

This period therefore manifests patterns of political and social behaviour which might appear to support the Weberian perspective on class. Workers were highly organised within the labour market and actively asserted their collective class organisation to improve wages and conditions. But their militancy did not extend beyond the workplace. In terms of political and social behaviour workers were motivated by non-class values. There was no mass perception that the social system itself was somehow geared to the interests of capital. What would be the Marxist response? It would probably be to stress the role of the state in sustaining the political and social conditions needed for capitalist production. Marxists, and some other historians as well, would argue there was a conscious shift in governmental priorities during the 1940s to forestall the type of social radicalism experienced at the end of the First World War. 'Full employment in a Free Society' was an antidote to more radical socialism.

The 1970s did witness a sharp change. The Conservative Government of Edward Heath sought to place legal controls on trade union activity, to manage the economy with somewhat higher levels of unemployment and to close down those sectors of state-controlled industry that might be conceived as loss-making. Government policies were met with fierce resistance from the trade union movement and ultimately defeated. Scottish trade unionists played a significant part. Shipyard workers on the Upper Clyde occupied their yards to stop closure in 1971 and thereby led the way for 200 other factory occupations across Britain. These occupations, and especially the UCS work-in, appear to have been largely instrumental in the government's 'U-turn' on industrial policy in March 1972. Scottish miners and engineering workers were also to the fore in a series of battles which effectively negated the government's Industrial Relations Act and provided the context for the Conservative's electoral defeat in 1974. The level of industrial stoppages during these years exceeded those of 1918 and 1919. The leadership of the movement was once more assumed by the shop stewards movement. Unofficial bodies such as the Liaison Committee for the Defence of Trade Unions sought to mobilise workers for wider class objectives, and there were series of mass one-day strikes, originally initiated by unofficial bodies, on political issues such as unemployment and welfare provision as well as solidarity strikes on behalf of other workers in struggle.

> EXERCISE 8
> What does the data on one-day 'political' strikes given below tell us about changes in class attitudes among Scottish workers and their trade unions during the 1970s and early 1980s? How does this compare with the period 1915–26?

The figures show that only a small minority of workers ever involved themselves in strike action on issues which were not immediately to their own economic benefit.

The numbers to do so did, however, increase sharply from the late 1960s to the mid 1970s, and remained at this level until the early 1980s. The figures also demonstrate that while the early political strikes were called by unofficial bodies, those during the later years of the 1970–74 Conservative government and also during the later years of the 1974–79 Labour governments were organised by official trade union bodies. In other words, over that period bodies representing all organised workers in these particular sectors, including on occasion the TUC and the STUC, had been won for the idea of using industrial action to influence government policy. Second, there is a broadening of issues. Initially 'political strikes' were on issues immediately concerning the legal position of the trade union movement (the 1969 White Paper In Place of Strife and the Conservative government's Industrial Relations Bill). Later, political strikes extended to questions of unemployment, economic policy and solidarity with other workers such as NHS staff and miners.

It is difficult to make direct comparison with the 1915–26 period. But you will remember that the initial numbers of workers coming out on the first day of the 1919 General Strike was estimated by the employers as only 28,000. The total number at the height of the strike was probably not beyond 300,000 – within a workforce almost identical in size to that of 1973 when 375,000 came out in Scotland.

TABLE 2: ONE-DAY STRIKES IN SCOTLAND DEFINED BY THE BOARD OF TRADE AS 'POLITICAL'.

Date	NUMBERS ON STRIKE	% OF TOTAL EMPLOYEES	ISSUE	ORGANISATION CALLING
Feb 1969	30,000	1.4	GOVERNMENT WHITE PAPER ON TU LAW	LIAISON COMMITTEE FOR DEFENCE OF TRADE UNIONS (LCDTU)
May 1969	30,000	1.4	SAME	LCDTU
Nov 1970	28,000	1.4	UNEMPLOYMENT	GLASGOW AEUW
Dec 1970	75,000	3.7	GOVERNMENT BILL ON TU LAW	LCDTU
Jan 1979	22,000	1.1	SAME	LCDTU
1 March 1971	150,000	7.4	SAME	ENGINEERING UNION
18 March 1971	150,000	7.4	SAME	ENGINEERING UNION
June 1971	100,000	5.0	CLOSURE OF UCS	UCS SHOP STEWARDS
Aug 1971	150,000	7.5	CLOSURE OF UCS	UCS SHOP STEWARDS
Nov 1971	75,000	3.7	UNEMPLOYMENT	SCOTTISH SHOP STEWARDS
Sept 1972	16,000	0.8	INDUSTRIAL RELATIONS ACT (IRA)	SCOTTISH SHOP STEWARDS
Dec 1972	NOT KNOWN	NOT KNOWN	FINES UNDER IRA	ENGINEERING UNION
May 1973	375,000	18.7	GOVERNMENT POLICY ON DEFLATION	TUC
Nov 1973	60,000	3.0	FINES UNDER IRA	ENGINEERING UNION
April 1974	27,000	1.3	FINES UNDER IRA	ENGINEERING UNION
March 1976	40,000	2.0	UNEMPLOYMENT	AEUW DISTRICT COMMITTEES
April 1977	NOT KNOWN	NOT KNOWN	PAY RESTRAINT	BRITISH LEYLAND SHOP STEWARDS
May 1980	188,000	9.4	GOVERNMENT POLICY ON DEFLATION	TUC
March 1981	100,000	5.3	GOVERNMENT POLICY	STUC

			ON DEFLATION	
Sept 1982	+150,000?	+7.9?	SUPPORT FOR NHS WORKERS	TUC
Feb 1984	NOT KNOWN	NOT KNOWN	SUPPORT FOR GCHQ WORKERS	TUC
March 1984	NOT KNOWN	NOT KNOWN	AGAINST ATTACKS ON LOCAL GOVERNMENT	TUC
May 1984	NOT KNOWN	NOT KNOWN	SUPPORT FOR MINERS	STUC

Source: This data comes, with the author's permission, from Alan Troup, 'The Mobilisation of and Response to Political Protest Strikes' (PhD Thesis, CNAA, 1987).

4.4 *Post-industrial Scotland: a state funeral for class politics?*

Between the mid-1970s and the mid-1990s Scottish manufacturing shed 300,000 jobs. By the 1990s manufacturing and mining together accounted for considerably less than 20% of the labour force. A significant number of the remaining manu-facturing jobs were in areas such as computer assembling which increasingly sought to exclude trade unions. Conversely, as manufacturing employment fell, service jobs increased – at least proportionately. By the 1990s, 60% of the workforce were employed in the service sector: half in the public sector and half in finance, distribution, catering and other services. Almost half of the total workforce was now made up of women – many in part-time jobs.

At the same time unemployment rose to levels more associated with the 1920s or the 1880s. Predictably, trade union membership fell back. By the end of the century only 36% of the employed workforce were unionised.

For the first part of this period, between the mid 1970s and the mid 1980s, levels of industrial action remained relatively high. The miners strike lasting from 1984 to 1985 formed a key turning point – rather like the General Strike and Lockout of 1926. Itself the biggest strike action of the twentieth century, the ultimate defeat of the miners in 1985 ended significant opposition to the imposition of legal restraints on the trade union movement and opened a period in which strike levels fell to their lowest this century. Some notable struggles did occur subsequently. The Caterpillar workers used the tactic of occupation to resist the closure of their factory in 1987. The offshore oil workers did the same in 1989 and 1990 in their bid for trade union recognition (Woolfson 1988; 1996). The largely female workforce of Timex electronics in Dundee fought back against a six month lock out in 1992 after they had refused cuts in wages and conditions. But none of these actions achieved their original objectives. And though the level of strike action increased in the second half of the 1990s as workers in the public services and newly privatised industries came under pressure, these actions were typically defensive and fought largely in isolation.

It could therefore be argued, on Weberian terms, that the wheel had come full circle. Class-based forms of social organisation, born of the Industrial Revolution, were now withering away. Society had moved on to a post-industrial phase in which consumption and individually-oriented services took the lead. The industrial strug-gles of the 1980s, on this view, represented the death throes of the old era.

This perspective might take further support from apparent changes in political behaviour. Class-aligned parties no longer dominated the political arena. Support for the Conservatives dropped from 40% to less than 20% over twenty years. The Labour Party abandoned class politics. Support for non-class parties, such as the SNP and, to a lesser extent, the Liberals, increased. On top of this new, non-party political, forms of political expression emerged. Social movements on issues such as the environment, gender equality, animal welfare and even the community-based opposition to the poll tax could all be seen as marking the opening of a new era in which class was no longer a significant point of social orientation (McCrone 1996; Harvie 1992).

But the Marxist answer would be easily found. These years, they would argue, saw a quite conscious change in ruling class assumptions. After the sharp class challenges of the 1970s, the Conservative policy makers decided to run the economy with much higher levels of employment and to use this opportunity to break trade union power (McCabe and Wallington 1988). The Conservatives also embarked on quite deliberate projects of social engineering to break up the community base of class solidarity. Council house sales, urban redevelopment, and new systems of local government taxation (especially the poll tax) were carefully designed to individualise people's perception of their relationship to the political system (McConnell 1995). Hence, it is argued, society did not change its basic class character. On the contrary, as a result of these policies, it became more unequal and far more directly dominated by those who owned and controlled the means of production (Westergaard 1996). What is more, its social composition became more proletarianised. Marxists would re-emphasise that their definition of working class encompasses all those who sell their labour power. This included those working in the services. The continuing erosion of small business and the self-employed professions consequently increased the total size of the group to whom class politics were relevant. So also did the *forms* of work organisation. These years saw much higher levels of (subjectively perceived) stress and insecurity in white collar and professional employment, the move to single status bargaining in much of the public sector, the transfer of large areas of employment into the private sector and the re-emergence of plant and workplace level bargaining (Knox 1992). Surveys of mass attitudes to wealth, ownership and power taken during the 1990s reveal the consequences. While 'class-type' attitudes were always more prevalent in Scotland (at around two-thirds of the population), there was a 5 to 10% swing across the country towards more anti-capitalist positions between 1990 and 1996 (Curtice 1997). Marxists would argue that, no less than those in the 1880s, conflicts of material interest were creating an environment in which the employed population would sooner or later become conscious of wider class objectives.

EXERCISE 9
Consider the 1996 figures for union density by region within Britain, given below. What do they tell us about the process of unionisation in Scotland?

TABLE 3: UNION DENSITY, 1996: PER CENT BY REGION OR COUNTRY

	ALL	PRIVATE	PUBLIC
All employees	31	21	61
England	30	20	60
Greater London	27	15	58
Rest of South East	23	15	50
East Anglia	25	18	46
South West	28	18	56
West Midlands	32	23	63
East Midlands	32	23	62
Yorks/Humberside	35	24	67
North-West	38	26	69
North	42	30	72
Wales	41	29	68
Scotland	36	22	68
Northern Ireland	41	27	68

The figures show Scotland to have a higher level of overall unionisation than most of England and Wales – but lower than the North and the North-West and Northern Ireland. On the other hand, Scotland is among those parts of the UK with a relatively low level of unionisation in private industry. To balance this it has one of the highest public sector rates, and the highest level anywhere of differential between public and private sector unionisation: 46%. On the face of it, the difference in unionisation in the two sectors might be taken to reflect the difference between level of unionisation which might exist 'naturally', if employees were under no pressures to the contrary, and what union organisers are able to manage in face of pressures from management in private industry. Scotland's two fastest growing industries, offshore oil and electronics, have displayed fairly determined anti-union policies.

REFERENCES TO BOOKS AND ARTICLES MENTIONED IN THE TEXT

Curtice, J 1997 'One Nation Again?', *in* Jowell, R, Curtice, J, Park, A, Brook, L and Thompson, K (eds), *British Social Attitudes, Thirteenth Report*, Aldershot, 1–15.

Dickson, T 1989 'Scotland is Different, OK?', *in* McCrone, D, Kendrick, S and Straw, P (eds), *The Making of Scotland: Nation, Culture and Social Change,* Edinburgh, 53–69.

Edgell, S 1993 *Class.* Oxford.

Foster, J 1992 'A Proletarian Nation? Occupation and Class since 1914', *in* Dickson, T and Treble, J (eds), *People and Society in Scotland. Volume III 1914–1990*, Edinburgh, 201–40.

Fraser, H 1988 *Conflict and Class: Scottish Workers 1700–1838.* Edinburgh.

Gray, R 1975 *The Labour Aristocracy in Victorian Edinburgh.* Oxford.

Harvie, C 1981 *No Gods and Precious Few Heroes.* London.

*Harvie, C 1992 'Scottish Politics', *in* Dickson, T and Treble, J (eds), *People and Society in Scotland. Volume III 1914–1990*, Edinburgh, 241–60.

Kendrick, S, Bechhofer, F and McCrone, D 1985 'Is Scotland Different?', *in* Newby, H, *Restructuring Capital*, London, 63–104.

*Knox, W 1992 'Class, Work and Trade Unionism in Scotland', *in* Dickson, T and Treble, J (eds) *People and Society in Scotland. Volume III 1914–1990*, Edinburgh, 108–37.

MacDougall, I 1978 *Labour Records in Scotland.* Edinburgh

Marx, K 1959 *Capital*, Vol III. Moscow.

McCabe, S and Wallington, P 1988 *The Police, Public Order and Civil Liberties.* London.

McConnell, A 1995 *State Policy Formation and the Origins of the Poll Tax.* Aldershot.

*McCrone, D 1992a 'Scottish Elites in the Twentieth century', *in* Dickson, T and Treble, J (eds), *People and Society in Scotland. Volume III 1914–1990*, Edinburgh, 174–200.

McCrone, D 1992b *Understanding Scotland: the Sociology of a Stateless Nation.* Edinburgh.

*McCrone, D 1996 'We're A' Jock Tamson's Bairns: Social Class in Twentieth Century Scotland', *in* Devine, T and Finlay, R (eds) *Scotland in the Twentieth Century,* Edinburgh, 102–21.

McIvor, A 1996 'Were Clydeside Employers More Autocratic?', *in* Kenefick, W and McIvor, A (eds), *The Roots of Red Clydeside 1910–1914?*, Edinburgh, 41–65.

McLean, I 1983 *The Legend of the Red Clydeside.* Oxford.

Melling, J 1990 'Whatever Happened to Red Clydeside?', *International Review of Social History* 35, 61–142.

Melling, J 1982 'Scottish Industrialists and the Changing Character of Class Relations in the Clyde Region', *in* Dickson, T (ed), *Capital and Class,* Edinburgh, 3–32.

Morris, R 1991 'Introduction', *in* Morris, R and McKinlay, A (eds) *The ILP on Clydeside 1893–1932,* Manchester, 1–19.

Paterson, L 1994 *The Autonomy of Scotland.* Edinburgh.

Reid, A 1985 'Dilution, Trade Unionism and the State in Britain During the First World War', *in* Tolliday, S and Zeitlin, J (eds), *Shopfloor Bargaining and the State,* Cambridge, 46–74.

Smith, J 1984 'Labour Tradition in Glasgow and Liverpool' *History Workshop Journal* 17, 32–56.

Shinwell, E 1973 *I've Lived Through it All.* London.

Smout, C 1986 *Century of the Scottish People.* London.

Strath, B 1986 *The Politics of De-Industrialisation.* London.

Weber, M 1961 *From Max Weber: Essays in Sociology.* London.

Westergaard, J 1996 *Who Gets What?: the Hardening of Class Inequality in the Late Twentieth Century.* London.

Woolfson C 1986 *The Politics of the UCS Work-In.* London.

Woolfson, C 1988 *Track Record: the Story of the Caterpillar Occupation.* London.

Woolfson, C 1996 *Paying for the Piper: Capital and Labour in Britain's Offshore Oil,* London.

Young, J 1979 *Rousing of the Scottish Working Class.* London.

RECOMMENDED FURTHER READING

Those references marked * in the above list are recommended further reading.

Education

Robert Anderson

One of the best-known dates in modern Scottish history is 1872, when the Education (Scotland) Act created a public educational system by transferring most existing schools to elected local school boards, with the Scotch Education Department (the SED: not renamed 'Scottish' until 1918) to supervise them. This was a landmark both in the growth of the modern state and in working-class life, since it made education compulsory for the first time. But was the 1872 Act the real beginning of public education, and what did it achieve? This is the first question to look at. After that we shall examine changes in the education of the élite in secondary schools and universities, and look at how in the twentieth century the different types of education were forged into a single system.

The chapter is divided into the following sections –

- The 1872 Act and working-class education
- The spread of education: statistical evidence
- Educating the élite
- The twentieth century
- The spirit of Scottish education
- The myth of the lad o' pairts

By working through these sections you will get a broad outline of developments since 1850, but the chapter will also show how detailed evidence can be used to test historical generalisations. Tables in the text provide exercises in interpreting statistics, and the written sources in the Documents volume are focused on educational policy in the early twentieth century as a case study.

Scotland's distinct educational system has commonly been seen as a mark of Scottish identity, and an area of life where Scotland can claim consistent superiority over England, particularly in such 'democratic' features as the relative absence of class barriers and the encouragement of social mobility. The 'lad o' pairts', the boy of humble origins from the small town or village, rising in life through education, has become a part of Scottish legend. One aim of this chapter is to encourage a critical attitude towards 'myths' of this kind, and to underline the complexities of historical interpretation. The Reader volume contains extracts from two essays which analyse the democratic myth and its impact on the image and reality of Scottish education. But first, you will find it useful to read Chapter 9 in Smout's (1986) *Century of the*

Scottish People and, if you have access to it, Corr's (1990a) chapter on education in *People and Society in Scotland. Volume II, 1830–1914.*

I. THE 1872 ACT AND WORKING-CLASS EDUCATION

Because we think of compulsory education as a natural part of childhood, and because so many children are still educated in the Victorian schools built by the school boards after 1872, it is easy to underestimate how widespread education was before then. As you will know from Donald Withrington's chapter in the first volume of this course, Scotland had been notably well served by its parish schools, financed by rates on landed property, which created a high level of basic literacy. But parish schools were established only in the countryside, and this was a weakness when large-scale migration to the towns began, and when rural parishes found their population swollen by factories and mines. The inadequacy of the parish schools, and the absence of any public authority in burghs with the duty of educating the masses, led to a large expansion of charitable and religious effort to fill the gap. Education and religion were intimately linked in the nineteenth century, partly because the churches saw this as a traditional field of activity, partly because they were competing for influence, and partly because religious teaching was seen, by politicians as well as churchmen, as a way of moralising the new working class and coping with the frightening social problems of the cities. In the 1830s the state began to give subsidies for building schools, and by 1846 this had evolved into a system of annual grants to schools which were run by qualified teachers and met minimal standards of quality.

Between 1850 and 1872, therefore, there was a distinctive phase of popular education in which schools were provided by voluntary bodies, but with a good deal of central direction and inspection. Schools were financed by parents' fees and voluntary contributions (especially from church congregations) as well as by state grants, and there were also many schools, of varying quality, which did not qualify for subsidy or did not seek it. The result was a very complicated patchwork of small schools – well over 5,000 in the 1860s, which reorganisation under school boards was to reduce to just over 3,000. The pre-1872 schools included ones run by the Roman Catholic and Episcopalian churches as well as the three presbyterian churches, along with free charitable schools, schools connected with collieries and works, and a dwindling number of 'adventure' schools run by private teachers. In the Highlands, where the parish system had always been inadequate because of poverty and scattered population, there were also many schools run by religiously-inspired 'Gaelic school societies'. Gaelic was used in these schools, though only to accelerate the learning of English.

For all the deficiencies of this diverse mass of schools, it was they which conquered the problem of literacy in the cities and industrial areas. The numbers attending school rose from 310,442 in 1851 to 515,353 in 1873 (Anderson 1995, 103: the precision of these figures is illusory, but they are the best we have). The Act was thus more a gap-filling than a pioneering measure, though the gaps were real enough;

many of them were revealed by the reports published in 1867–8 by the Argyll commission, an official inquiry set up to resolve the political and religious disputes which were obstructing new legislation. The voluntary system worked best where local resources were strong, and where parents, including the 'respectable' working class, could afford to pay reasonable school fees. It was less effective in the economically distressed Western Highlands and Islands, among the city poor, or in places where children were under pressure to leave school early to work in coalmines or jute and cotton mills. By making education compulsory, introducing school rates in burghs, and imposing common standards through school board administration, the 1872 Act evened out these inequalities.

The controversies which preceded it arose mainly from denominational rivalry, intensified by the Disruption in 1843 and by the growth of the Catholic community through Irish immigration. In the 1850s and 1860s the state gave its grants to all denominations impartially, but many Scots sought to return to the national, uniform system which the parish schools had embodied since the Reformation. The 1872 Act largely achieved this, but since it followed the similar Act for England and Wales in 1870, and seemed to give only a limited place to Scottish traditions like the teaching of Latin and other 'higher' subjects in parish schools, it was seen by some as an anglicising measure. (Historians have covered the Act and its background quite fully: for a range of views, see Bain 1978; Lenman and Stocks 1972; Myers 1972; Withrington 1972; Anderson 1995). The new state system also had a significant gap: though nearly all presbyterian schools were handed over to school boards, Catholic and Episcopalian schools were unwilling to give up their identity, and continued to be funded directly by the SED until 1918.

School boards, in each town and parish, were a feature of Scottish life for fifty years. They were elected on quite a wide franchise (including women, if they met the necessary property qualification), though the ministers, philanthropic individuals and industrialists who dominated the provision of schools before 1872 still had a strong voice on the new boards. By the 1900s, Labour members were also appearing. Under the direction of the SED, the boards carried out a large if unglamorous task – enforcing attendance, building schools on a large scale, keeping up with the curriculum as it moved beyond the 'three Rs', and, after 1908, providing medical inspection and school meals (for the example of Glasgow, see Roxburgh 1971; and for school building Stephen nd). School fees were abolished in 1890, and the period of compulsory education, originally fixed as five to thirteen, was raised to fourteen in 1883. This remained somewhat theoretical, because children could leave earlier if they had mastered the basics, but in 1901 the scope for exemption was drastically reduced, and fourteen became the real leaving age for most children. By the eve of the First World War, there were about 840,000 pupils in public elementary schools. These schools, with their austere buildings, large classes, and mechanical teaching routines, had become an integral part of daily life, and of the homogeneous working-class culture of industrial Scotland. They were not to change much until the 1960s, when a more relaxed pedagogy transformed primary education.

The history of primary education, especially in recent years, remains under-researched, but two issues have attracted historians. The first is girls' education. The parish schools had bequeathed a tradition of mixed education, and girls had not been barred from studying 'university' subjects like Latin and mathematics (Moore 1984). Most of the new schools founded in the towns were also mixed. But in an age when increasing stress was put on women's role in the family, there was a feeling that younger girls should be taught by women, especially as sewing was a compulsory subject for girls. Thus there was a movement towards separate girls' schools, usually founded and supervised by middle or upper class ladies, who thus had a new opportunity for public service. It was also linked with the rise of women within the teaching profession. The training given in the 'normal schools' or training colleges, which were run by the churches, provided an important avenue of social mobility for women, though, as Corr (1990a; 1995) emphasises, real equality was slow to arrive: men tended to monopolise senior posts, and women's salaries were markedly lower even after national salary scales were introduced in 1918. As the concept of the 'lad o' pairts' implied, the Scottish educational ethos was a highly gendered one *(ibid)*.

When the school boards took over, they usually abolished small girls' schools and built mixed schools, even if (as the inscriptions over the doors still remind us) boys and girls had separate entrances, and were kept apart except when actually in the classroom. There were also new curricular developments for girls, who studied subjects like cookery, laundrywork and 'domestic economy' while the boys took woodwork or elementary science. But while this segregation may be seen today as a sign of the lower status of girls, this was not the view taken by the pioneers of domestic economy, who saw it as a specifically female area of technical expertise – with its own training colleges in Edinburgh and Glasgow – making a distinctive contribution to social welfare by helping women run happy and healthy homes (see Corr 1983; 1990b, and for a slightly different interpretation, Moore 1992).

The second point which has attracted historians is the evolution of Catholic schools. After 1872 they continued to receive annual grants from the state, but had to pay for their own buildings. Large sacrifices were made despite the poverty of the Catholic community, and the number of schools rose from 65 in 1872 to 226 in 1918; one child in eight was in a Catholic school, though secondary education lagged behind for lack of resources. This position was felt as a grievance by Catholics, but the hierarchy's insistence on retaining direct control of the schools made any departure from the status quo politically difficult. It eventually came about in 1918, when the Education Act transferred Catholic schools to the *ad hoc* education authorities which replaced school boards (and which were themselves merged into the all-purpose local authorities in 1929). The religious character of the schools was guaranteed by the Act, as was the right of Catholics to have new schools built where a demand existed. This legislation remains in force, and has perpetuated a cultural separatism which provoked sectarian tensions both before and after 1918, and about whose merits Scottish opinion remains divided (Smout 1986, 226; for the history of Catholic schools see Kenneth 1968; Treble 1978; 1980; Fitzpatrick 1986).

2. THE SPREAD OF EDUCATION: STATISTICAL EVIDENCE

We can now look at some statistical evidence on literacy and school attendance to illustrate the significance and impact of the 1872 Act. Standardised data for literacy only became available in 1855, when civil registration of marriages began, and brides and bridegrooms had to either sign the register or make a mark. In 1855, 89% of men and 77% of women could sign, compared with 70% and 59% respectively in England and Wales, a substantial difference. Table 1 shows how the Scottish percentages changed at five-yearly intervals down to 1900.

TABLE 1: LITERACY OF BRIDES AND BRIDEGROOMS, 1855–1900

	MEN	WOMEN
1855	89	77
1860	90	78
1865	89	78
1870	90	80
1875	91	83
1880	92	85
1885	94	89
1890	96	93
1895	97	95
1900	98	97

Source: Anderson (1995, 305).

EXERCISE I
Men and women married ten to fifteen years after their schooling ended. Bearing this in mind, what does Table 1 tell us about the development of literacy in the nineteenth century and about the impact of the 1872 Act? What deficiencies do you think national percentages of this kind might have as evidence? And is a signature actually a good indication of 'literacy'?

- If the 1872 Act had a significant impact on the elimination of illiteracy, this should have been visible around 1885. In fact, change is continuous, though there is perhaps some effect on male literacy. The most striking movement shown by the figures is the closing of the gap between men and women, and this continues steadily from 1865, reflecting the state of education in the 1850s and the 1860s.
- National averages are artificial when there are significant local or regional variations (see Smout 1986, 216). As we have seen, education had particular weaknesses in the Western Highlands and the industrialised cities, and these areas had higher rates of illiteracy than the rural Lowlands, where literacy was virtually complete, and probably had been for many years before 1855.

Another difference which we know about (because marriages were classified by religious denomination) is that Catholics, many of them recent immigrants from Ireland, had higher illiteracy than Protestants. Combined with the effects of industrialisation, this led to particularly low figures in the west of Scotland.

• The most basic form of literacy is being able to read, but there has been much discussion among historians about how far signatures are a guide to this. Until the nineteenth century, reading and writing were taught as separate skills, with reading coming first, so literacy statistics of this kind probably underestimate reading ability. In particular, it had been more common for boys than girls to learn writing. So the closing of the gap between men and woman may simply reflect girls learning to write, now that schools insisted on both skills being taught together; women's ability to read may already have been much closer to men's, or even equal to it.

TABLE 2: SCHOOL ATTENDANCE AS A PERCENTAGE OF AGE-GROUP, 1871–1901

Age	1871		1881		1891		1901	
	B	G	B	G	B	G	B	G
3	2	2	3	3	2	2	1	1
4	9	9	12	11	13	12	10	10
5	52	48	51	48	58	56	64	62
6	76	73	82	80	88	87	95	95
7	87	84	93	91	95	94	100	99
8	91	89	95	94	96	96	100	100
9	92	89	96	95	97	97	100	100
10	90	88	96	95	96	96	100	100
11	84	83	95	94	95	95	100	99
12	70	72	90	90	86	87	97	98
13	41	40	65	67	59	63	82	85
14	23	22	32	34	30	32	33	37

Source: Anderson (1995, 234).

Table 2 is based on the national censuses, when parents were asked whether their children were attending school. It shows the percentage reported as doing so in each age-group.

EXERCISE 2
Looking particularly at the 1871 figures, what general conclusions would you come to about the extent of schooling? Is it possible to say how many years of attendance were typical? And bearing in mind the information about leaving ages given earlier, what does the table tell us about the impact of compulsory education? Do you see any other points of interest in these data? And finally, how reliable is this particular source likely to be?

- In 1871, when education was not legally compulsory, around 90% of children were attending school at ages eight to ten. The figures are consistently lower for girls, but the gap is much less than for literacy, which may again suggest that the difference was in what girls learnt rather than in whether they attended or not. These figures reinforce the point that the 1872 Act came at the end rather than the beginning of the establishment of mass schooling. But they do suggest that up to 10% of children were escaping school altogether. And even if most children were attending schools of some kind, the quality was very variable before 1872.

- In 1871 over 70% attended between ages six and twelve, which suggests the majority stayed for about six years. The better-off obviously stayed longer, while poorer children were probably only staying for three or four years, say from seven to ten or eleven. Pressure for children to work was crucial, and as with literacy there were marked local variations in school attendance, with mining and factory towns, and the west of Scotland generally, showing the lowest rates.

- Between 1871 and 1881, attendance rises in all years, but there is a particularly sharp jump at age twelve, reflecting the impact of compulsion. It is interesting that numbers also rise at ages thirteen and fourteen, which were then beyond the compulsory age (a school leaving age of thirteen meant that children could leave on their thirteenth birthday). By 1901, just before the leaving age of fourteen was fully enforced, over 80% of thirteen-year-olds were already at school. And a third of all Scottish children stayed on beyond their fourteenth birthday – something which may conflict with conventional views of Victorian education. From all this, one might argue either that compulsory education gave a strong stimulus to school attendance, or that it was only one factor in something which was happening anyway.

- You may have noticed that although education became legally compulsory at five, this was very slow to take effect. Scottish habits had been to start at six or even seven, and evidently the authorities did not enforce this aspect of the law very rigorously.

- Census forms have to be completed by every family, so this evidence should be very comprehensive. On the other hand, parents would be reluctant to admit that their children were not going to school, so the figures may give an over-favourable picture.

3. EDUCATING THE ÉLITE

In most countries in the nineteenth century, education systems developed on marked lines of social class, with little connection between 'popular' and 'élite' education. This was the trend in Scotland too, but it came into conflict with past traditions. The parish schools had taught Latin, and both they and the burgh schools run by town councils served a fairly wide social range and could feed boys into the universities. The universities did not have a rigid curriculum or a formal entrance examination, and offered an open and flexible type of education: although there was an approved curriculum, many students stayed for only a year or two, chose which lectures to attend, and took no examinations. By the mid-nineteenth century, formal graduation was the exception. But these traditions now came under pressure from two directions. On the one side, most of the new schools for the working class were purely elementary, taught by men and women trained in the techniques of instilling the 'three Rs', but lacking the university culture of the old parish schoolmasters. On the other, the growing middle classes were making their own educational demands.

The expansion of the middle class, including professional as well as business occupations, was as important a result of industrialisation as the growth of the working class. The Victorian period was marked by the growth of formal qualifications for professional men, by the creation of professional bodies to exclude the unqualified, and by the reign of written examinations. By the 1850s, this movement was in full flood, most strikingly shown by the Medical Act of 1858, which set up a United Kingdom register of doctors for which a university medical course was the essential qualification. Other examples were the introduction of competitive examination for the civil service, first in India, later for most branches, and new entrance qualifications for the Scottish legal profession. From 1854 the Faculty of Advocates required entrants to possess an arts degree, and other legal bodies followed suit with more modest educational requirements. As new professions developed, education became ever more vital to career plans, and since the Scottish middle class wished to compete on equal terms for posts in England and in the British Empire, Scottish schools and universities had to respond.

The question of 'anglicisation' has rather dominated discussion of Scottish university history, because of George Davie's very influential book *The Democratic Intellect* (1964: the argument is extended into the twentieth century in Davie 1986). The phrase 'democratic intellect' has passed into general use to indicate various features ascribed to Scottish education, but Davie's own work is centred on the university curriculum. He argues that the traditional general education based on philosophy was more democratic in spirit than the specialisation which replaced it by the end of the nineteenth century, as well as being more distinctively Scottish. Davie has become something of a cult figure for nationalist intellectuals, and has helped to create the widespread current view, apparent for example in discussions of school examinations, that 'breadth' is the characteristic feature of Scottish education. Historians have questioned many aspects of his argument (Anderson 1983; Carter and Withrington 1992), but this is not the place to pursue these issues. Both specialisation and anglicisation certainly happened, and anglicisation was also apparent in the growth of 'corporate life' in the universities, designed to give students a social as well as an intellectual training. Although most students lived at home or in lodgings until well after the Second World War, a new sense of community began in the 1880s with the foundation of Students' Representative Councils, the growth of student newspapers and societies, the popularity of volunteer military units, and the development of student sport (Anderson 1988).

The growing middle class was predominantly urban. Scottish towns were well provided with schools, but they did not necessarily meet the new needs. The burgh schools had expanded in the early nineteenth century, but seldom took boys beyond the age of fifteen or sixteen, which was the age of entry both for universities and for joining a professional or mercantile office. There were a few 'proprietary' schools like Edinburgh Academy (1824) and Glasgow Academy (1846), competing with the best burgh schools, but expensive and socially exclusive. There were numerous private schools, but without standardised examinations it was difficult for parents to judge their quality. In some cities, notably Edinburgh, there were wealthy endowments, but these were usually devoted (following the model of the seventeenth-century George Heriot's) to educating a handful of deserving children within the walls of a residential 'hospital'. By the 1860s there were demands for a thorough reorganisation of 'secondary' education (itself a new term) to use these resources more efficiently and provide greater uniformity. The Argyll commission revealed many of the deficiencies, and Scottish opinion generally felt that the state should take the lead in reform. The 1872 Act did transfer the burgh schools to the new school boards, but the orthodox view in London was that the state should not subsidise middle-class education, and no new funds were provided.

The secondary education movement was linked with a complex and often politically controversial process of university reform, marked by two Acts of Parliament in 1858 and 1889 (for details, see Anderson 1983). Some of the changes were constitutional, including the formation in 1860 of a single University of Aberdeen out of the formerly independent King's and Marischal Colleges. But the reformers were particularly concerned to raise the standards of teaching and research, to restore a fixed curriculum, to encourage graduation as the normal target for students, to introduce an entrance examination, and to raise the age of entry from fifteen or sixteen to seventeen or eighteen. This was largely achieved by the 1890s, and the new arts curriculum, with its combination of specialised and general education, and choice between Honours and Ordinary degrees, was to be long-lasting. Also very important was the development of medical education, which involved heavy expenditure on new chairs, equipment and buildings, and accounted for a high proportion of university students (nearly half at Edinburgh, over a quarter in Glasgow and Aberdeen), many of them from outside Scotland.

University reform was only possible because by 1900 the secondary schools had been reshaped to fit a standard model and had been given a new academic orientation. A key development was the creation of the Leaving Certificate in 1888, the ancestor of the Highers, which was equivalent to the university entry standard. This was the work of the SED, which acquired more autonomy after the creation of the Scottish Office in 1885. Its secretary between then and 1904, Henry Craik, was a powerful bureaucrat who was determined to improve secondary education, and succeeded in diverting public funds towards it; there was a regular state grant for secondary schools from 1892, ten years ahead of England. Other contributions to change were the statutory reform of educational endowments, whereby most of the residential hospitals were turned into large day schools, and action by school boards, which not only developed the old burgh schools into modern high schools, but also created 'higher grade' schools, notably in Glasgow (Roxburgh 1971), to serve the new suburban lower middle class.

57 Sir Henry Craik, Secretary of the Scottish Education Department, 1885-1904.
Scottish National Portrait Gallery.

The Argyll commission in the 1860s identified 59 public secondary schools with 14,879 pupils. By 1912 there were 249, with 38,312 pupils (19,611 boys and 18,701 girls). Of these 143 gave a full five-year course, and 106 a three-year or 'intermediate' one; 171 of the schools were free (Anderson 1983). Secondary education of uniform quality, leading both to the universities and to careers in business, was now available even in small towns, and in areas, notably the Highlands, where it had been lacking before. In the large cities, especially Edinburgh and Glasgow, the reforms of the 1870s and 1880s created a structure, linked intimately with middle-class life and careers, whose outlines are still visible today. Most private schools disappeared, leaving proprietary and endowed schools to share the market with the public high schools or higher grade schools, and subtle social differentiation was reinforced by the development of team games, especially rugby. But despite the appearance of a handful of Scottish 'public schools' on the English model, most middle-class parents preferred to use day schools tied into the social fabric of their city, a cultural difference between Scotland and England which remains significant (Anderson 1985a).

By 1900, too, an equal standard of education was available for middle-class girls. In 1850 small private schools still dominated the market, and the movement for a more academic girls' education did not take off until around 1870, twenty years later than in England. In the cities, Glasgow and Aberdeen school boards founded girls' high schools, and there were also proprietary schools and reformed endowed schools such as the two opened by the Edinburgh Merchant Company in 1870. Outside the cities, school boards continued the tradition of mixed middle-class schooling inherited from the burgh schools, a practice which continued to distinguish Scotland from England, and indeed from most countries at this time. A demand for women's university education first appeared in the late 1860s, and was met initially by 'Ladies' Educational Associations' in the university towns, whose part-time courses, often given by sympathetic university professors, could lead to degree-level diplomas. But the attempt in 1869 by Sophia Jex-Blake and others to enter Edinburgh University as medical students failed, partly because of hostility from professors and students, partly because the courts decided that women could not be admitted without a change in the law. Thus Scottish women had to wait until 1892, following the 1889 Act, to become matriculated students.

The number of women university students grew rapidly after 1900, and they made a distinctive contribution to university life (Moore 1991). By 1914 they formed about 23% of the total, a figure which was to rise in the 1920s, but to fall again in the 1930s, and not to change dramatically until new careers for women opened up after the Second World War. For the great majority of arts and science graduates went into teaching, and in medicine the formal admission of women was slow to lead to real equality, either in the classroom or in the professional opportunities open to graduates (Alexander 1987).

The remodelling of élite education in the late nineteenth century was a major achievement which allowed Scots to compete on equal terms with their English contemporaries, and one where the middle classes benefited as much as the working classes from the action of the state. But it meant that a loosely structured system had been replaced by sharper barriers between the sectors of education; universities, once open to anyone with minimal qualifications (including adults studying for themselves), now had to be approached through formal secondary education. It was the SED's policy to 'centralise' the latter wherever possible, and by 1900 the tradition of rural schools teaching 'higher' subjects was virtually extinct. Pupils from elementary schools could only climb the educational ladder (a favourite image of the time) if they transferred to secondary schools around the age of twelve, and there were both cultural and financial barriers which discouraged this. Although bursaries and scholarships did exist, and the Scottish Education Act of 1908 expanded their provision, they were awarded by competitive examination, so that parental ambition was the driving force rather than any systematic selection by merit.

But did this mean that opportunities were in fact restricted? Here we can look at some more data, on the social backgrounds of university students. Table 3 compares information on the occupations of students' fathers in the 1860s (from the Argyll report) and in 1910 (from matriculation records). The grouping of occupations is a broad one: most 'agricultural' parents were farmers, not crofters or labourers; most 'intermediate' ones were shopkeepers or clerks; in the 'working class' group, artisans and skilled workers far outnumbered factory workers, miners, or the unskilled.

58 Scotland Street Primary School. Crown Copyright: *Royal Commission on the Ancient and Historical Monuments of Scotland.*

TABLE 3: SOCIO-OCCUPATIONAL ORIGINS OF UNIVERSITY STUDENTS (%)

	1866			1910			
	EDINBURGH	ABERDEEN		GLASGOW		ABERDEEN	
	GLASGOW						
				M	W	M	W
Professional	35	30	29	26	27	20	24
Commercial/industrial	15	20	9	25	27	13	14
Agricultural	13	13	29	3	7	13	20
Intermediate	8	6	7	20	19	16	12
Working class	25	24	17	24	18	14	15

Source: Anderson 1983, 150–1, 310–15

EXERCISE 3

On the basis of this limited information, what changes seem to have taken place in the composition of the student population over fifty years? Can they be described as a broadening or a narrowing of access to the universities? What differences are apparent between the different universities? And did women students come from the same sort of backgrounds as men?

59 Dens Works: Exterior view of 'Baxter's old half-time school', built 1858. Inset portrait of schoolmaster, Andrew Strachan, *c.* 1914. *Dundee University Archives.*

- The 'intermediate' group were the main gainers by 1910, while within the middle class the business element had gained on the professional; the proportion of working-class students stayed much the same, or declined slightly. It looks therefore as if the systematic reorganisation of education did not lead to social restriction, but opened up new opportunities, though for the middle as much as the working class. More detailed figures from other sources give a slightly better picture of working-class representation in the 1900s (Anderson 1983; 1988; Robertson 1900), and poorer students were helped by the fund set up in 1900 by the Scottish-American millionaire Andrew Carnegie, which offered to pay Scottish students' tuition fees (Smout 1986, 224).

- The data reflect the industrial and commercial character of Glasgow and the rural hinterland of Aberdeen, as was natural when universities drew mainly on their own regions. As one would expect, the 'professional' percentage is high at Edinburgh in 1866, though the high proportion of working-class students is perhaps more surprising. Unfortunately there are no later figures for Edinburgh.

- Women came from broadly the same backgrounds as men, but were rather more middle class; there were also more from farming backgrounds. Among the working class, the 'scholarship boy' was a relatively familiar phenomenon, but it is not difficult to see why it took time for girls to be given the same encouragement.

Despite some shifting between different groups, the Scottish student body had a class composition which differed fundamentally from Oxford and Cambridge at the same time – though not necessarily from the newer English and Welsh universities. In fact, the balance in Scotland between middle and working class students was not to change much in the twentieth century, when university numbers expanded and secondary education became general (for the example of Glasgow see McDonald 1967, referred to by Smout 1986, 224–5). From one point of view, therefore, the Scottish universities were 'democratic' at a remarkably early stage. But we need to remember that before 1914 both secondary and university education were confined to a very small percentage of the age-group – probably about 4% completed secondary schooling, and 2% or less carried on to university level (Anderson 1985b; 1997). Working-class children did reach the universities, but their numbers were too small to make much of a dent on working-class experience. Attendance increased between the two World Wars – more in secondary schools, where numbers had doubled by 1939, than in universities – but it was not until 1945 that 'secondary education for all', followed by a huge expansion of further and higher education, brought about real democratisation. Before this could happen the separate popular and élite sectors, with bridges for individuals to cross from one to the other, had to be replaced by the idea more familiar today of successive stages – primary, secondary, tertiary – within a single system. The evolution of these changes is the subject of the next section, and at this point you should read Andrew McPherson's chapter in *People and Society in Scotland* (1992). *Volume III 1914–1990* and look at the documents for this section (**Documents 128 to 132**).

4. THE TWENTIETH CENTURY

The historical research carried out on Scottish education since the First World War is limited. The greatest focus – perhaps because this was also the main area of political conflict – has been on the policies of the SED, particularly the organisation of 'post-primary' education. This became a problem after 1901: once most children stayed at school until fourteen, the higher levels of elementary schooling needed recasting. Although the SED began to use the term 'primary' around this time, it still assumed that 'secondary' education was suitable only for a small minority. For those who stayed in the elementary school, advanced education was to be given in 'supplementary courses', which were given a strong vocational bias. This policy was formalised in 1903, and included a 'qualifying examination' at twelve to decide which courses a pupil could follow, which became part of Scottish educational folklore as the 'qualy'. The SED also encouraged the provision of evening 'continuation' classes for school leavers, and the Education Act of 1908 allowed school boards to make these compulsory for adolescents who left school with their education incomplete. This was never widely adopted, but the boards who did so included Glasgow, and Edinburgh was noted for its effective organisation of voluntary continuation classes. As in many aspects of technical and further education, it was Britain's trading and military rival, Germany, which provided the model.

The distinction between secondary and supplementary courses was criticised at the time as socially divisive, and the First World War created a mood of social progress which looked forward to a more generous approach. The 1918 Education Act proposed raising the leaving age to fifteen, and making continuation classes compulsory to sixteen, and later eighteen. But the post-war financial crisis meant that neither of these measures was implemented. Hopes were also dashed by the conservatism of the SED, whose controversial Circular 44 in 1921, followed by new regulations in 1923, reasserted the dualist policy. Supplementary courses were renamed 'advanced divisions', but were still denied secondary status, and most gave only two-year courses (Paterson 1983; Stocks 1995).

With the economic crisis of the inter-war years and the fall in the Scottish birth-rate, much of the dynamism apparent in educational developments before 1914 vanished. Yet though official policy did not change, at the grass roots the division between elementary and secondary schooling was gradually eroded. Most authorities moved towards a 'clean cut' at the age of twelve, and concentrated their advanced divisions in 'central' schools. In smaller towns, though the courses remained distinct, secondary and advanced education were often given together in socially comprehensive 'omnibus' schools. Parents themselves resisted narrow vocationalism, and pushed their children into academic schools even if they had no intention of completing a secondary course. This was now easier because under the 1918 Act all authorities had to offer free secondary schooling (though they could keep fees in selected schools, and in the cities did so). The Education Act of 1936 envisaged raising the leaving age to fifteen in 1939; the outbreak of war postponed this, but SED policy in the 1940s was to reclassify all post-primary education in either senior (five-year) or junior (three-year) secondary courses, and the leaving age was finally raised to fifteen in 1947 (and to sixteen in 1973).

Secondary education for all, at least in nomenclature, was thus achieved. But it was selective, and based on a 'twelve plus' examination (descendant of the 'qualy'), given scientific authority by the development of intelligence testing between the Wars. Most senior secondary schools had always been secondary, while junior secondaries were either new, or based on the former 'central' schools; there were big differences in the buildings, equipment, and qualifications of teachers. For some time after the War, this selective system seemed unchallenged, and the SED showed no independent desire to move away from it. The introduction of comprehensive schools in 1965 was thus an innovation in Scotland, even if the path had been smoothed by the omnibus schools. Comprehensive education has generally been regarded as a success in Scotland, unlike England, a difference which must partly reflect different legacies from the past. But at the time, the change was accompanied by controversy, especially in the cities, where it also involved the abolition of the surviving fee-paying schools, and the withdrawal of direct state grants to former endowed schools, which now passed with their middle-class clientèle into the independent sector.

Secondary education policy since the Second World War has been studied in depth, though by sociologists and political scientists as much as historians (Gray, McPherson and Raffe 1983; McPherson and Raab 1988). The War itself was more important for fuelling a long-term explosion of social and educational aspirations than for any immediate political consequences (Lloyd 1983; 1992). Selective secondary education eventually broke down because the expectations of families, and the disappearance of the old industrial economy, with its simple division of labour between a small middle class and a mass working class, undermined the assumption that an 'academic' education leading to examination qualifications could be reserved for a quarter or a third of the population. There was also a fundamental change in the career expectations of women. Even before the Robbins report of 1963, these forces were leading to the expansion of higher education. In the 1950s it still reached only about 4% of the age-group, but this rose to 15% by the 1970s, 40% by the 1990s. The demand was accommodated partly by creating new universities out of existing technical colleges, with two major creations, Strathclyde and Heriot-Watt, in the 1960s and a further wave of promotions in the 1990s. This was possible only because technical and continuation education, formerly scanty and under-funded outside the handful of 'central institutions' developed by the SED since 1900, grew after the War into a broader 'further education' sector with a network of local colleges.

5. THE SPIRIT OF SCOTTISH EDUCATION

This section will try to give more insight into the twentieth century by discussing some documents and debates. First of all, re-read Chapter 9 of Smout's *Century of the Scottish People* (1986) and do the following exercise.

> EXERCISE 4
> Smout's chapter is called 'The aims and failures of education'. Make a list of what he seems to regard as the failures.

You could distinguish several points here, but the main ones are:

- The system provided a basic education for the masses, but picked out only a very small élite for further education. This was true of the traditional system (Smout 1986, 212), but equally true after 1872, when the system was designed to meet the needs of the upper and middle classes (*ibid*, 218, 223).
- The opportunities given to selected individuals were 'meritocratic rather than democratic' (*ibid*, 212), and pride in the 'lad o' pairts' was a 'delusion' encouraged by middle-class spokesmen like Lyon Playfair (*ibid*, 217–18). There is more on this in Section 6, below.
- The development of secondary schools after 1872 actually restricted opportunity, especially in Edinburgh (*ibid*, 221–3). (Since Smout is here drawing on my own research, it is difficult to disagree! But I would argue that later developments redressed the balance by 1900.)
- The universities were similarly restrictive (*ibid*, 223–5). We have already looked at some evidence on this point. Smout seems to conclude that working-class opportunities did not actually decline, but did not increase either despite the growth of a more generally democratic society.
- Progressive educational ideas were neglected in Scotland, and the Scottish classroom remained 'grimly authoritarian and narrow' (*ibid*, 228).
- Scottish education encouraged social conformity and a spirit of deference – giving the working class an 'inferiority complex', according to AS Neill (*ibid* 218). Here Smout is endorsing comments by Hamish Paterson (1983, 198), and concludes that the history of education holds the key to 'some of the more depressing aspects of modern Scotland' (Smout 1986, 229).

AS Neill, incidentally, is more famous as the libertarian teacher who founded Summerhill school in England, but he was the son of a Scottish schoolmaster, and taught in a village school in Dumfriesshire at the beginning of the First World War. His book *A Dominie's Log* (1915) described his experiences, and is still well worth reading. It is also interesting to compare his critical views with the results of a recent oral history project which interviewed people brought up in the early twentieth century. This evidence suggests that education was valued by Scottish families, but that in practice few were able to use it to escape the limited social horizons which were the fate of the great majority (Jamieson 1990; Jamieson and Toynbee 1992).

Obviously Smout is going out of his way to challenge complacent or self-congratulatory views of Scottish education. You may find his judgements over-harsh, as do McPherson (1992) and Lindsay Paterson (1996), and you may have your own views on some of these points. But as a test, turn now to **Documents 128 to 132**, which concentrate on the period of Craik and Struthers' administration at the SED, described by Smout (1986, 225–7).

EXERCISE 5

Look at **Documents 128 and 130**. What is the most striking point common to these two circulars? How do you think they might be related to contemporary political events? Are there any other distinct points to comment on?

- The most striking point, I would say, is the idea of the state promoting social discipline and 'citizenship', both at school and – through cadet corps (1900) or continuation classes (1909) – among adolescent school-leavers.
- The first circular was issued during the Boer War (1899–1902), so its military emphasis may be understandable. But the 1909 circular also shows awareness of competition from other countries. This was all part of the so-called 'national efficiency' movement, which sought to strengthen Britain's industrial and military strength by improving the welfare and physical health of the young, especially after recruitment for the Boer War revealed the poor physical state of urban children. School meals and medical inspection were part of this move-ment, as was teaching 'domestic economy' to girls. The 1900 circular also reflects the personal ideas of Craik, who was a keen proponent of military service, and became a Unionist MP after retiring from the civil service.
- You may well think that boys are put in the forefront here, especially in 1900. You may also have noticed that in 1909 the term 'adolescence' is used, while in 1900 there is only a vaguer reference to boys 'at an important crisis in their lives'. The American psychologist Stanley Hall's book *Adolescence*, published in 1904, had made the concept fashionable.

EXERCISE 6

Read **Documents 129 and 131**. These are the circulars of 1903 and 1921 whose significance has been explained above. Do you think they support Smout's view of the limited aims of Scottish education? What comments would you make on the specific teaching programmes outlined in 1903? And how far had things changed by 1921?

- It is certainly true that secondary education is seen as suitable only for 'exceptional' pupils, and that education for the remainder is to have a strong vocational bias. There is an assumption that the slots in society into which children are to fit are already pre-determined at age twelve.

- Again, there is a concern with producing 'the useful citizen', and the education is to have general as well as vocational elements. The programmes, though utilitarian, seem quite progressive in their emphasis on observation and practical experience.
- The basic distinction between secondary and non-secondary education is reasserted in 1921. With its reference to the 'immemorial Scottish tradition', the SED claims that every child capable of getting secondary or university education is already doing so. On the other hand, it admits that the policy of 1903 has not been a success: the Supplementary Courses have low prestige, and parents prefer the 'intermediate' curriculum (ie the first three years of a secondary course) even when it is supposedly not suitable for their needs. But rather than abandoning the policy, the SED hopes that raising the leaving age to fifteen will breathe new life into it.

Finally, look at **Document 132**, a critique of SED policy by Simon S Laurie, an expert active in Scottish educational affairs since the 1860s, who had just retired as professor of education at Edinburgh University. He also acted as secretary to the Dick Bequest, an endowment which supported advanced education in rural schools in the North-East, and this extract is from his report to the governors on current proposals.

EXERCISE 7
How would you contrast the ideas of Laurie with SED policy in 1903?

- He is particularly concerned with rural children, and hostile to concentrating them in secondary centres. He thinks that secondary subjects should be taught by the rural schoolmasters (as in the traditional parish schools), and that the separation of education into two types is harmful.
- He believes that the primary school should be 'sacred to a liberal education', and is strongly anti-utilitarian. We can guess that he would be very hostile to the rural programme proposed in 1903. In fact the evidence suggests that few rural schools ever adopted that programme, because Laurie's anti-vocational attitudes were widely shared.
- He emphasises that education should train children in the 'moral and religious ideal of the nation to which they belong'. Does he mean Scotland, or Britain? At any rate, this approach looks old-fashioned when compared with the SED's emphasis on preparing children for their place in society.

6. THE MYTH OF THE LAD O' PAIRTS

Was the 'immemorial Scottish tradition' that no talented child would be denied educational opportunity really a 'delusion' as Smout suggests? The two essays included in the Reader (**Articles 42 and 43**) should help you to make up your mind about this, especially if you read them in full as originally published. My essay (**Article**

42) was concerned mainly with the creation in the nineteenth century of a literary myth about educational opportunity. I argue there (and no-one has yet disproved it!) that the term 'lad o' pairts' was an invention of the 1890s. McPherson (**Article 44**) is more concerned with the influence of the myth on policy in the twentieth century.

McPherson and I would agree, I think, on two things. First, a 'myth' is not necessarily untrue, but may idealise and crystallise an underlying reality. Such myths are often central to the identity and self-image of nations. Secondly, both my research on the nineteenth century and that of McPherson and others on recent years (Gray, McPherson and Raffe 1983; McPherson and Raab 1988) show that myths can have a creative as well as a negative influence. Belief in the superiority and democratic character of Scottish education may encourage complacency and legitimise the inequalities which actually exist, but it also provides an ideal against which new developments are measured, and a test by which harmful ones can be rejected. Thus in Scottish education, in a way not perhaps found in other countries, there is constant interplay between the past and the present. This adds to the complexity, but also to the interest, of studying its history.

REFERENCES AND FURTHER READING

This guidance on further reading covers the main topics, but is inevitably selective. A fuller bibliography, and a brief general survey, will be found in Anderson (1997), and more specialised bibliographies for the period before 1918 in Anderson (1983; 1995). Knox (1953) and Scotland (1969) are older general histories, and Bone (1967) and Humes and Paterson (1983) are useful collections of essays. Otherwise the titles of the books and articles are self-explanatory.

BOOKS AND ARTICLES MENTIONED IN THE TEXT

Alexander, W 1987 *First Ladies of Medicine: the Origins, Education and Destination of Early Women Medical Graduates of Glasgow University*. Glasgow.

*Anderson, RD 1983 *Education and Opportunity in Victorian Scotland: Schools and Universities*. Oxford.

*Anderson, RD 1985a 'Secondary schools and Scottish society in the nineteenth century', *Past and Present* 109, 176–203.

Anderson, RD 1985b 'Education and Society in Modern Scotland: a Comparative Perspective', *History of Education Quarterly* 25, 459–81.

*Anderson, RD 1985c 'In search of the "Lad of Parts": the mythical history of Scottish education', *History Workshop Journal* 19, 82–104.

Anderson, RD 1988 *The Student Community at Aberdeen, 1860–1939*. Aberdeen.

*Anderson, RD 1995 *Education and the Scottish People, 1750–1918*. Oxford.

Anderson, RD 1997 *Scottish Education since the Reformation*. Dundee.

Bain, WH 1978 '"Attacking the Citadel": James Moncreiff's proposals to reform Scottish education, 1851–69', *Scottish Educational Review* 10, 5–14.

Carter, JJ and Withrington, D (eds) 1992 *Scottish Universities: Distinctiveness and Diversity*. Edinburgh.

*Corr, H 1983 'The schoolgirls' curriculum and the ideology of the home, 1870–1914', *in* Glasgow Women's Studies Group, *Uncharted Lives: Extracts from Scottish Women's Experiences, 1850–1982,* Glasgow, 74–97.

*Corr, H 1990a 'An exploration into Scottish education', *in* Fraser, WH and Morris, RJ (eds) *People and Society in Scotland. Volume II 1830–1914,* Edinburgh, 290–309.

Corr, H 1990b '"Home-Rule" in Scotland: the teaching of housework in schools, 1872–1914', *in* Fewell, J and Paterson, F (eds), *Girls in their Prime: Scottish Education Revisited,* Edinburgh, 38–53.

Corr, H 1995 'Dominies and domination: Schoolteachers, masculinity and women in 19th century Scotland', *History Workshop Journal* 40, 151–64.

Davie, GE 1964 (2nd edn) *The Democratic Intellect: Scotland and her Universities in the Nineteenth Century.* Edinburgh.

Davie, GE 1986 *The Crisis of the Democratic Intellect: the Problem of Generalism and Specialisation in Twentieth-Century Scotland.* Edinburgh.

Fitzpatrick, TA 1986 *Catholic Secondary Education in South-West Scotland before 1972: its contribution to the change in status of the Catholic community of the area.* Aberdeen.

Gray, J, McPherson, A and Raffe, D 1983 *Reconstructions of secondary education: Theory, myth and practice since the War.* London.

Jamieson, L 1990 ' We All Left at 14: Boys' and girls' schooling circa 1900–1930', *in* Fewell, J and Paterson, F (eds), *Girls in their prime: Scottish education revisited,* Edinburgh, 16–37.

Jamieson, L and Toynbee, C 1992 *Country bairns: Growing up, 1900–1930.* Edinburgh.

Kenneth, Brother 1968 'The Education (Scotland) Act, 1918, in the making', *Innes Review* 19, 91–128.

*Lenman, B and Stocks, J 1972 'The beginnings of state education in Scotland, 1872–1885', *Scottish Educational Studies* 4, 93–106.

Lloyd, J 1983 'The Second World War and educational aspiration: some Scottish evidence', *Journal of Educational Administration and History* 15, 38–41.

Lloyd, J 1992 'The Scottish school system, educational reform and the Second World War', *in* Lowe, R (ed), *Education and the Second World War: Studies in schooling and social change,* London, 177–90.

McDonald, IJ 1967 'Untapped reservoirs of talent? Social class and opportunities in Scottish higher education, 1910–1960', *Scottish Educational Studies* 1, 52–8.

*McPherson 1992 'Schooling', *in* Dickson, T and Treble, JH (eds) *People and Society in Scotland. III. 1914–1990,* Edinburgh, 80–107.

McPherson, A and Raab, CD 1988 *Governing education: a sociology of policy since 1945.* Edinburgh.

Moore, L 1984 'Invisible scholars: Girls learning Latin and mathematics in the elementary public schools of Scotland before 1872', *History of Education* 13, 121–37.

Moore, L 1991 *Bajanellas and semilinas: Aberdeen University and the education of women, 1860–1920.* Aberdeen.

*Moore, L 1992 'Educating for the "Woman's Sphere": Domestic training versus intellectual discipline', *in* Breitenbach, E and Gordon, E (eds), *Out of bounds: Women in Scottish Society, 1800–1945,* Edinburgh, 10–41.

Myers, JD 1972 'Scottish Nationalism and the antecedents of the 1872 Education Act', *Scottish Educational Studies* 4, 71–92.

Paterson, HM 1983 'Incubus and ideology: The development of secondary schooling in Scotland, 1900–1939', *in* Humes, W and Paterson, H (eds) *Scottish culture and Scottish education, 1800–1980,* Edinburgh, 197–215.

*Paterson, L 1996 'Liberation or control: What are the Scottish education traditions of the twentieth century?', *in* Devine, TM and Finlay, RJ (eds), *Scotland in the Twentieth Century*, Edinburgh, 230–49.

Robertson, PL 1990 'The development of an urban university: Glasgow 1860–1914', *History of Education Quarterly* 30, 47–78.

Roxburgh, JM 1971 *The School Board of Glasgow, 1873–1919*. London.

*Smout, TC 1986 *A century of the Scottish people, 1830–1950*. London.

Stephen, WM nd *Fabric and function: a century of school building in Edinburgh, 1872–1972*. Edinburgh.

Stocks, J 1995 'The People versus the Department: the case of Circular 44', *Scottish Educational Review* 27, 48–60.

Treble, JH 1978 'The development of Roman Catholic education in Scotland, 1878–1978', *Innes Review* 29, 111–39.

Treble, JH 1980 'The working of the 1918 Education Act in Glasgow Archdiocese', *Innes Review* 31, 27–44.

Withrington, DJ 1972 'Towards a national system, 1867–72: the last years in the struggle for a Scottish Education Act', *Scottish Educational Studies* 4, 107–24.

FURTHER READING

Those articles marked * in the above list are recommended further reading, along with the following:

Bone, TR (ed) 1967 *Studies in the history of Scottish education, 1872–1939*. London.

Humes, W and Paterson, H (eds) 1983 *Scottish culture and Scottish education, 1800–1980*. Edinburgh.

Knox, HM 1953 *Two hundred and fifty years of Scottish education, 1696–1946*. Edinburgh.

Scotland, J 1969 *The history of Scottish education*. London.

Leisure and Recreation
—————————————————— *Robert A Lambert*

INTRODUCTION

Studies of the history of leisure and recreation in Scotland are in their infancy, indeed, there is no single comprehensive historical study to which the student might be directed. A bibliography of all books that mention developments in leisure pursuits would be massive, as the material is diverse. The most popular mass-participation sports such as football (Murray 1984) and rugby (Thorburn 1985) have been well covered, as have more regional sports such as shinty (Robertson 1994), sheepdog trialing (Halsall 1982) and the tradition of Highland games (Brander 1992). Many PhD theses from Scottish universities address very focused issues such as the history of music halls, cinemas and urban sports and often concentrate exclusively on Glasgow and Edinburgh. These studies tend to stand in isolation and contribute only a little to our general understanding of leisure and recreation in Scotland from 1850 to the present day.

To have split this chapter into 'outdoor recreation' and 'urban leisure' would have caused conceptual shortcomings, as these labels are not mutually exclusive. In addition, it would have divorced the activities from ideological, social, gender, ethnic and power-relations perspectives on how people spent their time. Thus, as well as providing an historical framework for the student, this chapter will subtly address thematic issues such as leisure and its relationship to class, ethnic culture, sectarianism, puritanism, technology and national identity. It is hoped that whilst reading this chapter and studying the associated documents and article you will remain flexible enough to identify these themes as they arise. The chapter is divided into the following sections:

- The first age of mass recreation
- Organised sport
- The visual and performing arts
- Drink and society: the delirium tremens
- Tourism, heritage and the 'Great Outdoors'
- Recreation for all
- The future

Much of the commentary will be speculative, primarily because a good deal of basic research remains to be done and because the subject matter has not attracted historians' interest. In conjunction with this chapter, students are urged to read the few existing survey chapters on leisure and recreation (Fraser 1995; Brown 1996; Smout 1994; Smith 1991; King 1987; Harvie 1994), whilst noting that all of this work is of recent origin.

1. THE FIRST AGE OF MASS RECREATION

The 1870s and 1880s saw the 'Industrialisation of Recreation' in Scotland. Instead of a leisure pursuit being something you did to pass the time, it became something that others were paid to organise on your behalf. This shift in emphasis came about as real incomes began to rise from the 1850s, and especially from the early 1870s. It was also linked to the shortening of the working day and the widespread acceptance of the Saturday half-holiday, first to the skilled workers, and by the 1890s to the unskilled. Improvements in social welfare, health and diet and working conditions contributed to the generation of excess energy within the working classes. Leisure was no longer the domain of the élite. In this changing social climate, leisure and recreation, along with developments in transportation, brought about the transformation of popular culture in Scotland. Community-led recreation, or that associated with local or regional amateur organisations, was replaced by national and/or professional organisations capable of catering for mass amusements, often on a highly organised and grand scale. Increasingly a tourist or day-excursionist industry was built upon the foundations of a burgeoning transport revolution, driven by steamships, railways and road improvements.

The Victorian steamers that once took the Glasgow masses for a summer's day outing 'doon the watter' have now gone, but they have left behind a scattering of ornate piers. Competition for fare prices on steamers in the Forth and Clyde dates back to the 1820s when prices fell as the steamship companies sought to widen their clientele from a middle class base to the 'respectable' working class. The cult of Victorian respectability pervaded these day excursions; they were to be a form of rational recreation, educational, healthy, and vigorous for the mind and body. In many cases, the excursion on the river was organised by an individual firm for its workers, a form of paternalism to foster staff loyalty and revive lagging spirits. Owners of businesses were well aware that a healthy body and spirit produced a reliable and productive worker. In such a fashion, coastal towns on the Clyde – Largs, Millport, Rothesay, Dunoon, Gourock and Ardrossan – became household names in Glasgow only decades after they were thought of as inaccessible by previous generations of urban Glaswegians. The old 'doon the watter' tradition allowed many to gaze at the Isle of Arran, tremble at the tortured channel of the Kyles of Bute, or marvel at the birdlife of Ailsa Craig. From the 1840s, day trippers from Fife could cross, for a single penny, to Granton or Newhaven (Fraser 1995). The most visible icon of this mass day-long migration from town to coast, is surely the most elaborate and ornate public toilet in Scotland, built of marble and cast iron and still standing on the pier head at Rothesay. In the Highlands people rode on mail steamers or paddle-steamers such as the *Linnet*, the *Gondolier*, the *Grenadier* and the *Lochiel* which ran through the Caledonian and Crinan canals in the 1880s on cruises to the Hebrides and Northern Isles (Thompson 1989, photographs 121–6).

The railways offered even more opportunity for 'getting about' and served both seaside resorts and more remote Highland spa towns. The success of Aberdour as a Fife resort was initially built on its steamboat connection to Edinburgh which brought holiday-makers and day trippers across the Forth. Rather late in 1890, as part of the Forth Bridge extension, Aberdour received a rail link to Glasgow and Edinburgh and the town rejoiced, although its lack of a golf course (until 1906) was seen to be a drawback (Simpson 1988). In the 1890s North Berwick had a fine reputation as a resort of clean water and modern sanitation, golf and other leisure facilities. Aberdour was noted by one observer in 1860 to have become, 'a neat, white-washed, swept and kept-tidy-for-summer-visitors kind of place' (Farnie 1860, 16). In the north a rail line from Inverness to Nairn opened in 1855 and was extended to join a line between Aberdeen and Keith in 1858, but the most crucial northern rail link came with the 1861 Act which allowed the construction of a rail line from Dunkeld over Drumochter and down the Spey Valley to Forres; it opened in 1863 as the Inverness and Perth Junction Railway ('the Highland Railway'). This Highland Railway had been founded by local enterprise and there continued to be a strong feeling of attachment to it by the communities it served well into the twentieth century, its moss-green engines and carriages busiest every August with shooting tenants (Grant 1980).

Thomas Cook of Leicester maintained that Scotland alone had transformed him from 'a cheap Excursion Conductor to a Tourist Organiser and Manager'. Cook began excursions in Scotland in 1846, arranging package tours in conjunction with special trains from England and linking up with steamers on the west coast of Scotland (Butler 1985). By 1860 Cook had conveyed some 50,000 tourists about Scotland – pleasure was the major theme of all of his accompanied tours. It was an added bonus for the Victorian tourist that the Queen was now seasonably resident on Deeside, and Cook was not shy to exploit this Royal link with the Highlands. In 1858 the *Illustrated London News* reported how a 'monster train of excursionists, under the guidance of Mr Cook of Leicester', encountered the Royal party en route for Balmoral at Dunbar rail station. 'All ranks joined in hearty cheer after cheer'; the carriage windows were let down; Queen Victoria and Prince Albert 'turned with smiling faces to the multitude', who continued their 'impromptu outburst of genuine loyalty' for five minutes and then tactfully withdrew. Some of the most popular organised mass excursions in Scotland were to admired landscape views, places of literary association such as Abbotsford House (Durie 1992), health spas and seaside resorts, or to places where one could perhaps catch a glimpse of the Royal family. Cook even took to disturbing the Queen at Balmoral in an effort to satisfy customer demand, as he recorded in 1859:

> . . . we pulled up opposite the Royal Castle . . . when the National Anthem was sung at about half past seven in the morning, a strong breeze wafting the sound direct to the Castle. One of our party, applying his opera glasses, declared that

he saw the Royal Prince Consort in his night-cap at a window, but for the accuracy of this vision we cannot vouch.

(Brendon 1992, 51–2)

2. ORGANISED SPORT

Calder (1994, 232) recently mused on the link between the nation and sport in a clever analysis of 'popular culture'. He spoke of the 'realness' of novels that focused on heavy industries on the verge of extinction and the associated all-male-culture in which class bitterness was combined with football, drink and gambling. He also spoke of the fantasy of a primordial Gaelic communalism (whilst describing Scotland today as a mongrel nation) constantly cheated and bullied by wicked Sassenachs, adding that, 'I don't mind people singing 'Flower of Scotland' in which our spacious country is reduced to a 'wee bit hill and glen', so long as that helps us to beat England at Rugby and get into the World Cup finals'. Armstrong and Osborne (1996, 154–61) have suggested that Scotland's obsession with sport is of a more intense hue than England's, and within a far smaller number of sports; 'a strong popular and more democratic character to Scottish sport'. That certainly is the case if we look at football which, by the First World War, was the form of sport most enjoyed by Scotsmen. The first club in Scotland was Queen's Park which was founded in 1867 from an association of YMCA members as a form of 'muscular Christianity'. Over the next twenty years the game took off. Partick Thistle and Ayr United were founded in 1868, Hearts and Greenock Morton in 1874, Hibernian in 1875, Falkirk in 1876, St Mirren in 1877, Clyde in 1878 and then Motherwell in 1886 and Aberdeen in 1903 (the latter team with Dundee United are now known as the 'New Firm'). Of the 'Old Firm' rivals, Rangers came into existence in 1872, and Celtic was founded in 1888 as a charitable organisation to raise money and provide free dinners and other relief for the poorest in the East End of Glasgow, especially for the Catholic parishes there. Hibernian was the first sectarian team in Scotland, the club's 1875 constitution stating that all players must be practising Catholics; in 1893 Hibs was reborn as a non-sectarian club, leaving the 'Old Firm' alone to forge and symbolise the traditional link between sport and sectarianism across the next hundred years (Murray 1984). Celtic became the champions of the Irish Catholic immigrants, and Rangers the flagship of the native Scottish Protestants who feared this influx.

EXERCISE 1

Why has football remained so popular as a spectator sport in Scotland? You should also read **Article 44** to answer this question.

As a spectator sport football had an enormous impact on urban recreation, especially as its growing popularity coincided with the spread of the Saturday half-holiday. By the 1920s and 1930s going to a football game was seen as an outlet for social and political frustrations and as an antidote to boredom at a time of

economic ills and high unemployment; the clubs themselves tacitly encouraged
sectarianism and its associated violence and disorder as a crowd-puller; the game's
links with betting and drinking were an enduring lure; 'it became part of the ritual
pattern of Glasgow male recreation' (Smout 1987, 152–6).

Early attendance statistics can be difficult to trace and verify, but we do know that
up to 1914 Celtic versus Rangers matches could attract crowds of 50,000 to 60,000,
whilst the international game against England attracted 102,000 to the New
Hampden in 1906, 121,452 in 1907 and 149,515 in 1937.

TABLE 1: SCOTTISH FOOTBALL LEAGUE ATTENDANCES.

Seasons:						
1961/2	1965/6	1971/2	1973/4	1984/5	1989/90	1995/96
5,140,400	4,089,900	4,232,900	3,719,200	2,504,900	3,574,800	3,550,200

Source: SFA.

EXERCISE 2

Look at Table 1 and keep in mind what you have just read in **Article 44**. Can
you think of any reasons why, from about 1950, annual figures for those
watching a live game of football have fluctuated both up and down?

Since 1950 the SFA League attendances have fluctuated in response to a steady
increase in ticket prices, the threat of hooliganism and the availability of the game on
television with action replay.

There are hopes that in the 1990s Scottish football across all the leagues will
become a family spectator game. Few have described the modern clash
between Celtic and Rangers and its social impact on both Scotland and
Ireland as well as Simon Kuper (1994) in *Football Against the Enemy* (see
Article 44).

The modern story of sport in Scotland is not all about football. Fittis, in his unique
1891 survey, *Sports and Pastimes of Scotland*, addressed the history and importance
of cricket (the Perth Cricket Club was formed in 1827 but the game was played on
Glasgow Green in 1817); of bowls and curling (the Royal Caledonian Curling Club
was born in 1838, the year of a hard winter) and golf (new courses were built across
the Highlands in the last twenty years of the nineteenth century). Fittis also provided
a historical framework for these sports by talking of the older tradition of game
playing in Scotland, including archery, the rustic sports of Lammas, caitch-ball, the
kiles, or foot racing (in 1870, a crowd of 25,000 watched a running race at the
recently opened Powderhall Stadium in Edinburgh; 20,000 watched a similar race in
1913). Some children's games of chance were universal such as 'pitch and toss' or
'odds or evens', and were still played in the 1940s and 1950s in the street; others
were regional such as the game of pape-a-go played with cherry pips in Hawick (Rae
1991); even in the 1950s and 1960s Glasgow dockers sometimes engaged in

spontaneous swimming races, foot races on the dockside and unofficial fights spiced up with a bet. The ritual gambling abuse of animals continued into our period. In 1835 a new cock-fighting pit which could hold 280 spectators was built in Glasgow in 1835 and in the 1860s cock-fighting was recorded in Hawick and Pollockshaws (Fraser 1995, 239). Cock-fighting was noted in Fife in the 1920s and 1930s. In the 1990s the covert 'sport' of badger-baiting is seeing a revival despite the presence of appointed wildlife police officers in each regional constabulary.

Rugby, with its passionate heartland centred around the Borders, remained an amateur game until 1995, representing the 'old school' ethos of the middle classes. In the second half of the nineteenth century the game, which spread from Rugby School in England, won converts in private schools and boarding schools in Edinburgh. Its only true popular democratic following has come from the Border towns where it has been seen as part of a tradition of rough athleticism harking back to the 'mass football' ('ba games') of the early nineteenth century (Thorburn 1985). Like football, international games against England attract the largest crowds to Murrayfield; in 1981, crowds totalling 205,323 watched Scotland's home Five Nations games. It is interesting to note which sports have been encouraged by some of the purpose-built, post-1950s, towns with no tradition to build on, and no town parks created by generous benefactors, such as Beveridge Park in Kirkcaldy. In 1952 Glenrothes Development Corporation saw the provision of recreational facilities as a matter of great urgency and petitioned Kirkcaldy District Council to provide a bowling green and tennis courts at Dovecot. The District Council, however, saw their pressing need to be only the laying out of Bighty Park, and so in 1953 the Glenrothes Recreational Facilities Advisory Committee decided to go it alone with the financial help of the Coal Industry Social Welfare Organisation (CISWO) in the expectation that large numbers of miners and their families were to be housed in Glenrothes. A CISWO Centre was opened in 1959 and has housed art exhibitions, flower shows, club dinners and dances. The second phase of the town's development, and the advent of Glenrothes District Council in 1961, saw the provision of a swimming pool (1970), golf course (1967), a pavilion (1964) and an assortment of sports fields. On 1 July 1971, HRH the Princess Anne opened the Fife Institute of Physical and Recreational Education in Glenrothes (Ferguson 1982, 75–7, 102–107).

3. THE VISUAL AND PERFORMING ARTS

Scots have always gone to the cinema more than their English neighbours, and although cinema audiences in the UK were declining after 1946 (with around 1.6 billion admissions), even in 1971 more Scots were attending per head of population than the British average. The cinema represented the apex of public leisure and is a part of a historical tradition that runs from the nineteenth century music halls and penny theatres to the out-of-town multiplex cinemas of the 1990s. In the 1930s the 'Great Indoors' had as much appeal as the 'Great Outdoors' – Carnegie investigators found that almost 80% of their sample of young unemployed went to the cinema at least once a week, and 25% more often: this compared with 15% who regularly went cycling and 6% who borrowed a book from a library (Smout 1987, 158). The first appearance of the moving image in Glasgow was in 1895. By 1914 the city could boast 57 cinemas and audiences continued to rise after 1929 when talking pictures began. The cinema age of the inter-war years reflected increased leisure time and greater spending power within the working class. More remote areas were served with travelling picture shows with the Kinematograph and lantern slides. Available cinema statistics are as follows:

TABLE 2: CINEMA ATTENDANCE.

Year	NO OF CINEMAS IN SCOTLAND	TOTAL CINEMA ADMISSIONS	NO OF SCOTS ATTENDING PER HEAD OF POPULATION	NO IN GB ATTENDING PER HEAD OF POPULATION
1951	601	182,100,000	35.7%	27.9%
1961	389	61,030,000	11.9%	8.7%
1971	194	19,468,000	3.7%	3.2%
1982	130	6,278,000		

Source: Department of Trade and Industry.

Cinema audiences began to fall after 1950 as the 'newness' of the medium began to wear off and in-home entertainment became widely available at a lower price in the shape of radio (the late 1930s) and television.

The popular entertainment culture of Scotland has its roots in older traditions and community values. Song, music and dance have always been popular. There are strong bonds of workplace friendship, rhythm and enjoyment from the singing of traditional waulking songs in the Outer Hebrides by groups of women at work (Campbell and Collinson 1977) to the importance of song and informal dance in the sphere of women's work in urban Scotland (Gordon and Breitenbach 1990). Before 1939 a woman's access to leisure pursuits was limited and her social life would revolve entirely around the home, the workplace or the street. Camaraderie and a common sense of unity were developed through gossip, jokes played upon male supervisors, dancing and even the singing of male football songs. The Scottish nursery rhyme forged a similar sense of common identity and pleasure in the playground (Montgomerie and Montgomerie 1948). In the more liberated atmosphere of the 1960s the dance culture formed an integral part of the rituals of courtship and sex, and for women living in an urban small flat with little privacy, it offered a sense of liberation, as Spring (1990) reveals:

> The girls looked superb in the half light, their very young faces heavily painted and their eyes black with mascara. Some wore lime green trouser-suits, others daring backless dresses. Their skirts and 'sexy wee black frocks' were all very short. Pat commented, as he pushed forward and was pushed back by the girls, that some dresses were so low: 'Ye can see their breakfasts'.

In the Highlands in the nineteenth century the social spectrum was often united in song and dance at ghillies' balls, country-dancing and ballad singing and Burns suppers. The traditional Gaelic community ceilidh may have been slipping out of use in the first half of the twentieth century but the Gaelic folk culture of piping, song and recitation was institutionally supported from 1891 by *An Comunn Gaidhealach*, surely a direct forefather of the 'Gaelic Renaissance' of the 1980s, which itself has spawned a decade of popular Gaelic film and music, television and radio programming (Lloyd-Jones 1980, 168–179).

From the Glasgow Orpheus Choir, founded in 1905, the performing arts in Scotland have always symbolised the participation between amateur and professional, best exemplified by the tradition begun in 1947 with the first International Festival of Music and Drama in Edinburgh and recently creatively carried forward by its own 'fringe'. Reputable variety theatres challenged the music halls in the 1890s by providing more cultured evenings out for the middle class, although the attraction of the music hall lingered on into the 1930s especially at the Glasgow Britannia. Industrial radicalism found cultural expression from 1920–1940 in co-operative theatre groups such as the St George's Co-operative Players in Glasgow, and more permanently in the Glasgow Unity Theatre with its Communist connections. This radical theatrical tradition has been continued with the productions of the touring 7:84 Company, most notably with the play *The Cheviot, the Stag and the Black, Black Oil* (MacLean and Carrell 1986). Amateur dramatic and operatic societies still thrive in local community halls and the tradition of pantomime is a popular family entertainment in the larger venues around Christmas. The 'quality' acts which once used to grace the stages of working men's clubs now have to vie with the popularity of Bingo for stage space, as do traditional cabaret acts, be they singers, comedians, ventriloquists or strippers; the attendance figures and thus spending power at these local clubs in the industrial regions still reflects local prosperity and employment trends, although Bingo and strippers perpetually generate large and vocal adult crowds of both sexes. Although the concept of 'clubland' will stay with us, the trend in the 1990s is for 'in-home entertainment without the atmosphere', more often than not fuelled by a six-pack from the off-licence.

4. DRINK AND SOCIETY: THE DELIRIUM TREMENS

The Scottish love for recreational drinking is well known across the globe, indeed, Scots have a reputation for being one of the hardest drinking peoples in the world. In the nineteenth century it was quite normal for the poverty of the working class to be attributed to their misuse and overuse of alcohol rather than to low wages. In the 1830s the population aged fifteen years and over was drinking, on average, just a little under a pint of whisky a week, about two-and-a-half gallons of whisky a year per head of the population (Smout 1987, 133–158; Smout and Wood 1991, 147–157). This figure was still at a gallon per head just prior to the First World War, and was only regulated during the conflict by taxation and the introduction of workable licensing laws. However, the abnormally high incidence of alcohol abuse in Scotland across this period should be considered as more than just a series of statistics, already well presented in other books (Smout 1987). It should rather be seen as part of a leisure tradition, not just restricted to urban Scotland, for it permeated all regions and all social classes (be it the 'tipsy laird' or the sodden Irish navvy). On the testimony of English visitors and tourists, Glasgow was seen to be the most drunken city in the Kingdom at the start of the twentieth century. The geologist Sir Archibald Geikie best explains why in describing Lowland towns:

> . . . tipsiness is a state of pleasure to be looked forward to with avidity, to be gained as rapidly and maintained as long as possible. To many wretched beings it offers a transient escape from the miseries of life, and brings the only moments of comparative happiness which they ever enjoy. They live a double life — one part in the gloom and hardship of the workaday world, and the other in the dreamland into which whisky introduces them'.
>
> (Smout and Wood 1991, 151–2)

Commentators also sought to highlight cultural differences in drinking habits. Geikie concluded that Highlanders drank steadily but could hold their drink, but Lowlanders drank quickly to obliterate family and workplace miseries. Writing in 1932, Edwin Muir found that the working class were noisy public drunks, whilst the middle classes drank behind closed doors (Muir 1935). Drink then was inexorably linked to all aspects of life. It often formed an element of apprentice-ship rites of passage in the workplace; it was linked with other leisure pursuits such as gambling, betting and going to football matches; it was used as a form of social entertainment in the home by the middle classes and to celebrate family events such as marriage or the birth of a child. In most commentators' descriptions of Scottish towns though, the central themes seemed to be the pauperised spirit drinker, the shebeen, rags, poverty, disease and death (Shadow 1858). King (1987) has shown how the young were attracted into the pub culture by providing singing clubs and 'free and easies' with a piano and separate saloon room. Flourishing in the 1870s, such establishments were removed by the efforts of the temperance movement by 1900.

EXERCISE 3

Do people go to a pub in the 1990s for much the same reasons as they did in the 1890s, or has the nature and role of the public house changed in the last century? How important has the temperance movement been in shaping an alternative to the 'recreation of the bottle?' Is drink now much more acceptable in the home as an aid to social entertainment than it used to be?

As a balance against the evils of drink and as an exercise in social control, the puritanical temperance societies of the second half of the nineteenth century also sought to offer recreational and leisure pursuits, but with a high moral tone. It was an experiment to control and suppress the 'rough culture' of drink, gambling, sexual promiscuity, street fighting and domestic violence (Brown 1996). Groups such as the Band of Hope (a children's movement) and the Rechabites held evening concerts, soirées and lectures hosted by youthful middle-class idealists. Temperance hotels and tea rooms (serving tea, coffee and sherbet) were established as places of cheery and sociable entertainment, an example of how rewarding and fulfilling life could be away from the bottle. Gangs of lads in Glasgow from the 1840s to the 1890s were provided with a sober leisure alternative in the Boys' Brigade (1883) and Young Men's Institutes across the city.

By the 1940s and 1950s beer had replaced whisky as the preferred Scottish drink, although the two were linked in the daring Glasgow game of 'shooting the craw' where a whisky was ordered first before a pint of stout, was consumed quickly whilst the stout was being laboriously poured, and the customer fled to the next pub, without paying for either.

In the last two decades the fashion in Scotland has been for theme pubs with 'happy hours', drink promotions and meals served all day to the whole family. The pub culture is now centred around additional leisure activities aside from drink; to survive in the market place a pub manager needs to have a karaoke machine, run a pub quiz and darts league, have a couple of snooker or pool tables and provide a supervised children's play area.

5. TOURISM, HERITAGE AND THE 'GREAT OUTDOORS'

From the early 1930s there were rapid developments in the way that people took holidays within Scotland, or came to appreciate their own nation's heritage and topographical beauty. It was a new era of popular tourism, of day trips sustained by better roads, improved rail networks and increased leisure time for working people. The motor car, the motor coach and omnibus offered a new spirit of freedom. Enthusiasts of motoring subscribed to the *SMT Magazine* which gave advice on the most popular car model to purchase and the best value for money (the Ford 8 car was for sale at just under £100 in the late 1930s) along with numerous suggestions for motoring holidays in Scotland. The summer of 1934 saw unprecedented numbers of holidaymakers using Scotland's roads. They were celebrated as 'very ordinary folk', reclaiming their right to look at Scotland's landscape; 'the liberation of the weekend crowd has come to stay', wrote MacLaren (1934). Some of the most popular articles in the *SMT Magazine* were those that charted accessible and beautiful drives in the Highlands, particularly on Speyside.

EXERCISE 4

Read **Document 135** which relates to tourism and its benefits (and potential drawbacks) in the 1930s. Has the tourist vision of Scotland changed over the last fifty or one hundred years? Or is the vision still one of tartan, shortbread, historic castles, malt whisky, golf, quaint B & B accommodation, grand scenery and a monster in Loch Ness? How has the motor car changed our personal mobility at holiday times or for just a weekend excursion? Why are the issues raised by Neil Gunn still being debated today in countless commissioned economic, financial and visitor impact surveys?

In the motoring literature of the 1930s there was a keen sense that the volume of holiday traffic using Scotland's roads was destined to increase year by year, that a motoring revolution had begun; after all, 'Scotland is the natural motoring paradise of Great Britain, alike in respect of scenic grandeur, sporting roads for the driver, and freedom for picnic meals', wrote the editors of the *Glasgow Herald* sponsored 1935 collection *Motoring in Scotland – A Touring Guide*. Central Belt bus companies were not to miss out on this new era of Highland holidays. In 1949, Alexander's Bus Services were advertising a service from Glasgow to Aviemore that took almost 7 hours and cost 14/3 (single) and 26/- (return). The service also ran from Stirling on a daily seasonal service. For the most complete set of motoring maps outside of London, enthusiasts were directed to William Porteous and Co of Glasgow (*Scottish Omnibus Annual* 1949). Ease of access to the northern Highlands had been helped by Inverness County Council's comprehensive scheme for the improvement of Highland roads in the late 1920s (Grant 1980, 17). The hillwalking recluse found this transport-aided mass rush to the glens a curse, as Matt Marshall (1933, 173) bemoaned:

> These motorists are rapidly making the roads impossible for trampers. One can't walk a hundred yards but a motor pulls up, a head sticks out, and a voice says, 'Jump in'.

60 The clash between nature, landscape conservation, traditional sporting rights and outdoor recreation: Young stag on path to Dorus Duaine, Invernate Forest, 21 September 1934. RM Adam. *By kind permission of the University of St Andrews Photographic Collection.*

There was of course an allied expansion in hotel accommodation for these visitors; in fact, in 1934 the *SMT Magazine* began its own 'Directory of Recommended British Hotels' in a similar fashion to that already done by the AA and RAC. No work has been done on the history of individual hotel companies (although a handful of archives do exist) and how they reacted to the vagaries of the new god tourism. There has been some limited work on visitors' books, in settings as diverse as the famous mountaineering retreat in the Cairngorms known as the Shelter Stone (Duncan 1926; 1930), to nineteenth-century shooting lodges (Packe 1950) and the Rowardennan Hotel near Ben Lomond (Hall 1933). Contemporary observations of hotel life are similarly scarce. In the summer of 1934, Edwin Muir found a Kingussie hotel to be full of middle-aged ladies from Glasgow taking afternoon tea, 'who sailed into the room like miniature battleships, and bore down on their chosen tables as if they were enemies to be ruthlessly breached'. He returned to his 1921 Standard car feeling that he, 'had seen a representative example of Scottish hotel life . . .' (Muir 1934, 188–9). In 1937, Neil Gunn penned a stinging attack on those who felt that tourism and its money was the sole solution to the economic ills of the Highlands; individuals he called, 'half-sycophant depending on the whims of a passing tourist'. His article should be seen as part of the wider debate about the somewhat inappropriate nature of earning a living through tourism in the Highlands, a debate that continues to rumble on today (Gunn 1937: see **Document 135**).

The growing prosperity and consumerism within Scottish society after the Second World War led to a rapid increase in the membership of voluntary organisations concerned with the protection of Scotland's historic (built) and natural heritage. During the nineteenth century a leisure visit to a historic house was a rare event for all but the élite, and it would often be to a house with literary associations such as Abbotsford House.

In the second half of the twentieth century, the distinctive 'Scottishness' of the National Trust for Scotland (1931), the Association for the Protection of Rural Scotland (1926), the Scottish Ornithologists Club (1936) and Scotland's Gardens Scheme (1931) attracted middle class financial support urged on by a dose of national pride; working class support came as the organisations matured and the facilities on offer widened. The growth of the leisure and recreational aspect of the heritage industry has been impressive, as the following tables reveal:

TABLE 3: NATIONAL TRUST FOR SCOTLAND MEMBERSHIP.

1964	1971	1981	1990	1992	1996
32,500	46,800	110,000	218,000	238,000	230,000

Source: Evans 1997, 197

TABLE 4: VISITS TO NATIONAL TRUST FOR SCOTLAND PROPERTIES.

1966/7	1969/70	1970/71	1972/3	1986	1991
649,800	748,500	755,000	1.03M	1.87M	2.08M

Source: National Trust for Scotland.

TABLE 5: VISITS TO ANCIENT MONUMENTS (SCOTLAND).

1967	1969	1971	1978	1996/7
1,422,500	1,613,200	1,948,600	2,406,100	2,900,000

Source: Department of the Environment (1967–78); Historic Scotland 1996/7

People came to view historic homes, castles, landscaped gardens and wild scenery, because for generations they had been excluded from these places; now for the cost of a subscription they could enjoy a day out in what was previously forbidden territory and most came to admire, not to criticise. There were of course people who did not want to be herded off a charabanc and into a castle and then an adjoining tea-room, and they sought solitude and pleasure in the mountains. They were amateur naturalists, botanists, geologists, photographers and ramblers (Lambert 1996), and to an extent they were scorned by the more aggressive mountaineering fraternity of the inter-war years (McNeish and Else 1994). We can trace the 'freedom to roam' and rights of way debate in Scotland back to the first half of the nineteenth century in the Edinburgh origins (1847) of the organisation that was to rename itself in 1884 as the Scottish Rights of Way and Recreation Society. Generations of 'stravagers and marauders' in Scotland (Aitken 1975) took heart from the society's legal triumphs and support after the celebrated Battle of Glen Tilt in 1847 and the Battle of Braemar in 1891 (Stephenson 1989; Anton 1991), when the right of the common man to wander at will in the Highlands confronted traditional landed sporting rights head on.

EXERCISE 5

Read **Document 133** (a piece of oral history work conducted amongst mountaineers) and **Document 134** (a poem from a bothy door). What do they tell us about both life in the city and the joy of walking in the mountains of Scotland? Think about the term 'escapism'; some achieve this by watching an Australian soap on television, others take to the hills or lochs.

By the 1930s and 1940s, as the National Park debate in Scotland (launched by *The Scots Magazine* in the late 1920s) raged on, the middle class mountaineer of the 1880s had been replaced by a new generation of adventurous unemployed (and employed) working class climbers escaping the drudgery and uncertainties of the industrial city. They met at night at the Craigallion fire near the loch in Milngavie, they read the poetry of Robert W Service and disliking youth hostel rules they slept in the hills on their climbs, in caves, barns and howffs (see **Document 133**). As Alastair Borthwick put it:

> You have to understand what Scotland was like in those days. It was a grim place . . . People were on the dole, there was absolutely no hope at all . . . and you were a youngster in this, you had been brought up to this, this was normal, this grimness, then suddenly to find this escape route, this climbing thing and it absolutely bowled you over. And the escape from the city at the weekend . . . It was an explosion, it was a wonderful thing.
>
> (MacLean 1980, 79)

In a similar vein, children from all over Britain visiting Glenmore Lodge in the Cairngorms in the late 1940s and 1950s wrote poetry and songs about their days' walking in the hills, which they read out at the regular Friday ceilidh evenings (Loader 1952: see **Document 134**).

6. RECREATION FOR ALL, 1950–2000

Trends in leisure and recreation can be more closely followed in the period after the Second World War, from the new availability of government statistics. The *Digest of Scottish Statistics* started to include leisure and social statistics in 1965, but by 1972 the *Scottish Abstract of Statistics* was including a wide range of leisure and

61 Aristocratic botanists with leisure time to pursue an amateur interest in natural history: Lady Elphinstone (sitting), Lord Elphinstone and Lady Colquhoun looking at Alpine Gentian, *Gentiana nivalis*, Ben Lawers, 25 July 1932. RM Adam. *By kind permission of the University of St Andrews Photographic Collection.*

recreational information, often supplied directly by sporting and recreational bodies themselves. This final section will make available a number of tables of statistics which reflect a wide and varied range of both indoor and outdoor leisure and sporting activities. A number of activities will be discussed in the text but the reader should also study the tables to identify additional trends in the way that Scots spend their leisure time, and to identify how external political, economic and social factors have shaped both the provision of leisure facilities and our responses to them. This section includes a vision of how we may be spending our leisure time at the dawn of the twenty-first century; historians after all, cannot always dwell in the past but must endeavour to inform of our future.

The Scottish countryside has seen a dramatic increase in the number of people visiting it and in the variety of leisure activities now permitted and arranged within it. On the lochs, rivers, hills and glens of Scotland it is now possible to enjoy an enormous range of recreational activities. MacLean (1996, 11) recently captured the new égalitarian nature of outdoor recreation:

> Look out of the car window at any Scottish mountain or heather-clad
> moorland . . . and the chances are you will see somebody doing something
> sporty, even if it just involves putting a packet of Jammy Dodgers into a
> rucksack before a brisk stroll in the hills. These are healthy, glowing people for
> whom the wild peaks and peaty bogs of our native land are such a familiar
> environment, when they get back to the office on Monday morning, they need a
> compass to find their desk.

We should be careful to treat this evidence with caution, for the 'reluctant adventurer' is just as well catered for, and many Scots find no interest in hillwalking, rambling, or studying natural history. The student of the history of recreation should be aware that in Scotland in the 1990s four out of every ten toys sold is a computer or video game. As people 'surf the Net' at cyber-cafés in Glasgow or Edinburgh, others surf the Atlantic off the Hebrides or northern coasts. The steady rise in those who pay for a television licence shows how addictive a form of leisure activity the infamous 'goggle-box' has become, with many children and adults watching hours and hours of TV each day.

TABLE 6: TELEVISION LICENCES.

Year	1951	1958	1961	1966	1971
Scotland only	200	600,000	1,007,000	1,253,100	1,468,200
GB	764,000		11,268,000		15,961,000

Source: Department of Trade and Industry.

It is extremely difficult to ascertain just how many people do venture into the 'Great Outdoors' in Scotland on a regular basis now. The Scottish Youth Hostels

Association, born in 1931 as a distinct entity from its English counterpart, has kept careful records of those staying overnight in its ever-increasing network of hostels across urban and rural Scotland (Moir 1933).

EXERCISE 6

Look at Table 7 'SYHA Overnight Stays'. What trends can you identify over the past thirty years in the country of origin of those using youth hostels in Scotland? Can you explain this changing nature of youth hostelling in Scotland?

TABLE 7: SYHA OVERNIGHT STAYS.

Year	1961	1966	1971	1980	1990
Total visitors	468,700	459,400	481,900	557,500	629,000
From Scotland	261,800	268,700	235,700	241,300	246,000
	(55.9%)	(58.5%)	(48.9%)	(43.2%)	(39.1%)
From England and Wales	140,900	113,900	116,000	98,100	121,400
	(30.1%)	(24.8%)	(24.1%)	(17.6%)	(19.3%)
Elsewhere	66,000	76,800	130,200	218,100	261,500
	(14.1%)	(16.7%)	(27%)	(39.2%)	(41.6%)

Source: Scottish Youth Hostels Association.

Table 7 shows that as the proportion of overseas visitors to hostels have increased, so the proportion of Scots using SYHA facilities has fallen steadily from 1971. This can best be explained by the emergence of enticing package holidays to Greece, Florida or Spain over the past two decades, especially as Scottish holidaymakers can now fly direct to these sun-kissed foreign shores from Glasgow or Edinburgh airports.

In recent decades, some Highland estates have reacted to the growing number of Scots seeking day-long countryside recreation, the most notable being Rothie-murchus Estate in the Cairngorms and Drimsynie Estate near Lochgoil. Rothie-murchus provides a wide range of organised and structured activities ranging from clay pigeon shooting and winter dog-sled racing, to off-road driving and farm tours; it also attracts those wanting to wander in the Cairngorms NNR or around the scenic Loch-an-Eilein. From around 1980 this estate has seen annual visitor numbers of 290/333,000 and in 1990 introduced corporate hospitality facilities after requests from within the business sector in Scotland. This fashion in the 1980s and 1990s for 'Corporate Recreation', whether it be at a paint-ball facility in a Central Belt woodland, or on a unity and confidence building course at an Outward Bound centre in the Highlands, continues the nineteenth-century paternalistic employer-employee relationship and will develop to become accepted workplace practice, merely recasting the traditional link between work culture and rational recreation (Scarlett 1988; Rothiemurchus Estate 1976–1995).

Outdoor sports that twenty years ago we may have viewed as fresh and innovative, such as some water sports, mountain-biking, orienteering (Climie

1990) and paragliding are now commonplace in Scotland's countryside, and the search to find alternative sports of daring and speed will continue. A Scottish Ski Club was formed in Edinburgh in 1907, which gave away skis to postmen and shepherds; with an upsurge of interest in the 1960s, there are now five centres of Scottish skiing which in the 1990s have to accommodate snowboarders as well as downhill, off-piste and slalom skiers. In 1913 the *Scottish Ski Club Magazine* captured the macho attraction of the sport:

> I glory in the victory over self and Nature . . . the greatest of all joys of ski-ing is
> the sense of limitless speed, the unfettered rush through the air at breakneck
> speed . . . Man is alone, gloriously alone against the inanimate universe . . . He
> alone is Man, for whose enjoyment and use Nature exists.
>
> (Smout 1991, 247)

EXERCISE 7

Identify some of the individual sports and leisure pursuits that you enjoy. Try and find out about the history of these activities in Scotland. How long have people been playing the particular sport? How popular or regional is it? Is it part of a tradition of recreation for certain classes of people? How is it funded or supported? How is it affected by wider issues such as conflicts over landuse, economics, government policy, and initiatives or technology. You can widen this picture by asking friends and family to suggest other leisure activities that they enjoy.

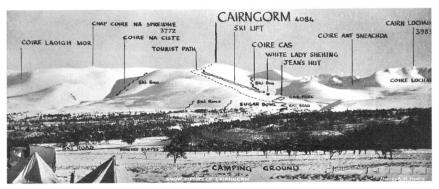

62 The Snow Fields of Cairngorm. Probably taken in the late 1950s or early 1960s around the time of the initial development of Cairn Gorm as a centre for Scottish skiing. Photograph by BH Humble made into postcard.

7. THE FUTURE

The 1990s are the age of the televised National Lottery and the ubiquitous Scratch Card, but the jury is still out as to the effect that these forms of recreational gambling are having on the poorest in Scottish society. Church and social welfare groups have already vocalised strong concerns that they are encouraging addictive and under-age gambling behaviour, although many charitable causes in Scotland benefit from payouts from the National Lottery Fund.

Of a far graver concern are the growing incidences of recreational drug abuse in Scotland be it heroin or Ecstasy tablets and the subsequent criminalisation of these alternative forms of leisure activities such as 'raves' and the drinking of 'Hooch' or 'Buckfast' in town centres (Brown 1996). From the 1970s, government has increasingly supported Scottish sporting initiative, and this is bound to continue with lottery funding being now available to individual targeted sports, and especially after the dismal performances of British athletes in the Atlanta Olympic Games of 1996. In the Scottish countryside ('the playground of the future'), recreation has become an important land use (sustainable or not), as well as a manifestation of social attitudes towards nature, an economic interest and a source of town-country conflict (Smith 1991). With a dramatic increase in leisure as a human activity, and as it comes into increasing conflict with other forms of land use – sporting rights, nature conservation or agriculture and forestry – so the history of countryside recreation deserves much more intensive research if we are to ever understand the dynamics of modern rural Scotland in the years to come.

REFERENCES TO BOOKS AND ARTICLES MENTIONED IN THE TEXT

Aitken, R 1975 'Stravagers and Marauders', *Scottish Mountaineering Club Journal* 30, No 6, 351–7.

Anton, S 1991 'Battles for Cairngorm Rights of Way', *Cairngorm Club Journal* 20, No 102, 23–29.

Armstrong, R and Osborne, BD 1996 *Scotch Obsessions*. Edinburgh.

Brander, M 1992 *The Essential Guide to Highland Games*. Edinburgh.

Brendon, P 1992 *Thomas Cook – 150 Years of Popular Tourism*. London.

*Brown, CG 1996 'Popular Culture and the Continuing Struggle for Rational Recreation', *in* Devine, TM and Finlay RJ (eds) *Scotland in the Twentieth Century*, Edinburgh, 210–29.

*Butler, RW 1985 'Evolution of Tourism in the Scottish Highlands', *Annals of Tourism Research* 12, 371–95.

Calder, A 1994 *Revolving Culture – Notes from the Scottish Republic*. London.

Campbell, JL and Collinson, F (eds) 1977 *Hebridean Folk Songs. II Waulking Songs from Barra, South Uist, Eriskay and Benbecula*. Oxford.

Climie, B 1990 *History of the Scottish Orienteering Association*. Elgin.

Duncan, JL 1926 'The Shelter Stone Visitors' Book', *Cairngorm Club Journal* 11, No 64, 212–213.

Duncan, JL 1930 'Visitors' Book at the Shelter Stone', *Cairngorm Club Journal* 12, No 69, 117–21.

*Durie, A 1992 'Tourism in Victorian Scotland: The Case of Abbotsford', *Scottish Economic and Social History* 12, 42–54.

Evans, D 1997 *A History of Nature Conservation in Britain*. London.

Farnie, H 1860 *The Fife Coast from Queensferry to Fifeness*. Cupar.

Ferguson, K 1982 *A History of Glenrothes*. Glenrothes.

*Fittis, RS 1891 *Sports and Pastimes of Scotland*. Wakefield (1975 edn).

*Fraser, WH 1995 'Developments in Leisure', *in* Fraser WH and Morris, RJ (eds) *People and Society in Scotland. Volume II 1830–1914*, Edinburgh, 236–64.

Glasgow Herald 1935 Motoring in Scotland – A Touring Guide. Glasgow.

Gordon, E and Breitenbach, E (eds) 1990 *The World is Ill Divided*. Edinburgh.

Grant, IF 1980 *Along a Highland Road*. London.

Gunn, NM 1937 '"Gentleman – the Tourist!" the New Highland Toast', *The Scots Magazine*, New Series 26, No 6, 410–15.

Hall, TS 1933 *Tramping Holidays in Scotland – Five Walking Tours Described in Detail*. London.

Halsall, E 1982 *Sheepdog Trials*. Cambridge.

Harvie, C 1994 'Sport and the Scottish State', *in* Jarvie, G and Walker, G (eds) *Scottish Sport in the Making of the Nation: Ninety Minute Patriots?*, Leicester, 43–57.

*King, E 1987 'Popular Culture in Glasgow', *in* Cage, RA (ed) *The Working Class in Glasgow 1750–1914*, London, 142–87.

Kuper, S 1995 *Football Against the Enemy*. London.

Lambert, RA 1996 '"Strathspey and Reel": Photography and the Cairngorms', *Inferno: St. Andrews Journal of Art History* 3, 68–81.

*Lloyd-Jones, ID 1980 'Culture in Scotland Since 1870', *in* Kellas, JG *Modern Scotland*, London, 168–76.

Loader, CM 1952 *Cairngorm Adventure at Glenmore Lodge – Scottish Centre of Outdoor Training*. Edinburgh.

MacLaren, M 1934 'The Freedom of the Countryside – Scotland and the Motor Age', *SMT Magazine* 13, No 6, 54–6.

MacLean, I 1980 'Mountain Men', *in* Kay, B (ed) *Odyssey – Voices from Scotland's Recent Past*, Edinburgh, 78–87.

MacLean, M and Carrell, C (eds) 1986 *As an Fhearann – From the Land: A Century of Images of the Scottish Highlands*. Edinburgh.

MacLean, N 1996 'Pick Your Kicks in the Great Outdoors', *The Sunday Times*, Travel Section, 22 September, 11.

*McNeish, C and Else, R 1994 *The Edge – One Hundred Years of Scottish Mountaineering*. London.

Marshall, M 1933 *The Travels of Tramp-Royal* . . . Edinburgh.

Moir, DG 1933 'Scottish Youth Hostels', *Cairngorm Club Journal* 13, No 74, 132–8.

Montgomerie, N and Montgomerie, W (eds) 1948 *Sandy Candy and Other Scottish Nursery Rhymes*. London.

*Muir, E 1996 *Scottish Journey*. Edinburgh (first published 1935).

*Murray, B 1984 *The Old Firm – Sectarianism, Sport and Society in Scotland*. Edinburgh.

Packe, AH 1950 'A Highland Visitors' Book', *Country Life*, February 10, 370–1.

Rae, JR 1991 'Pape-a-go Ploys', *The Scots Magazine* 135, No 4, 370–3.

*Robertson, J 1994 *Kingussie and the Caman – Follow Closely the Fame of Your Fathers*. Kingussie.

Rothiemurchus Estate 1976–1995 *Annual Reports* (published each year from 1976 to 1995 and onwards).

Scarlett, MH 1988 *In the Glens Where I Was Young*. Milton of Moy.

Scottish Omnibus Annual 1949. Edinburgh.

Shadow (pseud. Brown, Alexander) 1858 *Glasgow, 1858. Shadow's Midnight Scenes and Social Photographs*. Glasgow (1976 edition).

*Simpson, E 1988 'Aberdour: The Evolution of a Seaside Resort', *in* Cruickshank, G (ed) *A Sense of Place – Studies in Scottish Local History*, Edinburgh, 177–87.

*Smith, R 1991 'The Playground of the Future', *in* Magnusson, M and White, G (eds) *The Nature of Scotland – Landscape, Wildlife and People*, Edinburgh, 197–210.

Smout, TC 1987 *A Century of the Scottish People, 1830–1950*. London.

Smout, TC and Wood, S 1991 *Scottish Voices, 1745–1960*. London.

Smout, TC 1991 'The Highlands and the Roots of Green Consciousness, 1750–1990', *Proceedings of the British Academy* 76, 237–63.

*Smout, TC 1994 'Patterns of Culture', *in* Dickson, A and Treble, JH (eds) *People and Society in Scotland. Volume III 1914–1990*, Edinburgh, 261–81.

Spring, I 1990 *Phantom Village – The Myth of the New Glasgow*. Edinburgh.

Stephenson, T 1989 *Forbidden Land – The Struggle for Access to Mountain and Moorland*. Manchester.

*Thompson, F (ed) 1989 *Victorian and Edwardian Highlands from Old Photographs*. Edinburgh.

Thorburn, AMC 1985 *The Scottish Rugby Union – Official History*. Edinburgh.

FURTHER READING

Those references marked * in the above list are recommended further reading, along with the following:

All issues of the *Cairngorm Club Journal, Scottish Ski Club Journal, The Scots Magazine, Scottish Mountaineering Club Journal, SMT Magazine* (Scottish Motor Traction Co Ltd), *Take Note* (the magazine of the Scottish Tourist Board).

Aldous, K (ed) *Who's Who in the Environment – Scotland*. London and Battleby. SNH.

Baker, EA 1923 *The Highlands with Rope and Rucksack*. London.

Baker, EA 1933 *On Foot in the Highlands*. London.

Deal, W 1976 *A Guide to Forest Holidays in Great Britain and Ireland*. London.

Durie, AJ 1992 'Tourism and Commercial Photography in Victorian Scotland: the Rise and Fall of G.W. Wilson and Co., 1853–1908', *Northern Scotland* 12, 89–104.

Firsoff, VA 1949 *The Cairngorms on Foot and Ski*. London.

Haines, GH 1973 *Whose Countryside?* London.

Parke, H 1989 *Scottish Skiing Handbook*. Barr.

Smart, R 1988 'Famous throughout the world: Valentine and Sons Ltd, Dundee', *in* Fenton, A, Cheape, H, and Marshall, R (eds) *Review of Scottish Culture 4*, Edinburgh, 75–87.

Smout, TC 1983 'Tours in the Scottish Highlands from the eighteenth to the twentieth centuries', *Northern Scotland* 5, 99–121.

Culture and Identity
————————————————— *Christopher Harvie*

INTRODUCTION

There are two general ways to approach cultural studies. The first is historical, an extension of the history of ideas, paying special regard to the social conditions in which a society either accepted or rejected an ideology. This is broadly the line taken by Raymond Williams in *Culture and Society* (1958). The second approach, recently more salient, concentrates on the text and mode of discourse, language, symbolism, relationship to audience, and so on. In the Scottish situation the former has been central, because cultural factors have always had an exaggerated validity in a polity without an omnicompetent legislature.

But the second can't be dismissed. Perhaps the most influential writer ever to come out of Scotland – Adam Smith – was a rhetorician by training. He makes his point quite frequently not by rational persuasion but by the striking phrase or symbol – the pin factory to explain the division of labour, or the tradesmen who 'seldom meet together, even for merriment or diversion, but the conversation ends in a conspiracy against the public' (*The Wealth of Nations*, 1776, Book 1, Chapter 10, Part 2). Does the division of labour *always* produce such a startling output? Does every gathering of merchants hatch a cartel? Discourse-analysis can nurture the pretentious academic bore, creating a small but perfectly-formed specialism, but it can't be dispensed with, any more than the philosophy of history which highlights the relativism which determines 'historical fact'.

Above all, a sense of rhetoric and argument ought to make you suspicious of what follows. I will be insisting that Scottish 'culture' (very much Matthew Arnold's notion of 'high culture' as 'a study of perfection, and of harmonious perfection') has been an extension of politics by other means, rooted in the peculiar nature of Scottish civil society, and its Estates – like the Kirk and Law – which have had their own existence semi-independent of Parliament in London, and have radiated a sense of Scottish 'differentness' through associated literary and artistic activity. A 'surrogate politics' of Scottish institutions stands in for an absent parliament.

But because Scottish culture is so political, it imposes distinctive stresses on the individual: part of it is an artistic language and symbols which show its interpreters being broken – most notoriously by the tendency for the human identity to split into the hyper-rational and the near-bestial: James Hogg's *Justified Sinner* (1823), RL Stevenson's *Jekyll and Hyde* (1885), RD Laing's *The Divided Self* (1961). Contrast, for example, the Tory intellectual Walter Elliot's praise of what he christened 'democratic intellectualism' with the same society seen by another (admittedly older) politician, JM Robertson. And however multifaceted the Scottish personality, it found little place for women:

> [A society] wherein discipline is rigidly and ruthlessly enforced, but where criticism and attack are unflinching, continuous, and salt with a bitter and jealous humour. It is a heritage wherein intellect, speech and, above all, argument are the passports to the highest eminence in the land. These traditions we should study, and their histories are the annals of the parish, their ministers and their elders.
>
> (Elliot 1932, quoted in Coote 1965, 16)

> Before the Reformation they [the Scots] were vivacious, art loving, full of healthy life: since then they have become 'museless', as Mr Ruskin would say . . . Austerity and joyless gloom on the one hand produce their natural corrective in dissolute mirth and defiant licence on the other . . . A moral duality, so to speak, runs through this past Scottish life in a way that seems at time perplexing . . . I could lay my finger at this moment on half-a dozen small Scottish towns in which, for sheer lack of a theatre or any other recreation, a large proportion of the youths became unintellectual, sottish and dissolute. The more ambitious eagerly flock to the large towns; those left behind have no resource but the tap room.
>
> (Robertson 1886, 211)

What is from one angle stimulating is from another inhibiting and destructive. A classic example of this tension is Hugh Miller (**Document 136**). The journalist and geologist set store by a religious rationalism far superior to the deference of the English. But his remarkable autobiography *My Schools and Schoolmasters* (1850) shows a man living not just on the borderline of Saxon and Gael but on the edge of schizophrenia. Miller ended by shooting himself. Scottish culture during the industrial age *is* dualist: both nativist and cosmopolitan, adventurous and defensive. Look at Edwin Muir's poem 'Scotland 1941' (**Document 137**). Is your reaction at all comfortable, either with the Calvinist Scotland Muir rejects, or the more credulous feudal alternative?

My historical narrative is necessarily a very selective one with many cultural personalities left out – something which strengthens the argument for discourse-analysis! The reason for this is to concentrate on certain critical phases which affected the survival of Scotland as a 'culture-nation', a concept implying a political unit more prestigious than a French region or a German *Land*, and consequently an important concept in today's Europe. At the same time I want to examine how such a cultural politics treats individuals and groups who don't fit in. Think about Patrick Doyle in James Kelman's *A Disaffection*, a put-upon Glasgow teacher who achieves an epiphany, a mystical experience in which, for a matter of minutes, he becomes aware of his full humanity. Consider this in the context of Kurt Wittig's observation on the essence of Scots literature:

> "Naw kids I'm no kidding, it was an urge, like a magic spell had befallen me. It was as if these two pipes themselves were calling out to me to come on and play me come on and play me, so I lifted one up and what I did I just, okay, blew into it, and out came this long and deep sound that made me think of scores and scores of years and generations and generations of people all down through the ages, and this tune – not exactly a tune, more of a sound, the one kind of long sound that you could occasionally just pause from doing, then start again as if ye hadni stopped at all except when you came to the very end of it you would know about the pauses you did, they would all be a part of it. It was really beautiful weans and it made me think of magic. I'm no kidding ye on. Magic."
>
> (Kelman 1989, 298)

> The method by which he [Eric Linklater] achieves this total impression is that which GD Brown considered characteristic of the Scottish mind, and it is one which runs, as we ourselves have seen, through the whole Scottish literature: namely the flashing together of different pictures of vivid sensuousness to produce a new compound image highly charged with meaning – actual or metaphorical. It is because the pictures thus flashed together are themselves so incongruous that the final effect has the characteristic flavour of the grotesque.
>
> (Wittig 1958, 330)

Can this intense individualism be squared with the culture-politics of the earlier Estates? How does it differ from the feelings, say, induced by heroin in Irvine Welsh's *Trainspotting* (1994)? If we can work this one out, we might at least be able to fix *where* Scottish culture is, as Raymond Williams put it, 'measure the distance' between it and the varieties of our existence.

We will look at this topic under the following headings:

- 'Semi-Independence' and modern Scottish culture
- Disruptions
- 'North Britain' or the democratic intellect?
- Neotechnics versus ethnic nationalism
- The pathology of imperial unionism
- 'Seeing Scotland whole?'
- The Renaissance of the 1980s

When you have completed this chapter you should have gained an insight into the complex relationship between culture and identity.

1. 'SEMI-INDEPENDENCE' AND MODERN SCOTTISH CULTURE

A key paradigm of national cultural development is that of the Czech revisionist Marxist Miroslav Hroch, applied to nineteenth-century nationalist movements, from which Scotland was a notable absentee. If we update Hroch, do we see by the 1990s the belated completion of his first two stages of ethnic mobilisation: the intellectual movement and the capture of institutions? Are *Braveheart*, the bawling of 'Flower of Scotland' at rugby matches and the return of the Stone of Scone augurs – along with some opinion polls and SNP election successes – of the imminence of the third stage, the mass movement (Hroch 1985)? Or are the Scots still the 'ninety-minute patriots' whom Jim Sillars attacked in 1992?

Were Victorian Scots expressing a national identity of their own by moving *away* from ethnic nationalism, as the rest of Europe moved towards it? An ethnic element certainly existed, with 'Ancient Scottish constitution' historicists – Duncan MacNeill (1957) and Compton Mackenzie (1945) in the past, Murray Pittock (1991, Chapter 5) today – seeing continuity from the Declaration of Arbroath in 1320 via the aristocratic nationalism of the French/papal alliance, in which the nobility remained supreme, even after the Reformation. Their rights over the other Estates – law, kirk, burghs, universities – were defended by George Buchanan's aristocratic republicanism and by Andrew Fletcher's federal scheme for British union: anti-metropolitan but also deeply inegalitarian. But after 1745, this petered out.

Muir's poem (**Document 137**) mourns a patriotism of the sort that flared up into national rebirth in Poland, Hungary or Finland. This was done down, according to Colin Kidd, in *Subverting Scotland's Past* (1993), by Whig 'improvement', which also commodified the feelings it could not eradicate into the commercial 'culture' of Burns and Scott. Marx and Engels saw Scottish nationalism as assembled from the rubbish of pre-national cultures (Kidd 1993; Engels 1849). Pittock and Kidd can reanimate ethnicity because of the destruction of Marxism in 1989–91. But ethnic nationalism's subsequent short life makes this now seem less convincing. Nor is Kidd's equation of Scottish decline with the weakening of ethno-historical politics final.

But this wasn't only the ideological contender, as Muir makes plain:

> Till Knox and Melville clapped their preaching palms
> And bundled all the harvesters away.

Calvinism had a rational structure of social organisation which competed with ethnicity. 'Federal Calvinism' used the F-word in the sense of a covenant between God and man *and* man and man: a type of transcendental constitutionalism. Politically this meant the 'Godly Commonwealth' of the presbyterians, with authority devolved to the local oligarchies of kirk sessions and elders, the base of a pyramid of presbyteries and synods, culminating in the General Assembly of the Kirk, a concept which in the late seventeenth century also took root on the other side of the Atlantic (Williamson 1979, Chapter 3). As John Macmurray showed, this influenced the home rule movement in the 1940s and continues to affect modern politics:

> The British differentiation of the cultural from the political union had its main source in the historical accident by which a Scottish king inherited the English throne. It was confirmed by the failure of the English attempt – totalitarian in conception – to force episcopacy on Scotland. Scotland remained free in fellowship, with her own type of established religion and her own distinctive type of law . . . An epidemic of militant nationalism would not consolidate, but disrupt the political unity of Great Britain.
>
> (Macmurray 1950, 66)

Writing about British unity, David Marquand has stressed how the market, the 'universal pandar', dissolves existing conventions. The post-Union Scots adapted both the idea of the covenant and the country's own quasi-constitutional mechanisms – the Faculty of Advocates, the Convention of Royal Burghs, the General Assembly and the Universities – to contain the market and direct the social feelings which Adam Smith termed 'sympathy'. When Adam Ferguson talks of 'social bands' he uses a secular version of federal Calvinism to describe such institutions (Marquand 1995).

The Scots saw the 'fundamental law' of the Union broken, but most Scottish institutions survived, and created compensatory conventions in a state in which regulation was anyway minimal. Authority was courted, patronage and local autonomy being the *quid pro quo*. As the political community broadened, an innovative 'English' literature accompanied it whose cultural assumptions, Robert Crawford has argued, are really a Scottish invention. With access to administration and markets the threat of 'luxury and corruption' to the *polis* prompted a reorientation of politics to entrepreneurialism and socialisation, while the 'ballads of the nation' – Blind Harry's *Wallace* and Barbour's *Brus* – were replaced by the novel as constitutional convention, and by a new type of patriot (Crawford 1992, Chapter 1).

EXERCISE 1

Look at **Document 138**, an extract from *Rob Roy*, the most popular of all Sir Walter Scott's works in Scotland, on stage as well as in print, throughout the nineteenth century. How does it suggest a Scottish type of political fiction? Bailie Nicoll Jarvie is a Glasgow magistrate, cousin to the Highland rogue, and a successful businessman. What does Jarvie regard the Union as implying? What does he mean by honour and credit? Where do his loyalties lie?

This passage repays close reading. The eighteenth-century enlightenment repudiated Scotticisms for plain English and British patriotism. But in Jarvie's play of words there are Scotticisms *and* irony. Behind them here lies the concern that though economic success *had* to be the condition of the Union, it could also lead to the 'corruption' feared by both Adam Smith and Adam Ferguson. Jarvie is a specifically Glasgow patriot, quite different from a British nationalist. He lasted as an archetype for over a century; one of his fictional descendants was Dickson MacCunn in John Buchan's *Huntingtower* (1924).

The structures of Scottish society in the eighteenth century had supported 'improvement': socialisation and in particular religion and education – were 'reserved' to Scottish institutions. These eased economic development and preserved social sympathy, while the union controlled (rather than prevented) corruption and warded off external threat. Hume and Smith regarded cultural nationality as destructive, but thought the 'local or provincial state' best suited to economic development. 'Commodifying' culture made it harmless, while a peculiar diffused sovereignty traded parliamentary power for patronage and local autonomy (Smith 1776, 318; Phillipson 1969).

The Scottish 'traditional intelligentsia' – its charters confirmed by the Union-accelerated 'improvement'. Economic development was driven by landowners and advocates and the towns, individually and corporately: building harbours and new villages, promoting industry and regulating labour. The Kirk was also involved in education, poor relief, assembling statistics and extending social control. This transformed the Buchanan/Fletcher gentry ideal into a civic ideal. Edinburgh was changed from a congested slum to a capital for the political class of the Scottish 'estates', centralised and professionalised after the end of the heritable jurisdictions in 1747 (Fraser 1988; Fry 1993).

While Scotticisms were eradicated to enable Scots to colonise British public life, cultural goods were 'symbolically appropriated' notably by 'Ossian' MacPherson, Burns and Scott, into British cultural stock, just when 'print capitalism' evolved (Chapman 1993; Anderson 1982). This compound of efficiency and cultural nativism – what I have called 'red and black Scotland' – became during the long French Wars, 1793–1815, the Scottish element of Linda Colley's 'forging' of Britain (Colley 1992, 117–31). The paradox was that 'improvement' didn't mean secular-isation: while it gradually diminished the law and the aristocratic element of Scots autonomy, but enhanced the significance of the pillar most open to popular control: the presbyterian Kirk (Clark 1970).

2. DISRUPTIONS

I think we can only really understand Scottish culture in the nineteenth, and much of the twentieth, century when we realise the scale of the traumas which afflicted this 'semi-independent' settlement in the period up to 1843. In his *Break-up of Britain*, Tom Nairn (1977, 118–20) stressed the smoothness of the Scots intelligentsia making the transition to metropolis and empire. For George Davie (1990, 43) the end of the Scottish enlightenment involved a last flare-up in the 1830s, attempting to make 'the reform of the Union parliament the occasion for rescuing from corruption a two-kingdoms constitution distinctive of the country, placing the spiritual order once again on a level with the temporal'.

EXERCISE 2
What did Davie mean by this?

I think a clue is given when we compare a treatment of political theory from a later writer, John Buchan (**Document 139**), with extracts from the most articulate voice of the early nineteenth century, Thomas Carlyle (**Document 140**).

Obviously, the impression is of 'a sick state and an ailing people'. In the middle of their technological triumphs, the Scots' attempt to extend 'civic humanism' into the bourgeois epoch had come unstuck. John Galt and Thomas Carlyle's critiques imply reasons for this.

Galt applied 'the general principles of the philosophy of history' to 'the West' – the region bounded by Glasgow, Greenock and Ayr, following it from rural tranquillity to industrial insecurity (Scott 1985, 76). In *Annals of the Parish*, his study of a small Ayrshire village (based on the documentation of the *Statistical Account*), contract takes over from status, broadly 'improving' the community. But what is happening in *The Provost* (1822) and *The Member* (1832) (**Document 141**)?

Provost Pawkie *is* 'luxury and corruption'. Galt paralleled Scott's concern in the *Malagrowther Letters* (1826) with metropolitan assaults on Scottish distinctiveness. Scott's function as a national remembrancer and print capitalist, which seeded imitators throughout Europe, was marginalised by his near-paranoid Toryism. Galt was far subtler; his novels are constitutional documents as pivotal for Scotland as Bagehot and Trollope would later be for England. His 'rich diet of unspoken criticism' implies the supremacy of law over power, and the equation of law with community in a very European sense (Campbell 1981, 48). They are the foundation works of a popular political literature which ranges from Henry Cockburn's *Memorials of his Time* (1854) to William Alexander's *Johnnie Gibb of Gushetneuk* (1871), also carried on in the didactic output of the Kailyard, and a wealth of newspaper fiction and political commentary (Donaldson 1986, 9).

Carlyle represents another critical input, aggressive, perceptive and ultimately unbalanced. Does he share Ferguson and Galt's sense that society exists independently of party-political action? He was the contemporary of Thomas Chalmers and the ecumenical Edward Irving, whose universalist Catholic Apostolic Church presaged several attempts to re-erect secular versions of the Two Kingdoms ideology. Does he share their transcendentalism?

Carlyle respected the 'fire and strength' of the Calvinist tradition (**Document 140 b & f**) but he couldn't share the retreat into Calvinist fundamentalism that Chalmers implied, when 'mechanism' and the market were not just ravaging existing social relationships, but actually shattering people's ideas about identity (**Document 140d & e**).

The Disruption of 1843 was a traumatic Scottish setback. The 'ten years' conflict', the battle for control of the Kirk, which then directed Scottish educational and social policy, was a debate about a form of devolved Scottish government: characterising the Act of Union as a *basic law,* federal just as much as Calvinism was federal. JF Ferrier (1848) at the time, and the young Harold Laski (1917, 208) in his pluralist phase, recognised that this reading guaranteed the freedom of the Kirk. The church split weakened Scottish autonomy, and strengthened class and religious loyalties just when the railway and telegraph were cementing ties to the south, something reflected in Carlyle's criticism of the Railway Mania (**Document 140d**).

Ironically, the British élite's absorbent abilities made Carlyle the main inspirer of that didactic but persuasive tradition, the English realist novel, from Disraeli to Meredith (Harvie 1991a). This marked, in Joseph Schumpeter's sense, its success in the critical decade of the 1840s, in recruiting from the élites of the other nations – turning 'uneven development' into a positive advantage for the metropolis.

3. 'NORTH BRITAIN' OR THE DEMOCRATIC INTELLECT?

In contrast to nationalist activity on the Continent, climaxing in 1848, Victorian Scotland seemed resigned to British unity. The 1850s and 1860s could fairly be called 'North British'. An energetic attack on the Scots deductive philosophy was delivered by HT Buckle followed by John Stuart Mill on *Sir William Hamilton's Philosophy* (1864).

> EXERCISE 3
> Read the following quotation from Buckle and comment on what he sees as the deficiencies of Scots philosophy. How do you think this argument is carried on by later Liberals like JM Robertson (see quote in Introduction)?

The Scotch literature, notwithstanding its brilliancy, its power, and the splendid discoveries of which it was the vehicle, produced little or no effect on the nation at large . . . its method, both of investigation and of proof, was too refined to suit ordinary understandings. Therefore, upon ordinary understandings it was inoperative. In Scotland, as in ancient Greece, and in modern Germany, the intellectual classes, being essentially deductive, have been unable to influence the main body of the people. They have considered things at too great an altitude, and at too great a remove . . . In no civilised country is toleration so little understood . . . in none is the spirit of bigotry and persuasion so extensively diffused.

(Buckle 1861 465, 140)

The Scots are deductive, ie they proceed from a central, semi-mystical core of belief what the eighteenth-century enlightenment called 'common sense' – as a unifying principle. To Buckle, this makes them unscientific and dogmatic, while Robertson regards Scots religiosity as totally negative in its social consequences. He might almost be describing the parochialism of George Douglas Brown's 'Barbie'.

While the Westminster ethos was being distilled by Erskine May and Bagehot, the zenith years of the realist political novel provided a solid and supportive ethical-political culture, and the reform of Oxford and Cambridge a modernised political élite. Scots *were* ardent federalists, but in Canada and Australia. At home, autonomy continued along the route of a specifically Scottish style of administration. The Christian social civics of Chalmers and the 'modernist' theologian Thomas Erskine of Linlathen, frustrated by the Disruption in 1843, became secularised and transferred to the universities, as Davie described in 1961 in perhaps the leading text of post-war nationalism, *The Democratic Intellect*.

Tory nationalism, compounded of *Blackwoods* and Balmoral, radiated from every baronial mansion in the tones of Eton and Oxford, continuing the 'commodification' of Scottish identity and a militarism which was more salient than elsewhere in Britain. A brief Tory-nationalist phase in the 1850s later gave way to militant protestantism. '*Blackwoodsmen*' like WE Aytoun denounced Liberalism as wholly denationalised, yet it represented an economy which, with its large-scale exporting industries and commercial agriculture, was unusually market-oriented and thus *ipso facto* independent of London government. Scottish political culture favoured the Liberal high-mindedness of Gladstone. His sense of 'Christendom' ('international public right' diffused among the European nations) and of self-government (initially among religious groups; latterly among nations) accorded with the traditions of divided sovereignty, international trade and international law (Harvie 1989).

Laisser faire started to break down as a result of the land crisis after 1873. The county franchise, and interventions such as the Highland Land Act of 1885, presaged further measures in farming and housing, and the recovery of Scotland's Gaelic tradition, hitherto discriminated against (Hanham 1967; Harvie 1987). This sustained a professional administrative culture far different from that of the Oxbridge/Westminster élite because based more on theory than on ascriptive authority. Yet it was much affected by the rise of Hegelianism, with its attraction to the 'state-in-being'. *Essays in Philosophical Criticism*, edited by Andrew Seth and RB Haldane in memory of the Oxford philosopher TH Green in 1883, favoured welfarism and 'international public right', but Hegelians left and right did not view Scotland through pluralist lenses. Contrast Goethe writing to Carlyle in the 1820s with Georg Lukács writing of Scott throughout *The Historical Novel* (1936) as an English author. What had changed in the intervening period?

The effects of the best poets and aesthetic writers throughout the world have been directed towards the general characteristics of humanity . . . [but] one must study and make allowances for the peculiarities of each nation, in order to have real intercourse with it. The special characteristics of a people are like its language and currency. They facilitate exchange; indeed they first make exchange possible.

(Goethe 1832, cited in Froude 1885, 414–20)

For Marxists industrial Scotland was simply a variation of the superstructure above a solidly 'British' base. Seen from Scotland, the picture was different but in no orthodox way nationalistic. The evolving Scottish state and its 'democratic intellectualism' promoted and exported public service-based innovation, creating radically new institutions: some Scottish, but mostly British. Such figures as William (Lord) Weir and the National Grid, John Grierson and documentary film, John (Lord) Reith and the BBC, and Walter Elliot and agricultural planning, had their origins in the post-Hegelian Scottish universities. But how 'democratic' – in the participative sense – were their ideas (see extract from Elliot, above, Introduction)?

Not very. This is an intellectualism of achievement. This was backed up, and contradicted, by the theory of Professor James Lorimer, in which the civic notion of 'good' rather than 'popular' government – something derived from the enlightenment via Carlyle – is deeply engrained. In fact, if the writings of the Kailyard – JM Barrie, 'Ian MacLaren', SR Crockett – are examined closely, a humanistic reforming ethic emerges, but one in which Adam Smith's 'sympathy' is replaced with lashings of sentiment (Harvie 1991a).

Lorimer, by contrast, was a more European type of cultural nationalist. He defended the autonomy of the Scots universities, revived Scottish architecture – his restoration of Kellie Castle in Fife was the first attempt to get away from Balmoral and back to the spirit of Franco-Scottish architecture – and argued in favour of female suffrage and proportional representation. His plan of 1885 for a federal Europe in his *Institutes of the Law of Nations* was ground-breaking, a federalist enthusiasm shared by James Bryce's *The Holy Roman Empire* (1864) and his influential *American Commonwealth* (1889).

> The notion that the progress of the Anglo-Saxon race can take place only by the expansion of England, appears to me to belong to the exclusively English, or rather, I should say, to the London school of thought . . . [The Londoner] conceives that steam and electricity will . . . stamp out any pestilent traces of separate national life which may still linger in Scotland or in Ireland . . .
>
> The European legislature's tendency would be to protect and give freer scope to ethnic peculiarities, whilst their anti-national action would add to its strength . . . there seems every reason to anticipate that Scotland, at no distant period, will lay claim to that local autonomy for which Ireland has never ceased to cry out, and which her own incapacity for self-government can alone justify us in refusing her.
>
> (Lorimer 1885, 294–5)

The imperialist FS Oliver in schemes for 'home rule all round' echoed ideas of his friend John Buchan in his study of *Montrose* (1926) and his novel *Witch Wood* (1928). What implications had these schemes for Scottish nationality? How did they differ from contemporary European nationalism?

4. NEOTECHNICS VERSUS ETHNIC NATIONALISM

I think that there's a notion here of civic responsibilities which go beyond the boundaries of the nation, and thus are different from the *sacro egoismo* that characterised most late nineteenth-century nationalist movements. But this is unstraightforward, tangled up with imperialism on one hand and internationalism, either of a free trade or socialist sort, on the other.

A figure who embodied the ambiguity of this period was Sir Patrick Geddes (1854–1932), pioneer sociologist and regional planner.

EXERCISE 4
Look at the following two extracts from Geddes. What influences do you see from Adam Smith and Karl Marx? Are any new concepts being added?

The sorely needed knowledge, both of the natural and the social order, is approaching maturity; the long-delayed renaissance of art has begun, and the prolonged discord of these is changing into harmony; so that with these for guidance men shall no longer grind on in slavery to a false image of their lowest selves, miscalled self-interest, but at length as freemen, live in Sympathy and labour in the Synergy of the Race.

(Geddes 1884, cited in Macmillan 1992, 272)

Here, then, is the point: that the feudalism of the palace, the ecclesiasticism of the monastery, viewed from the contemporary economic view of history, which now takes precedence of the common romantic pictures of sword or cowl, are the two rival ways, temporal and spiritual, of exploiting the miller and his mill. In short, the economic maintenance, and therefore consciously or subconsciously the policy, of tower and abbey, of medieval Church or State, was very largely in terms of their rival or coadjusted grips upon the corn sack coming to the mill, their dips into the flour sack going out again.

(Geddes 1904, 130)

Geddes combined the 'sympathy' of Adam Smith with Comteian positivism, Carlyle-Ruskin social criticism, 'cosmopolitan' Celtic nationalism, and an interest in the power of economic possession derived from Marx, adding his own 'biocentric' concept of 'ecology'.

Originating in the Edinburgh Social Union in the 1880s, and greatly influencing such figures in architecture and town planning as Charles Rennie Mackintosh, Patrick Abercrombie and Lewis Mumford, Geddes' regional planning movement both exploited and criticised Empire – through his links with the proconsuls Lord Pentland and Lord Aberdeen *and* with Zionism, and Irish and Indian nationalism. When Hugh MacDiarmid added the international influences of 'modernism' – Pound, Spengler, Shestov (the Russian philosopher) and Joyce – to the 'Scottish renaissance', he was rehousing Geddes in a post-imperial Scotland (Meller 1990; Macmillan 1992; Gray 1992).

Geddes' paradigm fused nationality and urbanisation, drawing on evolutionary ideas and the contemporary problems of Scottish cities in which nearly half the population lived. Karl Miller has noted how fascinated Victorians – from Cockburn to Ruskin – were with the symbol of Venice (Miller 1966). 'Civics' was well-adapted to what resembled a west-coast floating republic from Bristol to Glasgow, dependent on the capital goods industries and steam traction. A confederation of huge multi-cultural cities, regional mineral-fields, and worldwide commercial contacts, this West Britain was Scots-dominated, and by 1910 Geddes regarded it as standing on the edge of a 'geotechnic' civics which would balance cultural nationalism, cosmo-politanism and technology (Harvie 1996).

'Civics' both in its Haldanite and Geddesian forms anticipated the 'social citizen-ship' of the welfare state – a political society democratic in recruitment although élitist in function. Hence its – and the Scots' – success in urban politics and colonial territories where first-comers tended to rule over natives and late-comers. These ideas about culture, technology and law go back to Roman and medieval precedents via Chalmers and Galt, but also draw on the fusion between sociology, religion and technology encountered among the revivers of Scottish anthropology in the late nineteenth century, such as JF MacLennan, Robertson Smith and JG Frazer as well as Geddes. Look, for example, at the way Robertson Smith reconciles the religious impulse with the advance of the scientific method:

> (On Robertson Smith) . . . Jesus comes on the scene, letting himself publicly be done to death to end the bizarre confusion of matter and spirit which had persisted from time immemorial, and at the same time to promote a renovation of the sacred ritual which would enable all members of the community, irrespective of wealth, to participate in the reanimating effects, public and private, of the religious experience.
>
> (Davie 1991, 135)

In Walter Elliot's *Toryism and the Twentieth Century* (1927) the sciences, social and physical, are assumed as the basis of expert government 'biology is the *logos* of Toryism' (Elliot 1927, 126). By contrast, attitudes to democracy and popular belief were much less confident.

EXERCISE 5

Read the following extract from Frazer's *The Golden Bough*. In what way do Frazer's doubts resemble those of Carlyle in **Document 140**?

It is not our business here to consider what bearing the permanent existence of such a solid layer of savagery beneath the surface of society, and unaffected by the superficial changes of religion and culture, has on the future of humanity. The dispassionate observer, whose studies have led him to plumb its depths, can

hardly regard it as otherwise than as a standing menace to civilisation. We seem
to move on a thin crust which may at any time be rent by the subterranean
forces slumbering below.

(Frazer 1892, 2)

While a great deal could be said here, the essential point is a fear of forces likely to
undermine existing social and cultural values; indirectly industrialisation, the
market and greater democracy.

5. THE PATHOLOGY OF IMPERIAL UNIONISM

As in the eighteenth century, the organic and traditional Scots intelligentsias
combined between 1880 and 1920 into a powerful hybrid of journalists, politicians
and social engineers whose Hebraic notion of 'The Law' was drawn from the 'shop'
of technology as well as biblical injunction – and enforced by the notion that
somewhere below the structures of society was something anomic and anarchic.
'You think that a wall as solid as the earth separates civilisation and Barbarism', says
the villain in the first of Buchan's thrillers, *The Power House* (1913), 'I tell you the
division is a thread, a sheet of glass . . .'
    Noel Annan (1960) noted that the semi-Scot, Rudyard Kipling, came close to the
'legislative ethos' of early European sociology: Max Weber, Emil Durkheim and
Vilfredo Pareto. But the Scots also had an aggravated tendency to dislocation.
    Any culture-derived ideology only indirectly connected to sovereign institutions
will tend, by opposing sympathy and emotion to an over-rigid mechanism, to
produce complete contradiction; something to which the Tory cultural nationalist
and political unionist - like Hogg, Stevenson or Buchan – is peculiarly prone (Harvie
1991b).

EXERCISE 6
Compare the extracts from JD Scott's novel *The End of an Old Song* (1953)
(**Document 142a**) and from Allan Massie writing two decades later. Both
retrospectively survey this period but whose song is actually ending?

. . . the world is for the big battalions. Small countries cannot withstand it,
especially when they are not protected by the barrier of a different language.
Their geographical fate determines their nature . . . Scotland will grow ever less
Scottish and ever less stimulating; we live in a withered culture. Sounds of energy
are the energy of a death-rattle. The Union may not have been the end of an
auld sang, but it led us into the last verse.

(Massie 1984, 112)

Scott's hero has decided to ditch both Scotland and Britain. Massie (1988) still sees
Britain as dominant. Yet he has also pointed out the gulf that can appear in the
imaginative writer who is also a political commentator. In the second guise he might

find himself commending a steelworks closure, but as novelist he would oppose it. Out of this can come two things: (i) an internal division when a rational (what the Franco-Scottish social anthropologist Emmanuel Todd (1988) calls an 'authoritarian') politics of community and family challenges individuality, and (ii) an unscrupulous opportunism battening on a more ascriptive establishment, as with Alastair Kerr.

An obsession with the collapse of rationalism – the *doppelgänger* from Hogg through Stevenson to RD Laing – creates plausible modern versions of Hogg's Gilmartin. Think of Lord Beaverbrook and Rupert Murdoch, born into Scottish religious politics and thereafter exhibiting all the solipsism of the 'Scotchman on the make'. In 1825 Sir Walter Scott wrote to JW Croker, 'If you unscotch us you will find us damned mischievous Englishmen' (Grierson 1935, 472). Political indirection has not just shadowed even the most dedicated careerists within the Union, it has also impregnated the way in which the Scots environment has been appraised **(Document 142b)**.

All right, I'm going to pause here, for the benefit of the 50% or so of my readers who ought at this point to be incandescent with fury. How many times has a woman been mentioned, so far? The problem with reconstructing a Scotland from the point of view of the institutions which maintained its distinctiveness was that they were almost exclusively male. The Estates, it goes without saying: the clubs, the volunteer movement, the engineers and councillors. Now there *is* a continuing series of lively, embattled women throughout the eighteenth and nineteenth centuries: Jane Porter, whose *The Scottish Chiefs* (1810) reanimated the Wallace legend; Susan Ferrier, whose novels have a raciness unencountered in Jane Austen; Marion Reid, the first feminist pamphleteer after Mary Wollstonecraft; the Countess of Sutherland (though not all of her tenants would agree). My point is this: the English, commercial structure of culture could actually admit women; the Scottish, being founded on legislative enactment, reinforced male privilege.

Now the implications of this are far-reaching and may help us to explain the foregoing psychosis: the preponderance of divisions between essentially male drives: legalism and physical power, intellect and emotion. The women avoided living, as Douglas Gifford puts it, 'as a divided self, within a divided family in a divided state'. But this tended to mean that they simply disappeared from the record. Only in the 1890s do Scotswomen – the MacDonald sisters, Phoebe Traquair, Jessie M King – start to carve out their own careers in art and interior decoration, and they tend to fit themselves into the sort of Kailyard niche, most notably occupied by Annie S Swan. When women again come back into the general cultural-political reckoning, during the Scottish renaissance of the inter-war years it's as personifications of Jung's *anima*, and various versions of this turn up. The irony is that both in the 1890s and in the 1930s the most prominent and eloquent woman symbols were both male-created: Fiona MacLeod and Chris Guthrie.

By the 1930s there were women writers, musicians and artists with well-defined and quite idiosyncratic personalities: Willa Muir, Catherine Carswell, Violet Jacob, Helen Cruikshank, and Naomi Mitchison. Their output has never been less than interesting, but it has to be looked for. It does not fit either into the world of the Estates, or into the world of metropolitan feminism. Only in the 1980s was it properly assessed.

6. 'SEEING SCOTLAND WHOLE?'

The real challenge to 'the grim, competitive little country' came with the enforced centralisation of World War I, and the zenith of Britain's imperial might, rapidly followed by two decades of unbroken economic recession. Autonomy lost out after 1920 to centralised collectivism, the replacement of administrative boards by Civil Service departments, and after the removal of anti-Tory Ireland from an increasingly Conservative Westminster, the marginalisation of constitutional issues. Economic collapse subverted 'civics' but so too did the ethnic nationalism of Versailles which produced the National Party of Scotland in 1928. The martyrs of Easter 1916 – Patrick Pearse and the Edinburgh-born James Connolly – became icons of the *literati*: MacDiarmid and Edwin Muir, enthusiasts like Ruaridh Erskine of Mar, and the occasional leftist maverick like John MacLean. In some ways nationalism publicised mass unemployment, housing deterioration, sectarianism, poor health and neglected education, in other ways it obscured it.

> EXERCISE 7
> Look at the first two extracts from Hugh MacDiarmid (**Document 143 a & b**) and his friend and collaborator in *The Scots Scene* (1934), Lewis Grassic Gibbon. Are they 'right' or 'left'?

That is The Land out there, under the sleet, churned and pelted there in the dark, the long rigs upturning their clayey faces to the spear-onset of the sleet. That is The Land, a dim vision this night of laggard fences and long-stretching rigs. And the voice of it – the true and unforgettable voice – you can hear on such a night as this as the dark comes down, the immemorial plaint of the peewit, flying lost. *That* is The Land – though not quite all. Those folk in the byre whose lantern light is a glimmer through the sleet as they muck and bed and tend the kye, and milk the milk into tin pails – they are The Land in as great a measure.

(Gibbon 1934, 67)

. . . this Nationalism was just another plan of the Tories to do down the common folk. Only this time 'twas to be done in kilts and hose, with bagpipes playing and a blether about Wallace, the English to be chased across the Border and the Scots to live on brose and baps.

(Gibbon 1934, 82)

MacDiarmid could almost be a clerical Tory like the Rev John White stoking up resentment against the immigrant Irish, and Gibbon's invocation of 'the Land' has an almost *Blut-und-Boden* (blood and soil) echo, which rather contradicts his scepticism about political nationalism.

The Depression allied the ethnic nationalists with collectivism of a sort. Further agencies of the welfarist type were invoked, not least in the plethora of civic bodies like the Scottish National Development Council set up in the 1930s. Social Credit, the nostrum of a Scottish engineer, CH Douglas, was for a time as influential within the Labour Party as within the NPS – or in Canada or New Zealand. Anti-bank propaganda perhaps appealed in a country whose banks shifted investments south in response to the slump: quite different from the peasant-based ideology of Ireland or the language struggle in Wales. Other radicals were sceptical about the whole project, or saw it in a far more dramatic context.

EXERCISE 8

Compare MacDiarmid (**Document 142 b & c**) with the following extract from Grassic Gibbon and with the extract from *Greenvoe* (**Document 144**). Where do these writers locate culture and nationalism, in time and place?

There the Covenanting folk had screamed and died while the gentry dined and danced in their lithe, warm halls. Chris stared at the places, sick and angry and sad for those folk she could never help now, that hatred of rulers and gentry a flame in her heart, John Guthrie's hate. Her folk and his they had been, those whose names stand graved in tragedy . . .

(Gibbon 1932–4, 464)

This is a tricky one. For MacDiarmid, Scotland is crucial, but as a means to an end, the superman's venture towards a sort of *totum scibile*. A lot of physical benefits for the Scots folk isn't something he envisages. Grassic Gibbon sees nationalism as a Tory con-trick. For Mackay Brown, in a much later piece, but one which looks back to Edwin Muir, and before him to the rituals of death and rebirth Frazer recorded in *The Golden Bough*, nationalism implies a revived medievalism, and also the regional variety of Scotland, exemplified by the history and landscape of his own Orkney. MacDiarmid's great attempt to 'see Scotland whole' actually resulted in the Scots seeing their country, and themselves (for the Scottish Renaissance had a psycho-analytical side to it as important as it's under-researched), as enormously various (Kimpel 1995).

The Scots' complex identity was not just exported, it could be repatriated. Carlyle, John Muir, Thomas Davidson and later Geddes had helped, via Lewis Mumford, to create the ideology of the American progressive movement which had its outcome in the New Deal (Anderson 1989). Its cultural programme – regional planning, people's history and political folksong – came back to the post-1945 Scottish radicals, via John Grierson, Alan Lomax and Hamish Henderson, *without* taking the usual route through London (Henderson 1993). Yet this 'progressivism' had centralist implications, depending either on the regional policy of Big Government or on working-class internationalism. This was added to the existing centralisation of welfare citizenship, in Reith's BBC or the 1935 Unemployment Assistance Board, and accelerated by the southward shift of the print media, although there were counter-currents, such as the continuing 'imperial federation' notions of the Beaverbrook papers. Labour's rapid growth provoked a Unionist-Liberal *anschluss*. But there was some non-political initiative from the likes of the Saltire Society, 'founded by a group of people who wished to set not a mere revival of the past, but a renewal of the life which made them, such as the Scots themselves experienced in the eighteenth century' (quoted in Reiach and Hurd 1944, 1).

The 'estates' shied from taking initiatives; though the Scottish National Development Corporation and a sequence of planning bodies owed much both to the Convention of Royal Burghs and the Scottish Office. This was followed in World War Two by the success of Tom Johnston's decentralisation, legislative as well as administrative, under the umbrella of his Scottish Council of State, which involved physical planning, energy, and the health service. What the Renaissance, and the linked political movement for administrative decentralisation, didn't achieve is noted by William Power and, almost half-a-century later, Alasdair Gray (**Document 145c**).

> Between an unreal Drumtochty and a too real St Rollox Scotland seemed to have
> vanished. Probably that was what made me fall so passionately, so obstinately, in
> love with her. She was my own country, for I seemed to have created Scotland
> out of books and songs. She was, in a sense, my Galatea. She was the Galatea of
> many Scots about that time.
>
> (Power 1937, 219)

Galatea was the idealised Scotland of the intellectuals; Agnes Owens' Mac is a symbol of the post-industrial reality: the ordinary 'wee man', a survivor, to whom solidarity matters more than success. Even if he had 'infinities within him', he was largely ignored by a culture which was, in its settings and in its socialising programme, largely oriented towards a rural Scotland in which scarcely a third of the country's people lived.

7. THE RENAISSANCE OF THE 1980S

Why leap ahead from World War II to the 1980s? Begin with Cairns Craig's judgement on the aftermath of the Referendum débâcle of 1979:

> Instead of political defeat leading to quiescence, it led directly into an explosion
> of cultural creativity, a creativity coming to terms with the origins of the political
> defeat and redefining the nation's conception of itself. The eighties have been one
> of the most significant decades of Scottish cultural self-definition in the past two
> centuries.
>
> (Craig 1989, 9)

Now look at the extracts from Kelman (above) and Gray (**Document 145b**) and compare these with Carlyle (**Document 140a**), Davie (two extracts, above) and MacDiarmid (**Document 143b**).

I hope that these suggest the way in which some of those who contributed to revival of the 1980s were consciously resuming the idea of a semi-independent culture. This was something only fitfully present, even in the Renaissance of the inter-war years, but was borne out by an unprecedented number of substantial synoptic projects about Scottish history and culture, of which this course is one, and without which this course couldn't have come into being. It was a movement which began in politics, but it was actually deepened and broadened through the setbacks which these encountered. Cultural life, subordinated to politics in the 1970s, then propelled the national movement in the following decade.

The initial nationalist revival in the 1960s was broadly generated by protest against what we now call deindustrialisation, though many of its activists were drawn from the old ILP and CND, and shared a modest input of 'small-is-beautiful' ideas with Plaid Cymru (Harvie 1993, 173–78). In the 1970s Labour's grudging conversion to devolution, and the failure of the Scottish anti-Common Market left in the referendum of 1975, led to irresolution, and the setback of 1 March 1979. But the evolution of a 'Scotland in Europe' position, adopted in 1988 by the SNP but echoed by the Labour and Liberal parties, which removed the threat of separation while capitalising on England's alienation from Brussels, both echoed and influenced marked cultural changes.

Culture became political because it was recognised as the country's major post-industrial endowment – in for example the art collections built up by industrialists such as Sir William Burrell, or the Edinburgh Festival. 'Scotland the Brand' could also mean, in the industrial and enterprise sphere, the advantageous – because subject to prestige rather than price considerations – marketing of such positional goods as tweeds, whisky and specialist foods (McCrone 1996). Effectively this meant that the Scots, latter-day Nicoll Jarvies, were identifying themselves as European 'bourgeois regionalists', and calibrating their history against a European rather than a British scale.

Did this mean a return to regarding the Union as a fundamental law? The language of *Scotland's Claim of Right* (1987), by specifically reopening the dual sovereignty issue which obsessed the Church of Scotland in 1842, and demanding entrenched clauses guaranteeing Scottish autonomy, reanimated earlier ideas about popular sovereignty (Mitchell 1996, 127–33).

The Scottish Constitutional Convention of March 1989 was one not-terribly-auspicious terminus of this (constitutionalism never has a very long shelf-life as a political issue). Was the *Charter for the Arts in Scotland* (1995) in which the transfer of cultural responsibility to the Scottish Office became the occasion for a sharp break with the overlordship of the London intelligentsia not more influential? Particularly when, at the same time, the dropping of ideas for English regional assemblies by the Labour Party postponed to infinity the prospect for a 'balanced' federal settlement (Campaign for a Scottish Assembly 1988).

Following the 1997 election and referendum the position is uncertain. Adopting Hroch's pattern, is Scotland about to evolve mass-movement nationalism, albeit thanks to the decline of Britishness as much as Scottish political evolution? Further, support for independence grew from about 20% in the mid-1970s to 35% in the 1990s. Support for the monarchy plummeted to the 50% mark. Yet while constitutional self awareness matured, the autonomy of the Scottish 'community' has deteriorated. In certain aspects – diet, drugs, violence, prostitution – its distinctiveness is negative. Irvine Welsh's Edinburgh junkies in *Trainspotting* (1994) convert the social critique of such as James Kelman into a glorification of deviant lifestyle as fashionable and toxic as Glasgow's razor-gangs of MacArthur and Long's *No Mean City* (1934). Glasgow's social bill for its drug problem is, at £500 million, rather bigger than the budget of Scottish Enterprise, while the Dunblane tragedy showed the extent to which a social psychopath could wheel and deal in local politics (*Scotland on Sunday*, 5 January 1994).

But the degree to which new Scottish approaches in the arts to the totality of a society have married themselves to politics, as a means towards an ecological integration of technics and civics – a concept pioneered by Patrick Geddes – is distinctive. To recover the trajectories of Scottish discourse on politics, religion, philosophy and culture – while British conventions deteriorate – brings autonomy perceptibly closer.

In the course of this chapter I have been concerned mainly with a political explanation, which regards culture as having a particular weight as a type of politics in a 'stateless nation'. To argue thus may, however, reduce imaginative writing to a merely functional role. So you will find in the reader volume two treatments of the same problem which analyse different discourses: Cairns Craig on the Scots novel in 1981 and Ursula Kimpel on Scots poetry in 1995 (**Articles 45 and 46**). I would like you to read both and compare them with my narrative before tackling the final exercise, variations on which might also appear as assignments or exam questions.

Towards the end of *Lanark*, Alasdair Gray ('Nastler') appears in the text to discuss his purposes in writing the book. His more optimistic view was that

> . . . what the Aeneid had been to the Roman Empire my epic would be to the Scottish Cooperative Wholesale Republic, one of the many hundreds of small peaceful socialist republics which would emerge (I thought) when all the big empires and corporations crumbled.

(Gray 1981, 492–3)

EXERCISE 9
Consider this, along with Gray's concluding passage (**Document 145a**), Patrick Doyle's epiphany in *A Disaffection* (above) and one illustration: Gray's panorama from *Lanark* (Illus 63). Then make the comparison with the country in 1945: 'Stands Scotland where it did?'

Frontispiece, Alasdair Gray, *Lanark* Book Four.

REFERENCES TO BOOKS AND ARTICLES MENTIONED IN THE TEXT

Anderson, B 1982 *Imagined Communities*. London.

Anderson, D 1989 *Lewis Mumford: an American Life*. New York.

Annan, N 1960 'Kipling's Place in the History of Ideas', *Victorian Studies* 3, 323–48.

Buckle, HT 1861 *History of Civilisation in England* Vol III. London.

Campbell, I 1981 *Kailyard*. Edinburgh.

Campaign for a Scottish Assembly 1988 *A Claim of Right for Scotland*.

Chapman, M 1993 *The Celts*. London.

Clark, I D 1970 'From Protest to Reaction: the Moderate Regime in the Church of Scotland, 1752–1805', *in* Phillipson, N and Mitchison, R, *Scotland in the Age of Improvement*, Edinburgh, 200–24.

Colley, L 1992 *Britons: The Forging of the Nation. 1688–1832*. Cambridge, Mass.

Craig, C 1989, 'Scotland ten years on', *Radical Scotland*, February/March, 9.

Crawford, R 1992 *Devolving English Literature*. Oxford.

Davie, GE 1961 *The Democratic Intellect: Scotland and her Universities in the Nineteenth Century*. Edinburgh.

Davie, GE 1990 *The Scottish Enlightenment and other essays*. Edinburgh.

*Donaldson, W 1986 *Popular Literature in Victorian Scotland: Language, Fiction and the Press*. Aberdeen.

Elliot, W 1927 *Toryism and the Twentieth Century*. London.

Elliot, W 1932 'Scotland's Political Heritage', in *A Scotsman's Heritage*, quoted in Coote, C 1965 *Companion of Honour*, London, 16.

Engels, F 'The Magyar Struggle', 13 January 1849, cited in Harvie, C 1994 *Scotland and Nationalism*, London, 11.

Ferrier, JF 1848 *Observations on Church and State*. Edinburgh.

Fraser, WH 1988 *Conflict and Class: Scottish Workers. 1700–1838*. Edinburgh.

Frazer, JG 1892 *The Golden Bough*. London.

Froude, JA 1885 *Carlyle's Early Life*. London.

Fry, M 1993 'The Disruption and the Union', *in* Brown, SJ and Fry, M (eds), *Scotland in the Age of the Disruption*, Edinburgh, 31–43.

Geddes, P 1904 *City Development: A Study of Parks, Gardens and Cultural Institutes*. Birmingham.

Gibbon 1932–4 *A Scots Quair*. London. Edinburgh.

Gibbon, LG 1934 'The Land', in *The Scottish Scene* (1934) rpt in Munro, IS (ed) 1967 *A Scots Hairst*, London, 67.

Gray, A 1981 *Lanark*. Edinburgh.

Gray, A 1992 *Why Scots Should Rule Scotland*. Edinburgh.

Grierson, Sir H (ed) 1935 *The Letters of Sir Walter Scott 1825–1826*. London. (Scott to Croker, 19 March, 1825).

Hanham, HJ 1967 'Mid-Victorian Scottish Nationalism: Romantic and Radical', *in* Robson, R (ed), *Ideas and Institutions of Victorian Britain*, London, 143–79.

*Harvie, C 1987 'Legalism, Myth and National Identity in Scotland in the Imperial Epoch', *Cencrastus* 26, 35–41.

Harvie, C 1989 'Gladstonianism, the Provinces, and Popular Political Culture', *in* Bellamy, R (ed), *Victorian Liberalism*, London, 152–74.

Harvie, C 1991a *The Centre of Things: Political Fiction in Britain from Disraeli to the Present*. London.

Harvie, C 1991b 'Second Thoughts of a Scotsman on the Make: Politics, Nationalism and Myth in John Buchan', *Scottish Historical Review*, 70, 31–54.
Harvie, C 1996 'Garron Top to Caer Gybi: Images of the Inland Sea', *The Irish Review* 19, 44–61.
Henderson, H 1993 *Alias MacAlias*. Edinburgh.
Hroch, M 1985 *Social Preconditions of National Revival in Europe*. Cambridge.
Kidd, C 1993 *Subverting Scotland's Past*. Oxford.
Kelman, J 1989 *A Disaffection*. London.
*Kimpel, U 1995 'Seeing Scotland Whole', *in* Fietz, L and Ludwig, H-W, *Poetry in the British Isles: Non-Metropolitan Perspectives*, Cardiff, 135–56.
Laski, H 1917 *Studies in the Problems of Sovereignty*. New Haven.
Lorimer, J 1885 *The Institutes of the Law of Nations*, Edinburgh and London.
McCrone, D 1996 *Scotland the Brand*. Edinburgh.
Mackenzie, C 1945 *The North Wind of Love*. London.
Macmillan, D 1992 *Art in Scotland*. Edinburgh.
Macmurray, J 1950 *Conditions of Freedom*. London.
MacNeill, DB 1957 *The Scottish Realm*. Glasgow.
Marquand, D 1995 'How United is the Modern United Kingdom?', *in* Grant, A and Stringer, K (eds), *Uniting the Kingdom*, London, 277–91.
Massie, A 1984 *One Night in Winter*. London.
Massie, A 1988 *The Novelist's View of the Market Economy*, Edinburgh. (= David Hume Institute: Occasional Paper 7).
Meller, H 1990 *Patrick Geddes: Social Evolutionist and City Planner*. London.
Nairn, T 1977 *The Break-up of Britain*. London.
Miller, K 1966 *Cockburn's Millennium*. London.
Mitchell, J 1996 *Strategies for Self-Government*. Edinburgh.
Phillipson, N 1969 'Nationalism and Ideology', *in* Wolfe, JN (ed), *Government and Nationalism in Scotland*, Edinburgh, 168–86.
Pittock, M 1991 *The Invention of Scotland: the Stuart Myth and the Scottish Identity, 1638 to the Present*. London.
Power, W 1937 *Should Auld Acquaintance*. London.
Reiach, A and Hurd, R 1944 *Building Scotland*. Edinburgh.
Robertson, JM 1886 *The Perversion of Scotland*. London.
Scott, PH 1985 *John Galt*. Edinburgh.
Smith, A 1776 *The Wealth of Nations*. Chicago.
Todd, E 1988 *The Conditions of Progress*. Oxford.
Williamson, A 1979 *Scottish National Consciousness in the Age of James VI*. Edinburgh.
Wittig, K 1958 *The Scottish Tradition in Literature*. Edinburgh.

FURTHER READING

Those references marked * in the above list are recommended further reading.

Index

Abercrombie, Patrick 136, 287
Agnew, Andrew 196
Agricultural Executive Committees 198, 203
Agricultural mechanisation 198–9, 203–5
Agriculture Act (1947) 204
Agriculture (Scotland) Act (1948) 204
Alexander, William 192, 283
American Civil War 76–8, 193
Argyll 50
Argyll commission 237, 243, 245–6
Association for the Protection of Rural Scotland 268
Atholl 183
Atomic Energy Authority 64
Aytoun, W.E. 285

Baldwin 15–18
Balfour, Arthur 8, 10, 57
Battle of Braemar 269
Battle of Glen Tilt 269
Beardmore, William 86
Bell, George 123
Bell, Patrick 190
Bessemer process 82–3
Board of Agriculture 9, 17, 59–60, 198
Board of Health 13, 15–17
Board of Lunacy 3
Board of Supervision 3, 5, 9, 48
Boothby, Bob 37
Borthwick, Alastair 270
British Empire 28–30, 35–6, 43
British Steel Corporation 89
Broadhurst, Henry 126
Brown, George 189
Bryce, James 286
Buchan, John 37, 282–3, 286, 289
Buchanan, Robert 147
Buckle, H.T. 284
Burrell, William 294

Cameron, Charles 54
Campbell of Islay 48
Campbell, John Francis 68
Campbell, Stephen 169
Cargill, John 37
Carlyle, Thomas 283–4, 292
Carmichael, Alexander 68
Carnegie, Andrew 248
Carswell, Catherine 291
Catholic schools 237–8
Catholicism 143–4, 147, 153, 155–9, 169, 226
Census of Scotland 120
Chalmers, Thomas 123, 147, 215, 283, 285, 288
Chamberlain, Neville 15
Chartism 214
Chartist Church 143
The Cheviot, the Stag and the Black, Black oil 69, 264
Church of Scotland 142–7, 149, 154, 236, 282–4
City of Glasgow Act (1891) 131
Civic Survey and Plan for Edinburgh 136
Clearance 48–9, 56, 69
Clyde Valley Plan 39
Clyde Valley Report (1946) 135
Clyde Workers' Committee 224–5
Coal industry 80–1, 83, 86–8, 121, 219–20, 225–6
Coal Industry Social Welfare Organisation (CISWO) 262
Cockburn, Henry 283
Collins, William 126, 130
Colonial Lands and Emigration Commission 50
Common Agricultural Policy 206–7
Common good fund 132
Communist Party 225
Congested Districts Board 9, 58–9
Connal, Michael 149

Conservative Party 42
Convention of Royal Burghs 7, 16, 281, 293
Cook, Thomas 259
Co-operative marketing boards 202
Cormack, John 158
Corn Production Act 198–9
County Education Authorities 144
Covenant movement 39
Cowan, Henry 35
Craik, Henry 243–4, 252
Crawford, Helen 183
Crofters' Commission 65–6
Crofters Holdings (Scotland) Act (1886) 57–60
Crofters Land Act (1919) 59–60
Crofters' Movement 54, 56
Crofting protests (Crofters' Wars) 8, 51–2, 54, 57, 59–60
Crofting Reform Act (1976) 66
Crowther commission 40
Cruikshank, Helen 291
Currie, Donald 223

Davidson, Thomas 292
Davitt, Michael 221
Dean of Guild 125–7, 130
Deer forests 50
Demographic changes 98–104, 116–17
    Highlands 47–8, 62–3, 69–70, 99–100
    urbanisation 121
Department of Health 1, 135
Development Areas 64
Development Programmes 64
Devolution 9–10, 21–2, 40–1, 294
Devolution referendum (1979) 42, 293–4
Digest of Scottish Statistics 270
Discharged Soldiers and Sailors Federation 225
Distribution of Industry Act (1945) 64
Divorce (Scotland) Act (1938) 170
Dollan, Agnes 183
Douglas, C.H. 292
Dounreay Experimental Reactor Establishment 64
Duff, Alexander 29

Eardley, Joan 137
Edinburgh Act (1866) 127
Edinburgh Evening Courant 133
Education Act (1908) 246, 249
Education Act (1918) 238, 249–50

Education Act (1936) 250
Education (Scotland) Act (1872) 235–7, 239, 241, 243
Electronics 91–2, 233
Elliot, Walter 202, 277–8, 286, 288
Emigration 48–50, 56, 61, 96, 100, 104–8, 117, 192, 196, 219
Emigration Advances Act (1851) 50
Erskine, Ruaridh 291
Erskine, Thomas 285
Estates 191–2, 199
European immigration 114–15
European Union 43, 70, 206–9, 294

Factory Acts 2, 166
Family Law (Scotland) Act (1985) 170
Federation of Celtic Societies 51
Ferguson, Harry 204
Ferguson System 204
Ferrier, J.F. 284
Ferrier, Susan 290
Fertility 111–13, 167–9, 172
Fife Institute of Physical and Recreational Education 262
Fisheries Board 3, 5
Football 158, 260–1, 280
Forestry Commission 199
Forward 224–5
Frazer, J.G. 288
Free Church 142–6, 192, 215

Gaelic 66–8, 264
Gaelic school societies 236
Gaelic Society of Inverness 51
Gallacher 227
Galt, John 283
Geddes, Patrick 136, 287–8, 295
Geikie, Archibald 265
Gibbon, Lewis Grassic 291–2
Gilchrist, Marion 166
Gilmour, John 15–17
Gladstone 5, 7, 285
Glasgow Boundaries Commission 131
Glasgow Empire Exhibition (1938) 37
Gordon, John 50
'Goschen formula' 8, 15
Goschen, George 8
Government Tractor Service 203
Gowans, James 126, 130
Graham, Billy 154
Gray, Alasdair 137, 293, 295
Great Famine 47–9, 99–100

Grierson, John 286, 292
Grieve, Robert 64
Gunn, Neil 68–9

Harcourt, William 7
Hardie, Agnes 183
Hardie, Keir 30–1, 36, 219, 221, 223
Hay, George Campbell 68
Health Insurance 12
Heath, Edward 40, 217, 229
Henderson, Hamish 292–3
Henery, Marion 183
Herbison, Margaret 183
Highland Development League 61
Highland Land Act (1885) 285
Highland Land Restoration League 221
Highlands and Islands Development
    Board 64, 135
Highlands and Islands Emigration
    Society 50
Highlands and Islands Medical Board 9,
    13
Hogg, James 277, 289–90
Hogge, J.M. 34
Home front 198
Home rule bill 14, 35–6
Housing 12, 14–15, 18, 110, 113, 122,
    124–30, 134–5, 195, 203, 205
Housing Act (1919) 16
Hunter, Alexander 29
Hydro Board (North of Scotland Hydro
    Electric Board) 2, 63

Immigration 96, 104–5, 113–15, 219
Improvement Acts 127
Improvers 194, 282
Independent Labour Party 14, 221, 224–
    5
Industrial zones 122–3, 136
Industrialisation 73–4, 81, 92–3, 188
Infectious diseases 125, 127
Inglis, Elsie Maud 166
Inglis, John 133
Irish home rule 9, 31–2
Irish Home Rule Bill 57
Irish immigration/immigrants 96, 113–
    14, 143, 155, 157, 219, 237, 240, 260
Irish Land Act (1881) 56–7
Iron industry 81–2, 87–9, 121, 219–20
Irving, Edward 283
Irwin, Margaret 166
Islam 147

Jacob, Violet 291
Jenkins, Robin 68–9
Jews 147
Jex-Blake, Sophia 245
Johnston, Tom 20–1, 38–9, 63, 293

Kelman, James 278
Ker, John 29–30
Kerrigan, Rose 183
Kilbrandon commission 40
King, Jessie M. 290
Kirk session system 143

Labour Party 18, 35–6, 42, 216, 221,
    226, 232
Laing, R.D. 277, 290
Land League 221
Land raids 60
Laski, Harold 284
Leaving Certificate 243
Lee, Jennie 183
Leverhulme 60–1
Liason Committee for the Defence of
    Trade Unions 229
Liberal Party 28, 33, 35, 214–15, 221,
    232
Littlejohn, Dr. 126–7
Livingstone, David 29
Livingstone, William 68
Lloyd George 12–13
Local Government Act (1894) 9
Local Government Board 12–13
Local Taxation (Customs and Excise)
    Act (1890) 194
Local Taxation Returns 120
Lomax, Alan 292
Lord Advocate 1, 3, 5–6
Lorimer, James 286
Lothian 7

MacArthur, Mary 166
Macaulay Institute 202
MacCaig, Norman 68
MacColla, Fionn 69
MacDiarmid, Hugh 38, 41, 287, 291–2
MacDonald 48
Macdonald, Alexander 219
Macfarlane, Donald 54
MacGrath, John 69
McHugh, Edward 52
McIlroy, Anne Louise 166
McIlvanney, William 137

Mackintosh, Charles Fraser 51, 54
Mackintosh, Charles Rennie 136, 287
Maclean, John 225–7, 291
MacLean, Sorley 68–9
MacLennan, J.F. 288
MacLeod of Dunvegan 48
MacNeill, John 3–4, 48, 50
MacPherson, Mary 68
Malcolm, Lavinia Laing 166
Mann, Jean 183
Mansholt Plan 207
Marjory, Katherine 183
Married Women's Property Act (1920) 162
Marwick, J.D. 131
Marzaroli, Oscar 137
Massie, A. 289
Matheson, James 48
Maxton, James 169
Maxwell, John Stirling 199
Mechanics Institutions 132
Medical Act (1858) 242
Medical Officer of Health 126
Migration, internal/temporary 51, 99–
   101, 104
Miller, Hugh 278
Miners strike 231
Mitchison, Naomi 291
Morden Institute 202
Muir, Edward 265, 268, 278, 280, 291
Muir, John 292
Muir, Willa 291
Mulock, Thomas 49
Multi-nationals 90–2
Mumford, Lewis 287, 292
Munro, Robert 12–13, 15–16
Murdoch, John 51–3
Murray, Eunice 166, 183

Napier Commission 54–7, 60
National Assistance Board 135
National Coal Board 88
National Federation of Women Workers
   166
National Insurance Act (1911) 134
National Reformer 134
National Trust for Scotland 268
Neill, A.S. 251
New Poor Law 2
North British Agriculturalist 189
North Sea Oil 42–3, 90–2, 233
Northern Ireland 158–9
Novar 14

Office of the Scottish Secretary 20
Oliver, F.S. 286
Orange Order 157
Ordnance Gazetteer of Scotland 120–1,
   123, 133
Orr, John Boyd 202

Paterson, Robert 126
Police Act (1862) 130
Police burghs 130–1
Poor Law 2–3, 12, 48, 134–5
Porter, Jane 290
Prison Board 3
Professional registration 242
Progressivism 33
Protestant Action 158

Radcliffe, Alexander 158
Railways 14, 58, 134, 259, 284
Ravenscraig Steel works 88–90, 137
Red Clyde 35, 215, 224, 226
Reform Act (1832) 2
Reid, John 132
Reid, Marion 290
Reith, John 286, 293
Relief Church 142
Rent Restriction Act 12
Respiratory diseases 110
Restoration of Pre-War Practices Act 175
Ridley, Nicholas 217–18
Robertson, J.M. 278
Rosebery 6–7, 29–30
Ross, Donald 49
Rowett Institute 202
Royal Burghs 125, 127, 132
Royal Commission on Scottish Housing
   12, 16, 125–7, 130
Rural Forum 208
Russell, J.B. 130

St Andrews House 19–20
Salisbury 7, 57
Saltire Society 293
Savings Banks 132
School-board system 144
Scotch (Scottish) Education Department
   (SED) 8, 235, 243, 246, 249, 252–3
Scotland's Gardens Scheme 268
Scotsman, The 134
Scott, J.D. 289
Scott, Walter 281–2, 290
Scottish Abstract of Statistics 270

Scottish Administration 1–2, 17
Scottish Boards 2–5, 8–9, 11, 15–17
Scottish burgh statistics 140–1
Scottish Constitutional Convention 294
Scottish Co-operative Women's Guild 169
Scottish Council for Industry and Development 39
Scottish Covenant Movement 21
Scottish Crofters Union (SCU) 66
Scottish Development Agency 135
Scottish Economic Committee 61–2
Scottish Farm Servants' Union 195, 198, 203
Scottish Home Department 1
Scottish National Development Council 292–3
Scottish National Health Insurance Commission 13
Scottish National Party (SNP) 18, 26, 40, 42, 232, 280, 291
Scottish Office 7, 13, 17–18, 20, 39–40, 135, 293
Scottish Ornithologists Club 268
Scottish Protestant League 158
Scottish Rights of Way and Recreation Society 269
Scottish Secretary 1, 6–8, 11–13, 16–18, 20
Scottish Select (Grand) Committee 10–11, 21
Scottish Special Housing Association (SSHA) 135
Scottish Trade Union Congress (STUC) 35, 64, 182
Scottish Unionist party 35
Scottish Women's Rural Institutes 196, 199
Secession Church 142
Sectarianism 157–8, 260–1
Shaw, Clarice McNab 183
Shaw, Thomas 29
Shinwell 217
Shipbuilding 82–9, 220, 226, 229
Siemens, William 82
Small Landholders Act (1911) 59–60
Smith, Adam 277, 281–2
Smith, Ian Crichton 69
Smith, James 190
Smith, John 68
Smith, Robertson 288
SMT Magazine 266, 268

Social Democratic Federation 220–1
Socialist League 220–1
Special Areas Act 18, 62
Spence, Basil 135
Steel Company of Scotland 82
Steel industry 82–3, 86–90, 219, 225–6
Stephens, Henry 189–90
Stevenson, R.L. 277, 289–90
Stewart, Eleanor 176
Stone of Destiny 39, 280
Stresa Conference 206
Students' Respresentative Councils 242
Sturrock, John 27, 150
Sunday schools 148, 151
Sutherland 48, 50, 290
Swan, Annie S. 290

Temperance Associations 132
Temperance societies 148, 151, 265–6
Tennant, Charles 82
Tennant, John 82
Textiles 76–9, 90, 121, 165–6, 177
Thatcher, Margaret 43, 149
Third Reform Bill (1884) 32
Town planning 136
Traquair, Phoebe 290
Treaty of Rome 206
Treaty of Westminster (1931) 36
Trevelyan, Charles 50
Trevelyan, George 5, 9–11
Tuberculosis 12, 110, 124, 202
'Turra Coo' incident 196

Unemployment 18, 100, 219–20, 226–7, 229, 231–2
Unemployment Assistance Board 135, 293
United Free Church 145, 149
United Presbyterian Church 142–6
United Trades Councils 220
Utilitarianism 2–3

Voluntary associations 132

Wage differentials, gendered 165–6, 174, 180, 238
Wages survey 165
Walker, Peter 218
Wason, Eugene 197
Weir, Molly 153
Weir, William 286
Welfare 12, 134–5

Welfare State 39, 43, 227
Welsh, Irvine 137, 279, 295
West of Scotland Agricultural College 194
Wheat Act (1932) 202
Wheatley Act 14
Wheatley, John 14, 169
Whooping cough 110

Wittig, Kurt 279
Womens Land Army 198, 203, 205
Women's Social and Political Union 166
Womens' Timber Corps 203
Woolen textiles 79
Wright, Patrick 194

Young Scots 33